50 YEARS
OF THE EUROPEAN CUP
AND CHAMPIONS LEAGUE

Scene: Istanbul's Ataturk stadium. **Occasion**: the 2005 Champions League Final, Liverpool versus Milan. **Time**: 45 minutes to kick-off. Alongside me is Jacques Ferran, last survivor of the *L'Equipe* editorial team who created the European Cup. He is transfixed by a magazine picture of the teams lining up at the first, 1956 final. **I ask**: 'Did you ever envisage where that would lead?' Ferran waves towards the TV screens and sponsor banners. **He says**: 'Personally, I don't like it but that's not important. What really matters is what happens on the pitch: the players and the football... and that remains as good and as dramatic as ever.'
KEIR RADNEDGE

First published in 2005

10 9 8 7 6 5 4 3 2 1

Copyright © Carlton Books Limited 2005
This edition published for Index Books Ltd 2006

A CIP catalogue record for this book is available from the British Library.

ISBN 10: 1-86200-384-X
ISBN 13: 978-1-86200-384-2

Commissioning Editor: Martin Corteel
Editor: Nigel Matheson
Project Art Director: Luke Griffin
Design: Jim Lockwood
Picture Research: Tom Wright
Production: Lisa French

Printed in Dubai

50 YEARS
OF THE EUROPEAN CUP AND CHAMPIONS LEAGUE

KEIR RADNEDGE

FEATURING INTERVIEWS WITH:

**SIR BOBBY CHARLTON · ALFREDO DI STEFANO · EUSEBIO
FRANZ BECKENBAUER · IAN RUSH · PAOLO MALDINI · ZINEDINE ZIDANE**

INDEX

Contents

6   SIR BOBBY CHARLTON

8   THE PIONEERS

12   THE 1950S

14   ALFREDO DI STEFANO

18   1955-1959

34   THE 1960S

36   EUSEBIO

40   1959-1969

80   THE 1970S

82   FRANZ BECKENBAUER

86   1969-1979

126   THE 1980S

128   IAN RUSH

132   1979-1989

172   THE 1990S

174   PAOLO MALDINI

178   1989-1999

232   THE 2000S

234   ZINEDINE ZIDANE

238   1999-2006

280   RECORDS

284   INDEX

RIGHT: **OLE-GUNNAR SOLSKJAER DAMAGED KNEE LIGAMENTS WITH HIS CELEBRATORY SLIDE AFTER SCORING THE WINNER AGAINST BAYERN IN 1999**

SIR BOBBY CHARLTON

Country: England

Position: Inside-forward

Born: 11 October, 1937

Club: Manchester United (England)

SIR BOBBY CHARLTON

Call it the European Cup – as we did in the early years – or the Champions League now that it has expanded to move with the times but, whatever the label, it remains the competition any big club with ambition wants to win.

The English football authorities would not let Chelsea enter in the first season, and they tried to stop us at Manchester United after we won the league in 1956. But Matt Busby, United's manager, knew better. He had vision. He believed that the European Cup represented the future of the game and he wanted United to be right in at the start. He got his way, we played and the rest, of course, is history.

Consider the identities of some of the other pioneers: Real Madrid, Milan, Juventus, Benfica, Barcelona... the biggest names both then and now. Of course it was a very different world then. The only live football on TV in England was the FA Cup Final once a year. Now we have live football almost every day. Worldwide broadcasting technology was in its infancy and satellite television was not even dreamed of.

I remember watching an early European match involving Real Madrid – it was the first time I'd seen them – on a tiny black-and-white set, and the picture kept breaking up. It was primitive compared with today, but for me, back then, it was like opening a window into another world.

The two-leg knockout system was successful because of the drama it brought, and playing under floodlights was also new. Those were always the most exciting matches either to play in or watch. There was nothing like it. As a young player, you never knew quite where you were going or what players or styles you would come up against – or what conditions.

I remember going to Hungary once to find that the Danube had flooded and the pitch was under water. It meant that we had to come all the way home and then go back again the next week. You would not have that now. Football today is so much more professional in every area, from communication and organization to nutrition and training.

English clubs learned a lot from going into Europe, and I'm sure the continental clubs and coaches learned things from us about attitude and so on. We all helped each other improve.

Off the pitch, we have seen enormous commercial progress. Football has exploded from being just one of several popular games into the majority game for the entire world. That has brought other responsibilities. You see it with all the big clubs and the leagues in France, Germany, Italy, Spain and England: professional football has to be run as a proper business. The increasing power and influence of television and sponsors has made itself felt but, on the plus side, their investment in football helps keep ticket prices at a level most fans can afford.

But it's romance, not profit, that sticks in the memory. For me, the pinnacle was winning the European Cup against Benfica at Wembley in 1968. It was such an emotional achievement, for Sir Matt in particular, because of what had happened to the club and so many of his players at Munich.

Yet when it comes to drama I would look elsewhere – a few weeks further back to the second leg of our semi-final that season against Real in Madrid. At Old Trafford, we had beaten them 1-0, but when we went back to Spain we were 3-1 down at half-time. The world seemed to be collapsing around us. But English teams always keep going, and somehow we got back to 3-2 and then 3-3 to reach the final. That was the most dramatic game I ever played in.

Can you imagine football without the European Cup? Of course not. This book is about 50 years which have changed the game for ever.

OPPOSITE: **BOBBY CHARLTON SURVIVED THE MUNICH DISASTER TO WIN THE EUROPEAN CUP IN 1968 WITH SIR MATT BUSBY'S REBUILT MANCHESTER UNITED**

THE EARLY DAYS

In the beginning... only the football mattered when 22 players, one referee, two linesmen and a few thousand fans populated the wooden stands at grounds in Vienna, Budapest and Prague

That was the essence of association football, not yet compromised by the twisting gaze of the commercial and media lens. Television was still an inventor's dream. Radio was primitive. Sponsorship was a word yet to be coined on 14 August, 1927.

This was the founding date of pan-European international competitive club football. The UEFA Champions League it was not; the European federation did not exist. Nor was it the *Coupe Européenne des Champions*; the French sports newspaper *L'Equipe*, which was to be instrumental in the formation of the competition, did not exist either.

Various one-off tournaments had been cobbled together in the previous 20 years to define club supremacy in one corner of Europe or another. The fledgling world federation, FIFA, had tinkered with the concept of a world club championship rather than a national team tournament. However, lacking money and the means of transport – motorways, jet aircraft, high-speed trains, the product of future decades – it gave up on the idea for the best part of a century.

It was love of football alone that breathed life into the Mitropa Cup, whose title was a contraction of Mitteleuropa, the German name for Central Europe; indeed, its reach

RIGHT: **VALENTINO MAZZOLA CAPTAINS ITALY AGAINST PORTUGAL IN GENEVA, 1949. HE WAS TO DIE A FEW MONTHS LATER WHEN THE PLANE CARRYING HIM AND OTHER MEMBERS OF THE TORINO SQUAD CRASHED OVER TURIN**

TOP RIGHT: **FERENC PUSKAS WHO MOVED FROM HONVED TO REAL MADRID TO TEAM UP WITH THE GREAT ALFREDO DI STEFANO**

owed everything to the historic Austro-Hungarian Empire and nothing to the nation-state jigsaw created in its place by the First World War.

The Cup's instigator was one of the greatest of the forefathers of international football. Hugo Meisl was born in what is now Ostrava but was the scion of a Jewish banking family and wealthy enough to live the dream in an age before lofty idealism was transformed into a term of derision.

Meisl became both general secretary of the Austrian federation and manager of its fabled 'Wunderteam'. He was an internationalist. That, for Meisl, was the only way forward. He mixed happily with counterparts and sometime rivals from Germany, Czechoslovakia, Switzerland, Italy and England, from where he imported the legendary coach Jimmy Hogan.

Meisl had more ambition than football had money. And the clubs, in the early years of continental professionalism, had more money than the federations. Logic thus dictated that the Mitropa Cup took off in the late 1920s and 1930s in a way that even the World Cup could not match.

An organizing committee was created by a founding meeting in Venice in July 1927. Two clubs each from Austria, Czechoslovakia, Hungary and Yugoslavia were entered: the champions and either runners-up or cup-winners.

Initially, Meisl wanted to run it on FA Cup lines. But, after consideration, he decided that the English formula did not meet his concept of sporting equality. Thus, he devised the now familiar home-and-away system, with victory decided on aggregate over two legs.

Meisl could not think of everything. In the goal-glut days immediately after the change in the offside law, he had not foreseen that clubs might end up all square. Sparta Prague and Hungaria of Budapest (later Voros Lobogo/Red Banner and then MTK) drew their 1927 semi-final 2–2, 0–0. A frightened referee tossed a coin and Hungaria, to their fury, were eliminated. Sparta went through to beat Rapid Vienna and become the first holders of the Mitropa Cup.

Sparta won 6–2 in Prague and lost 2–1 in Vienna, where their rugged tackling provoked a hail of stones, fruit and bottles from the crowd. Centre-half Karel Kada was carried off after being knocked out by one such missile, and demonstrations continued long after the final whistle. Familiar fury, indeed.

The Mitropa grew just as the Champions Cup would grow. Initial critics from neighbouring nations recognized the error of their ways and hurried on board. The Cup grew both in size and in status. The richer clubs went fishing in

foreign oceans for their players. Juventus, with one eye on Serie A and one on the Mitropa, imported a bevy of Argentines in vain; Bologna went scouting in Uruguay and were rewarded with success in 1932 and 1934: they were Italy's only inter-war winners.

Winning mattered with an intensity to match today's standards. It was more about glory than financial rewards. FK Austria's Matthias Sindelar, his country's greatest-ever player, is said to have travelled to the winning finals of 1932 and 1936 on the same tram as his adoring fans. Sparta meanwhile had raised the largesse to persuade Belgian forward Raymond Braine to sacrifice a World Cup opportunity in 1934 because his own federation frowned on professionalism.

The idyll faded after a decade. Meisl died in 1937, which was also the last year in which Austrian clubs competed before independence was forfeited the following spring in Hitler's Greater German *Anschluss*. One further year and Sindelar, artistic, free-scoring symbol of Mitropa football, died in his home after a mysterious gas leak.

The Mitropa Cup lived on in name but not spirit. It was 'captured' by the communist-controlled federations of post-war Soviet eastern Europe and, even before slipping away in 1992, had been reduced to an embarrassing joust between the reluctant reserve teams of second division champions.

But the legacy was priceless. The Mitropa spelled

international club glamour, 'defining the market' long before bright young things talked in such terms, demonstrating that great clubs need the grand stage for which domestic duelling is insufficient.

Four years after the end of the Second World War – and a year before FIFA had revived the World Cup – the federations of Italy, Spain, France and Portugal launched their own club competition. European clubs could not afford hefty travel costs, so the Latin Cup was staged at the end of every season in each country by turn. Direct knockout was the system: two semi-finals, a third place play-off and a final. Every four years, the competition points were totalled per nation. Spain took overall honours in 1949–52 and 1953–57.

That was immaterial. What lives on, even beyond fading memory of outstanding matches, is the Latin Cup's legacy of an interim international stage for the likes of Real Madrid, Milan, Benfica, Barcelona and Reims. Also there is the regret that the greatest club team of the era never competed.

Torino, champions of Italy five seasons in a row, sent a mixture of reserves and youth-team graduates to the 1949 Latin Cup. One month earlier their entire first-team squad had been wiped out. Some 12 Italian internationals were among the 18 players killed when the plane bringing them

home from Lisbon, after a warm-up testimonial against Benfica, swooped through mist and rain into the perimeter wall of Turin's Superga basilica.

The deaths of Italy's captain Valentino Mazzola and his team-mates was only the first such tragedy. But football would never be daunted from breaking down its own – and politicians' – international barriers. Post-war technology, an ironic byproduct of the demands of battle, provided the means for revolution with high-powered focused floodlighting. Football could now be played both day and night.

Pioneering promotional work in England was led by Wolverhampton Wanderers. Manager Stan Cullis, a former England centre-half, was a devoted proponent of the physical long-ball game, but he recognized that the future was international. Hence Wolves invited Moscow Spartak and Hungary's Honved to Molineux for prestige friendlies in November and December 1954.

Honved brought all their star soldiers, including the great inside-forwards Ferenc Puskas and Sandor Kocsis as well as right-half Jozsef Bozsik. They led 2–0 then lost 3–2 on a pitch which Cullis, deliberately, had half-flooded before the game. Next morning's headline in the *Daily Mail* hailed Wolves as 'Champions of the World'.

L'Equipe editor Gabriel Hanot, sitting at his desk in Paris, was not amused.

RIGHT: **BEFORE THE DAYS OF PRIVATE JETS AND SLEEK COACHES, PLAYERS USED TO ROUGH IT, WHILING AWAY LONG JOURNEYS PLAYING CARDS. THIS IS WOLVES IN 1963**

OPPOSITE: **WOLVES STALWART STAN CULLIS LEADS OUT HIS SIDE AT MOLINEUX. AN ADVOCATE OF THE LONG-BALL GAME, HE HAD HIS OWN WAYS OF DEALING WITH 'FANCY' FOREIGN FOOTBALLERS**

1950S

FOOTBALL'S NEW HORIZONS

The 1950s were a mere half-decade as far as the European Champions Cup was concerned. But it laid a foundation for a sporting edifice which changed the game, its balance of power and its finance. Out in front, on and off the pitch, were Real Madrid. They won the Cup for the first five years of its existence, including those four initial seasons of its inaugural decade. The most powerful initial challenge came from two of Spain's Latin neighbours. Reims from France were twice runners-up, in 1956 and 1959, with the Italian clubs Fiorentina and Milan the silver medallists in the intervening seasons. Alfredo Di Stefano was the defining individual.

RIGHT: **THE VERY FIRST FINAL: REAL MADRID VERSUS REIMS IN THE PARC DES PRINCES IN 1956. THE FRENCH SIDE RACED INTO A 2-0 LEAD, THEN IT WAS 3-1, BUT MADRID STORMED BACK TO WIN 4-3, SETTING THEIR BENCHMARK FOR THE FUTURE**

ALFREDO DI STEFANO

Country: Argentina and Spain

Position: Centre-forward

Born: 4 July, 1926

Clubs: River Plate,
Huracan, River Plate
(Argentina), Real Madrid,
Espanol (Spain)

ALFREDO DI STEFANO

No one believes me now when I tell them that Real Madrid, when I joined in 1953, had gone so many years without winning the league that hardly anyone could remember the last time. Not that it bothered me. I just thought this was the club of the capital of Spain, with a fantastic stadium and lots of great players before me. We had a duty to be the best.

I was determined to do something very special. I did not come for the money, I came to achieve.

When I had arrived in Barcelona from South America that May, no one knew whether I was to play there or for Real Madrid. They both claimed to have bought me. At one stage, there was even talk of loaning me to Juventus. I got fed up with it all. I told Barcelona I was getting the next flight back to Buenos Aires. But then in the September, Santiago Bernabeu, the Real president, pulled some strings somewhere, so I went to Madrid. I went to play for two years, signed initially for four and stayed all my life.

The day we arrived, I had to dump my family on the steps of the hotel and go straight to the stadium for a spot of training, a steak for lunch and a game that afternoon against a French club, Nancy.

I was not too keen. I had been sitting around in Barcelona for three months. In all that time, I had not trained properly and I had played only three friendlies. The stadium was being redeveloped and you would not believe the state of the pitch! On top of that, I was worried about what had happened to my family. It was all a bit of disaster and we lost 4-2. Still, I scored a goal with a header.

That was on the Wednesday and, four days later, I made my league debut at home to Santander. We won 4-2 and I scored again, though I still felt disorientated because I knew about as much about my team-mates as I did about the opposition - nothing.

Of course, that changed. We won the championship both in that first season and then in my second, which qualified us for the new European Champions Cup. This was a big deal and we made it even bigger by winning it for the first five years. Joan Gaspart, who was briefly president of Barcelona years later, said that our first five European Cup wins were worthless because the opposition in the 1950s and early 1960s was so weak. But what did he know? He did not have to play against them.

In the first campaign, we played Partizan in the snow in Belgrade. When we beat them, the fans threw snowballs at us. One hit our coach, Pepe Villalonga, on the back and knocked him over. There was a stone in the snowball. If it had hit him on the head, it would have killed him.

Against Nice next season, we started to develop our style. Villalonga told me to stay up in attack, but we knew it was not working. We used to talk a lot on the pitch about the state of the game and what had to be done. I dropped

LEFT: **ALFREDO DI STEFANO IN THE COLOURS OF ESPANOL AFTER LEAVING REAL MADRID IN 1964**

back towards midfield, but because I was quick we did not lose anything in attack.

I remember the final against Milan in 1958 when Paco Gento scored the winner in extra time. I still don't know how the ball went in because there were so many people in the penalty area. Then Bernabeu signed Ferenc Puskas. It proved a wonderful choice, though Hector Rial did not like it much because he could not adapt to playing inside-right instead of inside-left.

It was in that 1958–59 season that I was sent off for the first time, against Besiktas, for dissent because I got fed up with their goalkeeper's time-wasting. We had to beat Atletico in a play-off in the semi-final – Kopa and Mateos were fantastic – and Reims again in the final, just as we had in the first cup in 1956.

We had an outstanding team with extraordinary individuals. We also had high standards. Nothing upsets me now as much as seeing a player applaud a team-mate who has missed a crucial pass. In my day, we would have killed for such an appalling mistake. We always had a core of South American players – myself, Rial, Santamaria and so on – so we had the ideal mixture of South American technique and European pace. We developed a distinctive style because we could keep the ball until something opened up for us.

That was why we were champions of Spain, Europe and the world. That was why for every home match the ground was full, with 125,000 spectators, which was the capacity then. People had laughed at Bernabeu when he planned the stadium in the 1940s. But he was proved right. He had built a stadium that big because he knew he could get the people to fill it.

Bernabeu was a great president – the best. He set the standard. For example, when I was at Barcelona, they gave me a nice car, but I had to give it up when I moved to Madrid. Real Madrid players were not supposed to own cars. No ostentation was allowed. Bernabeu was quite conservative: no cars, no moustaches, no beards and later no long hair either. Every game we knew we were ambassadors for the club – and we played a lot of games.

People talk about world tours as if they're something new, but we used to do two or three every year. We'd play friendlies half a world away. We'd start in Uruguay and finish up in New York. We even went up as far as Vancouver one year. Then we would go back down to play River Plate or Boca Juniors. We used to fly in airplanes that took years off your life. I used to complain that I had signed a contract to play football, not to run rings around the world.

We did not get paid anything to compare with today, but I cannot complain. We earned what we were worth in different times. I can remember ex-players in my day saying how much more we earned than they did. It's always been the same.

People said that the team which beat Eintracht Frankfurt in 1960 was the 'team of Di Stefano and Puskas', but this was untrue. I have never changed my view: football is a team game and everybody in the side depends on everyone else. For example, in the 1960 semi-finals we beat Barcelona. They had better individuals than us, but we were the better team.

It's collective responsibility both when you win and when you lose – and in the end, of course, we lost, for reasons there is no point in pursuing now. But I have no regrets. I am delighted with all the titles and trophies I won – much more than I could ever have dreamed of. I had a wonderful career.

Later, it was a great honour when Florentino Perez invited me to be honorary president. But I still believe the strength of Real Madrid is the way the club maintains a pride in its history without losing sight of present-day priorities. Some clubs spend too much time looking back. Real Madrid is not like that.

Reputations do not win matches and trophies, only goals can do that.

LEFT: DI STEFANO WON
FIVE EUROPEAN CUPS AND
WAS SURELY ONE OF THE
GREATEST ALL-ROUND
PLAYERS EVER TO GRACE
THE COMPETITION

TOWARDS A BETTER TOMORROW

In the decade after World War II, the format for the brave new world of European football was open to discussion. At club level, Real Madrid had friends in high places and were able to pull strings

Alfredo Stefano Di Stefano Lauhle arrived in Madrid at 10.30 on the morning of 23 September 1953. With him, on the sleeper train from Barcelona, were wife Sara and their two daughters. Today the greatest footballer in the world would be enveloped in a locust swarm brandishing cameras, voice recorders and notebooks. Instead, at Atocha railway station, a tired and somewhat bewildered footballer and his young family were greeted by two reluctant officials from the local football club, Real Madrid.

Di Stefano had been born in Argentina, rose as a teenager with his father's old club River Plate, then took advantage of the explosive strike of Argentine players in 1949 to fly off and join Millonarios of Bogota in their pirate professional league in Colombia.

Later Millonarios took their 'blue ballet' to Europe to make money from prestige friendlies – which is how Real Madrid president Santiago Bernabeu came to spot Di Stefano at the club's 50th anniversary tournament in 1952.

Acquiring him was not easy. Madrid agreed a deal with Millonarios, while Barcelona agreed terms with his official club River Plate. In the end – and to cut a long and fairly poisonous story short – Bernabeu pulled strings within the government of the dictator, General Francisco Franco, to snatch his man from Barcelona's grasp.

Di Stefano had trained with Barcelona, alongside their great Hungarian émigré inside-forward Ladislav Kubala, for three months before Bernabeu's coup. Hence his bewilderment on arriving at Atocha station to be met by Real officials. On the pitch, however, Di Stefano knew exactly what was wanted. His first season climaxed with Madrid winning the league title for the first time in 21 years. They repeated the magic a year later. This was the most significant league title in the history of the club, because it earned Madrid an invitation to Paris for the meeting which created the European Champions Club Cup.

Gabriel Hanot, former French international full-back and editor of the daily sports newspaper *L'Equipe*, had called the meeting. He had been irritated by the English media's assumption of world-dominating status for Wolves after their friendly victories over Hungarians and Russians.

Along with colleagues Jacques Goddet, Jacques van Ryswick and future *France Football* editor Jacques Ferran, he went down the road pursued by Hugo Meisl in Vienna 30 years earlier.

Some 18 clubs – among them Real Madrid, Reims, Milan, Spartak Prague (formerly and later Sparta), Anderlecht and Chelsea – answered his call. Some 15 attended a founding meeting at the Ambassador Hotel in Paris to agree a fledgling constitution and the knockout format: two legs, home and away, with aggregate winners proceeding to the next round and with the first final to be staged, naturally, in Paris at the old Parc des Princes. Each subsequent final would be hosted by the previous season's winners.

Hanot was not alone in dreaming of a new international club competition. Swiss pools supremo Ernst Thommen and FA general secretary Stanley Rous had already put their heads together to create the International Inter-Cities' Fairs Cup. But Hanot had the advantage in that entry to his European Cup was based entirely on the sporting merit conferred by winning league titles.

The Fairs Cup, with teams chosen from clubs in a given city, staggered into life and the first edition took three years to progress to a final in 1958 in which Barcelona thrashed a London Select. By that time it was too late for the Fairs Cup; the Champions Cup had gained a pre-eminence that would never be threatened.

Quickly Hanot and his assistants found the workload and the political complications too much to handle. With a mixture of pride, regret and relief, they ceded administrative authority to the one-year-old European federation, UEFA – whose first officers were delighted to be handed a ready-made *raison d'être*.

Not all the founder clubs had ended up as domestic champions and not all of them dived in. Chelsea had qualified as champions of England but were then forbidden to compete by the Football League for fear of fixture problems.

The first match was played on the sunny Sunday afternoon of 4 September 1955 in Lisbon between Sporting Clube de Portugal and the Yugoslav club Partizan Belgrade. The first goal was scored, after 14 minutes in front of a

BELOW: RAYMOND KOPA, THE BRILLIANT REIMS CENTRE-FORWARD, ON ARRIVAL IN EDINBURGH FOR THE SECOND LEG OF THE SEMI-FINAL AGAINST HIBERNIAN. A FEW MONTHS LATER, HE JOINED REAL MADRID...

30,000 crowd, by Sporting's Joao Baptista Martins in a tempestuous 3-3 draw. Four days later, Real Madrid launched themselves into football history by winning 2-0 away to Switzerland's Servette in Geneva. Madrid's first goal was scored by their right-half and captain, Miguel Munoz. Madrid cruised through comfortably with a 5-0 win back in their magnificent stadium, named after Bernabeu, their inspirational president. Di Stefano scored twice.

Other first-round winners were Reims, Milan, one-time Mitropa Cup-winners Rapid Vienna, Hibernian of Scotland, Djurgarden of Sweden and Hungary's Voros Lobogo. The quarter-finals saw victories for Reims over Voros Lobogo, Milan over Rapid, Hibernian over Djurgarden and Madrid over Partizan.

Madrid very nearly did not make it. The first problem was political. Franco's Spain had denied diplomatic relations to all Soviet bloc countries. Officially, Yugoslav passport-holders could not enter Spain. Bernabeu pulled more strings. Partizan's players and officials were smuggled into Spain through a side gate at Barajas airport, bypassing customs and passport controls. Their 'reward' was a 4-0 thrashing.

But in the snow and ice of Belgrade in late January the tables were turned. Partizan's inspiration was tearaway centre-forward Milos Milutinovic, elder brother of Bora, the future World Cup managerial mercenary. At 3-0, Milutinovic shot past Madrid goalkeeper Juanito Alonso only to see the ball stick in the goal-line slush. Madrid scrambled the ball clear and went into the semi-finals. Their players rolled in the snow in delight. Inside-left Jose Hector Rial breathed an icy sigh of relief. His contribution in Belgrade had been to miss a penalty.

REAL MADRID START THE BALL ROLLING

Raymond Kopa laced his boots ahead of the 1956 European Cup Final with his head in a whirl. He was the finest French footballer of his generation, considered even as potentially the greatest of all time. He, more than anyone else, had been responsible for the stylish performances, inevitably labelled champagne football, which had brought Reims to the inaugural Champions Cup Final.

Yet, there and then in the Parc des Princes, which would become a second home for Reims in Europe, he already knew that the following season he would be playing for the team he faced that night: Real Madrid.

Reims had beaten Hibernian 2–0, 1–0 in a tight semi-final, while Madrid had come through against even tougher opponents in Milan. The Italians had needed two contentious penalties converted by Giorgio dal Monte to win 2–1 in a largely deserted San Siro stadium. Madrid, 4–2 winners at home, reached the final 5–4 on aggregate.

On 13 June Madrid, coached by Spaniard Jose Villalonga, were at full strength: the acrobatic Alonso in goal; Atienza, Marquitos and Lesmes a ruthless back three; Munoz and sharp-tackling Jose-Maria Zarraga at wing-half; Joseito and the electric-heeled Francisco Gento on the wings; Ramon Marsal and Rial the inside-forwards; and the peerless Di Stefano wearing the centre-forward's traditional No. 9 but with a licence to roam the entire pitch.

At this time, no other player so effectively combined individual expertise with an all-embracing ability to organise a team to play to his command.

Reims considered themselves international veterans with a track record of success. They had beaten Milan 3–0 in Lisbon in 1954 to win the Latin Cup, their victory sparked by a superb solo goal by young left-winger Francis Meano. It was his last goal for Reims. On returning home he was killed in a high-speed car crash along with six other people including his wife, father and best friend.

Without Meano, Reims returned to the Latin Cup Final in 1955, only to lose 2–0 to Madrid, for whom the big Argentine, Rial, scored both goals. It was an ill-starred

RIGHT: **EUROPEAN PIONEERS REAL MADRID POSE FOR THE TRADITIONAL TEAM SHOT BEFORE THE FIRST-EVER FINAL – AS EVER, DI STEFANO IS AT THE CENTRE OF THE ACTION**

PARC des PRINCES
13 JUIN
1956

FINALE
DE LA COUPE
DES CLUBS

Champions Européens

MADRID
REIMS

PROGRAMME
OFFICIEL
DE LA FEDERATION
FRANÇAISE DE FOOTBALL

édité par
FOOTBALL

PRIX :
60 Francs

omen for the European showdown a year later. Also weighing on Reims coach Albert Batteux was the absence of his right-half Armand Penverne, ruled out for three months by a cartilage injury in the days before the 'miracle' of arthroscopy.

Then there was the Kopa question. Madrid and Reims had secretly agreed the transfer back in mid-March. Kopa had even made a guest appearance for Madrid, scoring twice, in a 4–2 friendly win over the Brazilian club Vasco da Gama a week before the European final.

Thus Madrid should have understood the threat he posed as a Hungarian-style, deep-lying centre-forward. Should... but did not.

Kopa's corner presented Penverne's deputy Michel Leblond with the first goal on six minutes, while Meano's replacement, Jean Templin, struck a second on ten. Reims paused to catch their breath, only to be caught first by Di Stefano and then by Rial: 2–2 after half an hour.

Just after the hour Kopa's free-kick was turned in by Michel Hidalgo, future manager of France, to restore Reims's lead. Not for long. Marquitos charged forwards out of central defence, exchanged passes with Rial and

Di Stefano, took a lucky rebound off Templin and thumped home another equalizer for 3–3.

Now Real's hard work on the training pitch paid off. Rial had joined Madrid a year later than Di Stefano after rivalling him as the star player among the pirates of Colombia, where Rial led Santa Fe, deadly rivals to Millonarios.

What Rial lacked in pace he made up for in footballing intelligence. It was Rial who was credited with turning Gento, through footballing wisdom and verbal prompting, from an unpredictable shaft of lightning into the finest left-winger in the world.

Their intuitive understanding paid off on 79 minutes. Gento accelerated away down the left and Rial read the intention to perfection. The man, whose missed penalty in Belgrade very nearly cost Madrid everything, timed his run perfectly to convert the winger's near-post cross.

Real Madrid's winning goal had brought a superb final and a dramatic inaugural season to a thrilling conclusion. After returning home to Spain, Di Stefano celebrated by buying his first car. Back in Manchester, Matt Busby was thinking big. He was determined that no one would keep him off the road to Europe.

WEDNESDAY 13 JUNE 1956
PARC DES PRINCES, PARIS

REAL MADRID   4
DI STEFANO 15, RIAL 30, 79,
MARQUITOS 71

REIMS   3
LEBLOND 6, TEMPLIN 10, HIDALGO 62

HT: 2–2. ATT: 38,239, REF: ELLIS (ENG)

REAL MADRID:
ALONSO - ATIENZA, MARQUITOS,
LESMES - MUNOZ*, ZARRAGA -
JOSEITO, MARSAL, DI STEFANO, RIAL,
GENTO. COACH: VILLALONGA.

REIMS:
JACQUET - ZIMNY, JONQUET*,
GIRAUDO - LEBLOND, SIATKA -
HIDALGO, GLOWACKI, KOPA, BLIARD,
TEMPLIN. COACH: BATTEUX.

*CAPTAIN

BELOW: **ALFREDO DI STEFANO BEARS DOWN ON GOAL AS JACQUET RACES OUT TO THWART HIM. THE ARGENTINE SCORED MADRID'S FIRST GOAL AND WAS A DOMINANT FORCE IN THE GAME**

UNITED ENTER THE FRAY

The future of top-level football lay in Europe. This much was obvious to Matt Busby, who defied the Football League to take his team abroad in a year when revolution turned Honved into exiles

England's football commanded wide respect in the game in the late 1950s despite the thrashings by Ferenc Puskas's Hungary in 1953 and 1954 and the embarrassing World Cup defeat by the United States in 1950. English referees were also reckoned to be the best in the world: many went out to referee high-tension league derbies in Argentina and Brazil in the early 1950s, and Arthur Ellis had been appointed to control the inaugural Champions Cup Final.

All that was missing was English engagement in Europe: an old story and not only in football terms.

Manchester United had different ideas. Their manager, Matt Busby, felt he had been granted a glimpse into the future after the competition's first season. When his magnificent young team of so-called 'Busby Babes' won the Football League in 1956 he had no doubt that Europe was the route to follow.

The Football League told United not to enter. United

defied this injunction. Busby said: 'We don't fear congestion of fixtures. We have at least 18 players who can play in the first team without noticeably weakening us.' The 18 included the left-back and captain Roger Byrne, wing-halves Eddie Colman and the magnificent Duncan Edwards, centre-forward Tommy Taylor, a record signing at £29,999, wingers John Berry and David Pegg plus inside-forwards Billy Whelan, Dennis Viollet and the teenage Bobby Charlton.

United proved Busby's point in their opening tie by thrashing Belgian champions Anderlecht, which made it a painful homecoming for their manager, the former Blackburn goalkeeper Bill Gormlie. United won 2–0 in Brussels and by an imposing 10–0 back at Maine Road, their temporary European home from home while Old Trafford's floodlighting was installed. Viollet scored four, Taylor three.

Borussia Dortmund were beaten next and then the Basque club Bilbao, who had previously seen off the ageing greats of Hungary's army team, Honved.

Bilbao, coached by Kubala's Slovak father-in-law Ferdinand Daucik, had won 3–2 at home. Before the return could be staged, however, the Hungarian revolution erupted back in Budapest.

Honved's players decided not to go back to Hungary and arranged for the return with Bilbao to be played in Brussels. But in the Heysel stadium everything went wrong. The weather was freezing and, early on, goalkeeper Lajos Farago was injured. Substitutes not being permitted, left-winger Zoltan Czibor had to go in goal, and the 10 men of Honved could only draw 3–3.

Elimination left Honved in limbo. The players summoned their wives and children from Budapest and organized fund-raising friendlies in Italy, Portugal and Spain, although the Hungarian federation tried to block them through FIFA at every turn. They even took their circus on tour to Brazil, but when they returned to Europe reality cut in. Half the team voted to go home while the rest decided to try to find clubs and build new lives in western Europe.

Bilbao, meanwhile, fell to United in a memorable quarter-final. In Spain, on a quagmire of a pitch, the

RIGHT: MATT BUSBY, MANAGER OF MANCHESTER UNITED, AT RINGWAY AIRPORT, MANCHESTER, BEFORE LEAVING FOR COLOGNE AND THE DRAW FOR THE SEMI-FINALS OF THE CHAMPIONS CUP

Basques led 3–0 at half-time, then 5–2 before Whelan pulled one more back with a remarkable solo effort. With ominous presentiment, United's players helped clear snow and ice off their plane for the return journey. They then completed the comeback with a straightforward 3–0 dispatch at home to earn a semi-final against Real Madrid.

The holders had not enjoyed an easy ride, particularly against Rapid Vienna in the second round. Madrid won 4–2 at home but lost 3–1 in the Prater stadium within sight of the giant ferris wheel made famous by Carol Reed's film *The Third Man*. Veteran defender Ernst Happel scored a hat-trick from two free-kicks and a penalty.

If away goals had then counted double, Madrid would have been dead and buried. Instead level aggregate scores meant a play-off.

Madrid 'persuaded' Rapid to play back in the Bernabeu and duly won 2–0. Nice were defeated home and away, so the semi-finals lined up the old masters from Madrid against the young pretenders from Manchester and, in the other half, Red Star Belgrade against the iron-clad defence of Italy's Fiorentina.

One goal from Maurilio Prini was all that the *Viola* needed. Coach Fulvio Bernardini planned it that way. The previous season Fiorentina had conceded a mere 20 goals in 34 league games and would have completed the season unbeaten in Serie A had they not slipped up in their last match.

The Madrid–Manchester semi-final was a total contrast, a duel between teams from very different footballing cultures, sharing enormous mutual respect: United marvelled at Di Stefano's relentless energy and vision, while Madrid took the young giant Edwards to their hearts. Greater experience – plus goals from Rial, Di Stefano and Enrique Mateos – brought Madrid a 3–1 win in the Bernabeu. United thought they could turn the tie around, as they had against Bilbao. But Madrid were in a different class. Within 32 minutes of the kick-off at Maine Road they led 2–0 through Kopa and Rial. United, true to their perpetual nature, fought back but only for a 2–2 draw.

REAL BEAT FIORENTINA IN STREET FIGHT

Matt Busby, unlike many other English club managers who scorned anything from beyond their own shores, never saw any point in hiding his admiration for Madrid and Di Stefano.

But he also remained fervently convinced that his young team represented the European Cup's future.

United's average age had barely risen above the low

THURSDAY 30 MAY 1957
BERNABEU, MADRID

REAL MADRID   2
DI STEFANO 70 PEN, GENTO 76

FIORENTINA   0

HT: 0-0. ATT: 120,000.
REF: HORN (HOL)

REAL MADRID:
ALONSO - TORRES, MARQUITOS,
LESMES - MUNOZ*, ZARRAGA - KOPA,
MATEOS, DI STEFANO, RIAL, GENTO.
COACH: VILLALONGA.

FIORENTINA:
SARTI - MAGNINI, ORZAN, CERVATO* -
SCARAMUCCI, SEGATO - JULINHO,
GRATTON, VIRGILI, MONTUORI, PRINI.
COACH: BERNARDINI.

*CAPTAIN

20s, whereas Fiorentina and Madrid were at the other end of the scale as they lined up in the afternoon sunshine in the Estadio Bernabeu. The original rules and regulations had specified that each year's winners should host the next final: Madrid's early dominance soon saw that idea consigned to the dustbin.

Madrid showed three changes compared with Paris 12 months earlier. Kopa, nicknamed 'the little Napoleon of football' by a Spanish newspaper after inspiring France's 2–1 win over Spain in Madrid in spring 1955, was on the right wing; quick-tempered goal poacher Enrique Mateos was his inside-right; and Miguel Torres had been taken on loan from Zaragoza to cover an injury crisis at right-back.

Torres later boasted that he had earned more in six months in Madrid than in all the rest of his career. That was fortunate. When he returned to Zaragoza in the summer he had to sit out the first half of the following season because of loan transfer restrictions.

Fiorentina's tactic was classic and simple: Bernardini, a pre-war international, relied on a safety-first defence, a hard-working phalanx in midfield and the attacking inspiration of Brazil's Julinho at outside-right, 'Pecos Bill' Virgili at centre-forward – so-called for his love of cowboy comics – and the underrated Argentine, Miguel Montuori, at inside-left.

It was a system devised to win, not entertain. Madrid pressed forwards repeatedly and Fiorentina threw them back. 'It was more akin to a street fight,' said founding father Gabriel Hanot.

Di Stefano worked harder than anyone to unlock the Italian defence, but in the end it was Gento's pace which cut them open. He scored a second, clinching goal himself after Di Stefano had opened Madrid's account from a penalty awarded by Dutch referee Leo Horn following a trip on Mateos by right-back Ardico Magnini. Goalkeeper Giuliano Sarti was well beaten; he would take his revenge, though not for another seven years.

Di Stefano, by now, had added yet another title to his fast-growing collection. In mid season he had been voted European Footballer of the Year in succession to Stanley Matthews. The poll was organized for the second year by the Paris magazine *France Football*, weekly sister to the daily *L'Equipe*.

Di Stefano qualified as 'European' by virtue of having assumed Spanish citizenship, and thus could even play for the national team – which he would do on 31 occasions, scoring a then record 23 goals. Di Stefano was 'Total Football' personified. One moment he was defending in his own penalty area, the next organizing his midfield, the next scoring from the edge of the opponents' six-yard box.

His longevity would prove a problem at Madrid for Kopa, who was shunted out to the right wing. For others, however, pursuit of the European Cup's holy grail would have far, far worse in store.

LEFT: **ALFREDO DI STEFANO FIRES HIS PENALTY PAST GIULIANO SARTI, WHO LOOKS TO BE A LONG WAY OFF HIS LINE**

THE SHADOW OF TRAGEDY

Aggrieved at past defeat, Milan set their sights on overhauling Real Madrid with a furious campaign of recruitment. But this campaign will always be remembered for the death of the Busby Babes

Milan are the older of the two Milanese clubs, founded in 1899 and thus nine years senior to splintering Internazionale. In the inter-war years Milano – the name change enforced by Benito Mussolini's *fascisti* – were second best in the city. At the start of the 1950s, however, new money and renewed ambition revived *rossoneri* (red and black) pride.

President Andrea Rizzoli sent his scouts far and wide. Sweden provided the greatest inside-forward trio in the club's history in Gunnar Gren, Gunnar Nordahl and Nils Liedholm. As they aged, so South America filled the gaps through the Argentine left-wing partnership of Ernesto Grillo and Tito Cucchiaroni alongside the Uruguayan world record signing Juan Alberto Schiaffino, the 1950 World Cup-winner who came from Penarol of Montevideo for a then staggering fee of £72,000.

The supporting cast was Italian and included a promising young full-back or central defender named Cesare Maldini.

Milan believed they should have beaten Real Madrid in the 1956 semi-finals and that Madrid's European crown rightly belonged to them. Their revenge campaign began falteringly; they needed a first-round play-off to beat Rapid Vienna. Elsewhere Benfica marked their Champions Cup debut with a 3-1 aggregate defeat by Sevilla and Manchester United put nine goals past Shamrock Rovers over two legs. Real Madrid's holders were awarded a bye into the second round, where they beat Antwerp 2-1 away, 6-0 at home with a Rial hat-trick.

The other major players also marched on. Manchester United, featuring more youngsters in the centre-half Mark Jones, right-winger Ken Morgans and inside forward Colin Webster, overcame Czechoslovak army club Dukla Prague and their astute left-half Jozef Masopust; Grillo scored twice for Milan against Rangers at Ibrox on the way to a 6-1 aggregate success; new Dutch entrants Ajax Amsterdam had the reflexes of goalkeeper Eddie Pieters-Graafland to thank for their victory over Wismut Chemnitz.

RIGHT: THE BERNABEU STADIUM IN MADRID, WAS BUILT IN 1947 AND WAS CONSIDERED THE GREATEST FOOTBALL GROUND IN THE WORLD WITH A CAPACITY OF 74,309. THIS PHOTOGRAPH WAS TAKEN IN 1957, THREE YEARS AFTER THE FIRST EXTENSION WAS ADDED

In the quarter-finals even the long arms of Pieters-Graafland were no match for the attacking verve of Vasas Budapest, who thrashed Ajax's part-timers 2-2, 4-0; Milan, without the injured Schiaffino both away and home, overcame Borussia Dortmund 1-1, 4-1 with Grillo again on target; Madrid humiliated their fellow Spaniards from Sevilla 2-2, 8-0. Di Stefano struck four in the Bernabeu.

But the most memorable quarter-final was between Red Star Belgrade and Manchester United. Red Star were an outstanding side with a ballet-dancer in goal in Vladimir Beara, a gypsy playmaker in Dragoslav Sekularac and a left-winger in Bora Kostic who packed one of the most thunderous shots in European football. United won only 2-1 at home after being 1-0 down at half-time and recovering with goals from Charlton and Colman. That was 14 January 1958.

So to Belgrade. Back in December bad weather had seen United struggle to find flights back from Prague in time for their weekend league fixture. This time, to eliminate any such risk, United decided to charter their own plane.

It was Charlton's first European trip and he was the first-half hero, scoring two superb goals as United went 3-0 ahead. Red Star refused to concede. Kostic scored once, Lazar Tasic converted a penalty and Viollet deflected a Kostic free-kick past 'keeper Harry Gregg. But only two minutes remained and United clung on.

The next day, 6 February, United flew for home and stopped to refuel at Munich's cold, snowy Riem airport. They landed shortly after 2.00 pm and the party of club officials, led by Busby, players, journalists and crew returned to the plane half an hour later. Twice, accelerating down the runway, captain James Thain aborted the take-off. The passengers returned to the airport lounge while attention was given to a 'slight technical fault'.

The third attempt to take off saw the Elizabethan pass the point of no return without leaving the ground. It careered through the perimeter fence, striking two small huts and a tree on its deathly path.

The sad tale has been told and retold many times: of the heroism shown by, among others, Gregg and a *Daily Mail* photographer, Peter Howard, in rescuing people from the wreckage; and of the eventual death toll of 23, including eight journalists and eight players – captain Byrne, Colman, Jones, Whelan, Taylor, David Pegg, reserve full-back Geoff Bent and, after fighting on for 15 days, Edwards.

Amazingly, 13 days after the disaster, United put a team back together to beat Sheffield Wednesday 3-0 in the FA Cup. Three months on, in mid-May, they took up the semi-final legacy of the original Babes, only to lose, not surprisingly, to Milan. Veteran signing Ernie Taylor and crash survivor Viollet scored the goals in a 2-1 win at Old Trafford. But in the return the emotion of the away trip and the guile of Schiaffino, Liedholm and co proved too much.

Milan won 4-0 and were delighted that Madrid had dispatched Vasas 4-2 overall in the other semi-final. Di Stefano scored a first-leg hat-trick, but Milan coach Gipo Viani believed the Argentine's best days were behind him.

REAL TRUMP MILAN

Gipo Viani was the Milan coach who had concentrated so intently on the European Cup that Serie A issues had fallen by the wayside.

Milan, champions by a clear six points in 1957, had slipped to a mid-table ninth after winding up their league campaign just four days before the trip to the Heysel stadium in Brussels to combat hat-trick-chasing Real Madrid.

Their last league fixture was wreathed in controversy. Milan, with nothing at stake, were home to relegation-threatened Genoa, who needed a big win to survive. What transpired produced national outcry.

Viani lined up Grillo at inside-left but rested his three other star forwards: Schiaffino, Liedholm and Cucchiaroni. Genoa duly won 5–1 in the San Siro to finish a safe 12th, just two points behind the European finalists. Left-winger Paolo Barison scored three of Genoa's goals to earn a summer move to Milan.

Milan had to win in Brussels, not only for the sake of their pride but in order to return to the European Cup the following season.

Madrid lined up in the shadow of the Atomium, which still survives from that year's International Expo, with no such concern. They had won 2–1 at Zaragoza the previous weekend to secure their sixth league title.

Goalkeeper Lorenzo Buffon took the blame for Milan's five-goal beating by Genoa and was replaced by Narciso Soldan; Madrid had Alonso back, not only in goal but as captain, and lined up Joseito – with only five league games that season to his name – at inside-right in place of the injured Ramon Marsal. Madrid also had a new coach: the former Argentina inside-forward Luis Carniglia.

The first half was all Milan, but they found their progress towards goal thwarted apparently at every step by Di Stefano – the ultimate exponent of 'Total Football' long before the term was coined. The next day an Italian journalist wrote: 'For an hour he played Milan on his own. Is this man a god?'

The inevitable happened almost on the hour when Schiaffino finished off a quicksilver interpassing move with Liedholm and Grillo to open the scoring. Di Stefano, naturally, levelled, only for Grillo to restore Milan's advantage. A minute later, as Italian players called to their bench to check the time, Rial punished the momentary lapse of concentration by equalizing again.

The European Cup Final thus went into an extra half-hour for the first time in its history. Milan inevitably began to tire and Gento exploded out through the mist on the Madrid left wing.

Once, he went past three flagging defenders only to see his cross wasted. The next time, he cut inside and smacked a shot against a post. Then, two minutes into the second half of extra time, it was third time lucky; again Gento cut inside and this time his fizzing drive surprised Soldan at the near post. Years later, Gento conceded in time-honoured fashion: 'I just hit it and hoped.'

'Madrid may still be European champions but they need rejuvenating,' wrote a French journalist to general approval. No one dreamed that the future would see Madrid lifted to another level by an overweight 31-year-old who had not kicked a ball in anger for 18 months.

COUPE DES CLUBS CHAMPIONS
EUROPESE BEKER DER LANDSKAMPIOENEN

1958

REAL MADRID - AC MILAN

STADE DU HEYSEL / HEIZELSTADION

28-05-1958: BRUXELLES
BRUSSEL

PROGRAMME OFFICIEL / OFFICIEEL PROGRAMMA : 5 BF

ABOVE: **REAL LEVEL THE SCORES ONCE MORE AS NARCISO SOLDAN FLAPS AT EMPTY AIR**

LEFT: **REAL'S JOSEITO AND MILAN'S RADICE CHALLENGE FOR A LOOSE BALL**

THE YEAR OF REVOLUTION

It was Pele who coined the expression 'The Beautiful Game' and teams throughout Europe were inspired to emulate the Brazilians after their World Cup win. However, old enmities were not forgotten...

The summer of 1958 marked a watershed in not only European but world football. In June Brazil became the first nation to win the World Cup outside their own continent when they triumphed in Sweden.

They prompted new tactical awareness with their 4–2–4 system and won new respect through the established talents of playmaker Didi and the explosive emergence of outside-right Garrincha and the 17-year-old inside-left Edson Arantes do Nascimento, aka Pele.

Europe's resistance was led by two Frenchmen: Raymond Kopa and Just Fontaine, the man Reims had bought to fill the gap left by the little man's departure for Madrid in the summer of 1956.

Kopa, restricted to the right wing at Madrid by Di Stefano's centre-field dominance, was the creative genius behind a majority of Fontaine's record-breaking 13 goals in Sweden. The sum total of French World Cup inspiration and

Champions Cup victory with Madrid earned Kopa the 1958 European Footballer of the Year prize. But he was a loser where Madrid's internal politics were concerned.

Ferenc Puskas, scorer of 83 international goals in 84 games from inside-left, was one of the three members of Hungary's 'magical Magyars' who had decided to stay in western Europe after the collapse of the 1956 revolution back in Budapest.

The Hungarian federation attempted to ban Puskas, left-winger Zoltan Czibor and inside-right Sandor Kocsis for life from signing anywhere else. But other forces were at work behind the scenes.

Ladislav Kubala, the darling of Barcelona, had fled Hungary almost a decade earlier and built an admired new football life in Spain. He persuaded Barcelona to sign Kocsis and Czibor, while Puskas was rescued by Emil Osterreicher, the former Honved technical director who was now on the

RIGHT: ATLETICO MADRID GOAL-KEEPER PAZOS MAKES AN AMAZING FLYING SAVE FROM REAL MADRID'S RAYMOND KOPA IN THE METROPOLITANO IN ONE OF ONLY FOUR DERBIES BETWEEN TEAMS FROM THE SAME CITY SO FAR PLAYED IN THE EUROPEAN CUP

Real Madrid payroll. It was a major gamble, as Puskas was now past 30 and overweight through inaction. The gamble paid off, however, when the Hungarian averaged nearly a goal a game in his first season in the Spanish league.

The European challenge to Madrid's crown appeared to be led by Italy's Juventus, by the Fontaine-fired Reims and by Madrid's neighbours and Spanish runners-up Atletico.

Manchester United were invited to compete in a gesture of sympathy and support from UEFA. The Football League refused permission; an FA appeal panel approved United's entry; then a joint FA-League commission rejected it again. England's challenge thus remained with Wolves, whose floodlit exploits back in late 1954 had inspired the competition's creation.

Hearts made their bow for Scotland, hoping to emulate the semi-final achievements of Edinburgh neighbours Hibernian in 1956 while at least improving on the early-round exits of Rangers in 1957 and 1958. However, they lost 6-3 on aggregate to Standard Liege in the qualifying round.

Football is a funny game, at all levels. Juventus expected to crush Austria's Wiener Sportclub. The attacking partnership of the outrageous Argentine showman Omar Sivori and the Welsh 'gentle giant' John Charles had overwhelmed the rest of Serie A. For good measure Sivori added a hat-trick in the opening 3-1 win over the Austrians, an unknown quantity at this stage of the competition.

He again went through his range of technical trickery in the first half-hour of the return in Vienna's Prater stadium. Then, against the run of play and to the Austrians' own surprise, they took the lead through a speculative free-kick from Karl Skerlan. Juventus lost their heads and also their control. Wiener led 3-0 at half-time and finished 7-0 winners. Josef Hammerl scored a hat-trick. It took Juve years to recover their European confidence.

There were no such problems for Reims and Fontaine. Later Fontaine would be forced into premature retirement after twice breaking a leg, but while he was fit he was lethal. He scored six goals against Ards, two against Palloseura Helsinki and two more against Standard Liege. Young Boys Berne concentrated so hard on stopping Fontaine in the semi-final that they forgot about two-goal Roger Piantoni and Armand Penverne. Reims, beaten 1-0 in Berne, turned the tables 3-0 at home.

Wolves were a disappointment despite benefiting from a first-round bye before being drawn against West Germany's Schalke. German football was part-time and lacked a national league. Each regional league played out its own championship with the winners meeting in an end-

of-season play-off series. Schalke had triumphed 3-0 over a Hamburg side led by an energetic young centre-forward named Uwe Seeler.

Left-winger Berni Klodt, who had scored twice against Hamburg, struck a decisive goal in the first-round play-off win over BK Copenhagen. He did not score against Wolves but his wing play opened up their defence both at Molineux and back in the mining citadel of Gelsenkirchen deep in the heart of the Ruhr. Schalke matched two goals from Peter Broadbent to draw 2-2 away then won 2-1 at home. In the quarter-finals, however, they lost 0-3, 1-1 to Atletico Madrid.

Atletico had pounced, after the World Cup finals, to sign Brazil's pugnacious centre-forward Vava. He scored in both legs against Schalke and posed a major threat to Real when the neighbours were drawn together in the semi-finals.

Madrid had found this title defence the most bruising. Di Stefano was sent off in the opening win over Turkey's Besiktas, and Puskas was dismissed in the subsequent defeat of Wiener SK. The Hungarian, who had trained alone for months to sweat off most of the extra kilos, made amends with the first-leg winner when Real edged Atletico 2-1 in the Bernabeu stadium.

Not far across town, in Atletico's Metropolitano, left-winger Enrique Collar struck back painfully. If away goals had counted double, Madrid would have gone out. Instead the play-off option provided the opportunity for a 2-1 win in neutral Zaragoza.

Di Stefano and Puskas scored the goals; Kopa would now face his old club in the final in Stuttgart.

FOURTH TIME LUCKY FOR REAL

Unrest was stirring behind the scenes at Madrid. Much of it swirled around the Argentine coach Luis Carniglia, who was being squeezed by directors and technical staff on the one hand and by senior players on the other. All of this was further complicated by injury concerns.

On that score at least, Reims came into the final with the advantage of fitness and a settled team.

Robert Jonquet was the commanding centre-back who had anchored France's defence in their run to third place at the 1958 World Cup.

Indeed, it was only after he was injured that France had succumbed to Brazil in the semi-finals. World Cup half-back partner Penverne wanted to make up for having missed the 1956 European Cup Final; Bruno Rodzik was a powerful raiding full-back; Rene Bliard and Roger Piantoni goalscoring inside-forwards; Jean Vincent an aggressive and pacy left-winger.

Carniglia knew them all well. He had played in France with Nice in the early 1950s and was a long-term sparring partner of the Remois and their coach Albert Batteux.

His first problem was in goal. Juanito Alonso had been taken ill, which led to a recall for Rogelio Dominguez, who had played only five league games. Injury-prone left-back Rafael Lesmes had been hurt again in the play-off win over Atletico, so Carniglia shifted back his captain, Jose Maria Zarraga and drafted in young Antonio Ruiz as defensive left-half.

The usual five-man Madrid attack was Kopa, Rial or Mateos, Di Stefano, Puskas and Gento. But Puskas had a slight leg strain which had hampered him the previous week in a cup-tie against Sevilla. So, for all his magnificent first-season 21 goals in 24 league games, he was omitted.

Gabriel Hanot noted that Carniglia did not want to repeat the mistake made by Hungary in playing a half-fit Puskas in the 1954 World Cup Final. Then he added, caustically: 'It's a safe bet that, if Rial were Hungarian and Puskas Argentine, Madrid's line-up would look somewhat different.'

Not that it mattered. Madrid won comfortably, remarkably so considering that they played half the match with 10 fit men after Kopa suffered a serious knee injury when taken down from behind by Vincent. Kopa, furious, refused to accept his compatriot's apology after the game. Perhaps he already sensed – correctly, as it turned out – that this injury would dog him for the rest of his career.

The final's outcome was soon decided. Inside the second minute Bliard misplaced a pass, Penverne hesitated and Zarraga sent in Enrique Mateos to open the scoring. On 12 minutes, Mateos was brought down by Jonquet. Dominique Colonna made a fine save to the victim's penalty, diving to his right, but was at fault when Di Stefano shot Madrid 2-0 ahead early in the second half.

Gento had a goal disallowed for taking a free-kick before the referee had signalled but it mattered not. Madrid were champions of Europe for a fourth time, while Di Stefano was on his way to a second European Footballer of the Year accolade in three seasons; Kopa, winner in 1958, would be his runner-up.

Carniglia danced in delight on the touchline, little knowing that another Argentine had already, in effect, put him out of a job. Early in the season, to the fury of president Santiago Bernabeu, Madrid had lost away to Barcelona 4-0. Barcelona went on to win the league that season while their coach, Helenio Herrera, would go on to haunt Madrid for years to come.

RIGHT: **THE LEGENDARY JUST FONTAINE CHALLENGES REAL GOALKEEPER DOMINGUEZ FOR THE BALL**

OPPOSITE: **REAL CAPTAIN JOSE ZARRAGA BASKS IN THE REFLECTED GLORY OF REAL'S FOURTH EUROPEAN CUP VICTORY IN A ROW**

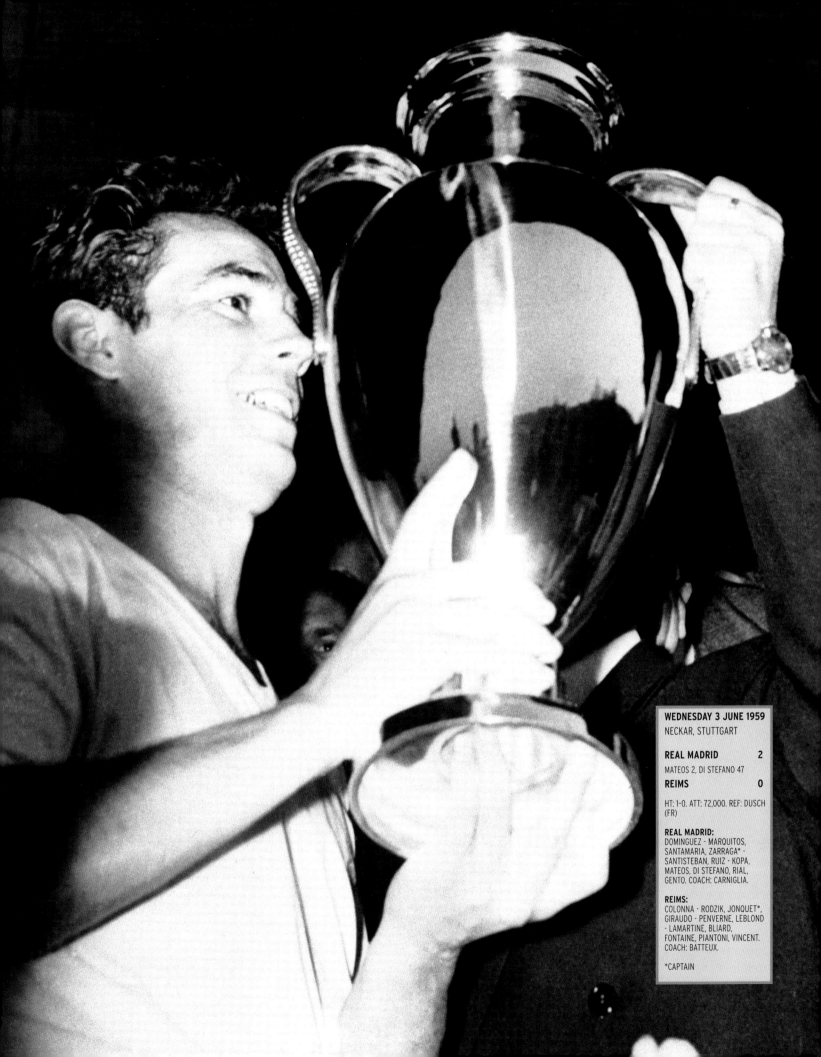

WEDNESDAY 3 JUNE 1959
NECKAR, STUTTGART

REAL MADRID   **2**
MATEOS 2, DI STEFANO 47
REIMS   **0**

HT: 1-0. ATT: 72,000. REF: DUSCH
(FR)

REAL MADRID:
DOMINGUEZ - MARQUITOS,
SANTAMARIA, ZARRAGA* -
SANTISTEBAN, RUIZ - KOPA,
MATEOS, DI STEFANO, RIAL,
GENTO. COACH: CARNIGLIA.

REIMS:
COLONNA - RODZIK, JONQUET*,
GIRAUDO - PENVERNE, LEBLOND
- LAMARTINE, BLIARD,
FONTAINE, PIANTONI, VINCENT.
COACH: BATTEUX.

*CAPTAIN

1960s

THE DECADE THAT SWUNG

The 1960s proved a decade of extremes for the European Champions Cup. Real Madrid began it wreathed in glory, only to be toppled by their old Spanish rivals Barcelona – who failed to capitalize on their achievement. Instead, it was Portugal's Benfica and the exciting Eusebio who briefly ruled the continent before being overtaken, in turn, by Italian pragmatism as represented by Milan and Internazionale. Latin Europe's domination then retreated in the face of a British invasion led by Celtic before Manchester United triumphantly sealed their own circle of fate. But already a new dawn was being promised by the Dutchmen of Ajax Amsterdam.

RIGHT: **MATT BUSBY REVIVES MANCHESTER UNITED'S SPIRITS DURING THE 1968 FINAL JUST BEFORE EXTRA TIME BEGINS. IN THE BACKGROUND, YOU CAN SEE THE BENFICA PLAYERS. UNITED WON 4-1 IN THE END**

EUSEBIO
(Eusebio da Silva Ferreira)

Country: Portugal

Position: Striker

Born: 25 January, 1942

Clubs: Sporting Lourenco
  Marques (Mozambique),
  Benfica (Portugal), Boston
  Minutemen (US), Monterrey
  (Mexico), Toronto Metros
  (Canada), Las Vegas
  Quicksilver (US), Beira-Mar
  (Portugal)

EUSEBIO

I am always surprised how many people continue to remember me, more than 40 years after winning the Champions Cup with Benfica.

A few years ago, the French presented me with the Borotra Trophy, which is a fair-play award in memory of their old tennis player. I was amazed. I thought my days for receiving trophies finished 30 years ago when the goals stopped.

Then, when Benfica built their new stadium for the European Championship finals in 2004, there was a suggestion that it might have been named after me – which would have been a great honour but not something I really wanted.

A football stadium is about a club and its fans; it's not just about one individual.

I was proud enough a few years earlier when they put a statue of me at the stadium entrance. In Portugal, people normally do not receive any sort of homage until they are dead, but I am very much alive and that was honour enough.

Many great experiences came my way through football. The 1966 World Cup, when we reached the semi-finals in England, was a wonderful moment. But that was a one-off tournament. The prolonged high point was pulling on the red shirt of Benfica every week for a decade – once I had finally made it to Lisbon, that is.

Mozambique was still a Portuguese colony when I was a kid, and I played for Sporting Clube of Lourenco Marques, the capital, which is now known as Maputo. They were a sort of nursery club. We all knew that, if we were any good, one of the big Portuguese clubs would come in. The complication in my case was that both Sporting and Benfica wanted me.

Benfica made the first offer, and that was fine, but Lourenco Marques would not release me. So, even after I went to Lisbon and settled into the Benfica players' home, I could not play for them – even though I travelled to all their away games in the European Cup that season.

Finally, everything was sorted out eight days before we were to play Barcelona in the 1961 Champions Cup final. I thought I might have a chance of playing, but it turned out that UEFA had brought in a three-month transfer delay, so I was still ineligible.

In fact, I did not even go to the game. I had to listen to it on the radio because our coach, Bela Guttmann, wanted to keep me for a cup tie against Vitoria Setubal the next weekend. It's not a happy memory.

We lost and, though I scored a goal, I also missed a penalty which might have got us a play-off.*

My international baptism was not in the Champions Cup but in that year's end-of-season Paris Tournament, which was very prestigious in those days. We beat Anderlecht 2–1 in our semi-final – and I scored – and then we played the

LEFT: **EUSEBIO BEFORE PORTUGAL'S WORLD CUP QUARTER-FINAL AGAINST NORTH KOREA AT GOODISON IN 1966**

Brazilian club Santos, who had Pele playing for them, in the final.

Now, for me, Pele was the finest footballer of them all. He played in an era which had so many great players, yet he stood head and shoulders above them all.

He was the complete player in every respect, as well as being a very kindly human being. I have not seen anyone to compare, so imagine how I felt being on the same pitch with him for the first time.

Guttmann did not put me in the starting line-up. But after half an hour when we were losing 5-0 (!), he sent me on in place of Joaquin Santana. We would have needed a miracle, so I felt under no pressure and, perhaps because of that, I scored a hat-trick. In the end we lost 6-3, which was not so bad in the circumstances.

After that everything moved very fast. I scored again in the World Club Cup defeat against Penarol – we lost over there, in Uruguay, to a dubious penalty. Then I began my Portugal career in the qualifiers for the 1962 World Cup against Luxembourg and then against England at Wembley, the 'cathedral' of football.

Next we had the European Cup to defend, and this time I was in the team from the start.

I was lucky over the next 10 years to go all over Europe both as a player and just as me, Eusebio. But I have never met fans who are more passionate about football than the Portuguese. We soak up anything and everything about the game.

Look at the media here. We have three daily sports newspapers whose pages are mostly all about football. Not only that, but one daily sports paper sells more copies each day than any other newspaper of any sort.

Looking back, I think we built a lot of the legend of Portuguese football then. Before Benfica, Real Madrid had been the only club to have won the European Cup, so we were up at that level. We surpassed them, too, by beating them 5-3 in the 1962 final in Amsterdam. That was the game in which we were 3-2 down at half-time but Guttmann told us in the dressing room: 'Don't worry about a thing – we've got this all sewn up.'

That was when I was first called the Black Panther. Frankly, I did not like it, because there was a violent, revolutionary group in the United States with the same name. But it was meant as a compliment and I had no choice but to get used to it.

I did not like being called the 'European Pele' either. I thought that was disrespectful. Would Pele have appreciated being called 'America's Eusebio'? I doubt it somehow.

We should have beaten both Milan in the 1963 final and Inter in 1965. I have to say we could not begrudge Manchester United in 1968, even though my miss just before the end of the 90 minutes was probably the blackest moment of my career.

But with the Italian clubs it was different. Against Milan over-confidence meant we lost a game in which I scored first and which we had all but won; against Inter I needed a painkilling injection before the game and I played badly.

We also suffered crucial injuries during both finals in the days before substitutes were permitted. Luck was not with us.

Sometimes football is like that.

* The goalkeeper who saved Eusebio's first senior competitive penalty was Felix Mourinho, father of Jose Mourinho, now Chelsea manager

OPPOSITE: **KNOWN AS THE BLACK PANTHER, EUSEBIO WAS VOTED EUROPEAN FOOTBALLER OF THE YEAR IN 1965; HE WAS ALSO TOP SCORER IN THE 1966 WORLD CUP FINALS**

THE BRAIN GAME

The old-fashioned virtues of English football were put to the test as Barcelona took on Wolves. In a new tactical era, team play came to the fore as Eintracht Frankfurt stole almost unnoticed into the final

Wolverhampton Wanderers were back, determined to get it right this time. Their famous floodlit friendlies had prompted the creation of the European Champions Cup, but they had let themselves down badly the previous season. Manager Stan Cullis believed in the winning qualities of traditional English football, in spite of the evidence provided by Hungary and Real Madrid. For him, strength in defence, hard work in midfield, versatile inside-forwards and pacy wingers provided the hardware.

Wolves were changing. Billy Wright had retired, virtually overnight, after returning from England's summer tour to the Americas to find that Cullis was grooming George Showell to take his place in the heart of defence. The veteran left-winger Jimmy Mullen, one of the heroes against Honved and Spartak, had also been removed from the attacking equation.

RIGHT: RON FLOWERS SHAKES HANDS WITH LUIS SUAREZ AFTER BARCELONA HAD BEATEN WOLVES 4-0 IN THE NOU CAMP IN FRONT OF A CROWD OF 80,000. WOLVES LOST THE SECOND LEG 5-2 AT HOME

Reviewing the field ahead of the draw, Cullis picked out Real Madrid and Milan as dangers, with Spanish champions Barcelona and Scotland's Rangers threats further down the field. No one – in England, Spain or Italy – stopped to worry about the German champions Eintracht Frankfurt.

Wolves started in East Germany against the army club, Vorwarts, from East Berlin. The communist takeover of eastern European had revolutionized sports administration. The main ministries and public utilities had either swallowed up the independent pre-war clubs or created new ones in their own authoritarian image. But the gain in financial subsidies was balanced, negatively, by the loss of foreign influences in both coaching and player sectors.

The ability of army clubs throughout eastern Europe to order conscripts into their playing ranks brought league titles aplenty for Vorwarts in the German Democratic Republic, Legia in Poland, Dukla in Czechoslovakia, CDNA (later CSKA) in Bulgaria, CCA (later Steaua) in Romania and Partizani in Albania, though not, oddly, CSKA in Russia.

Vorwarts played like good soldiers obeying orders: all discipline, no individual flair. They edged Wolves 2-1 at home and lost 2-0 at Molineux. The England inside-forward Peter Broadbent scored both away and home.

The next step was an emotional one: to Belgrade to play Red Star, last opponents of the Busby Babes before the Munich disaster. Six of the Red Star team who drew 3-3 with United now faced Wolves, including Beara, Sekularac, Tasic and Kostic. Again the outcome was a draw, this time 1-1, and Jimmy Murray scored twice as Wolves rampaged home 3-0 in the return.

That meant the quarter-finals and a meeting with Barcelona. The rest of the world had yet to fall for the Catalan 'romance' but their pedigree was clear.

They had triumphed in the first Fairs Cup in 1958, had won five Spanish league titles in nine seasons and boasted some of the world's finest players in the Hungarians Kubala, Sandor Kocsis and Zoltan Czibor, Brazil's Evaristo de Macedo and arguably Spain's greatest-ever player, Luis Suarez, who later played with Internazionale.

Wielding a demanding conductor's baton was a coach

who had been born in Morocco, brought up in Argentina, played in France then made his coaching name in Spain: Helenio Herrera.

'The Magician', as he enjoyed being known, introduced rotation decades before the term was conceived. Against weak opponents he played inside-forwards at wing-half; against tough opponents he included an extra wing-half at inside-forward.

Every match was different, every tactic adjusted to suit the opposition and the occasion.

Now it was Wolves' turn to be intimidated by the four-square cliffs of the Nou Camp. Barcelona trounced them 4–0. It was a cosmopolitan collapse. Paraguayan winger Ramon Villaverde scored two, Kubala and Evaristo the others.

Herrera held back Kocsis, one of the scourges of England in 1953 and 1954, for the return. Wolves, predictably, threw caution to the Molineux winds and Barcelona hit them remorselessly on the break –

time and time again. Villaverde scored again and Kocsis claimed the other four. Barcelona won 5–2 on the night and 9–2 on aggregate; Wolves have never appeared in the competition since.

Barcelona, having earlier beaten Milan, considered themselves favourites to deprive Madrid of their European crown just as they had deposed Real as champions of Spain. Years later Di Stefano acknowledged: 'They had the better individuals,' then added after a pause, 'but we had the better team.'

Herrera's personal feud with Kubala meant that the Hungarian watched both legs of the semi-final from the stand. The result was the same: Madrid won 3–1 both in the Bernabeu and in the Nou Camp. Furious Barcelona fans chased Herrera down the Ramblas and out of town.

Madrid's opposition in the final would be the first non-Latin team to grace the event: unconsidered, underrated Eintracht Frankfurt.

ABOVE: RANGERS ARE ALL AT SEA AS THEY DISCOVER THEY CANNOT MATCH EINTRACHT FRANKFURT FOR PACE OR TECHNIQUE. THEY EVENTUALLY LOST 6–1 IN FRANKFURT AND BY 6–3 AT IBROX IN A ONE-SIDED SEMI-FINAL

THE GREATEST-EVER FINAL

Real Madrid and Eintracht Frankfurt will be forever linked together by events over 90 minutes on the Glasgow evening of May 18, 1960. 'The greatest game ever played' is the label which has sealed the legend down the years.

For fans in the twenty-first century, watching flickering grey-and-white images, the recording offers a dreamy, slow-motion quality.

Oceanic expanses of pitch open up between players, and the protection for two hapless and helpless goalkeepers is vague, to say the least.

But greatness is born of context and nothing like it had been seen before. Developments in training systems in particular and nutrition in general would change the face of association football. But without Real Madrid and the glamour of this one match the European Cup would not have sparked the international awakening of commercial and media giants.

The outcome was a surprise to the record 127,621 crowd jamming Hampden. Frankfurt had pulverized Glasgow's own

Rangers in the semi-finals: winning 6–1 in the Waldstadion and 6–3 at Ibrox. Their inspiration stemmed from a veteran of West Germany's 1954 World Cup-winning party: inside-left and captain Alfred Pfaff.

Madrid's make-up had changed on and off the pitch. At the instigation of the players, the club had replaced short-lived Paraguayan coach Fleitas Solich with Miguel Munoz, their cup-winning captain from 1956 and 1957.

Kopa had gone home to Reims in the summer of 1959, amid controversy. Originally he had agreed to stay until 1960 but then, ahead of time, sorted out his own delayed deal with Reims. Bernabeu was furious, insisting Kopa go immediately.

Bernabeu liked to buy a new superstar each summer; Florentino Perez and his *Galacticos*, 50 years later, would be nothing new. Di Stefano, Rial and Santamaria were all now Spanish citizens which left vacancies for two new foreign players. Madrid filled both from Brazil with inside-right Didi and right-winger Canario.

WEDNESDAY 18 MAY 1960
HAMPDEN PARK, GLASGOW

REAL MADRID   **7**
DI STEFANO 26, 29, 74, PUSKAS 44, 56
PEN, 60, 71

EINTRACHT FRANKFURT   **3**
KRESS 18, STEIN 72, 76

HT: 3-1. ATT: 127,621.
REF: MOWAT (SCOT)

REAL MADRID:
DOMINGUEZ – MARQUITOS, SANTA-
MARIA, PACHIN – VIDAL, ZARRAGA* –
CANARIO, DEL SOL, DI STEFANO,
PUSKAS, GENTO. COACH: MUNOZ.

EINTRACHT FRANKFURT:
LOY – LUTZ, EIGENBRODT, HOFER –
WEILBACHER, STINKA – KRESS,
LINDNER, STEIN, PFAFF*, MEIER.
COACH: OSSWALD.

*CAPTAIN.

Didi had been the playmaker of Brazil's World Cup-winners in Sweden in 1958 and would repeat his magic in Chile in 1962.

But his Madrid stay was a disaster. Di Stefano was supposed to have welcomed him with the words: 'They say you've come to replace me; well, you're too old and you're not good enough.' The story may be apocryphal, but, if nothing else, Didi hated the pace of Spanish football.

He never played even one European tie before being loaned out to Valencia, then sold back to Rio's Botafogo. Madrid, after misfiring for months in midfield, replaced him just before the Barcelona semi-final with the tireless Luis Del Sol from Betis. He proved, in effect, to be Di Stefano's new legs and completed the perfect football jigsaw.

In Hampden's vast old bowl, Madrid went a goal down to Richard Kress before hitting back gloriously. The ball flowed from one white shirt to another, with Di Stefano linking every phase of play and Puskas deadly at the attacking apex. Di Stefano scored three, Puskas four; Stein replied with a late consolation double for Frankfurt. Watching players, managers and media cast around desperately in search of new superlatives.

LEFT: ALL-WHITE ON THE NIGHT: REAL'S PLAYERS CELEBRATE VICTORY ON THE LEGENDARY EVENING WHEN GOALS RAINED DOWN ON GLASGOW

LEFT: VAST NUMBERS OF FANS ROLL UP AT HAMPDEN PARK BEFORE THE CHAMPIONS CUP FINAL IN 1960. A RECORD CROWD OF 127,621 WAS TO SEE ONE OF THE GREATEST GAMES EVER PLAYED

1960-61

THE EAGLES HAVE LANDED

Football's spotlight turned further west with the arrival of Benfica as a major European power. They started as also-rans but picked up momentum as likely contenders dropped like flies along the way

Different times, different rules. Italy and Spain, increasingly concerned about the failings of their national teams, tightened restrictions on player imports. This trend was not one, however, to worry the champions of Portugal.

Benfica, the Eagles of Lisbon, had never signed a foreign player, but foreign coaches were a different matter. The man who led them into the 1960–61 Champions Cup was Bela Guttmann, a wandering Hungarian who had been on the coaching staff of the Magical Magyars in the early 1950s.

Guttmann had once, famously, been sacked by Milan while they were top of the table; during a spell in Brazil he claimed to have taught the future World Cup winners the 4-2-4 system. On arrival at Benfica, however, he decided his players were better suited to the traditional WM.

That did not go down well with players converted to 4-2-4 by Guttmann's Brazilian predecessor, Otto Gloria. In particular, it was not to the liking of midfield general Mario Coluna. He resented being 'restricted' to the inside-left channel. But Guttmann's gift was in knowing players better than they knew themselves; he also converted Jose Augusto from a creative centre-forward into the best right-winger in Europe after Kopa.

Benfica were not reckoned to be among the likely winners at the time of the draw. Major contenders were Reims, with Kopa and Fontaine reunited, Barcelona, Juventus, Red Star and Hamburg, plus England's Burnley. And, of course, Real Madrid.

The holders had their usual bye through the opening round. The *Merengues* put the time to profitable use by winning the inaugural World Club Cup. Madrid held Penarol of Uruguay goalless in the Montevideo rain then thrashed them 5-1 back in Madrid. By that time, Di Stefano, Puskas and co were already thinking ahead to their Champions Cup defence: they would open against Barcelona.

Open... and close. Herrera having gone to Internazionale, Kubala was restored to primacy at the Nou Camp. His creative partnership with Suarez, in support of Kocsis and Evaristo up front, flared triumphantly. Suarez scored twice, once from a penalty, in the 2-2 draw in Madrid. Kubala then dropped back on the Barcelona right wing to smother the threat of Gento in the return. Madrid, with Pachin a limping passenger for much of the game, had three goals disallowed by referee Reg Leafe and lost 2-1.

RIGHT: **ENGLISH REFEREE REG LEAFE DISALLOWS A GOAL TO THE VISIBLE DISBELIEF OF GENTO, PUSKAS AND VIDAL DURING THE SECOND-ROUND SECOND LEG AGAINST BARCELONA**

'UEFA people didn't like us dominating "their" cup,' said a jaundiced Di Stefano later. 'That's why they got English referees to make sure we didn't. After all, English referees were supposed to be the best. No one would suspect anything.'

With Madrid gone, the cup was perceived as a shoo-in for Barcelona. The pyramid of power was built to their design. In the semi-finals Barcelona beat Hamburg, who had defeated the home-grown purists of Burnley – who had previously beaten Reims; injuries kept Fontaine out of the first leg, Kopa out of the second.

Juventus, meanwhile, committed defensive suicide all on their own in the first round, losing 4-1 to CDNA in Bulgaria after winning 2-0 at home.

The signs were ominous for Barcelona in their semi-final. Hamburg were built on the bullish attacking fire of Uwe Seeler, the pace of left-winger Gerd Dorfel and the half-back support of Seeler's elder brother, Dieter. Even though Dieter missed the semi-final, after breaking a leg in a league game, Hamburg nearly upset the Barcelona dream.

Evaristo scored the lone goal in the Nou Camp, but goals from Peter Wulf and Uwe Seeler back in Germany put Hamburg on course for the final with 90 seconds left. Then Kocsis lived up to his nickname of 'Golden Head' to level the aggregate. The away-goals rule was yet to be adopted, so the teams had to play off at the Heysel stadium in Brussels. A lone goal from Evaristo settled it. All that was left for Barcelona was the academic matter of beating Benfica in the final in Berne.

Benfica possessed talented players who had grown in stature and confidence with each succeeding round as they dismissed Hearts, Hungary's Ujpest, Denmark's Aarhus and Rapid Vienna, their semi-final opponents, who lost the first leg 3-0 in Lisbon.

The second leg of the semi, in Vienna, was abandoned two minutes from time, at 1-1, after referee Leafe refused the hosts a penalty. Hundreds of furious fans besieged the stadium offices for more than two hours before police came to the rescue of both Leafe and Benfica's finalists. Rapid were later banned from European competition for three seasons.

A number of Benfica's team, including Coluna, had been discovered in Africa, in Mozambique and Angola; but because these were colonies their footballers did not count as foreigners in Portugal. Another was Jose Aguas, the Benfica captain and centre-forward. In Angola he had earned local fame as a teenaged lion-hunter. Benfica had brought him to Lisbon and taught him to hunt goals.

BENFICA'S VICTORY AGAINST THE ODDS

Barcelona did not arrive in Berne in the best of shape. Ljubisa Brocic had succeeded Herrera as coach the previous summer and then been replaced by Enrique Orizaola after a mid-season dip in form. The escalating costs of building the Nou Camp had also weighed on the club; Luis Suarez, reigning European Footballer of the Year, was playing his last game before a world record £210,000 transfer to rejoin Helenio Herrera at Internazionale of Milan.

Kubala was also at the end of his contract and considering his options. He was almost 34 and had a portfolio of offers from Spain to Canada to Argentina, where River Plate had a one-year contract waiting. Meanwhile veteran skipper and left-half Juan Segarra had injured a knee in a league match the previous weekend; and goalkeeper Antonio Ramallets had not been the same since being hit for four by England at Wembley the previous autumn.

Worst of all was the superstition factor. Seven years earlier Sandor Kocsis and Zoltan Czibor had lined up in this same old wooden stadium for Hungary against West Germany in the 1954 World Cup Final. Hungary were far greater favourites then than even Barcelona now, but they had lost 3–2; it was the Magical Magyars' first defeat in four years – in the match which mattered the most.

For the first time, a European final failed to attract a capacity crowd. At 33,000 the Wankdorf was almost 15,000 below its limit. The perceived predictability of the result had failed to enthrall and draw the neutral Swiss.

In the event they missed a classic. Barcelona took that predictable lead on 20 minutes. Suarez crossed into the heart of the Benfica goal area where Kocsis rose above Germano to head home. It was a classic headed goal from the greatest exponent of the art.

Within 10 minutes Benfica had turned the game on its head. Domiciano Cavem crossed from the left, and Ramallets let the ball drift past him, freeing a surprised Aguas to push the equalizer over the line.

Another 90 seconds and Benfica were 2–1 up. Augusto mis-hit his shot, centre-back Enrique Gensana misheaded it backwards and Ramallets flapped out a hand. The ball flew up against the cross-bar and the goalkeeper pushed it out. Too late. The Swiss referee had already whistled for the goal and signalled a restart.

Europacup
Final
Barcelona
Benfica Lisboa

RIGHT: SPANISH DOMINANCE CAME TO AN END AGAINST PORTUGUESE SIDE BENFICA IN JUNE 1961. HERE ANGELO CHESTS THE BALL OFF THE LINE AS 'KEEPER ALBERTO COSTA PEREIRA LOOKS ON, ALONG WITH A NUMBER OF PHOTOGRAPHERS

WEDNESDAY 31 MAY 1961
WANKDORF, BERNE

BENFICA   3
AGUAS 30, RAMALLETS OG 31,
COLUNA 54

BARCELONA   2
KOCSIS 20, CZIBOR 75

HT: 2-1. ATT: 33,000.
REF: DIENST (SWITZ)

BENFICA:
COSTA PEREIRA - MARIO JOAO,
GERMANO, ANGELO - NETO, CRUZ -
JOSE AUGUSTO, SANTANA, AGUAS*,
COLUNA, CAVEM.
COACH: GUTTMANN.

BARCELONA:
RAMALLETS* - FONCHO, GENSANA,
GRACIA - VERGES, GARAY - KUBALA,
KOCSIS, EVARISTO, SUAREZ, CZIBOR.
COACH: ORIZAOLA.

*CAPTAIN.

LEFT: **SKIPPER JOSE AGUAS HOLDS THE EUROPEAN CUP ALOFT AFTER THE EUROPEAN CUP FINAL IN THE WANKDORF**

Five years later that same official, Gottfried Dienst, would referee the 1966 World Cup Final in which he validated – with the assistance of Soviet linesman Tofik Bakhramov – a crucial goal by Geoff Hurst whose shot also ricocheted off the cross-bar.

Ten minutes into the second half, Cavem crossed from the left once more and Coluna shot home first time from 25 yards. At 3-1 down Barcelona's nightmares were coming true.

Suarez had faded out, so Kubala drifted into the centre of midfield and provided Czibor with the left-wing service of which he had been starved. The Hungarian sliced the Benfica cover to shreds. Kubala saw a shot hit one post, dance across goal and ricochet back into play off the other upright; Kocsis had a header cleared off the goal-line.

A quarter of an hour from time Czibor smacked home a second goal for Barcelona. He had scored in the 1954 World Cup Final, too. Then, as now, the score was 3-2. Then, as now, he and Kocsis finished with losers' medals.

'That was our peak,' said Guttmann. 'I'm not sure we can repeat it.' But that was to ignore the potential of a young reserve named Eusebio da Silva Ferreira.

THE NEW SOPHISTICATION

Formations were shuffled as European sides sought to capture a little of the magic Brazil had brought to the game. Real Madrid rang the changes as the draw set them on a collision course with Benfica

While the 1950s had been a golden age of creative football, the 1960s would prove an era of increasing negativity in which the importance of not losing outweighed the importance of winning.

Tactical shifts went into overdrive. Even England caught the trend. In the autumn of 1960 manager Walter Winterbottom adopted Brazil's 4-2-4 with a midfield run by right-half Bobby Robson and inside-left Johnny Haynes.

The results were remarkable. England scored 44 goals in eight games. Italian clubs took note. Welshman John Charles was an established legend in his own air space at Juventus. Now he was joined by England centre-forward Gerry Hitchens at Internazionale and Jimmy Greaves at Milan.

Workmanlike Hitchens stayed for a decade; Greaves, hating the dictatorship of coach Nereo Rocco, flew home after scoring nine goals in 12 games. A rising star at Chelsea, he returned for £99,999 to Tottenham; manager Bill Nicholson deliberately refused to make this goal-poacher supreme the English game's first £100,000 footballer.

Greaves strengthened a Spurs side who had, the previous May, become the first league and FA Cup double-winners of the twentieth century.

But he had to wait three months before he could play in the Champions Cup. UEFA had introduced a registration 'gap' to prevent any repetition of Real Madrid's overnight acquisitions of Miguel Torres in 1957 and Luis del Sol in 1960.

Even with Greaves in the stands, Tottenham did not do so badly, although it was far from easy. They were 4-0 down against Gornik in Poland in the first round but snatched back two late goals, then crushed the Poles 8-1 at White Hart Lane. Flying winger Cliff Jones scored a hat-trick on the first of the glory, glory nights.

Members of the Fleet Street press were not being immodest in suggesting that Spurs had the potential beating of all the rest.

Feyenoord lost 4-2 on aggregate, as did Dukla Prague in the quarter-finals. Nicholson and his loquacious Northern Irish captain Danny Blanchflower used reserve wing-half Tony Marchi – back from a defensive education in Italy with Torino – as an extra defender for the away leg.

Joining Spurs in the semi were holders Benfica, former holders Real Madrid and the first Belgians to reach the last four, Standard Liege. The luck of the draw fell to Madrid, who snagged Standard; Tottenham drew Benfica.

Madrid had rung the changes in the bid to regain 'their' cup. New faces had joined Del Sol to help prop up the ageing legs of Di Stefano, Puskas, Gento and Santamaria. Unfortunately, the new faces did not include the one Madrid needed most. Sweden's Agne Simonsson had been signed as potential successor to Di Stefano but had failed to establish either his personality in the dressing room or his authority on the pitch.

Even so, class told as Madrid opened with an easy win over Hungary's Vasas in a tie set amid a diplomatic frenzy.

RIGHT: THE GREAT EUSEBIO PLAYS KEEPY-UPPY DURING A BREAK FROM TRAINING AT THE WHITE CITY STADIUM BEFORE THE MATCH WITH TOTTENHAM HOTSPUR

ABOVE: JOSE AGUAS SCORES
PAST TOTTENHAM'S BILL BROWN
IN THE SECOND LEG OF THE
SEMI-FINAL. SPURS WON 2-1
BUT IT WASN'T ENOUGH

The Hungarian authorities equivocated over what greeting might await Puskas on his first return to Budapest since the revolution, so he sat out the first leg back in Madrid; president Santiago Bernabeu did, however, succeed in negotiating an exit visa for Kubala's ageing mother (proving that the Madrid-Barcelona relationship is not always what it may appear).

Madrid put five goals past Vasas – three from the ex-Barcelona winger Justo Tejada – then 12 past BK1913 Odense (three each for Di Stefano and Puskas).

But after winning 1-0 away to Juventus in the quarter-final opener, they suffered their first European home defeat by the same margin in the return. Argentine Omar Sivori, Juve's European Footballer of the Year, scored the historic goal.

Sivori hated flying, so Juventus took the train from Turin to Paris for the play-off in the Parc des Princes. Ice and snow delayed their arrival and they appeared still half asleep when Felo put Madrid ahead within minutes of the kick-off. Santamaria gave Charles a 90-minute kicking and Madrid saw it out 3-1.

Standard's victims on the way to the semi-finals included Rangers, against whom Irish inside-forward Johnny Crossan scored twice. Crossan had built a continental career, first with Sparta Rotterdam, after being barred from the English game over a transfer wrangle. But his Belgians were no match for Madrid, losing both home and away and failing to score.

Benfica had started the season with defeat by Penarol in the World Club Cup but their attack had been powered up by the remarkable Eusebio. The youngster from Mozambique had made a stunning substitute's debut against Pele's Santos in the 1961 Paris tournament, then lit up Wembley for Portugal in a World Cup qualifier.

He scored his first Champions Cup goals in Benfica's opening defeat of FK Austria and followed up with two more against Nurnberg. He failed to score against Spurs in the semi-finals, but Aguas and Jose Augusto (twice) did the damage in Lisbon – despite the Marchi Plan – and Aguas struck early on back at White Hart Lane. Spurs, driven on heroically by left-half Dave Mackay, stormed back to win but only by 2-1.

EUSEBIO INSPIRES BENFICA VICTORY

Hindsight suggests that the 1962 European Cup Final was better even than 1960. Madrid's demolition of Eintracht Frankfurt had turned into an exhibition, whereas the 1962 reverse against Benfica was a full-blooded contest all the way from the first minute to the last.

Benfica benefited from stability. At inside-right Eusebio had more than filled the gap left by the brief internment of Joaquin Santana, suspected of links to an African freedom movement; another highly talented youth product in Antonio Simoes had been brought through at outside-left; while the powerful-running Cavem had dropped back to the role of attacking right-half.

Madrid had a new goalkeeper in Jose Araquistain, signed from Real Sociedad in exchange for the loans of Simonsson and the illness-struck outside-right Chus Herrera; Tejada, briefly one of the most successful of the rare handful to travel from Barcelona to Madrid, was a short-term solution to the right-wing problem.

But Del Sol was playing virtually his last game; Madrid had already agreed a sale to Juventus and hoped to use the money to persuade Santos to part with the one player worthy of filling Di Stefano's boots: Pele.

Santos, poised to win the South American Copa Libertadores and the World Club Cup two years in a row, said no. Madrid would be left to soldier on with their ageing army.

Not that age appeared to be a great problem when leavened with experience and outstanding natural talent.

RIGHT: **BENFICA GOALKEEPER COSTA PEREIRA LEAPS TO COLLECT FROM TEAM-MATE GERMANO WITH REAL'S FERENC PUSKAS IN THE OFFING**

WEDNESDAY 2 MAY 1962
OLYMPIC, AMSTERDAM

BENFICA   5
AGUAS 25, CAVEM 34, COLUNA 61,
EUSEBIO 68 PEN, 78

REAL MADRID   3
PUSKAS 17, 23, 38

HT: 2-3. ATT: 68,000. REF: HORN (HOL)

BENFICA:
COSTA PEREIRA - MARIO JOAO,
GERMANO, ANGELO - CAVEM, CRUZ -
JOSE AUGUSTO, EUSEBIO, AGUAS*,
COLUNA, SIMOES.
COACH: GUTTMANN.

REAL MADRID:
ARAQUISTAIN - CASADO,
SANTAMARIA, PACHIN, MIERA - FELO,
DI STEFANO, DEL SOL - TEJADA,
PUSKAS, GENTO*.
COACH: MUNOZ.

*CAPTAIN.

LEFT: EUSEBIO KISSES THE CUP
IN THE BENFICA DRESSING ROOM
AFTER THE 5-3 VICTORY OVER
REAL MADRID

Benfica began as if they intended to run the legs of Madrid in the first 20 minutes. Instead they were caught extended. Di Stefano lofted a clearance out of defence and Puskas galloped from almost halfway before leaving Alberto Costa Pereira without a hope.

Six minutes later Puskas, again from the edge of the penalty area in a shooting context where he had no equal, beat Costa Pereira with a shot which swerved then bounced and spun away from the goalkeeper.

Fortunately for Benfica, Aguas pulled one back almost immediately from close range after a Eusebio drive had ricocheted back off a post. Domiciano Cavem equalized with a 25-yard drive – a goal which Araquistain later blamed on inadequate floodlighting. No matter, Puskas completed his 21-minute hat-trick by restoring Madrid's lead.

At White Hart Lane, in the semi-finals, it was Benfica who had borne the brunt of a second-half rally. Now the boot was on the other foot. They answered the challenge superbly, raising the tempo and equalizing again, this time with another long-range thunderbolt from Coluna. Helpless, Araquistain could do little but stand and watch.

With the match and the cup in the balance, Madrid right-back Pedro Casado was injured and limped out on to the wing. Luck was flowing in the wrong direction. Tejada headed against the cross-bar; referee Leo Horn turned down a penalty claim; and Di Stefano saw a shot rattle against Costa Pereira's legs with the goalkeeper floundering.

Benfica went back down the other end and Eusebio thundered two match-winning goals beyond shell-shocked Araquistain in the space of three minutes: one from a penalty, one from a free-kick.

Benfica were European champions for the second and, as it turned out, the last time.

ABOVE: BENFICA COACH BELA
GUTTMANN IS SAID TO HAVE
INVENTED THE 4-2-4
FORMATION WHICH HE TAUGHT
TO THE BRAZILIAN NATIONAL
SIDE DURING THE 1950S

ITALIANS ON THE COUNTER-STRIKE

Goals rained in as the strong mercilessly ripped apart the defences of the weak in the first round. Milan emérged at the head of the food chain as the Italians sought to win the European Cup for the first time

ABOVE: **IPSWICH TOWN'S TED PHILLIPS RISES ABOVE FLORIANA'S LOLLY DEBATTISTA TO SCORE ONE OF HIS TEAM'S FOUR GOALS**

Italy had been punching below its weight. Milan had been runners-up once, in 1958, and semi-finalists back in 1956, when a mere smattering of fans spread themselves around the gaunt concrete bowl of San Siro.

The Champions Cup had been little more than a curiosity. An embarrassing one for Juventus. *La Vecchia Signora* (The Old Lady) may have stunned Serie A with the understanding, intuition and goals of John Charles and Omar Sivori, but her beauty had left Europe cold. Fiorentina had reached the final in a one-off assault in 1956–57. But no other Italian club had had a look-in. This was the context in which Milan returned to the fray in autumn 1962.

Benfica were now recognized as worthy champions. The 1961 triumph had been considered a fleeting oddity. Now,

even though Bela Guttmann had left and Aguas was winding down, they were accepted as the team to beat. Milan and Real Madrid were more challengers than contenders. Surprising Ipswich Town, pragmatically fashioned by future England manager Alf Ramsey, were not expected to last long. Similarly, little was expected of Scotland's Dundee, managed by Bob Shankly, whose brother Bill was south of the border breathing life and fire back into Liverpool.

Barely apparent at the time was the rising force of Benelux football. Feyenoord from Rotterdam returned for a second successive season. Eddy Pieters-Grafland in goal had been a Champions Cup pioneer in the late 1950s with Ajax; Coen Moulijn was a 'thinking' outside-left; Reiner Kreyermaat a steamrolling right-half.

Out of Belgium came Anderlecht. Few clubs had learned their lessons so avidly. This was not the naïve outfit put to the 12-goal sword by Manchester United in 1957. Now they had their own Hungarian émigré in goalkeeper Arpad Fazekas; outstanding home-grown defenders in Laurent Verbiest and Martin Lippens; a sharp-thinking, bespectacled general in Jef Jurion; and a striker in Paul Van Himst who was destined to become his country's greatest-ever footballer.

Anderlecht were bound together by French coach Pierre Sinibaldi, a pre-Kopa star at Reims, in a 4-2-4 system based on perpetual possession of the ball plus an offside trap. The surprise factor was immense, and beyond Real Madrid in the first round. The Spanish season had not started when rusty Real were shocked to be held 3-3 at home, then defeated 1-0 in Brussels. Jurion struck the late, late winner.

Elsewhere, goals rained in. Milan hit eight in their first leg against Union Luxembourg, with their Brazilian centre-forward Jose Altafini scoring five. Dundee put eight past the woeful West Germans of Koln at Dens Park. Ipswich topped that by smacking a round 10 past Floriana of Malta to complete a 14-1 aggregate; Ray Crawford scored two in Malta and five back at Portman Road.

Benfica and Reims alone were granted byes into the second round, where Kopa scored twice as the French hit back from first-leg defeat to overwhelm FK Austria. It was all down to Kopa now; Fontaine, having twice broken a leg, would never play again.

The holders eased gently into their defence, with Eusebio ever more greedy for goals. He scored in the initial 1-1 draw at Norrkoping in Sweden and claimed his first European hat-trick in the return.

The rest of the round went according to the status quo. That included Milan's beating of Ipswich by 3-0, 1-2. Left-winger Paolo Barison was their main man. He scored twice at the San Siro and once more at Portman Road. He also scored again in the 8-1 dismissal of Galatasaray which secured a semi-final against Dundee.

Bob Shankly's team mixed experience with power and potential. Ian Ure was a tower of strength in central defence; Gordon Smith on the right wing brought to bear the experience he had garnered from Hibs' run to the 1956 semis; and inside-left Alan Gilzean rampaged at will. The future Tottenham favourite struck a second-round hat-trick against Sporting Lisbon and two more goals in the shock Heysel win which punctured the Anderlecht bubble in the quarters.

Feyenoord also sprang a surprising away win over Reims courtesy of a long-range cracker from Kreyermaat which secured a semi-final against Benfica. Mario Coluna, now back as the fulcrum in Benfica's reversion to 4-2-4 under Chilean coach Fernando Riera, scored twice to see off Dukla Prague.

Portuguese skill proved too much for Dutch determination in the one semi-final, while Dundee had their own bubble punctured in the San Siro. Milan, held 1-1 in the first half, ran away after the break to win 5-1. Wingers Bruno Mora and the unstoppable Barison scored two apiece. Gilzean signed off with the academic winning strike back in Scotland as Milan carried the tie 5-2.

For Barison it would prove a bitter-sweet victory.

LEFT: **EUSEBIO OF BENFICA (LEFT) HAMMERS THE BALL PAST VELDHOEN OF FEYENOORD DURING THEIR SEMI-FINAL**

Final 1963

RIGHT: **AC MILAN'S JOSE ALTAFINI PLANTS THE WINNER BEYOND COSTA PEREIRA**

WEDNESDAY 22 MAY 1963
WEMBLEY, LONDON

MILAN   **2**
ALTAFINI 58, 66

BENFICA   **1**
EUSEBIO 18

HT: 0-1. ATT: 45,000.
REF: HOLLAND (ENG)

MILAN:
GHEZZI - C. MALDINI* - DAVID,
BENITEZ, TREBBI - DINO SANI,
TRAPATTONI, PIVATELLI - MORA,
ALTAFINI, RIVERA.
COACH: ROCCO.

BENFICA:
COSTA PEREIRA - CAVEM, HUMBERTO,
RAUL, CRUZ - SANTANA, COLUNA* -
JOSE AUGUSTO, TORRES, EUSEBIO,
SIMOES.
COACH: RIERA.

*CAPTAIN.

MILAN TRIUMPH BY HOOK OR BY CROOK

Eleven months earlier Fernando Riera had been hailed as the finest coach in the world. He had turned a disparate bunch of Chilean footballers into a unified national team worthy of hosts' status at the World Cup.

Chile had lost to Brazil in the semi-finals but finished a proud third. Riera was immediately snapped up by Benfica to succeed retirement-bound Guttmann. His reign started ominously badly with a spectacular double-leg defeat by Pele's Santos in the World Club Cup.

But if this Eusebio-fired Benfica were not the best club side in the world, they were the finest in Europe. Their European Cup ambition was to emulate Real's five consecutive triumphs. As they walked out at Wembley in the afternoon sunshine, the dream appeared perfectly reasonable.

Riera sent out his 'usual' line-up, with the giant Jose Torres now leading the line in place of Aguas. It did not

occur to the Chilean that his opposite number might not be playing by the same gentlemanly rules.

Nereo Rocco was a rough, tough sergeant-major of a coach. His disciplinary ferocity had driven Jimmy Greaves out of Milan early in the previous season. But the Brazilian anchor Dino Sani and the classically gifted youngster Gianni Rivera coped equably.

The defence was marshalled by Cesare Maldini, now the captain and the only survivor from Milan's beaten finalists of 1958. The attack was led by Jose Altafini. He and Dino Sani had been team-mates in reserve when Brazil won the 1958 World Cup. Not that it was obvious from the squad lists. Back in Brazil Altafini was known as Mazzola because of his resemblance to the captain of Torino who had died in the 1949 Superga air disaster.

To everyone's surprise - above all, the player's -

Barison was missing when Milan walked out. Rocco preferred an ageing centre-forward turned midfielder in Gino Pivatelli. His task was simple: to mark Coluna out of the game.

The task of policing Eusebio had gone to Giovanni Trapattoni, famed as the one man who could put Pele out of a game by fair means rather than foul. But coping with Eusebio proved beyond even 'Trap' and Benfica went in one up at half-time.

Substitutes not being permitted, Rocco could not change his personnel during the interval. All he did was put the Peruvian, Victor Benitez, on to Eusebio and tell his players to close down their direct opponents more effectively. Pivatelli did exactly that, catching Coluna late and awkwardly. Coluna limped through the rest of the match and Benfica fell apart.

Now Rivera, the teenager whose half-share had cost Milan £65,000 from Alessandria back in 1959, glided into his own. His nimble footwork created both the equalizer and then the winner for Altafini. The Brazilian collected his second more by luck than judgement. Rivera had sent him away from the centre circle, and his first shot struck Costa Pereira's legs but rebounded conveniently for Altafini to score at the second attempt. It was his 14th goal of the campaign, two more than the previous record set by Puskas in 1959–60. Milan had won. Barison was forgotten as Maldini, wearing a borrowed shirt (as he had given his away), raised the European Cup high: the first Italian to do so. Rocco's tactical acumen had won the day. But his cynical pragmatism was nothing compared with what was to come.

ABOVE: **MILAN'S CESARE MALDINI TAKES THE BALL OFF BENFICA'S EUSEBIO ON THE EDGE OF MILAN'S PENALTY AREA**

LEFT: **MALDINI LIFTS THE EUROPEAN CUP AT THE TOP OF THE FAMOUS 39 STEPS**

THE SCIENCE OF SHUTTING UP SHOP

With Alfredo Di Stefano and Ferenc Puskas slipping into their footballing dotage, the game's philosophy took a defensive turn as Helenio Herrera's Inter Milan set foot on the road to success

Everton won the league in England, Real Madrid in Spain, Benfica in Portugal, Rangers in Scotland, PSV Eindhoven in Holland, Standard Liege in Belgium... and Internazionale in Italy for the first time in nine years.

What was important was not only securing the *scudetto* but the manner in which it was achieved. Helenio Herrera may have pulled all the attacking strings at Barcelona, but in Italy he had become the high priest of defensive football.

To be fair, Herrera had not changed his mind the moment Barcelona fans chased him out of town and into the arms of Inter's oil tycoon owner Angelo Moratti back in 1960. But impatient Inter had gone through 13 coaches in five years before Herrera marched in, and he knew that something very different was needed.

Initially, he threw men forward. Quickly he found Inter being caught on the break by inferior teams. That was when

RIGHT: **MASTER OF** *CATENACCIO*, **HELENIO HERRERA PICTURED UNDER THE FLOODLIGHTS OF THE PRATER STADIUM DURING INTER MILAN VERSUS REAL MADRID**

he changed tack. But imposing iron discipline demanded players who were prepared to adhere slavishly to his tactical discipline, to join in bonding dressing-room huddles with all hands on the ball, to swear commitment.

Kubala, at Barcelona, had dismissed all these typical Herrera motivational tactics as mumbo-jumbo.

Di Stefano thought the same while working under Herrera for Spain at the 1962 World Cup finals; centre-forward Antonio Valentin Angelillo felt the same again at Inter.

He was one of the infamous 'angels with dirty faces' who had quit Argentina for Italy after the spectacular Copa America victory of 1957; fans back home still believe their defections cost Argentina the 1958 World Cup.

But money talked. Angelillo had gone to Inter, Sivori to Juventus and Humberto Maschio to Bologna. In time all three were also to play for Italy.

Angelillo had set a Serie A scoring record with his 33 goals in 1958–59. But that was not enough for Herrera. So Angelillo was among a dozen players shipped out over the next three years.

Herrera knew what he wanted: the ultimate in *catenaccio*, the bolt defence with a sweeper and single-minded man-for-man marking.

Everton's ill fortune was to be drawn against Inter in the first round. The first leg was at Goodison. Only two foreigners were permitted in Italian teams in Serie A and Herrera's first choices were Luis Suarez in midfield and Brazilian right-winger Jair.

Specifically for Europe, though, Inter had signed the rugged German wing-half Horst Szymaniak. He helped shut up shop for a goalless draw at Goodison; Jair scored the only goal of the tie back in Milan.

The financial support of the ruling Grimaldi family was not enough to save Monaco against Inter in the second round; the nucleus of what would be the 1966 runners-up team was not enough to save Partizan Belgrade in the quarter-finals; and a couple of future World Cup silver-medallists could not carry the day for Borussia Dortmund in the semi-finals.

Hans Tilkowski was the Dortmund goalkeeper, and Lothar Emmerich a goalscoring hammer of an outside-left. He hit Lyn Oslo for a first-round hat-trick.

Next time out Dortmund lost only 2–1 away to Benfica, then humiliated the ex-champions 5–0 back in the Ruhr at Rote Erde; this time centre-forward Franz Brungs scored the hat-trick.

The other ex-champions, Real Madrid, had better luck.

Frenchman Lucien Muller, another Reims graduate, was now Di Stefano's aide-de-camp in midfield and Amancio Amaro a darting new outside-right.

But the old boys remained a danger: Di Stefano was being slowed by sciatica, but Puskas, despite some extra kilos, was still lethal in front of goal. He scored the lone winner away to Rangers at Ibrox in the first round and then a hat-trick in their 6–0 win back in Madrid.

Next up were holders Milan. But not the tight, confident Milan of the previous May. Rocco had been replaced as coach by Madrid's old boss, Luis Carniglia; Amarildo, Pele's World Cup-winning deputy with Brazil in Chile in 1962, had been added to the attack.

The mix had not worked against Santos in the World Club Cup, and it did not work against Madrid, even though the Spaniards had Felix Ruiz carried off with a fractured collar-bone during the first leg, which they won 4–1. Amancio, Puskas, Di Stefano and Gento scored the goals.

Injury robbed Milan of Gianni Rivera in attack and Cesare Maldini in defence for the second leg. They won 2–0 but it was not quite enough. Madrid cruised past Zurich in the semis and thus flew on to Vienna for the final against a very different challenge from Milan.

ABOVE: WITH NO LITTLE GLEE, UEFA PRESIDENT GUSTAV WIEDERKEHR, HELPED BY JOSE CRAHAY, MAKES THE DRAW FOR THE NEXT ROUND OF THE CHAMPIONS CUP

27. MAI 1964
EUROPACUP-FINALSPIEL

Preis S 3.-

F. C. INTERNAZIONALE MILANO –
REAL MADRID C. F.

HERAUSGEGEBEN VOM ÖSTERREICHISCHEN FUSSBALL-BUND
IM AUFTRAG DER U.E.F.A.

ABOVE: **MADRID DEFENDER
PACHIN HEADS CLEAR FROM
INTER'S MILANI AS LUIS
SUAREZ LOOKS ON**

HERRERA PLOTS REAL'S DOWNFALL

Jose Santamaria chased Luis Suarez's lofted clearance out of the Inter defence. Normally he would have volleyed it into the stand. Not now. Time was running out. He gambled on hooking it back over his shoulder. The ball struck an Inter forward full in the chest and he accelerated clear to shoot home Inter's decisive third goal. It was counter-attacking opportunism the classic Italian way. The goalscorer was Sandrino Mazzola.

Calcio's curse down the years has also been its blessing. Succeeding generations have produced twin

attacking superstars who inflamed the *tifosi* to a polemical passion over their ability, or usually inability, to pool their talents for the greater glory of the *Azzurri*.

Most recently the anti-partnership comprised Francesco Totti and Alessandro del Piero; before them it was Roberto Baggio and Gianluca Vialli; originally Mazzola and Gianni Rivera.

Rivera was the classical creator; Mazzola the king of open spaces. Together, and with the application of tactical common sense, they should have been lethal in tandem. Yet

tireless attacking pursuit and Mazzola all the rest.

Mazzola had been born on November 8, 1942, five and a half years before the Torino air disaster in which his father, Italy captain Valentino, was killed along with 17 of his team-mates.

He was always considered destined for stardom, but not with his father's old club. His mother had long since moved to Milan, where Sandro was taken under the Inter youth wing by former double World Cup-winner Giuseppe Meazza.

Herrera appreciated Mazzola's pace, strength and strong nerves. He was his father's son.

Elsewhere Herrera plotted to perfection. Burgnich would stick to Gento, Facchetti to Amancio, Guarneri to Puskas. Szymaniak was omitted; Herrera preferred to sacrifice Carlo Tagnin to the 90-minute task of pursuing and harassing Di Stefano.

Madrid had more of the possession but failed to create clear openings. Inter had too much all-round strength against the ageing, fading stars from the Spanish capital. Two minutes before half-time Facchetti caught Amancio dawdling and fed Mazzola. His snap shot bounced awkwardly in front of Jose Vicente, the Madrid 'keeper, and slithered through his grasp into the net.

Vicente was at fault again after half-time with the speculative shot from Milani which provided Inter with their second goal. Felo pulled one back, finally breaching Inter's defence from a corner. But time was running out as Santamaria chased Suarez's lofted clearance...

Herrera, at last, was champion of Europe. Madrid's consolation was to contribute Ignacio Zoco and Amancio to the Spanish European Championship victory over the Soviet Union. Even then, Spain's key player would be the controlling, commanding Luis Suarez.

WEDNESDAY 27 MAY 1964
PRATER, VIENNA

INTERNAZIONALE   3
MAZZOLA 43, 76, MILANI 62

REAL MADRID   1
FELO 69

HT: 1-0. ATT: 72,000. REF: STOLL (AUS)

INTERNAZIONALE:
SARTI - PICCHI* - BURGNICH, GUARNERI, FACCHETTI - TAGNIN, SUAREZ, CORSO - JAIR, MAZZOLA, MILANI.
COACH: HERRERA.

REAL MADRID:
VICENTE - ISIDRO, SANTAMARIA, ZOCO, PACHIN - MULLER, DI STEFANO, FELO - AMANCIO, PUSKAS, GENTO*.
COACH: MUNOZ.

*CAPTAIN.

even when Italy reached the 1970 World Cup Final they were used only in the notorious *staffetta*, as substitutes one for the other. They were not only cross-town rivals but also friends. But Mazzola, throughout the 1960s, had the better support.

Giuliano Sarti, a European runner-up with Fiorentina in 1957, was an ice-cool goalkeeper; Tarcisio Burgnich and Giacinto Facchetti were pacy, ruthless full-backs; Aristide Guarneri an effective stopper; protecting them all was Armando Picchi, a ruthless sweeper rarely if ever to be found even level with his back line.

Suarez and the unpredictable Mariolino Corso provided the creative force, Jair attacking pace, Aurelio Milani

BELOW: TARCISIO BURGNICH AND GIACINTO FACCHETTI, INTER'S HARDBITTEN FULL-BACKS, POSE FOR A VICTORY PORTRAIT

THE QUALITY OF MERSEY

Under the guidance of Bill Shankly with his Boot Room philosophy, Liverpool rumbled into life as a team to be feared in Europe. But the Reds had a lot to learn and were put to the sword in the semis

The blue half of the proud scouser city of Liverpool had already earned a crack at the European Cup and the Toffee Men of Everton had come unstuck at the first hurdle. Now the Reds had their chance. It was the era of Beatlemania and the Merseybeat and Liverpool, under the unique managerial leadership of Bill Shankly, caught the rhythm to perfection.

Indeed, long after the Beatles had all gone their separate ways, Liverpool would still be conducting the English football orchestra in continental competition. Shankly with his assistant and then successor Bob Paisley breathed a 90-minute fire into their teams and players which matched the new-fangled all-red strip.

For two decades they would be admired and feared in equal measure across Europe in the Champions Cup, the Cup-Winners' Cup and the Fairs/UEFA Cup. In that time, Shankly, Paisley and co-conspirators from the 'Boot Room', such as Joe Fagan and Roy Evans, constructed a style of play which mixed the best of British with continental cream.

Liverpool used craft and skill to maintain possession as the foundation from which to launch the attacking weapons of eager pace and ruthless finishing. Shankly and Paisley were loyal to their players but even more loyal to the club. Great club servants would be ruthlessly replaced by youngsters who had often been signed for significant sums and then stuck in the reserves for a year to learn 'the Liverpool way'.

Shankly's ferocious commitment was summed up by his most renowned aphorism: 'People say football is a matter of life and death. Well, they're wrong. It's more serious than that.'

Tactical sophistication and a more pragmatic balance between defence and attack would come with time and took longer to assimilate than that first season in the Champions Cup.

Liverpool, in 1964, had won their first league title in 17 years. They lined up for the draw alongside a phalanx of European old boys: Rangers, Red Star, Rapid, Anderlecht,

RIGHT: DUKLA PRAGUE'S JOSEF MASOPUST TURNS AWAY AFTER SCORING AGAINST REAL MADRID IN THE SECOND LEG OF THE SECOND ROUND, BUT IT WAS A CASE OF TOO LITTLE TOO LATE FOLLOWING AMANCIO'S HAT-TRICK AT THE BERNABEU

Dukla, Gornik, Real Madrid, Benfica and Internazionale.

In those days, long before seeding was introduced, the luck of the draw held sway. Thus Red Star went out immediately to Rangers, who then disposed of Rapid. Dukla saw off Gornik after a first-round play-off but lost to Madrid, whose new hero Amancio scored a hat-trick in the Bernabeu first leg. Madrid then crashed to Benfica, losing 5-1 in Lisbon and winning only 2-1 back in the Bernabeu, where Puskas missed a penalty.

Where was Di Stefano when they needed him? He had gone, at the end of the previous season, after refusing to concede to president Santiago Bernabeu that age had caught up with him. He had scored a record 49 Champions Cup goals in 141 games. Ironically, he left Madrid on a free transfer for a two-year spell with Espanol of Barcelona, where Kubala was player-coach; Kubala... who could have been his original team-mate along the Diagonal at Barcelona.

Benfica scored five without reply in the semi-final against the Hungarians of Vasas Gyor, astutely guided by 1950s legend Nandor Hidegkuti. That lifted them into the final in Milan where, to Portuguese fury, they found Inter waiting – on their home ground.

Inter qualified for their title defence as holders. They had lost the Italian league crown in 1964 amid controversy. Bologna had led throughout the spring but were then penalized nine points after half a dozen players failed dope tests. Bologna's lawyers ultimately had the charges and punishments thrown out, but the disruption cost them dear. Inter finished level on points before Bologna, spearheaded by Denmark's Harald Nielsen and West Germany's Helmut Haller, had the last laugh by winning a title play-off in Rome.

Ironically, Bologna were knocked out of Europe, by Anderlecht in a first-round play-off, before Inter had even started their campaign. Once they did, Dinamo Bucharest were crushed 6-0, 1-0 and Rangers outclassed 3-1, 0-1. Now it was Liverpool's turn to face Herrera's mystic machine in the semi-final.

Liverpool roared into the game fresh from their FA Cup Final triumph over Leeds. Injured heroes Gerry Byrne and Gordon Milne paraded the trophy around Anfield before kick-off, and the Kop greeted Inter with choruses of 'Go back to Italy' to the tune of 'Santa Lucia'.

Inter were experienced but this was something new. Roger Hunt swept Liverpool ahead on four minutes. Inter snapped back through Mazzola, but further home goals from Ian Callaghan and Ian St John were the least Liverpool deserved. Full-back Chris Lawler had a goal disallowed.

Inter's experience told, however, in the second leg. Corso scored on eight minutes, direct from what Spanish referee Jose Ortiz de Mendibil had signalled as an indirect free-kick. One minute later, Peiro punished 'keeper Tommy Lawrence's habit of bouncing the ball from hands held at head height; Peiro nicked the ball as it dropped and pumped it into the goal.

Level on aggregate, Inter had achieved the minimum of a play-off. It was not needed. Midway through the second half Facchetti strode up out of nowhere and ripped a superb, winning third goal beyond Lawrence.

ABOVE: LIVERPOOL'S ROGER HUNT FALLS UNDER THE CHALLENGE OF INTER MILAN'S GUARNERI AND LUIS SUAREZ AS ARMANDO PICCHI APPEALS TO THE REFEREE

INTER BECOME CHAMPIONS IN THE RAIN

ABOVE: BENFICA'S EUSEBIO TRIES
TO GET HOLD OF THE BALL AS
ARMANDO PICCHI (6) PREPARES
TO INTERVENE. EVERYTHING
FELL APART FOR THE
PORTUGUESE SIDE AS THEY
SUBSIDED TO DEFEAT AMID
TORRENTIAL CLOUDBURSTS

In the wake of Inter's victory over Liverpool, Benfica redoubled their efforts to persuade UEFA to change the venue for the final. Elek Schwartz, the Romanian coach who had succeeded Fernando Riera, told friends: 'If we play in Milan they will not let us win, no matter how long the game has to last.'

His fears were not only about the effects of crowd pressure on the referee and his linesmen; nor was he even concerned about suggestions that certain referees were awarded more Italian ties than others.

Behind-the-scenes whispers were building up about the scope of Inter's match preparation, which apparently stretched beyond merely the players. Their generous hospitality to officials was well known, though Inter were not the only club to fall into that category. The question related to where that generosity might stop.

Branko Tesanic, the Czech referee of their semi-final return against Borussia Dortmund the previous season, had admitted while on a Mediterranean holiday that 'someone from Inter' footed the bill. The match had been memorable

not only for Inter's win but for the way in which the referee had overlooked a bad foul by Suarez on the Dortmund wing-half 'Hoppy' Kurrat.

First Benfica threatened a boycott. UEFA responded with a threat of its own of a hefty fine plus suspension from one or more subsequent competitions.

Benfica responded that they would send their youth team. UEFA repeated the party line and pointed out that, with 80,000 tickets already sold, it would hold Benfica liable for any claims from fans, broadcasters and advertisers.

Grumpily, reluctantly, Benfica duly turned up to play. The match should never have gone ahead. Not because of

shenanigans behind the scenes but because of the weather. Storms had battered Milan during the day and the San Siro pitch was not so much a quagmire as a lake. The water had been unable to soak into the hard ground and lay on the surface, glistening in the reflection of the floodlights and speckled with continuing rain.

Both teams splashed hopelessly through the first half. Then, with three minutes to go to half-time, Mariolino Corso and Sandro Mazzola managed for once to put together a couple of passes and Jair's angled shot slipped through the hands and legs of Alberto Costa Pereira.

Worse was to come for the veteran goalkeeper from Angola. Early in the second half he injured a leg and insisted he could not play on. Centre-half Germano, limping after an early injury of his own, went in goal. He was rarely troubled by Inter. Joaquin Peiro went closest to a second goal when he hit a post. At the other end Eusebio tried the occasional hopeful shot, but Giuliano Sarti was mostly as untroubled as the stand-in at the opposite end.

Inter celebrated as if they had staged a six-goal special. This summer, as in the previous year, they again went on to defeat Argentina's Independiente to retain the World Club Cup. Herrera appeared to have European and world football in an iron grip. Fortunately, not everyone thought so.

THURSDAY 27 MAY 1965
SAN SIRO, MILAN

INTERNAZIONALE	1
JAIR 42	

BENFICA	0

HT: 1-0. ATT: 80,000. REF: DIENST (SWITZ)

INTERNAZIONALE:
SARTI - PICCHI* - BURGNICH, GUARNERI, FACCHETTI - BEDIN, SUAREZ, CORSO - JAIR, MAZZOLA, PEIRO.
COACH: HERRERA.

BENFICA:
COSTA PEREIRA - CAVEM, GERMANO, RAUL, CRUZ - NETO, COLUNA* - JOSE AUGUSTO, EUSEBIO, TORRES, SIMOES.
COACH: SCHWARTZ.

*CAPTAIN.

GATECRASHING THE BIRTHDAY BASH

As the competition entered its second decade, it was time for reflection: the old guard remained but there were new faces on the scene. And Manchester United made their first bow since Munich...

Celebrating its tenth birthday, the European Champions Cup was being led into a new decade by a new generation. In the five years between 1965 and 1969, the Champions Cup was won by five different clubs. Italian and, shortly, English would be the languages of success, rather than Spanish, Portuguese and French.

Of course, Spain still had a trick or two up its sleeve courtesy of Real Madrid, while French creative influence was still making itself felt even if its teams were not. Jules Rimet's World Cup was about to be hosted by England, while Henri Delaunay's European Championship had sprung modestly to life with initial victories for the Soviet Union and Spain.

Not that the established powers had been overthrown. The 1965-66 entry included Inter as both holders and Italian champions – no place now for the runners-up, loudly though Bologna complained – along with Real Madrid, Feyenoord, Anderlecht, Partizan Belgade, Benfica and Manchester United.

This was United's first appearance since they had been refused permission by the English authorities to accept a sympathy place in 1958-59; their first competitive entry since the semi-final defeat by Milan in the wake of the Munich air crash.

Matt Busby was back in charge. He had not shrunk from buying big before when he needed to: hence the

RIGHT: BENFICA'S TALL STRIKER JOSE TORRES HOLDS THE BALL ALOFT IN TRIUMPH AFTER SCORING IN THE 3-2 DEFEAT AT OLD TRAFFORD. UNITED WON 8-3 ON AGGREGATE

strengthening of the Busby Babes with Tommy Taylor and Harry Gregg. Now he had used the transfer market to help shortcut the rebuilding process, most notably with the £125,000 rescue of Denis Law from Torino.

Bobby Charlton and Bill Foulkes were stalwarts from the pre-Munich era aided and abetted by a 20-year-old one-off from Northern Ireland named George Best.

Probably the greatest night of Best's entire career was March 9, 1966, in the Estadio da Luz in Lisbon when he ran Benfica ragged. United, 3–2 winners at home in the first leg, scored a 5–1 triumph which ranks among the greatest single match displays in the history of all European club football.

Best scored twice in the first 12 minutes and John Connelly made it three in 15. Paddy Crerand and Charlton completed the 5–1 annihilation while, just for good measure, United even provided Benfica's only strike with Shay Brennan's own goal.

'When we drew Partizan in the semi-final we thought we were already in the final,' said Law, years later. But United had overlooked the Slavs' path to the last four. Many of their players had been battle-hardened in the 1960 Nations Cup and the 1962 World Cup: Yugoslavia had reached the final in one, the semi-finals in the other.

To face United had meant beating the burgeoning youth of Nantes, the bad-tempered, hard-edged Germans of Werder Bremen and old Mitropa Cup heroes Sparta Prague. In Belgrade Law missed from the edge of the six-yard box and United lost 2–0. At Old Trafford, missing Best through injury, United won by an insufficient 1–0 after 'keeper Milutin Soskic pushed a Nobby Stiles cross-shot into his own net.

Partizan, having surprised themselves by reaching the final, were equally surprised to learn that their opponents would not be holders Inter, as expected – but Real Madrid.

Inter had made few changes once Herrera had established command. Gianfranco Bedin was now the 'attacking' wing-half, and hard-working Angelo Domenghini had ousted the erratic Brazilian Jair on the right wing, but Mazzola, Suarez and Corso had gone from strength to strength. Dinamo Bucharest and Ferencvaros – despite the graceful Florian Albert – proved easy meat en route to the semi-finals.

This was a very different Real Madrid – nicknamed the 'Ye-ye' team to suit the Beatle era.

These days Santamaria and Puskas were wheeled out chiefly for money-making prestige friendlies, though Puskas did score four times in the 5–0 first-round thrashing of Feyenoord.

LEFT: MANCHESTER UNITED'S DENIS LAW PRESENTS EUSEBIO WITH THE *BALLON D'OR* AS EUROPEAN FOOTBALLER OF THE YEAR. UNITED THEN PRECEDED TO SLAUGHTER BENFICA 5–1

After that initial flurry the baton was passed to energetic newcomers such as inside-forward Amancio, midfielder Pirri and a new deep-lying centre-forward in Ramon Moreno Grosso. Only full-back Pachin and skipper Gento, of the old guard, remained first choices with coach Miguel Munoz.

Gento was on target when Madrid beat Kilmarnock 5–1 in the second round and claimed two more in the quarter-final defeat of Anderlecht.

But few critics gave Madrid's mixture of the old and the new much chance against Inter in the semis – not even after a 1–0 win at home, in which Gento crossed for Pirri to score.

Madrid had their backs to the wall in Milan, where Hungarian referee Gyorgy Vadas resisted Inter pressure on and off the pitch. Real had lost the Spanish league crown to neighbours Atletico. Thus they had to win the Cup to maintain their record of perpetual entry. Gento again provided a lethal cross which Amancio converted. Facchetti levelled 13 minutes from time, but goalkeeper Jose Araquistain – making belated amends for his disastrous 1962 final – kept everything else out.

Inter's stultifying reign was over.

REAL MAKE IT A RECORD SIX

Partizan were the first eastern European club to reach the Champions Cup final and only the second non-Latin contenders, after Germany's Eintracht Frankfurt in 1960. They were not, however, new to Europe and they had plenty to play for.

The Slav army club had competed in the first European Cup in 1955–56, despite not being domestic champions, and had enjoyed the honour of playing Sporting in Lisbon in the very first match. They and neighbours Red Star provided the nucleus of an outstanding national team.

Now their players intended using the springboard of European Cup progress to further their own careers in western Europe. The Yugoslav authorities were the first in communist-controlled eastern Europe to permit transfers abroad, albeit only for players who were over 28 and had given honourable service to the domestic cause at club and national team level.

Thus, within a couple of years of playing the final against Madrid in the Heysel in Brussels, Partizan would lose goalkeeper Soskic, full-back Fahrudin Jusufi, inside-forwards Vladimir Kovacevic and Milan Galic, plus left-half Velibor Vasovic to the west.

Vasovic captained Partizan, Francisco Gento captained Madrid. The referee was West Germany's Rudolf Kreitlein, who would be catapulted into legend six weeks later after sending off Argentina's captain Antonio Rattin in an infamous World Cup quarter-final against England at Wembley.

Partizan's tactic was simple: they wanted a quick early goal so they could then sit back and frustrate Madrid just as they had frustrated Manchester United's probably better attack in the semi-finals.

They pounded forwards from the start, and Jose Araquistain enjoyed a charmed life in the Madrid goal. After 20 minutes or so the initial storm blew itself out, Gento got a grip in midfield and Ramon Grosso missed the best chance on the counter-attack, shooting wide from in front of goal and with time to spare.

Eleven minutes into the second half Partizan went ahead. Josip Pirmajer curled in a corner and Vasovic used his height and power to goalscoring purpose.

Vasovic immediately ran back into the centre of defence and the rest of his team followed him. Madrid attacked with increasing frenzy. On 71 minutes Grosso put in Amancio for the equalizer. Six more minutes and right-

winger Fernando Serena – who had promised the Spanish newspaper reporters that he would score the winner – kept his promise from 25 yards with his 'wrong' left foot.

Real Madrid, for the sixth time, were champions of Europe and were allowed to keep the original trophy. Gento had won his record sixth cup, Pachin a second; Araquistain, Ignacio Zoco and Amancio each had a winners' medal to offset his losers' bauble from 1962 or 1964.

Intriguingly, for a club who had leaned so heavily on star imports, Madrid had won with a team of 11 Spaniards. It was the first time a home-born team had won the European Cup. Colonial Benfica, although their players had been Portuguese citizens, could not have said the same in 1961 or 1962.

Partizan left with nothing, except those soon-to-be-realized dreams of long, lucrative contracts in western Europe.

WEDNESDAY 11 MAY 1966
HEYSEL, BRUSSELS

REAL MADRID   2
AMANCIO 70, SERENA 76

PARTIZAN BELGRADE   1
VASOVIC 55

HT: 0-0. ATT: 55,000.
REF: KREITLEIN (WG)

REAL MADRID:
ARAQUISTAIN - PACHIN, DE FELIPE,
ZOCO, SACHIS - PIRRI, GROSSO,
VELAZQUEZ - SERENA, AMANCIO,
GENTO*.
COACH: MUNOZ.

PARTIZAN BELGRADE:
SOSKIC - JUSUFI, RASOVIC, VASOVIC*,
MIHAJLOVIC - BECEJAC, KOVACEVIC -
BAJIC, HASANAGIC, GALIC, PIRMAJER.
COACH: GEGIC.

*CAPTAIN.

LEFT: **PARTIZAN'S GOALKEEPER MILUTIN SOSKIC LOOKS BACK IN ANGER AND DESPAIR AS AMANCIO'S EQUALIZER NESTLES GENTLY IN THE BACK OF THE NET**

LEFT: **IN THE SHADOW OF THE ATOMIUM, SOSKIC CATCHES THE BALL SAFELY IN HIS HANDS. THE GOALKEEPER MADE MORE THAN 400 STARTS FOR PARTIZAN AND LATER PLAYED OVER 200 TIMES FOR FC KOLN**

GLASGOW'S PASSION PLAYERS

Celtic exploded from nowhere to power their way towards European football's most glittering prize, while Liverpool fell to an emerging Ajax side inspired by the precocious Johan Cruyff

In May 1967 Celtic became the first British club to win the Champions Cup, a high water mark to which the Bhoys have dreamed of returning ever since. But the Scottish game has changed beyond recognition and, arguably, for the worse where competition is concerned.

Celtic had qualified for the Champions Cup by winning the Scottish league title in 1966 for the first time in 12 years. They were the fifth different club to win the championship in seven seasons – after Hearts, Rangers (three times), Dundee and Kilmarnock – which says much about the competitive nature of Scottish football at that time.

In terms of cosmopolitan skill, the Celtic of the mid-1960s could not have competed with the Celtic of the new millennium.

But winning the Scottish title was a far more robust challenge and Jock Stein's team were much sharper, competitively. Of course Stein also happened to be the greatest modern manager in Scottish football.

He had gained an invaluable insight into what worked and what did not from a spell as reserve-team manager at Celtic in the early 1950s. That was where he first exercised his guiding control over ambitious young players such as Billy McNeill, later his captain. Impressive spells as

RIGHT: **THE NET BULGES AS BILLY MCNEILL'S HEADER FLIES PAST VOJVODINA NOVISAD'S GOAL-KEEPER IN THE 90TH MINUTE TO GIVE CELTIC AN AGGREGATE LEAD. BOBBY MURDOCH (L) AND STEVE CHALMERS (2ND R) WATCH ON**

manager in his own right at Dunfermline Athletic and Hibernian persuaded Celtic to bring him back as boss in the spring of 1965.

Stein's second coming was a culture shock. For one thing, he was a Protestant – although Celtic, for all their well-established Roman Catholic roots, had never been such a closed shop as Old Firm rivals Rangers on the other side of the sectarian divide.

In practical terms, Stein insisted on running the team himself, a contrast to the laissez-faire regime previously in place where chairman Robert Kelly 'assisted' long-serving manager Jimmy McGrory. The value of that arrangement was clear from the simple fact that, before Stein's arrival, Celtic's last trophy success had been the Scottish Cup way back in 1954.

Celtic's progress from no one to someone in the Champions Cup within nine months shocked the continent. But beaten opponents along the way such as FC Zurich – for whom veteran player-coach Ladislav Kubala made his last European appearance – Nantes, Vojvodina Novisad and Dukla Prague, had only themselves to blame. Celtic had reached the semi-finals of the Cup-Winners' Cup in both of the two previous seasons and learned hard but significant lessons from last-four defeats by first MTK Budapest and then Liverpool.

Losing to MTK, after taking a three-goal lead to Budapest, had taught Celtic's players that nothing in Europe could be taken for granted; losing to Liverpool, after dominating the first leg, taught them that chances had to be taken with a ruthless efficiency unfamiliar to the Scottish League.

To that effect, Stein strengthened his team during the autumn of 1966 by splashing £30,000 on Hearts striker Willie Wallace.

He envisaged Wallace replacing ageing Steve Chalmers and teaming up alongside top-scoring Joe McBride. But barely had Wallace arrived than McBride suffered a knee injury which was to blight his career.

To compound the blow, an administrative blunder meant that Wallace was not registered in time for the quarter-final against Vojvodina.

Bobby Lennox stood in as Chalmers' partner instead against the team who impressed Celtic's players more than any other that season.

Celtic lost 1–0 in Yugoslavia and won 2–0 at home. Chalmers scored the first and McNeill headed the winner in the last minute to avert a Rotterdam play-off.

The quarter-finals also saw the exit of holders Real Madrid, who lost 1–0 away and 2–0 at home to Internazionale, with Helenio Herrera savouring vengeance for the previous season's semi-final defeat.

The Madrid media speculated after the tie that Real wanted HH to replace Munoz, but he enjoyed both power and perfect working conditions without interference at Inter: even the Bernabeu, for Herrera, would have been a comedown after the San Siro.

CSKA Sofia reached the semi-finals for the first time by cruising easily past Northern Ireland's Linfield, while further eastern European progress was attained by Dukla in defeating Ajax Amsterdam.

The Dutch, coached by their former centre-forward Rinus Michels, had sprung an earlier sensation by famously demolishing Liverpool 5–1 in the old Olympic stadium. The Reds' manager Bill Shankly, blaming Amsterdam fog rather than Ajax finesse, predicted hellfire vengeance back at Anfield.

The Liverpool floodlights, however, only lit up the enormous potential of young visitors such as Johan Cruyff and Piet Keizer. Roger Hunt scored twice, but so did Cruyff, and Liverpool fell 7–3 on aggregate.

Dukla then beat Ajax, after which their ageing legs creaked to a defeated standstill against Celtic, while Facchetti scored in both semi-final legs before Inter edged out CSKA with a lone Renato Capellini winner in a play-off in Bologna.

Scottish passion would meet Italian pragmatism in Lisbon, the city where the European Cup had started just 13 years earlier.

ABOVE: 'JINKY' JIMMY JOHNSTONE SCORES THE FIRST GOAL AT PARKHEAD AGAINST DUKLA PRAGUE IN THE SEMI-FINAL FIRST LEG

TRIUMPH OF THE LISBON LIONS

Some 27 years after Celtic made British football history, a Lisbon newspaper revealed a proposal to flatten the Estadio Nacional beneath a glass and steel complex for new Portuguese government ministries.

Conveniently, the plan was almost swamped by news from the European Championship, which Portugal was hosting at the time. That was probably fortunate. If the plan had been reported back in Glasgow, the invasion of protest might have dwarfed the number of fans already present for Euro 2004.

Pride of place in Celtic's history will always go to the crowning glory when skipper Billy McNeill – abandoned to

LISBOA
25 DE MAIO DE 1967
ESTÁDIO NACIONAL

FINAL DA
XII TAÇA DOS CLUBES
CAMPEÕES EUROPEUS

PROGRAMA OFICIAL
PREÇO: 2 ESCUDOS

INTER — CELTIC
ITÁLIA   ESCÓCIA

RIGHT: **CELTIC CELEBRATE WITH FANS AFTER THE GAME – (FROM THE LEFT), TOMMY GEMMELL, JOHN HUGHES AND BOBBY LENNOX. ALL CELTIC'S PLAYERS WERE BORN WITHIN A 30-MILE RADIUS OF CELTIC PARK**

ABOVE: **PHOTOGRAPHER'S EYE
VIEW OF TOMMY GEMMELL'S
25-YARD EQUALIZER AGAINST
INTER MILAN**

the presentation by his team-mates amid green-and-white mayhem – raised the new European Cup over the marble edifice built by the dictator Antonio Salazar.

This was the city which had hosted the first game in the history of the Champions Cup, between Sporting and Partizan; the city from which Benfica and Eusebio had exploded on to the European football stage; the city with no sympathy for Internazionale and Helenio Herrera. Portuguese fans had bitter memories of how they had, they believed, been cheated out of a fair chance to regain the cup in 1965 on the half-flooded San Siro pitch.

Herrera's luck had started to turn. He was as meticulous as ever in preparation, lining up his first team in training matches against reserves set up Celtic-style, right down to the shorts numbers, Celtic's idiosyncratic way of resisting the imposition of shirt numbers as long as possible.

The previous weekend Inter had lost their Italian league crown and thus the right to a Champions Cup return; they had lost Brazilian right-winger Jair to a knee injury and Spanish playmaker Luis Suarez to a thigh strain. Suarez was now 32, his form was ebbing, but his presence carried a worth all of its own; his absence was a serious psychological blow.

No such problems for Celtic. McBride remained a long-term absentee. But everyone else was there: from 36-year-old Ronnie Simpson in goal, via well-balanced full-backs Jim Craig and Tommy Gemmell, 'Caesar' McNeill in the heart of defence, and converted inside-forward Bobby Murdoch at right-half, to the archetypal 'tanner ball-player' Jimmy Johnstone on the right wing.

The Estadio Nacional not only lacked a stand on one side of the pitch, it also lacked floodlights. Thus Inter and Celtic kicked off in the mid-afternoon heat. Within six minutes Celtic's players were even hotter under their collars. Craig brought down Renato Cappellini, sent wide into the penalty box by Sandro Mazzola, and referee Kurt Tschenscher awarded a penalty. Celtic's players were furious.

Most realized later, after reviewing a television rerun, that it was indeed a foul, but at the time the pursuit of an equalizer for Mazzola's penalty conversion was fuelled by a spirit of righteous indignation. Giuliano Sarti was kept busier than for many a long match as Celtic's tireless forward movement created shooting space for the midfield support.

One such raid, on 62 minutes, provided the equalizer as Gemmell thrashed home Craig's cross from 25 yards. That was it. As Bobby Lennox said later: 'Their heads went down. We knew then we were going to win it.' Chalmers, the veteran leader who should have been cast among the reserves, deflected home the inevitable winner with eight minutes left.

Two weeks later came the ultimate tribute: Celtic played, and beat, Real Madrid in Di Stefano's farewell testimonial match at the Bernabeu. Ring out the Spanish old, ring in the Scottish new.

THURSDAY 25 MAY 1967
ESTADIO NACIONAL, LISBON

CELTIC	**2**
GEMMELL 62, CHALMERS 83

INTERNAZIONALE	**1**
MAZZOLA 6 PEN

HT: 0-1. ATT: 55,000. REF:
TSCHENSCHER (WG)

CELTIC:
SIMPSON - CRAIG, MCNEILL*, CLARK,
GEMMELL - MURDOCH, AULD -
JOHNSTONE, WALLACE, CHALMERS,
LENNOX.
MANAGER: STEIN.

INTERNAZIONALE:
SARTI - PICCHI* - BURGNICH,
GUARNERI, FACCHETTI - BEDIN,
BICICLI, CORSO - DOMENGHINI,
MAZZOLA, CAPPELLINI.
COACH: HERRERA.

*CAPTAIN.

MATT BUSBY'S HOLY GRAIL

Innovative rule changes were the order of the day as UEFA attempted to slipstream the competition. And in the footsteps of Celtic, Manchester United made their bid for the European crown

Ten seasons after the Munich air disaster Manchester United were back yet again. They had fallen, to their own gaping disbelief, in the 1966 semi-finals. Now Matt Busby was once again in hot pursuit of his holy grail. But a significant change in the balance of power between English and European football had occurred in the meantime.

England's double thrashing by Hungary in 1953 and 1954 had raised questions about everything from coaching to equipment. The awful realization that England no longer ruled the football waves was driven home by repeated failures in the fledgling European club competitions.

A London Select in 1958 and Birmingham City in 1960 had reached the finals of the Fairs Cup before Tottenham, in 1963, became the first English club to win a European trophy, the Cup-Winners' Cup – carrying it off with plenty of goals and no little style.

The following year, 1964, Denis Law of Manchester United and Scotland became the first British winner of the European Footballer of the Year prize. Even more significant was Bobby Charlton's *Ballon d'Or* in 1966, off the back of England's World Cup triumph.

English football was back at the world pinnacle, and command of the Jules Rimet trophy provided solid gold

RIGHT: MANCHESTER UNITED'S LEGENDARY NUMBER 7 GEORGE BEST TURNS AWAY IN TRIUMPH AFTER SCORING THE ONLY GOAL IN THE HOME LEG OF THE SEMI-FINAL AGAINST REAL MADRID. THE AWAY LEG ENDED 3-3

evidence of that fact. Celtic had broken a psychological barrier by proving that British clubs could beat Europe's best, and Manchester United duly squared the circle.

United were appropriate candidates to be the first English winners. They had been England's first entrants, had blazed the trail and paid the greatest sacrifice on that Munich runway in 1958.

Bobby Charlton thought it was fated that Manchester United would win the 1968 European Cup after the dramatic semi-final with Real Madrid. United enjoyed one tangible advantage in that the final was being played at Wembley.

Busby felt he owed it to the memory of his Babes to complete the European journey they had begun. To do so at Wembley, of all places, 10 years after Munich, was almost too symbolic for fiction. Of course, it was not that simple.

UEFA had drafted new regulations. A simple seeding system kept apart previous finalists or their domestic cousins in the opening round, while play-offs were scrapped up to the quarter-finals.

Teams who finished level on aggregate after second-leg extra time were thrown to the mercy of a toss of a coin. Most important, the away-goals rule was introduced, which often removes the need for extra-time.

Celtic, never mind the seeding, lost their grip on the cup immediately. They lost 2–1 at home to Dynamo Kiev, the long-awaited first Soviet entrants, and drew 1–1 in Ukraine, from where they flew home to Glasgow grumbling about dirty tricks.

It was a poor omen for Celtic's even more painful defeat by Racing of Argentina in the mayhem of the World Club Cup.

The away-goals rule was of instant help to Benfica against Glentoran of Northern Ireland, while Real Madrid needed extra time to edge Ajax. Political sensitivities still raised the occasional complication: ultra-communist Albania refused to recognize West Germany, so Dinamo Tirana's withdrawal offered progress to Eintracht Braunschweig thanks to a walkover.

United had no problem in disposing of Hibernians of Malta 4–0, 0–0. The four goals were shared two apiece by Law and David Sadler.

Veteran skipper Gento, having scored one against Ajax, scored in each leg of Madrid's second-round disposal of Denmark's Hvidovre, while Sweden's briefly sparkling Roger Magnusson scored Juventus's lone winner in their defeat of Rapid Bucharest. Eusebio struck as Benfica beat Saint-Etienne. Czech striker Vaclav Masek hit five of Sparta Prague's six goals against Anderlecht.

United had it tougher in beating Sarajevo: they drew 0–0 in Yugoslavia and won 2–1 at Old Trafford with goals from wingers John Aston and George Best.

That same 2–1 aggregate saw United past Gornik Zabrze, earlier conquerors of Kiev, in the quarter-finals, while Juventus needed a play-off to beat Braunschweig, with Magnusson again the match-winner.

An Amancio hat-trick lifted Madrid past Sparta, and Eusebio scored two in Benfica's defeat of Vasas Budapest. The Black Panther also managed one in each leg as Benfica beat Juventus in the semis to qualify for their fifth final in eight seasons.

United reached Wembley by the skin of their teeth and via a match which Charlton, years later, described as 'the most memorable individual match of my career'.

Old memories from different eras on both sides were renewed by the semi-final pairing of United with Real Madrid. Suspended Amancio missed the first leg at Old Trafford and Madrid, lacking his counter-attacking edge, conceded a lone goal to Best.

That did not appear enough as Madrid stormed back with three of their own in the first half in the Bernabeu. But when their storm blew over United raised one of their own: Ignacio Zoco had earlier put through his own goal, David Sadler scored a second, and Munich survivor Bill Foulkes – to the amazement of his team-mates – somehow found himself up in attack to level the scores at 3–3.

One headline proclaimed: '90 minutes from glory' – wrongly, as it turned out, by 30 minutes.

ABOVE: GUSTAV WIEDERKEHR, PRESIDENT OF UEFA, PRESENTS THE ORIGINAL EUROPEAN CUP TO SANTIAGO BERNABEU. MADRID WERE ALLOWED TO KEEP THE TROPHY AFTER WINNING IT SIX TIMES

FOOTBALL'S GODS SMILE ON UNITED

The red-and-white colour clash plus the demands of television in the black-and-white era meant that neither United nor Benfica could play in their favoured colours. Benfica wore all-white, United all-blue. But the blues at the end were reserved solely for the Portuguese.

Two years earlier England had beaten Portugal 2–1 in this same Wembley stadium in the World Cup semi-finals. United brought two of England's heroes, Bobby Charlton and combative half-back Nobby Stiles, while Benfica fielded six of Portugal's line-up that day: Jose Augusto, Jaime Graça (whom they had signed after the World Cup) and Mario Coluna in midfield, plus forwards Eusebio, Jose Torres and Antonio Simoes.

Benfica were also now under the command of the roly-poly Brazilian, Otto Gloria, who had masterminded Portugal's best-ever World Cup campaign.

Not that United were short of Wembley experience, but they were missing one of their most potent forces in Denis Law. The Scot had been awarded his first international selection by Busby who had later spent a then club record £125,000 in bringing him home from Torino. But Law missed the match that mattered above all. An ongoing knee problem meant he had played in only three of the qualifying ties, and he watched the final from his hospital bed.

David Sadler took Law's place to good tactical effect, although his individual contribution would be overshadowed by that of left-winger John Aston – playing his finest game for United – and birthday boy Brian Kidd, 19 on the big day.

United's team was completed by England reserve Alex Stepney in goal, loyal club men Shay Brennan and Tony Dunne at full-back, Foulkes in the heart of defence, tough but perceptive Scot Pat Crerand at right-half and the irrepressible Best nominally on the right wing.

If United needed any more good omens, Italian referee Concetto Lo Bello had been in charge of their 5–1 thrashing

EUROPEAN CHAMPION CLUBS' CUP

BENFICA F.C.   MANCHESTER UNITED

FINAL

ORGANISED BY THE FOOTBALL ASSOCIATION ON BEHALF OF THE UNION DES ASSOCIATIONS EUROPEENNES DE FOOTBALL

WEDNESDAY MAY 29th 1968

Kick-off 7·45 p.m.

OFFICIAL PROGRAMME   ONE SHILLING

WEMBLEY EMPIRE STADIUM

RIGHT: MANCHESTER UNITED'S BOBBY CHARLTON CELEBRATES AS HIS SHOT FLIES INTO THE NET BEYOND BENFICA GOALKEEPER JOSE HENRIQUE FOR UNITED'S THIRD GOAL

of Benfica in the Estadio da Luz two seasons earlier.

The first half, scrappy and fitful, ended goalless and without much between the sides, although Eusebio once set Stepney's cross-bar twanging. Seven minutes into the second half, United went ahead as Charlton glanced in Sadler's cross for one of his rare headed goals.

Benfica, though significantly older, found fresh legs in pursuit of parity and Graça equalized after Jose Torres had tormented United in the air to redirect Jose Augusto's cross.

Eusebio, in the closing minutes, should have won the game for Benfica. First, forced wide, he shot comparatively weakly at Stepney. Then, clear through the centre and far more dangerous, he thundered in another drive on goal. Fortunately, Eusebio targeted his shot on goal too accurately: it struck Stepney full in the chest and he managed to hold on.

Benfica heads went down and were not raised by the whistle for extra time. Fate was against them. Three goals in seven minutes in extra time, from Best, Kidd and Charlton again, brought the European Cup to England for the first time and to Manchester United for the first time amid tears of emotional, memory-scarred joy... and relief.

WEDNESDAY 29 MAY 1968
WEMBLEY, LONDON

MANCHESTER UNITED   **4**
CHARLTON 54, 98, BEST 92, KIDD 95
BENFICA   **1**
JAIME GRAÇA 78

HT: 0-0. AFTER EXTRA TIME (90 MIN: 1-1). ATT: 100,000. REF: LO BELLO (IT)

MANCHESTER UNITED:
STEPNEY - BRENNAN, FOULKES, STILES, DUNNE - CRERAND, CHARLTON*, SADLER - BEST, KIDD, ASTON.
MANAGER: BUSBY.

BENFICA:
HENRIQUE - ADOLFO, HUMBERTO, JACINTO, CRUZ - JOSE AUGUSTO, JAIME GRAÇA, COLUNA* - EUSEBIO, TORRES, SIMOES.
COACH: GLORIA.

*CAPTAIN.

LEFT: MATT BUSBY PROVIDES WORDS OF INSPIRATION TO HIS PLAYERS AS THEY GET READY FOR ONE LAST EFFORT. SEVERAL PLAYERS WRITHE WITH CRAMP AS GEORGE BEST (7) PREPARES HIMSELF FOR DECISIVE ACTION

NO SUBSTITUTES FOR CLASS

Soviet tanks brought an end to the Prague Spring and football's administrators felt the chill when they had to keep East and West apart. But it was an Italian goalkeeper who stole the headlines...

In the international days before multiple substitutions, in the days before overburdened qualifying schedules, in the days when friendlies were not meaningless but played for prestige and pride, many fine footballers were never rewarded even once with a game for their national team.

The expanding European club competitions thus offered an alternative route to international achievement and recognition. One such player to follow this route was the best goalkeeper never to play for Italy: Fabio Cudicini.

He had moved north to Milan, after long years at Roma, to fill a void left by pre-eminent contemporaries such as the gawky, awkward Giorgio Ghezzi and the luckless Lorenzo Buffon – whose battle scars included a nose fracture after a collision with England's Johnny Haynes and whose nephew, Gianluigi Buffon, would far outstrip his uncle's 15 caps.

Cudicini had triumphed in the Fairs Cup with Roma in 1961 and then won the Cup-winners Cup with Milan in 1968 against Hamburg. Now he had the chance to become the first

BELOW: **DUTCH ARMS GO UP IN UNISON AS SPARTAK PLAYERS TURN ON THEIR GOALKEEPER IN RECRIMINATION – 3-0 TO AJAX...**

player to boast a winners' medal in all three European cups.

Politics intervened before even the start of term. Soviet tanks, supported by Warsaw Pact partners, had rolled into Czechoslovakia to bring an abrupt end to Alexander Dubcek's 'Prague Spring'. Celtic then refused to play Ferencvaros of Hungary in the first round, so UEFA organized a new draw, keeping eastern and western European clubs apart.

The Warsaw Pact federations announced that they were withdrawing their clubs in protest. In the event, Yugoslavia, by now a communist outsider, defied Soviet requests to toe the line and Red Star Belgrade played on. So did Steaua Bucharest from Romania as well as Czechoslovakia's Spartak Trnava – who beat Steaua 5-3 on aggregate in the first round.

Elsewhere, Manchester United put 10 goals past Waterford from the Irish Republic, with Denis Law making up for lost time by scoring all three in the first leg and four out of seven in the return. Neighbours Manchester City were not so fortunate. A fine side put together by Joe Mercer and Malcolm Allison went out narrowly but immediately to Turkey's Fenerbahce.

Celtic averted an upset of their own against Saint-Etienne after losing the first leg 2-0 in France. Benfica put eight goals past Valur of Iceland, Ajax scored five against Nurnberg, Real Madrid 12 against Limassol and Milan five against Malmo: two for 1963 survivor Gianni Rivera, two for new striker Pierino Prati and one for the Italo-Brazilian centre-forward Angelo Benedetto Sormani.

The imbalance in the draw meant that Milan and Benfica benefited from byes through to the second round. There was no such luck for Real Madrid: they played, and lost on away goals to, Rapid Vienna.

Everything else went according to plan: Ajax won 2-0 both home and away against Fenerbahce, Law scored twice more in United's defeat of Anderlecht, and Jimmy Johnstone – a reluctant flyer – turned in a two-goal display which inspired Celtic's 5-1 home win over Red Star; manager Jock Stein had promised that Johnstone could skip the Belgrade trip if he turned on the first-leg style.

Ironically, the Czechoslovaks of Trnava thumped Finland's Lahden Reipas 9-1 away and 7-1 at home. They followed up with a quarter-final win over AEK Athens to reach the semis along with Milan (victors at Celtic on the tie's lone goal from Prati), United (3-0, 0-0 winners against Rapid) and Ajax (for whom Johan Cruyff scored at home and away against Benfica).

Ajax had the luck of the draw in the semi-finals. Trnava were well drilled and skilful, but Ajax boasted greater individual class, with the youth of Cruyff, Suurbier and Keizer complemented by the experience of Henk Groot, Bennie Muller and the former Partizan Belgrade anchor, Velibor Vasovic.

Ajax won 3-0 at home, with Cruyff scoring his sixth of the campaign, and clung on at 2-0 down in Czechoslovakia for victory on aggregate.

Milan against United had been most observers' dream final. Milan had rebuilt since the 1963 victory over Benfica. Rivera, the inspirational playmaker, and wing-half Giovanni Trapattoni were the lone survivors from that side.

United had not had an easy time. They had lost a foul-strewn battle with the notoriously cynical Estudiantes de La Plata in the World Club Cup, when Stiles was sent off in the first leg and Best in the second. Best's consolation was to be voted European Footballer of the Year, the third United player to be so honoured in five seasons.

Another expulsion was awaiting in Milan, where midfielder John Fitzpatrick's sending-off contributed to a 2-0 defeat by goals from Sormani and the veteran Swede, Kurt Hamrin.

Milan brought a siege mentality to Old Trafford. Goalkeeper Cudicini threw his huge frame right and left in defiance, just as son Carlo would do years later.

He needed some luck, notably after Denis Law's shot appeared to have crossed the line before it was finally cleared. Since Charlton had already scored, that would have levelled the tie. But French referee Roger Machin waved play on.

Cudicini returned to Milan sporting a large bruise on the back of his head as a souvenir of the crucial second-half moment, when passions bubbled over and he was felled by a missile from the crowd.

This was the first season in which substitutes had been permitted, but coach Nereo Rocco was happy for the match – and United's momentum – to be interrupted while Cudicini was revived and put back on his road into the history books.

LEFT: BRIAN KIDD LIES ON THE TURF AT OLD TRAFFORD AS NOBBY STILES REMONSTRATES WITH MILAN'S GIOVANNI LODETTI. MANCHESTER UNITED WON 1-0, BUT IT WAS NOT ENOUGH TO OVERHAUL THE 2-0 DEFICIT FROM THE SAN SIRO. TWO DAYS LATER, MATT BUSBY WALKED AWAY FROM THE CLUB FOR EVER

ITALY'S OLD MASTERS PAINT MADRID RED

Ajax, the first Dutch club to reach the final, stood for the future. Milan, with five players crowding 30 or over, represented the present and the past. Their team had been born of the impatience to provide an instant response to the world domination of Internazionale.

Gianni Rivera was at his peak, one of European football's greatest creative footballers, who would go on to become, briefly, club president as well as a member of parliament. Later that year he would be voted in as European Footballer of the Year.

In 1963 Rivera's passes had opened the way to goal for Jose Altafini. Now he played up to another Brazilian and a Swede. Angelo Sormani had been brought to Italy from among the substitutes at Santos and was thus lumbered with the label of 'Pele's reserve'. Italian parentage helped

earn him seven caps and a world record transfer of £250,000 from Mantova to Roma, who then almost went bust – not for the first or the last time – through financial irresponsibility.

Thus Sormani ended up at Milan alongside Hamrin, who had thought his trophy-winning days were over after a decade at Fiorentina had earned him a then club record 150 goals.

Ajax planned for Sormani and Hamrin, but not for the virtuosity which Pierino Prati brought to this one night in Madrid. Prati was unfortunate in that his career coincided with that of Cagliari's great left-side striker Luigi Riva. Thus he won only 14 caps for Italy spread over six years and, like Cudicini, can look back with happier memories on his club career.

RIGHT: **THE BEAUTIFULLY BALANCED JOHAN CRUYFF LEAVES ANOTHER DEFENDER IN HIS WAKE BUT HE CAN'T TAKE AJAX TO VICTORY ALL ON HIS OWN**

WEDNESDAY 28 MAY 1969
BERNABEU, MADRID

MILAN   **4**
PRATI 7, 39, 74, SORMANI 66

AJAX AMSTERDAM   **1**
VASOVIC 61 PEN

HT: 2-0. ATT: 50,000. REF: ORTIZ DE
MENDIBIL (SP)

MILAN:
CUDICINI - MALATRASI - ANQUILLETTI,
ROSATO, TRAPATTONI, SCHNELLINGER -
LODETTI, RIVERA* - HAMRIN, SORMANI,
PRATI. COACH: ROCCO.

AJAX AMSTERDAM:
BALS - SUURBIER (MULLER 46),
HULSHOFF, VASOVIC*, VAN
DUIVENDOBE - PRONK, GROOT
(NUNINGA 46) - SWART, CRUYFF,
DANIELSSON, KEIZER.
COACH: MICHELS.

*CAPTAIN.

LEFT: AC MILAN'S BRAZILIAN
FORWARD ANGELO SORMANI
HOLDS UP THE EUROPEAN CUP
IN THE BERNABEU BEFORE
BEING ENGULFED BY
JUBILANT FANS

The Bernabeu had hosted the final once before: in 1957, when hosts Real had beaten Italy's Fiorentina. But there was little chance of an Italian defeat this time, once Prati had converted assists from both Sormani and his captain Rivera before half-time. Left-winger Piet Keizer observed later that his directors and coaching staff had been 'a little naïve' about Italian gamesmanship on and off the pitch.

Spanish referee Ortiz de Mendibil had infuriated Liverpool in Milan four years earlier, but this time he whistled it straight down the line for a penalty to Ajax on the hour after Keizer had been tripped. Skipper Velibor Vasovic, formerly of Partizan, rattled home the spot kick to become the first man to score for two different clubs in a Champions Cup Final.

Not that it made any difference to the outcome. Milan, irritated out of their shell, struck twice more through Sormani and Prati. The left-winger thus became the first man to score a hat-trick in a Champions Cup Final since Ferenc Puskas against Benfica in 1962.

Years later, the Ajax coach, Rinus Michels, recalled the final in typically blunt fashion: 'We lost because we were not good enough. We were building our team. It was good enough to win everything in Holland but not yet everything in Europe.'

In fact, as well as losing the Champions Cup Final that year, Ajax had already conceded their Dutch crown to Rotterdam rivals Feyenoord, who were also about to steal their European thunder.

1970S

THE NEW NORTH-SOUTH DIVIDE

The 1970s saw the European Champions Cup leave Latin Europe behind. Holland seized command for four years courtesy of Feyenoord and Ajax, but then the primacy of Johan Cruyff's vibrant 'total football' was usurped by the rule of law imposed by Franz Beckenbauer and Bayern Munich – the first German winners. German football proved internationally dominant. Beckenbauer also led his men to glory in both the European Championship and World Cup before England struck back at club level through Liverpool. But only Brian Clough's red-clad archers from Nottingham Forest, plotting their ambush through the English back door, proved capable of silencing the Kop.

RIGHT: AJAX WON THE EUROPEAN CUP THREE TIMES IN A ROW, THE FIRST TEAM TO DO SO SINCE REAL MADRID. HERE THEY LINE UP BEFORE THE FINAL WITH JUVENTUS IN 1973, THEIR LYRICAL SWANSONG BEFORE A LENGTHY FALLOW PERIOD

FRANZ BECKENBAUER

Country: Germany

Position: Sweeper

Born: 11 September 1945

Clubs: SC Munich 1906,
Bayern Munich, New York
Cosmos, SV Hamburg

FRANZ BECKENBAUER

'Please, don't let the ball fly out of the ground,' I was thinking in the last seconds of extra time in the 1974 final. We were losing 1-0 to Atletico Madrid and 'Katsche' Schwarzenbeck was bringing the ball through in midfield and setting himself to shoot. It was not his job and never his speciality. I feared it was all over. At least, if the ball stayed in play, we might have a few more seconds...

Of course he shot from more than 30 metres and somehow the ball flew past the goalkeeper and into the net for our equaliser. It had to be a fluke. But it was the perfect fluke because immediately afterwards the referee blew the final whistle. As it turned out, we would not have had any more time. It was that or nothing – and, of course, we were relieved to rescue the draw and the replay.

We won that 4-0, the first of our three Champions Cups. We were physically the stronger for the replay but the key to it was psychological. Atletico's players were mentally broken because they had put one hand on the trophy only to see it prised away at the last moment. For us, it worked the opposite way: we were still flying high after pulling it back.

There were no penalties to settle a drawn final in those days; UEFA only changed the rules afterwards. But we needed a penalty shoot-out to beat Atvidaberg when we launched our defence the next season. I even converted our last penalty, though I rarely got involved in the shootouts. We believed penalties were the responsibility of the forwards. Anyway, I was always too polite. I was content to step aside for whoever wanted to take a kick.

We had a wonderful side. Six of us were in the national team who won the World Cup that year: Sepp Maier, Gerd Muller, Schwarzenbeck, Paul Breitner, Uli Hoeness and myself. We were also German champions and would have won the cup final, too, if it had not been for the referee. More success than that is impossible. From then on, however, it was all downhill.

Internationally, we stayed on top of our game but back home we could not focus. Six weeks after we beat Holland

2-1 in the World Cup Final, we lost 6-0 to Offenbach on the opening day of the Bundesliga. We had a string of injuries and, because we had won so much, everyone was gunning for us.

In Europe, it was different. The return with Atvidaberg was one of our most memorable games. We had won 3-1 at home, then went 3-0 down in Sweden before Hoeness scored the all-important goal which earned us extra time and penalties.

Equally memorable were our games against Dynamo Dresden. It was the first time West and East German clubs had come out of the hat together. We won 4-3 in Munich and drew 3-3 in Dresden, which was only half the story.

An Italian club had warned us that, when they played over there, something was put in their food and they could hardly run during the game. So Wilhelm Neudecker and Robert Schwan, our president and manager, decided that instead of staying the night before the game in the GDR, we would stop on the West side of the border.

LEFT: BECKENBAUER MODELLED HIMSELF ON GIACINTO FACCHETTI, THE ATTACKING LEFT-BACK OF INTER MILAN

Our decision was a big issue at the time which went to the highest political and diplomatic levels. But Neudecker and Schwan refused to budge and we got our way. We did the same a year later against Magdeburg, also from the GDR, and then everyone was much more relaxed about it.

But we were not fooling ourselves. We knew we were past our best and needed to play a more tactical game because football is not only about using your legs, it's also about using your brain. That was how we managed to beat both Leeds in the 1975 final, then Saint-Etienne in 1976.

The key to it was our Bavarian axis of Maier in goal, myself as *libero* and Muller at centre-forward. Then we had a hard-running midfield with Franz Roth, Bernd Durnberger or Jupp Kapellmann, plus other world-class players like Hoeness. He and Conny Torstensson, or later Karl-Heinz Rummenigge, hung back a little deeper than Muller who was our attack leader.

Muller was sensational, a phenomenon. When I brought the ball out of defence, you could see the anticipation in the muscles in his legs. He had a speed off the mark I have never seen in any other player. He would have scored 80 goals a season in today's Bundesliga, twice as many as in his heyday. Back then, Muller always had two defenders trampling all over him but you never see double-marking nowadays. He would had much more room in which to work.

I had been developing my own role as *libero* since I was a youth player. I modelled myself on Giacinto Facchetti, the Internazionale left-back, who was always overlapping up the wing. That was revolutionary because 40 years ago everyone held his position much more rigidly than today.

The more I watched Facchetti, the more I realised that I could employ the same tactic through the middle. What he could do in a narrow corridor on the left I could do to better effect with so much more room in which to work through the centre of the pitch. So that is what I did whenever the state of the game permitted.

To make it work, I needed a loyal assistant to sit tight in defence and Schwarzenbeck did exactly that except, thankfully of course, against Atletico.

Our greatest rivals in the 1970s had been Ajax. They were world class in the three years before Johan Cruyff went to Barcelona. In the 1973 quarter-finals, they beat us 4–0 in Amsterdam. That was a black day. Maier made three mistakes in one match for the only time in his career and they punished each one.

In time, of course, Liverpool followed us which left the Latin Europeans out in the cold throughout the 1970s.

Twice I nearly went to play in Italy. First, Internazionale wanted me in 1966, but then Italy lost to North Korea in the World Cup and the federation blamed it on all the foreign players and shut the borders. I would have gone if I could have, not only because of the top-class players there, but also, of course, for the money. One Sunday I flew down from Munich to watch the Milan derby. It was fantastic to be in an 80,000 crowd for just a club game, while at Bayern we still played in the little old Grunwald stadium. Later AC Milan also tried to sign me, but it fell through. A pity. I would like to have tried the Italian experience.

Pele was the greatest player of my era and, in Europe, Bobby Charlton, Eusebio, George Best... there were so many, unlike nowadays when I would pick out only Ronaldinho and Ronaldo.

Of course the game has changed. Players are fitter and far more professional in every aspect of their preparation. Also, the 'stage' has improved enormously. The footballs are better and so are the pitches. We played on potato fields which were green only in July and August; today's players have super pitches all year round.

But... today's player must be conscious of his behaviour every waking minute. If he lets his guard slip for a moment, the media and public are on his case. Today's players live in glass houses, while we lived a comparatively normal daily life.

On balance, I am glad I played then rather than now.

LEFT: BECKENBAUER
WAS THE PUPPET MASTER,
PULLING THE STRINGS
WHICH EARNED WEST
GERMANY AND BAYERN
MUNICH EVERY
MAJOR PRIZE

HAPPINESS IS TROPHY-SHAPED

Under Ernst Happel, Feyenoord outstripped rivals Ajax to make the final. Their opponents were the winners of the Battle of Britain, as Celtic's Cavaliers took on the Roundheads of Leeds United

Headline-writers found easy alliteration to celebrate Feyenoord's achievement as the Cup's first Dutch winners in May 1970. The descriptive focus settled on their coach: Ernst Franz Hermann Happel.

He was, repeatedly, dubbed 'Happy Happel' in headlines, introductions and picture captions. But easy words bore little relation to reality: Happel was a dour disciplinarian, ever wary of the natural law balancing good fortune with bad, triumph with defeat.

Happel was Austrian, born in 1925, two years before the Mitropa Cup. As a boy, he supported Rapid Vienna and he grew up to become one of their most resolute players. He even became the first player to score a European hat-trick against Real Madrid, with two free-kicks and a penalty in a first-round tie in 1956 – only for Madrid to trump his hat-trick in the subsequent play-off.

'Our organization was not up to the job,' said Happel years later. It was a mistake he would not permit once he had taken up coaching. In that respect Happel was more in the mode of Helenio Herrera than in the developing trend of charismatic, personality managers – exemplified in England by Liverpool's Bill Shankly.

Feyenoord had the easiest of starts: drawn against KR Reykjavik, they saved the Icelanders money by playing both legs in Rotterdam.

Sweden's Ove Kindvall scored a hat-trick in the opening 12-2 win and two more in the 4-0 'return'. One of the opening dozen was struck by full-back Wim Van Duivendobe who had joined Feyenoord after collecting a runners-up medal four months earlier with Ajax.

'Ajax had the better individuals,' said Van Duivendobe later, 'but Feyenoord, just then, were the better all-round team.'

They were not the only first-rounders to hit double figures. Don Revie's Leeds United – prepared on a steady diet of dossiers and carpet bowls – put 10 past Norway's Lyn Oslo without reply at Elland Road. Mick Jones scored a hat-trick that night and added another when Leeds won 6-0 in Oslo.

Real Madrid – with Paco Gento still at No. 11 – put 14 past Olympiakos Nicosia over two legs while Celtic, showing only a modicum of change since Lisbon, saw off Basel more modestly. A goal from Tommy Gemmell in the 2-0 aggregate win proved that he had not lost his attacking flair.

Milan opened their defence with a 5-0, 3-0 win over Avenir of Luxembourg. The ties were moved forward to assist the Italians in their World Club Cup clash with Argentina's Estudiantes de La Plata, in which Milan triumphed but at heavy cost.

They won 3-0 in Milan easily enough, then held out in La Plata, despite losing a bruising battle 2-1, for a 4-2 aggregate win. Franco-Argentine centre-forward Nestor Combin had his nose broken and Pierino Prati was callously kicked in the back while lying on the pitch receiving treatment to a bruised ankle.

That battering to legs and morale lowered Milan's resistance for the European challenge of Feyenoord. Gianni Rivera was injured and substituted before half-time in the first leg in which the *Rossoneri* lacked the energy to press home the advantage provided by an early goal from Combin. Rivera

RIGHT: AS A COACH AND PLAYER, ERNST HAPPEL WON 17 NATIONAL AND INTERNATIONAL TITLES AS WELL AS TAKING HOLLAND TO RUNNERS UP IN THE WORLD CUP IN ARGENTINA IN 1978. IN TRIBUTE, THE FORMER PRATER STADIUM IN VIENNA NOW BEARS HIS NAME

missed the return and Feyenoord won more easily than the tallies of Wim Jansen and Wim van Hanegem suggest.

Italy's own champions, Fiorentina, survived one round further before falling to Celtic in the quarter-finals, where Feyenoord again scored a 2-1 overall win, this time against Vorwarts of East Berlin. Leeds got the better by 2-0 of a Standard Liege side who had beaten Real Madrid 3-2 in the Bernabeu.

Feyenoord duly profited from a semi-final draw against the Polish outsiders of Legia Warsaw, while most European Cup eyes were focused on the so-called 'Battle of Britain' between Leeds and Celtic.

Leeds were revelling for the first time in the status of English champions. They were playing at their peak, with the inspirational Billy Bremner and Johnny Giles driving midfield and Allan 'Sniffer' Clarke, Mick Jones and Peter Lorimer an effective trio up front.

Manager Revie had changed their kit from blue and gold to all-white, like that of Real Madrid, a permanent reminder

that he set his standards as high as the best. But Leeds' achievements under Revie barely disguised a malevolence which denied them the credit their fine football deserved. They were never the most popular of teams.

Celtic were fortunate. They travelled to Elland Road to find Leeds playing their eighth game in 14 days in vain pursuit of the treble of League, FA Cup and Champions Cup. Leeds missed the wing-half steel of the injured Norman Hunter and never recovered from Celtic's winning strike by George Connelly inside 45 seconds.

Demand for tickets was so high that the return was switched from Parkhead to Hampden, where a European record gate of 136,505 saw Leeds level early on through skipper Billy Bremner, only to succumb to quickfire second-half strikes from John Hughes and Bobby Murdoch.

Celtic manager Jock Stein was jubilant, understandably. After all, he had stated in his programme notes that whoever emerged victorious from this British epic would be favourites for the final.

ABOVE: CELTIC GOALKEEPER EVAN WILLIAMS WATCHES A 40-YARDER FROM BILLY BREMNER HIT THE NET TO SILENCE THE 136,505-STRONG CROWD, A RECORD ATTENDANCE FOR THE EUROPEAN CUP

FEYENOORD TOPPLE MIGHTY CELTIC

Experience and track record confirmed manager Jock Stein's confident scribblings about the likely outcome in Milan. Celtic had won in 1967 and Lisbon cornerstones remained in the shape of skipper Billy McNeill, goal-scoring left-back Tommy Gemmell, midfielders Bobby Murdoch and Bertie Auld, wingers Jimmy Johnstone and Bobby Lennox and strikers Willie Wallace and John Hughes.

The over-confidence of the Scots extended to the media. Dutch clubs had won nothing and the rest of the continent was oblivious to the magical spell being conjured by Ajax in Amsterdam and the pacy pragmatism emanating from PSV in Eindhoven.

Celtic's players agreed later that their own publicity had lulled them into believing that the hardest part had been defeating Leeds and that Feyenoord would be overawed by the San Siro occasion.

That was to ignore, fatally, not only Feyenoord's ability and coach Ernst Happel's organization but also the fact that the Dutchmen had faced Milan in the San Siro earlier in the season in a far more intimidating atmosphere than the green-and-red-tinged neutrality of the final.

Celtic lined up seven Lisbon winners. Feyenoord responded with a goalkeeper, in Eddy Pieters-Graafland, who had been playing European cup football in the late 1950s, a superbly resilient defensive rock in skipper Rinus Israel, two underrated playmakers in Wim Jansen and Austrian Franz Hasil, plus Ove Kindvall up front and veteran Coen Moulijn on the left wing.

Moulijn, now 33, was rated by many as the greatest Dutch footballer since Faas Wilkes in the early 1950s. His left-wing talent was not pure pace in the manner of a Paco Gento or energy in the style of Antonio Simoes, but guile. When he needed pace he could find enough, but above all he had an eye for a gap and the passing accuracy to pierce it.

Not that this was instantly evident in Milan, where Celtic went ahead inside the opening half hour. Murdoch took a quick, short free-kick and Gemmell thumped the ball beyond Pieters-Graafland. Celtic, even more certain of laying hands on a second European Cup in four seasons, were still in dream mode when Israel headed home two minutes later.

Happel was low-key in the Feyenoord dressing-room at half-time, insisting that his players hold the ball up in midfield, control the pace and thus drain the passion from

Celtic's game. Van Hanegem and Hasil did precisely that, Moulijn began to drift into dangerous spaces and Celtic wavered.

The final went into extra time for only the third time in the competition's history but the second time in three seasons. Celtic had arrived there courtesy of the reflexes of goalkeeper Evan Williams, but might still have won it had Hughes not fluffed an opening as the clock ticked down.

WEDNESDAY 6 MAY 1970
SAN SIRO, MILAN

FEYENOORD   2
ISRAEL 32, KINDVALL 116

CELTIC   1
GEMMELL 30

AFTER EXTRA TIME, HT: 1-1, 90 MIN: 1-1. ATT: 53,187. REF: LO BELLO (IT)

FEYENOORD:
PIETERS-GRAAFLAND - ROMEIJN (HAAK 107), ISRAEL*, LASEROMS, VAN DUIVENDOBE - JANSEN, HASIL, VAN HANEGEM - WERY, KINDVALL, MOULIJN.
COACH: HAPPEL.

CELTIC:
WILLIAMS - HAY, MCNEILL*, BROGAN, GEMMELL - MURDOCH, AULD (CONNELLY 77) - JOHNSTONE, WALLACE, J. HUGHES, LENNOX.
MANAGER: STEIN.

*CAPTAIN.

A replay was looming when, with three minutes to go, Kindvall chased a long, looping clearance out of the Feyenoord midfield. The ball might have eluded him and bounced out for a goal-kick, but the wavering arm of the luckless McNeill, stumbling back, took the pace off the ball. Referee Concetto Lo Bello allowed the advantage and Kindvall fired his sixth goal of the campaign.

It was also the goal which brought more than 200,000 people on to the streets of Rotterdam the next day to welcome home the first Dutch champions of Europe. Even Happel almost smiled.

ABOVE: **FEYENOORD PLAYERS RUN OVER TO THEIR FANS WITH THE EUROPEAN CUP AFTER THEIR 2-1 VICTORY OVER CELTIC**

LEFT: **RINUS ISRAEL (3) TURNS AWAY AFTER SCORING HIS SIDE'S OPENER IN THE SAN SIRO. ISRAEL WAS LATER PICTURED ON A DUTCH STAMP TO COMMEMORATE THE VICTORY**

HISTORY'S GOLDEN THREADS

Brazil had taken football to new heights when they won the 1970 World Cup final but now there was a new talent, the gawky son of a cleaner in Ajax's offices, to lead Europe's great revival

1970-71

Threads of history weave an unbroken path through the tale of the Champions Cup. Ajax Amsterdam can trace their golden thread right back to Hugo Meisl, one of European football's leading administrators between the wars and founder of the Mitropa Cup.

Meisl's younger brother, Willy, had found his way to England as a refugee from the Nazis in the late 1930s after Hugo's death. In London, in 1955, this other Meisl published *Soccer Revolution*, which stands as a milestone among football books.

Soccer Revolution traced the international development of the game and concluded by peering into the future. Meisl predicted that the advent of television would bring about a demand for higher standards of entertainment and greater physical, tactical and technical expertise.

This would also put an end to the old rigidity of playing positions. Every player should be an all-rounder, said Meisl. 'A really fine footballer will be almost equally good in several positions and far from bad in all of them. He will have to be able to tackle any task workmanlike, because that will form the very basis of the new tactics.'

Meisl called his system of the future 'The Whirl'. Sadly he died in 1968, just too early to see it brought to life as 'Total Football' by Ajax.

'The Ajax way' has come, with the passing of time, to say less about style and more about administration: the efficient rounding-up of talented kids, the refined selection process, and their education both scholastic and sporting on the way to the pinnacle of the European game.

In the early 1970s, however, the flowering of Dutch talent was a remarkable force of natural brilliance whose appreciation was visual rather than academic.

Dutch football had embraced professionalism only in the mid-1950s, and even a decade later many of the stars who played in Europe for Ajax, Feyenoord and their domestic rivals were part-timers.

But the influence of European competition and the advent of television changed the focus.

Ajax appreciated the potential when they signed the

English manager Vic Buckingham. In 1964 he gave a first-team debut to a gawky 17-year-old centre-forward named Johannes Hendrikus Cruyff, the son of a cleaner in the club offices.

Even as a teenager, Cruyff was opinionated and sharp-tempered. Early on, he incurred an international ban for lashing out at the veteran East German referee Rudi Glockner. But his talent was beyond compare; arguably Cruyff was the greatest footballer raised in post-war European football.

The 1968–69 European campaign, which saw a nervy Ajax conclusively beaten by Milan in the final, was a practice run. Between late 1970 and the summer of 1973 Ajax dominated European club football with a style and élan which earned comparison with the best of Real Madrid.

Not that they were among initial favourites in the late summer of 1970, when Europe was reeling from the World Cup-winning brilliance of a Brazilian team inspired by Pele, Tostao, Jairzinho, Gerson and Carlos Alberto. After that extravaganza, the subsequent opening round of the Champions Cup seemed very dull fare.

RIGHT: **THE PORTLY FERENC PUSKAS TRAINING AT WEMBLEY WHEN HE WAS COACH OF PANATHINAIKOS. AS A PLAYER, HE SCORED 83 GOALS IN 84 MATCHES FOR HUNGARY AND WON THE EUROPEAN CUP FOUR TIMES WITH REAL MADRID**

Easy starts were accepted as the norm by Everton for England (Alan Ball scoring a hat-trick against Keflavik), Borussia Monchengladbach for Germany, Celtic for Scotland (Harry Hood hitting three against KPV Kokkolan), Cagliari for Italy and Atletico Madrid for Spain; neighbours Real were absent for the first time.

Ajax began inauspiciously against the politically reclusive Albanians of Nendori Tirana.

A double from defender Wim Suurbier earned them a 2-2 draw in the most hard-line of communist capitals and strikes from wingers Sjaack Swart and Piet Keizer brought a 2-0 win in Amsterdam.

Feyenoord were not so fortunate. The holders were held 1-1 at home, to their own surprise, by UT Arad – an unfashionable side even by Romanian standards – and could only draw 0-0 away.

Thus Arad went through on the away-goals rule. Feyenoord could not even push them to the newly introduced settlement lottery of the penalty shoot-out.

The honour of being the Cup's first shoot-out winners went to Everton, who defeated Borussia 4-3 on penalties after 1-1 draws in Bokelberg and at Goodison.

Everton's inability to win matches then cost them dear in the quarter-finals, when they lost on away goals to Panathinaikos from Athens.

The underrated Greeks then achieved the shock of the season with a dramatic turnaround of their semi-final against Red Star.

The Slavs thought they were through to their first final after winning 4-1 in Belgrade. But two goals from tall centre-forward Antonis Antoniadis inspired a 3-0 home win which carried the Greeks through on away goals.

Ajax met them at Wembley, having beaten Basel 5-1, then both Celtic and Atletico Madrid by 3-1.

Ajax were about to embark on a prolific three-year run in which their 'Total Football' would re-establish the supremacy of the European game and enthral the world. Cruyff had scored only one of their 15 goals along the way. Now the time had come for the new hero to cross swords with an old one.

ABOVE: AJAX'S BARRY HULSHOFF CAN NOT STOP CELTIC'S JIMMY JOHNSTONE FROM SCORING A CONSOLATION GOAL FOR CELTIC. THE GLASGOW CLUB WON 1-0 IN THE SECOND LEG, AFTER LOSING 3-0 IN AMSTERDAM

EUROPEAN CHAMPION CLUBS' CUP

AJAX v PANATHINAIKOS
(AMSTERDAM) (ATHENS)

ΠΑΟ

FINAL 1908

ORGANISED BY THE
FOOTBALL ASSOCIATION
on behalf of the
UNION DES ASSOCIATIONS
EUROPEENNES DE FOOTBALL

WEDNESDAY, 2nd JUNE, 1971 Kick-off 7.45 p.m.

OFFICIAL PROGRAMME 10p

Empire WEMBLEY Stadium

ABOVE RIGHT: GERRIT MUHREN
OF AJAX RAISES HIS ARMS IN
TRIUMPH AS ARIE HAAN (NOT
IN PICTURE) SCORES THE
CLINCHING GOAL AGAINST
PANATHINAIKOS

BELOW-PAR AJAX STILL RUN THE SHOW

Walking out at Wembley was a nostalgic experience for the Panathinaikos coach. Ferenc Puskas had entered Wembley legend in 1953 with Hungary and gone back there a decade later with a FIFA World XI in the all-star match which celebrated the centenary of the Football Association. While Panathinaikos was his major European appointment as a coach, this final also proved the pinnacle of his managerial career.

The same could not be said of Rinus Michels on the Ajax bench. Michels had been a powerful, if raw, centre-forward

for Holland in the mid 1950s. But Michels the coach was nothing like Michels the player; as a coach he was intuitive, sensitive, inventive and inspirational. He and his headstrong young players did not always see eye to eye: they fell out frequently over issues ranging from bonuses to training camps. But Michels knew their potential and all he wanted was to ensure that they profited from the genius of the greatest single generation in Dutch football history.

This Ajax was not quite the finished product. Three great young players in injured left-back Rudi Krol,

Panathinaikos put their hope in the craft of playmaker Mimis Domazos and the aerial ability of Anton Antoniadis. But Ajax had far more style and understanding and were adept at that fluid interchanging of position which ripped gaping holes in the tightest of defences.

They were not at their best but, even below par, proved too much for Panathinaikos.

As early as the fifth minute, Piet Keizer, who had passed a late fitness test, opened the way for Dick Van Dijk to make the most of his appearance in place of the injured Krol.

At half-time Ajax were upset when Nico Rijnders collapsed. He was quickly revived but had to be substituted, as did the leg-weary Swaart. The latter was replaced by Haan, who marked the start of his long-term stint at the heart of Dutch football by scoring the decisive second goal three minutes from time.

Cruyff sparked the attack which ended with Haan's shot being deflected home by defender Anthimos Kapsis. Ajax walked up the 39 steps to claim the prize which would be theirs for two more years. Panathinaikos, however, flew home to an enthusiastic reception for having reached the final.

For Kapsis, the pleasure of having a European winners' medal in the family would come 33 years later when his son, Michalis, helped Greece win Euro 2004 in Portugal.

ABOVE: SKIPPER VELIBOR VASOVIC HOLDS THE EUROPEAN CUP ALOFT, AS GOALKEEPER HEINZ STUY AWAITS HIS TURN TO CLUTCH SILVERWARE AND MILK THE APPLAUSE

midfielder Arie Haan and striker Johnny Rep were waiting in the wings as veterans Velibor Vasovic in defence and Jackie Swaart on the right wing were just going over the hill. Michels was to leave after the Wembley win, lured away to Barcelona; it would be left to another to apply the final gloss. But he went with the laurels of a worthy European champion.

Greek fans made more noise than the Dutch on a Wembley Wednesday afternoon. The cacophony which had greeted Everton in Athens had been described as 'frightening' by the English champions' manager, Howard Kendall. At Wembley it was muffled somewhat by the pitch perimeter ring and the greyhound track inside the old Empire Stadium.

WEDNESDAY 2 JUNE 1971
WEMBLEY, LONDON

AJAX AMSTERDAM   **2**
VAN DIJK 5, HAAN 87

PANATHINAIKOS   **0**

HT: 1-0. ATT: 90,000.
REF: TAYLOR (ENG)

AJAX:
STUY - SUURBIER, HULSHOFF, VASOVIC*, RIJNDERS (BLANKENBURG 46) - G. MUHREN, VAN DIJK, NEESKENS - SWART (HAAN 46), CRUYFF, KEIZER. COACH: MICHELS.

PANATHINAIKOS:
EKONOMOPOULOS - TOMARAS, KAMARAS, SOURPIS, VLAHOS - ELEFTERAKIS, DOMAZOS*, GRAMOS, KAPSIS - FILAKOURIS, ANTONIADIS. COACH: PUSKAS.

*CAPTAIN.

1971-72

PRESSING MATTERS FOR INTER

All hell broke loose when Inter played Borussia Monchengladbach and someone threw a Coke can from the crowd. Meanwhile, the magisterial Johan Cruyff was conducting play for a brilliant Ajax side

Roberto Boninsegna, centre-forward of the Italian national side who finished runners-up to Brazil in the 1970 Mexico World Cup, lay flat out as mayhem broke out in Borussia Monchengladbach's Bokelberg stadium.

Less than half an hour had gone in the first leg of the second-round match between Borussia and Inter. Near to Boninsegna lay a Coca-Cola can, blamed for the most controversial crowd incident thus far in the Champions Cup.

A steady rise in spectator unrest had been noted before the start of the season by UEFA's general secretary Hans Bangerter. A formal warning had been issued to all competing clubs that punishments ranging from fines to result-reversals would be imposed for further incidents. The warning, like many others issued by UEFA regarding the increasingly complex issue of hooliganism, had little effect. Telling the clubs seemed pointless to many when it was fans who were to blame.

Borussia, a fast-rising force in German club football, and Inter had both been unhappy with the second-round draw. The absence of effective seeding meant that one of these two clubs, both serious contenders for the trophy, faced a disappointingly early exit.

The first leg was staged at Bokelberg on 20 October. Both sides were confident.

Borussia relied on the pressing style preached by their so-called 'master coach' Hennes Weisweiler and the individual talents of defenders Berti Vogts and Luggi Muller, playmaker Gunter Netzer, workhorse Herbert Wimmer and striker Jupp Heynckes.

RIGHT: **HORST BLANKENBURG AND JOHAN CRUYFF PLAY CARDS ON THE EVE OF THEIR EUROPEAN CUP TIE WITH ARSENAL IN LONDON**

Inter looked to half a dozen veterans from the 1970 World Cup who included European Cup-winning survivors in Tarcisio Burgnich, Giacinto Facchetti and Gianfranco Bedin at the back, plus Sandro Mazzola, Jair da Costa and Mario Corso further forward.

The tackles flew in steep and sharp. Borussia went ahead on 19 minutes through Heynckes, Boninsegna levelled on 19 and Ulrich Le Fevre restored the Germans' lead two minutes later. Then, on 29 minutes, Boninsegna was apparently felled by a missile thrown from the crowd and all hell broke loose.

Inter skipper Mazzola handed the offending can to the officials as proof of the assault, Boninsegna was carried off and the Italians lost their collective heads. Le Fevre, Netzer and Heynckes scored three more German goals before half-time, when Inter substituted keeper Lido Vieri.

Since Boninsegna had already been replaced – and only two substitutes were then allowed – Inter were reduced to 10 men when Jair was injured in the second half. They ended up with nine since Corso was sent off five minutes from the end for pushing referee Jef Dorpmans, by which time Netzer and Klaus-Dieter Sieloff (penalty) had pushed the winning margin to 7-1.

The fall-out was immense. The Germans accused Boninsegna of play-acting and claimed that the can had been thrown on the pitch earlier in the game.

Inter – of all people! – accused the Germans of intimidatory tactics on and off the pitch and demanded that UEFA award them the game by a 2-0 or 3-0 margin.

In the end, UEFA went down the middle of road, annulled the result and ordered a replay at a different German venue. This took place in Berlin after the second leg in Milan which Inter won 4-2 with Boninsegna and Jair on the scoresheet.

A crowd of 84,000 was as good as gold in Berlin's Olympic stadium for the replayed first leg which ended goalless. Borussia's luck was right out. They missed a penalty and lost Muller with a broken leg after he mistimed a tackle on Boninsegna.

Inter thus went forward into the next round on a 4-2 aggregate and a wave of bad feeling.

They squeezed past Standard Liege on the away-goals rule in the quarter-finals and frustrated Celtic on penalties after two goalless games in the semis. 'Dixie' Deans, on as substitute for a youthful Kenny Dalglish, missed the crucial first spot-kick.

Buoyed by their previous success in persuading the authorities to intervene on their behalf, Inter launched another protest on finding that they would be playing holders Ajax in Holland, albeit in Rotterdam. UEFA, this time, was having none of it.

Ajax had beaten Dynamo Dresden 2-0, 0-0 in the first round, Marseille 2-1, 4-0 in the second, Cup newcomers Arsenal 2-1, 1-0 in the quarters, and Benfica 1-0, 0-0 in the semis.

Arsenal, winners of the Fairs Cup in 1970, had qualified for the Champions Cup for the first time by virtue of winning the English league and FA Cup double in 1971 under the low-key management of Bertie Mee.

They were absolutely delighted to return from Amsterdam with 'only' a 2-1 defeat, but that was before class told its own tale back at Highbury, though Ajax owed victory, oddly, to an own goal by Mee's sometime successor, George Graham.

Cruyff, crowned European Footballer of the Year the previous December after his emergent exploits in 1971, managed not one of Ajax's goals along the way – though his contribution, as he both led the line and faded back to organize play, was more magisterial than ever. He was saving his goals for the right occasion.

ABOVE: ARSENAL GOALKEEPER BOB WILSON LOOKS ON IN HORROR AS GEORGE GRAHAM'S PASS-BACK ELUDES HIM AND ROLLS TOWARDS THE NET. AJAX'S ARIE HAAN WILLS THE BALL HOME

AJAX TAKE INTER TO THE CLEANERS

Ajax's ego-driven young stars were shocked rigid when president Jaap Van Praag had introduced Stefan Kovacs as coach in place of Barcelona-bound Rinus Michels.

They had mixed feelings about Michels's departure; they had crossed swords with him, but he was also a father figure whom they respected.

Kovacs was a scarcely known Romanian whose short grey hair and squat build marked him out as anything but a football man.

'How do you like the length of our hair?' the players asked him on his first day, ready to challenge some stereotypically authoritarian East European response. 'I've been employed as a football coach not a hairdresser,' Kovacs told them, sensing the tension and knowing there was more to come.

Kovacs let the staff run the first training sessions while he observed from the touchline. Suddenly, out of a group of players, a football was fizzed directly at Kovacs at around knee height. He raised his right foot, brought the ball down smoothly out of its flight, trapped it and then knocked it back.

No one taunted him again after that. He had passed the test, made his point and went on to take Ajax to new heights. Kovacs was the man who completed the job Michels had started by bringing 'Total Football' to its zenith.

He compensated for giving Johan Cruyff freedom to roam back and across the pitch by encouraging technically adept defenders such as Wim Suurbier, Ruud Krol and Horst Blankenburg to advance in whatever direction the game took them. They could take that risk knowing that midfielders Johan Neeskens, Arie Haan and Gerrie Muhren could 'read' themselves back to fill the gaps.

Ajax had been worried about taking on Inter in the home stadium of their greatest Dutch rivals, Feyenoord. They half-expected a spectator backlash. But such fears proved groundless. Ajax were playing for the glory of Dutch sport and for the greater good of association football in general. Inter claimed victim status: they were missing Mario Corso from midfield because of the year-long ban which had followed his expulsion in Monchengladbach and were playing in their opponents' back yard. However, Inter had benefited similarly from playing Benfica in Milan in the 1965 final. To the neutrals, this was payback time.

The pattern was predictable. Inter, coached by their ex-international wing-half Gianni Invernizzi, fell back in Herrera-esque style. They conceded the initiative to Ajax and waited patiently for a chance to hit them on the break. It never came.

Inter reached half-time safely, but the interval disturbed their concentration. Invernizzi had confessed before the game that his greatest concern was how Ajax's raiding defenders might penetrate Inter's orthodox man-marking system. His concern was justified. Three minutes after the restart Suurbier crossed from the right, 'keeper Ivano Bordon fumbled and Cruyff stretched out a leg to jab home the opening goal.

Inter, at last, moved Sandro Mazzola forward behind Roberto Boninsegna, but the longer it lasted, the more dangerously exposed Inter became. Ultimately Piet Keizer eluded two defenders on the left and crossed for Cruyff to rise and glance home his, and his team's, second goal.

The red-and-white banners were unfurled to hail the finest club team on the planet. They were champions of Europe (again), champions of Holland as well as domestic cup-winners and duly added the World Club Cup and the new European Supercup to their rapidly expanding trophy cabinets.

'Total Football' meant total domination.

FINALE EUROPA-CUP · PRIJS 50 CENT
INTERNAZIONALE - AJAX

STADION FEYENOORD ROTTERDAM · WOENSDAG 31 MEI 1972

RIGHT: IF HOLLAND WAS THE NATION THAT GAVE THE WORLD TOTAL FOOTBALL, THEN JOHAN CRUYFF (RIGHT) WAS THE SUPREME TOTAL FOOTBALLER

OPPOSITE PAGE: THREE TIMES EUROPEAN FOOTBALLER OF THE YEAR, JOHAN CRUYFF HANGS ON TO THE CHAMPIONS CUP WITH HIS USUAL ELAN

WEDNESDAY 31 MAY 1972

DE KUIJP, ROTTERDAM

AJAX AMSTERDAM   **2**
CRUYFF 48, 77

INTERNAZIONALE   **0**

HT: 0-0. ATT: 61,000. REF: HELIES (FR)

AJAX:
STUY - SUURBIER, BLANKENBURG,
HULSHOFF, KROL - NEESKENS, HAAN,
G. MUHREN - SWART, CRUYFF,
KEIZER*.
COACH: KOVACS.

INTER:
BORDON - BELLUGI - BURGNICH,
GIUBERTONI (BERTINI 12), FACCHETTI -
BEDIN, ORIALI, MAZZOLA*,
FRUSTALUPI - JAIR (PELLIZZARO 58),
BONINSEGNA.
COACH: INVERNIZZI.

*CAPTAIN.

THE GOLDEN DAYS OF CRUYFF & CO

Total Football continued to dominate as Ajax went for their third win in a row, disposing of Bayern Munich and Real Madrid in stylish fashion on their way to confront the Old Lady of Turin in the final

The climactic and concluding third term of Ajax's reign over world club football was marked by a clash of philosophies within the European game as the old guard came to increasingly tetchy grips with the new.

Ajax, on the one hand, underlined their class and confidence by dismantling both Bayern Munich (the future) and Real Madrid (the past) on the grand march to a European Cup hat-trick.

But Bayern's hunger was to be fuelled by a defeat which infuriated players such as Franz Beckenbauer, Gerd Muller and Uli Hoeness, all of whom had already attained the status of European champions at national team level in 1972.

Madrid had returned to 'their' competition for the first time in three seasons after Spanish ambition had been modestly represented by Atletico Madrid and then a Valencia side coached by Madrid's old inspiration, Alfredo di Stefano.

Juventus were also back for the first time in five seasons, trying once again to exorcize their European demons. Record champions of Italy they may have been, but Europe was proving a perpetual puzzle for the Old Lady of Turin.

RIGHT: TWO GIANTS OF THE EUROPEAN GAME, FRANZ BECKENBAUER AND JOHAN CRUYFF, APPEAR TO BE MAKING EXACTLY THE SAME POINT TO TEAM-MATES DURING THE FIRST LEG OF THE QUARTER-FINAL IN AMSTERDAM

This season also saw the arrival on the Champions Cup scene of Brian Clough, manager then of newcomers Derby County. His was a household name in England, but so far nowhere else, and his idiosyncratic style and humour were lost on football observers from the other side of the English Channel. His football precepts were based on the highest standards, but this sometimes tipped over into a self-righteousness which created waves both on and off the pitch – as events in the 1973 semi-finals would demonstrate.

Progress to that stage, when Derby faced Juventus and Ajax totally humbled Madrid, was comparatively straightforward for both.

The first round saw home and away victories for Madrid against Keflavik, for Celtic against a then virtually unknown Norwegian club called Rosenborg Trondheim, Dynamo Kiev against Wacker Innsbruck, Derby against Zeljeznicar of Yugoslavia and Magdeburg against Finland's TPs.

Bayern Munich, Juventus and Benfica all came through safely in the end after first-leg frights against Galatasaray, Marseille and Malmo respectively.

Ajax benefited from the holders' customary first-round bye to battle their way to victory in the World Club Cup. Their duel with Independiente of Argentina, however, left physical and mental scars which were still raw five years later when Holland reached the World Cup finals back in the land of the River Plate.

Regaining their composure, Ajax put three goals past CSKA Sofia both away and home in the second round. Bayern, Kiev, Juventus and Real Madrid all took advantage of being kept apart, but Britain's hopefuls had mixed fortunes. Celtic went out after a 3–0 defeat away to Ujpest in Budapest which was more comprehensive than the scoreline suggests. Manager Jock Stein credited goalkeeper Evan Williams with saving the Bhoys from a far heavier defeat.

For Derby it was a different story. Clough was never going to be intimidated by Eusebio and Benfica, who hated the tight, noisy confines of the old Baseball Ground and were demolished 3–0. Roy McFarland, Kevin Hector and John McGovern scored the first-half goals which so comprehensively undermined Portuguese confidence that the Rams were able to claim a goalless draw in Lisbon after withstanding an initial 20-minute storm.

Now the going got tougher. Juventus edged Ujpest on away goals, while Real Madrid beat a winter-rusty Kiev largely thanks to the defiant magnificence of young goalkeeper Mariano Garcia Remon in the first leg; for the rest of his playing career – and beyond, into coaching the

club 30 years later – he would be known as 'the Odessa cat'. Derby found the unfashionable Czechoslovaks of Spartak Trnava a stiffer test than boastful Benfica. They lost 1–0 away but recovered at home with two second-half goals in 11 minutes from striker Hector.

Ajax, meanwhile, thrashed Bayern 4–1, 1–2. The tie had been billed as the ultimate gladiators' duel between Johan Cruyff and Franz Beckenbauer, Bayern's skipper and creative sweeper. The first half in Amsterdam's Olympic stadium ended goalless but the second half was no contest. Arie Haan (two) and Gerrie Muhren scored three goals in 13 minutes, while Cruyff added a deft finishing touch of a fourth with two minutes remaining. Cruyff, claiming a minor knee injury, was thus free to absent himself from the second leg, which Bayern won by a merely academic 2–1.

Ajax maintained their domineering work in the semis when they beat Real 2–1 in Amsterdam and 1–0 in Madrid. The margin could have been greater in the Spanish capital, where Muhren undertook a keepy-uppy exercise to demonstrate exactly how much respect Ajax had for the history books.

For a second successive season they would face Italian opposition in the final. Juventus had qualified for the final for the first time after beating Derby in a semi which prompted Clough's infamous tirade about '****ing, cheating Italians'.

ABOVE: **ARIE HAAN DRIVES FORWARD ONCE MORE AGAINST REAL MADRID IN THE STADION DE MEER, AMSTERDAM, IN THE FIRST LEG OF THE SEMI-FINAL**

AJAX MAKE IT A HAT-TRICK OF WINS

The first Champions Cup Final in eastern Europe, in the Yugoslav capital of Belgrade, saw Ajax play the very finest football of their entire reign. They went ahead through striker Johnny Rep after barely four minutes and followed up with some of the most fluid, inventive football ever seen in a European final before or since. They turned Juventus inside out, upside down and back to front. They played such wonderful sweeping football in the first half that they could have won by a hatful of goals. But it was almost as if they became bored by their own domination.

Juventus had gained extra spark along the qualifying route by the sensibly restricted use of the veteran Brazilian, Jose Altafini, Milan's two-goal hero in the 1963 defeat of Benfica.

In the final, however, he was played from the start, which was a mistake by coach Cestmir Vycpalek.

Juve would have done better to begin cautiously then introduce Altafini if and when they needed to chase the game or spring a tactical surprise. Instead, by the closing stages when Juve needed to push, his legs had gone.

Juve had a solid backbone. Dino Zoff would be Italy's goalkeeper-captain when they won the World Cup nine years later; Roberto Bettega would one day become Juve's chief executive, and Fabio Capello a trophy-gathering coach with Juve, Milan and Real Madrid.

But the here and now belonged to Ajax, albeit only by that single goal. Juventus could do nothing, on or off the pitch – and it was off the pitch where the ongoing contention remains.

Back in the mid-1960s Internazionale's European Cup victories had been shaded by suggestions that their general manager, Italo Allodi, was a little too hospitable to referees. Not that Inter were found to be alone in that regard. Match officials also enjoyed the fawning attention to be found in Madrid, and years later, after the advent of the Champions League, a trail of fur coats would cost Dynamo Kiev expulsion from Europe.

Inter's fade-out and the rise of Juventus coincided with the adept Allodi's switch from the one club to the other. Derby had been scandalized by events during their semi-final against Juventus.

The German forward, Helmut Haller, had provoked Brian Clough's fury by visiting German referee Gerhard Schulenberg in his dressing-room both before the match and at half-time in Juve's 3–1 win.

Worse was to come. It transpired after the second leg that the Portuguese referee, Francisco Lobo, had reported to his federation an approach by a Hungarian agent, Dezso Solti, suggesting that he might usefully favour Juventus. The referee did no such thing, even awarding Derby a penalty which Alan Hinton missed, although he did also send off centre-forward Roger Davies.

UEFA, pressed hard by the English media, exonerated Juventus and Allodi while declaring Solti *persona non grata*.

Fortunately, there was nothing Solti could have done to

counter the magnificence of Ajax's football in the final. That the score remained only 1–0 was because, after the whirling first 20 minutes, which Willy Meisl would have loved, Ajax appeared wearied by their own superlatives.

The Dutch would go on to win the World Club Cup again and the European Supercup once more but without the remarkable Cruyff. In the late summer of 1973 he was sold to Barcelona, rejoining Rinus Michels for a then world record fee of £922,000.

The Spanish federation sanctioned the deal even though it was concluded after their own transfer deadline. Cruyff was that important – as Ajax's own, uncontrollable fall from grace would prove.

LEFT: **WEARING THE BLACK-AND-WHITE SHIRTS OF THEIR DEFEATED OPPONENTS JUVENTUS, AJAX LOOK DRAINED AFTER A BRILLIANT PERFORMANCE IN BELGRADE WHERE THEY PLAYED SOME OF THE BEST FOOTBALL EVER SEEN IN A EUROPEAN FINAL**

LEFT: **DINO ZOFF CAN ONLY WATCH AS THE BALL FLIES BEYOND HIM AND INTO THE NET IN THE 4TH MINUTE. THE SCORER WAS JOHNNY REP**

WEDNESDAY 30 MAY 1973
CRVENA ZVEZDA, BELGRADE

AJAX AMSTERDAM   **1**
REP 4

JUVENTUS   **0**

HT: 1–0. ATT: 93,000.
REF: GUGULOVIC (YUG)

AJAX:
STUY - SUURBIER, BLANKENBURG, HULSHOFF, KROL - NEESKENS, HAAN, G. MUHREN - CRUYFF - REP, KEIZER*.
COACH: KOVACS.

JUVENTUS:
ZOFF - SALVADORE* - LONGOBUCCO, MORINI, MARCHETTI - CAUSIO (CUCCUREDDU 78), FURINO, CAPELLO - ALTAFINI, ANASTASI, BETTEGA (HALLER 63).
COACH: VYCPALEK.

*CAPTAIN.

GERMANY'S FOOTBALLING MIRACLE

The complexities of German history had held up the development of football but now the nation was firing on all cylinders with the emergence of Bayern Munich alongside the national side...

The scale of German achievement in 1973–74 – crowned by triumphs for Bayern Munich in the Champions Cup and West Germany in the World Cup – can be measured by historical reference.

Germany had been a modest power within the context of European football between the wars, when Italy, Austria, Hungary and Czechoslovakia were the finest of the non-British brigade.

In Germany, football had struggled initially to make inroads. The traditional sports culture clubs had long shut out the upstart footballers, while distance hindered the development of an integrated competitive structure. Germany, after all, stretched 900 miles from the Saar in the west to Breslau deep into what is now Poland.

Historic echoes of the span of German sport linger on. Today visitors to southern Poland find that Wroclaw's old stadium owes its 'Olympic' title to the matches the city hosted for the 1936 Berlin Games. Only then it was known as Breslau.

Adolf Hitler's national socialist regime added to the complexity by prohibiting professional sport.

This was only a precursor, however, of the state-imposed 'amateur' system prevalent throughout communist Europe after the Second World War.

Ambitious clubs found ways and means. The heroes of Schalke, from the pit town of Gelsenkirchen in the industrial Ruhr, were paid as miners but never took the caged plunge below ground.

Leagues were organized in geographical regions, with the championship decided by a series of end-of-season play-offs. That system remained fixed in place after the war, partly because of Allied-imposed travel restrictions as well as the Soviet Union's decision to carve out the German Democratic Republic.

Such restrictive conditions only magnify the stunning achievement of the 1954 World Cup win. Regionalization meant that Germany could not afford full-time football, so its clubs could not compete effectively in Europe until 1963–64, when the launch of the unified, professional Bundesliga changed everything.

In 1966 Borussia Dortmund became the first German club to win a European trophy, the Cup-Winners' Cup. Bayern Munich, not Bundesliga founders but promoted two year later, emulated that example the following season.

No fewer than three of the players who scored a 1–0 extra-time win over Rangers in Nurnberg were in the Bayern side who won the Champions Cup in 1974 and also in the West Germany team who won both the 1972 European Championship and the 1974 World Cup: goalkeeper Sepp Maier, central defender Franz Beckenbauer and centre-forward Gerd Muller, possibly the greatest goal-poacher of all time.

By the time Bayern set out to avenge their crushing defeat by Ajax in the spring of 1973, their ranks had been strengthened by the arrivals of attacking left-back Paul Breitner, stopper Hans-Georg Schwarzenbeck and support forward Uli Hoeness.

When the draw was made in the mid-summer of 1973, Ajax were hot favourites.

By the time they took the field against CSKA Sofia, the glitter had gone. Johan Cruyff had been sold to Barcelona and the difference he made could be counted in goals. The holders had beaten CSKA 6–1 on aggregate in the previous season's second round; this time they lost 2–1. Ajax were history.

RIGHT: EVEN THE EAST GERMANS GOT IN ON THE FOOTBALLING BOOM AS JURGEN SPARWASSER SCORES HIS HISTORIC WORLD CUP WINNER AGAINST WEST GERMANY IN THE FAMOUS 1–0 VICTORY. IT'S A HAIR-RAISING MOMENT FOR GOALKEEPER SEPP MAIER

Bayern were not the only contenders for their crown. Previous winners with an avenging hunger were Celtic and Benfica, while Liverpool, Juventus and Atletico Madrid were the other heavyweights lining up to be the new top dogs of European football.

But heavyweights can prove ponderous. In the first round, Juventus fell to a Dynamo Dresden side boasting half the East German team en route for a first (and last) World Cup appearance.

The second round saw Liverpool beaten both away and home by Red Star, while Benfica were dismissed by Ujpest Dozsa.

Celtic beat TPs Turku 9–1 overall, Vejle of Denmark 1–0 – after being held goalless at home – and Basel 6–5 after extra time to reach the semi-finals. Insufficient for the Swiss were two goals scored in the first leg by a run-of-the-mill midfielder named Ottmar Hitzfeld.

Atletico had a powerful Argentine flavour. Coach Juan Carlos Lorenzo had led his country at the 1966 World Cup, where they lost notoriously to England in a quarter-final marked by the expulsion of captain Antonio Rattin.

Lorenzo believed in discipline, caution and disrupting the opponents' game by whatever means came to hand, often literally – as Galatasaray after extra time, Dinamo Bucharest, Red Star and Celtic all found out. Dinamo were left with the historic consolation that their 11–0 first-round second-leg thrashing of Crusaders provided the Cup's only instance of two players, Dudu Georgescu and Radu Nunweiler, scoring four goals in one match.

At Parkhead, Atletico had Argentine Ruben Ayala and 'Panadero' Diaz plus substitute Quique all sent off while battling out (again literally) a goalless draw. Goals from Jose Eulogio Garate and veteran midfielder Adelardo collapsed Celtic late in the return.

Atletico were in the final for the first time, confident of emerging finally from beneath the shadow of Real.

BELOW: ATLETICO MADRID'S ADELARDO SANCHEZ GOES LOOKING FOR CELTIC'S JIMMY JOHNSTONE. THE SPANISH SIDE HAD THREE MEN SENT OFF AT PARKHEAD IN A GOALLESS DRAW BUT WON THE SECOND LEG OF THE SEMI-FINAL 2–0

BAYERN WIN THE FIRST-EVER REPLAY

Only once in football history has one country won both the World Cup and the European Champions Cup in the same season. West Germany was that country and this was the season. Strange icing was added to the cake by the achievement of Magdeburg in becoming the first and last East German club to win a European trophy; even if only 5,638, the smallest final crowd in European club history, turned up at the Feyenoord stadium in Rotterdam to watch Jurgen Sparwasser and his comrades see off Milan in the final of the Cup-Winners' Cup.

The names of Sparwasser, Martin Hoffmann and Jurgen Pommerenke loomed large in the German Democratic Republic but possessed little resonance next to those of the tennis-playing Sepp Maier, the footballing Kaiser Franz Beckenbauer and 'Der Bomber' Gerd Muller. Yet Bayern very nearly did not make it past the opening round...

Initial opposition was provided by modest Swedish outfit Atvidaberg. Bayern strolled imperiously to a 3–1 home win with two goals from Muller, then lost by the same margin in Sweden. Blond forward Conny Torstensson ran Beckenbauer and co ragged and was rewarded with two goals. Fortunately for the Germans he could not take all the penalties in the shoot-out and Bayern squeaked through 4–3.

A few weeks later, at the end of the Swedish season, Torstensson became a Bayern Munich player. He was ineligible for the historic second-round duel with Dresden,

Finale de la Coupe des Clubs Champions Européens

Finale van de Beker der Europese Landskampioenen

Club ATLETICO de MADRID
F. C. BAYERN MUNCHEN

15·5·1974

RIGHT: **GERD MULLER AND ULI HOENESS, WHO TOOK IT IN TURN TO SCORE THE GOALS AGAINST MADRID'S SECOND SIDE**

but a goal in each leg from Muller helped Bayern edge through 7–6 on aggregate. Torstensson was available for the quarter-final against CSKA and struck twice in the opening 4–1 win over the conquerors of Ajax. He also scored once both away and home against Ujpest in the semi-finals. Muller, to his and his fans' surprise, was being overshadowed.

Muller was also overshadowed in the final by the close marking of Atletico's Juan Carlos Heredia and Eusebio Bejerano. So was Uli Hoeness and also, for once, Torstensson, who had a poor game in the Heysel stadium in Brussels.

Atletico, despite missing three players through suspension, went ahead seven minutes from the end of extra time through a superb, curling free-kick from Luis Aragones; his footballing skills aroused far greater unanimity than his opinions on racism some 30 years later.

With the last touch of the match it fell not to Muller, Beckenbauer, Breitner or Torstensson but to rugged centre-back Schwarzenbeck to keep Bayern's hopes alive. He took a desperate dip from 30 yards and 'keeper Miguel Reina stood motionless as the equalizer thundered in.

For the first time, the final went to a replay. It was also the last time, as within a year the replay option was scrapped.

In truth, suspension-weakened Atletico had played above themselves in the first match. The replay, back in the Heysel two days later, was a step too far. Hoeness and Muller each scored twice. Beckenbauer became the first German captain to hold aloft the Champions Cup just as, back in his Olympic stadium in Munich a mere 51 days later, he would hoist, in similar fashion, the World Cup.

Torstensson, that time, would have no role to play.

BELOW LEFT: **BAYERN MUNICH CAPTAIN FRANZ 'DER KAISER' BECKENBAUER LIFTS THE EUROPEAN CUP FOLLOWING HIS TEAM'S MAGNIFICENT 4–0 WIN. JOHNNY HANSEN AND GERD MULLER LINE UP BEHIND HIM**

WEDNESDAY 15 MAY 1974
HEYSEL, BRUSSELS

BAYERN MUNICH   1
SCHWARZENBECK 120

ATLETICO MADRID   1
LUIS ARAGONES 113

AFTER EXTRA TIME
HT: 0–0. 90 MIN: 0–0. ATT: 65,000.
REF: LORAUX (BEL)

BAYERN:
MAIER - HANSEN, SCHWARZENBECK, BECKENBAUER*, BREITNER - ROTH, ZOBEL, KAPELLMANN - TORSTENSSON (DURNBERGER 76), G. MULLER, HOENESS.
COACH: LATTEK.

ATLETICO:
REINA - MELO, HEREDIA, EUSEBIO, CAPON - ADELARDO*, IRURETA, SALCEDO (ALBERTO 91) - UFARTE (BECERRA 69), LUIS, GARATE.
COACH: LORENZO.

REPLAY
FRIDAY 17 MAY 1974
HEYSEL, BRUSSELS

BAYERN MUNICH   4
HOENESS 28, 81, MULLER 57, 70

ATLETICO MADRID   0

HT: 1–0. ATT: 23,000.
REF: DELCOURT (BEL)

BAYERN:
MAIER - HANSEN, SCHWARZENBECK, BECKENBAUER*, BREITNER - ROTH, ZOBEL, KAPELLMANN - TORSTENSSON, G. MULLER, HOENESS.
COACH: LATTEK.

ATLETICO:
REINA - MELO, HEREDIA, EUSEBIO, CAPON - ADELARDO* (BENEGAS 61), IRURETA, SALCEDO - UFARTE (BECERRA 65), LUIS, GARATE.
COACH: LORENZO.

*CAPTAIN.

A CASE FOR THE FLYING DOCTOR

Bayern changed horses in midstream when they replaced Udo Lattek with Dettmar Cramer. Leeds were another club in uproar, having ended Brian Clough's reign at Elland Road after 44 days

For English football, the 1973-74 season had been depressing in the extreme. Liverpool had failed to live up to their own ambitions in the Champions Cup, Tottenham had lost to Feyenoord in a hooligan-marred UEFA Cup Final and England had failed to qualify for the World Cup finals after a night of high drama against Poland at Wembley.

Sir Alf Ramsey was duly removed as England manager, to be succeeded by Don Revie, supremely confident after guiding Leeds to the second league title of his reign. But to defend their domestic crown and challenge in Europe the Leeds board sprang one of the most spectacularly ill-starred appointments imaginable in Brian Clough.

Every English football fan recognized that Clough and Revie were at opposite ends of the spectrum in terms of personal style, managerial method and footballing standards. Clough was about flamboyance and pure football; Revie was about discipline and the result.

Clough, particularly in those years bridged by his previous success with Derby and later triumphs with Nottingham Forest, was also possessed of a divisive arrogance. Winning over his sceptical new squad was never on the cards after one early lecture in which he told Billy Bremner, Johnny Giles and co to throw away all the medals they had won by cheating.

Unsurprisingly, Leeds did not start the season well. They had to wait a month before claiming their first win, 1-0 at home to Birmingham City. That was the season when newly promoted Carlisle - ultimately to be relegated - had gone off like a rocket. Clough strode into the press room after the Birmingham game, demanded to know the Carlisle score and, on learning that they had won, boasted: 'We'll walk it.'

Instead he was the one who did the walking a fortnight later after 44 days in charge and less than a week before Leeds' Champions Cup opener at home to Zurich. Assistant Maurice Lindsay took temporary charge and Leeds won 4-1 with goals from Allan Clarke (two), Peter Lorimer and Joe Jordan. The tie was subsequently won 5-3 on aggregate, and in round two Leeds took on Ujpest Dozsa, under the managership of former England full-back Jimmy Armfield.

The remainder of the Champions Cup field, sorted by a primitive seeding system, was not exactly vintage. Celtic were fading fast, the glamour of Benfica and Real Madrid was missing, and Bayern had hit a flat patch which prompted the mid-season replacement of Udo Lattek by world football's own 'flying doctor', Dettmar Cramer. Italy was not represented, champions Lazio having been suspended from Europe after a UEFA Cup dust-up with Ipswich.

Eleven first-round goals against Northern Ireland's Coleraine - four of them for Lex Schoenmaker - persuaded Feyenoord to dream of repeating their 1970 success. They had reckoned without their fellow countrymen. Against Barcelona, the tactical nous of Rinus Michels, the energy of Johan Neeskens and the guiding craft of Johan Cruyff inflicted a 0-0, 3-0 defeat. Blond left-winger Charly Rexach scored a hat-trick in the Nou Camp; Cruyff created all three.

RIGHT: TERRY YORATH WATCHES FROM THE GROUND AS ALLAN CLARKE'S SHOT BEATS SADURNI FOR LEEDS' SECOND GOAL IN THE MATCH AGAINST BARCELONA AT ELLAND ROAD

Leeds saw off Ujpest 5–1 overall, despite the first-leg expulsion of the erratic ball-juggler Duncan McKenzie, with central defender Gordon McQueen scoring in both legs. This was more like the old Leeds.

Bayern came through after another East German duel. The European Supercup was not played this year: the second-round draw matching Bayern with Magdeburg rendered the new trophy redundant. At half-time in the first leg Magdeburg appeared on the brink of a major shock. They led 2–0 through an own goal from Johnny Hansen and a further strike from Jurgen Sparwasser, right on the interval.

Bayern should have been awake to Sparwasser; four months earlier he had scored the historic goal in Hamburg with which East Germany beat West Germany in their group match in the World Cup finals.

Just as Gerd Muller's nose for goal had pulled West Germany around in the World Cup, so it pulled Bayern around against Magdeburg. He scored twice in 18 minutes after the interval in a 3–2 revival win and then twice again as Bayern won 2–1 in front of a curious crowd of 33,734 in East Germany.

The quarter-final draw was perfect for most of the big guns of western Europe who were matched against ring-rusty eastern European and Scandinavian opposition. Only Leeds drew comparative neighbours in Anderlecht and, with David Stewart proving a more than capable deputy for David Harvey – injured in a car crash – won both home and away.

Barcelona believed this was to be the season in which they would lay their European Cup jinx. In vain. In their semi-final against Leeds they conceded early goals both at Elland Road and back in the Nou Camp, first to Billy Bremner, then to Peter Lorimer. Despite a numerical advantage gained by the second-leg expulsion of McQueen, they faded away 3–2 overall. Leeds' prize was a trip to the newly rebuilt Parc des Princes to face Bayern.

LEFT: COACH DETTMAR CRAMER WHO WAS KNOWN BY SEVERAL NICKNAMES IN GERMANY – 'NAPOLEON', 'THE PROFESSOR' AND 'FOOTBALL'S POPE'

MULLER SENDS LEEDS ON THEIR WAY

Bayern Munich had been disappointed but not surprised to be excluded from the Bundesliga on its launch in 1963. Under the presidency of Wilhelm Neudecker and Yugoslav coach Tschik Cajkovski, they quickly forged their way up out of the regional league system with a mixture of cultured football and hard graft.

Not that Neudecker and Cajkovski always saw eye to eye. Neudecker prided himself on being able to spot a player, but Cajkovski was not impressed when Neudecker showed off his chunky new acquisition. Cajkovski yelled: 'You can't expect me to put that little elephant in among my thoroughbreds!'

But Neudecker pulled rank and Cajkovski did as he was told. He never regretted it either.

Neudecker's 'little elephant' turned out to be Gerd Muller, one of the most prodigious marksmen in modern European football history.

Muller scored a record 365 goals in 427 Bundesliga games for Bayern, his only German club, and a further 68 in 62 appearances for West Germany, including the winner in the 1974 World Cup Final.

But Muller was far more than a goal-poacher or a 'scorer of little goals', as acclaimed by national manager Helmut Schon.

He was also an outstanding all-round footballer with a capacity for both organization and vision which was rarely noted – or, for that matter, needed. But the 1975 Champions Cup Final was different, through force of barely appreciated circumstance.

To revisit reports of the time is to find the stories of two entirely different matches. The one issue on which all agreed was that Leeds' fans disgraced themselves in the closing minutes. Fury at defeat boiled over into a hooligan exhibition with plastic seats ripped out and flipped down on to the pitch surrounding Sepp Maier's goal.

Leeds were subsequently banned from European competition for four years – a ban which Armfield, single-handedly, without support from the Leeds hierarchy, persuaded UEFA to halve.

From the Leeds perspective, the match should have been done and dusted by half-time. Referee Michel Kitabdjian rejected appeals for two penalties – one for a trip on Allan Clarke, another for hands by Franz Beckenbauer. In the 66th minute, Leeds believed that justice had been done when Peter Lorimer beat Maier, but

Kitabdjian disallowed the 'goal', ruling that midfielder Billy Bremner had been standing offside in front of Maier, interfering with play.

Five minutes later Franz Roth scored Bayern's first goal, and seven minutes from the end Muller grabbed their second. It was the trigger for Leeds fans to lose all self-control, and the French riot police waded in for the start of a night-long running battle through the streets of south-west Paris.

The Bayern perspective was very different. Paul Breitner had been sold the previous summer to Real Madrid

RIGHT: **GOALKEEPER DAVE STEWART, DAVID HARVEY'S BACK-UP AT LEEDS UNITED, KNEELS DOWN IN DESPAIR AS BAYERN MUNICH'S PLAYERS WHEEL AWAY IN DELIGHT AFTER MULLER SCORES THE CLINCHER**

F.C.Bayern/Leeds
Munich · United

and replaced by Bjorn Andersson. After only four minutes, however, the Swede was fouled, kicked on the ground while awaiting treatment and had to be substituted; then Uli Hoeness was hurt and, after limping on for the next half-hour, was himself replaced before the interval by Klaus Wunder.

Dettmar Cramer pushed Wunder forwards as a lone striker, pulled Conny Torstensson deep to buttress midfield and withdrew Muller into an unaccustomed linking role.

Positioning himself fearlessly in the eye of the Leeds midfield, Muller demanded possession, held up the ball, drew colleagues into prime supporting positions and sought to spark Wunder's pressure-relieving pace up in attack.

That he also struck the decisive second goal was no more nor less than he deserved.

ABOVE: LEEDS FANS RIOT AT PARC DES PRINCES. THE CLOSING STAGES OF THE 1975 FINAL WERE MARRED BY VIOLENCE AND BAYERN'S LAP OF HONOUR WAS DISRUPTED BY SEATS THROWN BY SPECTATORS

WEDNESDAY 28 MAY 1975
PARC DES PRINCES, PARIS

BAYERN MUNICH	**2**
ROTH 71, MULLER 81	
LEEDS UNITED	**0**

HT: 0-0. ATT: 48,000.
REF: KITABDJIAN (FR)

BAYERN:
MAIER - B. ANDERSSON (WEISS 4), SCHWARZENBECK, BECKENBAUER*, DURNBERGER - ZOBEL, ROTH, KAPELLMANN - TORSTENSSON, G. MULLER, HOENESS (WUNDER 42). COACH: CRAMER.

LEEDS:
STEWART - REANEY, MADELEY, HUNTER, F. GRAY - BREMNER*, GILES, YORATH (E. GRAY 80) - LORIMER, A. CLARKE, JORDAN. MANAGER: ARMFIELD.

*CAPTAIN.

RENAISSANCE OF THE FRENCH GAME

The Champions Cup was invented by Frenchmen but, since Reims in the 1950s, none of their teams had made it to the final. Saint-Etienne looked as if they might end this sad state of affairs

Years had passed since French football had had anything of which to boast. The glory of the national team had faded into memories of third place at the 1958 World Cup, and the once great Reims had not merely vanished from the Champions Cup in the early 1960s, they had suffered the double humiliation of relegation and bankruptcy.

Raymond Kopa had argued his way through the closing, injury-riddled seasons of his career, and Just Fontaine – forced by leg fractures into premature retirement – had been briefly leader of the players' union and then national coach before settling for the comfort of media punditry. France had not appeared at the World Cup finals since their first-round exit from England in 1966.

Then, in the mid-1970s, came the stirrings of revival. The federation lured Stefan Kovacs from Ajax to bring a new eye to the task of national manager. And a football-mad factory boss down in provincial Saint-Etienne put his money behind the local team in a way which was, in that era, unheard of.

Roger Rocher would eventually end up behind bars for playing too fast and too loose with his club's cash. But *Les Verts* (the greens) of Saint-Etienne not only rekindled French football pride; they would also provide a springboard to international glory for Michel Platini.

Ironically, the only Frenchman acclaimed three times as European Footballer of the Year was not yet in on the Saint-Etienne story. He was still playing in the south-eastern shadows of Nancy-Lorraine.

Saint-Etienne had collected their first league title in 1957, their second in 1964, then four in a row from 1967 to 1970. The manager was Albert Batteux, Reims' boss in the 1950s. But even he could not work a European miracle. Four times they went out in the first round, on the other two occasions in the second.

By the time Saint-Etienne regained domestic primacy, in 1974, red-haired centre-back Roby Herbin had become an equally inspiring coach, and imported experience had been added in Yugoslav 'keeper Yvan Curkovic and Argentine defender Oswaldo Piazza.

Their composure and confidence fired up impressionable young Frenchmen such as centre-back Christian Lopez, midfield terrier Dominique Bathenay, playmaker Jean-Michel Larque and brothers Herve and Patrick Revelli in attack. In due course they would be joined by a precocious talent who needed no lessons in self-confidence: the eel-like winger Dominique Rocheteau.

In 1974-75 Sporting of Lisbon, Hajduk Split and Ruch Chorzow were turned over in dramatic style before Bayern proved too wily in the semi-finals. The next season, *Les Verts* went one better.

KB Kobenhavn (beaten 5–1 overall) and Rangers (4–1) provided few initial problems. But the quarter-final pairing with Dynamo Kiev was something else.

Kiev were one of Europe's class acts, high technical ability having been honed with a scientifically refined preparation programme developed by former Soviet left-winger Valeri Lobanovsky. The previous year they had won the Cup-Winners' Cup on the back of the attacking brilliance of goal-scoring left-winger Oleg Blokhin, who had

RIGHT: OSWALDO PIAZZA, SAINT-ETIENNE'S OUTSTANDING ARGENTINE DEFENDER, STRUTS HIS STUFF DOWN THE WING AGAINST DYNAMO KIEV

duly earned the European Footballer of the Year accolade.

At 23, Blokhin was considered a Soviet Cruyff. But the biggest hurdle for Blokhin, as with all Soviet and eastern European teams in Europe, was the long, icy winter which left them ring-rusty and perpetually vulnerable against match-fit western Europeans in the quarter-finals.

The first leg against Saint-Etienne was staged, not in chilly Kiev, but in the warmer climes of Simferopol in the Crimea. That suited Kiev, who would have won by a landslide, instead of merely 2–0, had it not been for the acrobatic brilliance of Curkovic in goal.

The Stade Geoffroy-Guichard was developing a reputation as a European Cup inferno, but Kiev survived the first half of the return unscathed.

Twenty minutes into the second half, still goalless, they were poised for the *coup de grâce*. Blokhin slalomed off into the distance, past full-back Gerard Janvion, past Lopez, and closed in on Curkovic. He had two options:

to chip the goalkeeper or square to the unmarked Vladimir Onishenko. For some unknown reason the European Footballer of the Year did neither: he hesitated and tried to dribble one more time around Lopez... who dispossessed him and cleared to safety.

At this precise moment, Kiev heads went down, French spirits rose.

Piazza picked up the clearance and found Patrick Revelli. He swept the ball on up to brother Herve, who dispatched it low beyond 'keeper Yevgeni Rudakov's flailing hands. Seven minutes later Larque rifled home a free-kick to earn extra time in which the 21-year-old Rocheteau snatched the French winner.

Larque scored the only goal of the two semi-final games against PSV Eindhoven, and Saint-Etienne thus became the first French club in 17 years to reach the final of the event Frenchmen had dreamed up... apparently for the rest of Europe to enjoy.

ABOVE: **SAINT-ETIENNE'S JEAN-MICHEL LARQUE** IN THE PROCESS OF BENDING A FREE-KICK ROUND THE WALL AGAINST PSV EINDHOVEN TO TAKE THE TIE INTO EXTRA TIME

SWANSONG FOR BAYERN'S FADING STARS

Bayern Munich were cracking up. Winning the World Cup for West Germany in 1974 had doused a little of the fire. Franz Beckenbauer remained omnipotent, gliding forwards out of central defence, but Gerd Muller had retired from the national team and Uli Hoeness had struggled against injury. A talented successor had cost a mere £4,500 from Borussia Lippstadt, but Karl-Heinz Rummenigge was still learning his trade. Challengers were not in short supply. Each time, however, Bayern managed to raise their game for the one-off occasion.

Benfica's new generation put seven goals past Fenerbahce and six past Ujpest, but then collapsed 5–1 to

Bayern in Munich; Muller scored two, Rummenigge one. Borussia Monchengladbach were rising to challenge Bayern at home and abroad, but they had sold playmaker Gunter Netzer to Real Madrid, who edged them on away goals in the quarter-finals.

The media fuss was enormous when Madrid, with Netzer and Paul Breitner, drew Bayern in the semi-finals.

Madrid, bossed by charismatic Yugoslav Miljan Miljanic, had defeated Derby – now managed by former Tottenham hero Dave Mackay – in a see-saw quarter-final. A hat-trick, with two penalties, from ex-Arsenal star Charlie George had secured a 4–1 home win for Derby, who were naïve enough

RIGHT: **BAYERN CAPTAIN FRANZ BECKENBAUER ENJOYS HIS MOMENT OF CROWNING GLORY AT HAMPDEN PARK. BECKENBAUER INVENTED THE ROLE OF ATTACKING SWEEPER AND WON THREE EUROPEAN CUPS. HE IS ALSO THE ONLY MAN TO HAVE WON THE WORLD CUP BOTH AS CAPTAIN AND MANAGER**

to think it was all over. In Madrid George scored again, but the matchless Santillana tormented them in the air and scored twice in a 5–1 extra-time extravaganza.

Madrid were thus semi-final favourites against Bayern, but Beckenbauer shut down the attacking avenues in a 1–1 draw in the Bernabeu and Muller was his deadly old self – twice – in Munich.

The final was staged at Hampden, where Madrid and Eintracht Frankfurt had left an explosion of memories in 1960. By contrast, Bayern against Saint-Etienne left little but a string of regrets: regrets that Bayern won despite playing dreary, negative football and regrets that, even when Saint-Etienne did break through, the posts came to the holders' rescue. Saint-Etienne were handicapped from the outset by an injury which Rocheteau, their new

romantic idol, had collected in the semi-final defeat of PSV Eindhoven. Coach Roby Herbin decided to put him on the substitutes' bench in case of emergency.

Saint-Etienne started brightly against a German side who were nervy both on and off the pitch. Security had been stepped up amid fears of a terrorist attack following the prison death of the German urban guerrilla leader Ulrike Meinhof.

Muller had a goal disallowed for offside – wrongly, TV showed – in a first half largely controlled by the French. Twice they hit the posts. One stunning near miss flew in from 25 yards from left-winger Christian Sarramagna, who played like a man possessed.

But the green storm was blowing itself out by the 57th minute when Franz Roth – match-winner against Rangers in the 1967 Cup-Winners' Cup Final – reminded the Scottish audience of his ability to strike decisively for goal.

Herbin threw on Rocheteau for the last 10 minutes. One mazy dribble took him past five defenders to the byline, but somehow Bayern survived to celebrate what proved to be their swansong.

They would beat Brazil's Cruzeiro to win the World Club Cup, but the magic was fading. Less then six weeks after winning at Hampden, Maier, Beckenbauer, Schwarzenbeck and Hoeness were in the West German side deprived of their European Championship crown by Czechoslovakia in a penalty shoot-out in the final in Belgrade.

Going, going...

WEDNESDAY 12 MAY 1976
HAMPDEN PARK, GLASGOW

BAYERN MUNICH   1
ROTH 57

SAINT-ETIENNE   0

HT: 0–0. ATT: 54,684.
REF: PALOTAI (HUN)

BAYERN:
MAIER – HANSEN, SCHWARZENBECK, BECKENBAUER*, HORSMANN – KAPELLMANN, ROTH, DURNBERGER – RUMMENIGGE, G. MULLER, HOENESS. COACH: CRAMER.

SAINT-ETIENNE:
CURKOVIC – JANVION, PIAZZA, LOPEZ, REPELLINI – SANTINI, LARQUE*, BATHENAY – P. REVELLI, H. REVELLI, SARRAMAGNA (ROCHETEAU 82). COACH: HERBIN.
*CAPTAIN.

BELOW: **STRIKER GERD MULLER HOMES IN ON GOAL BUT GOALKEEPER YVAN CURKOVIC SUCCEEDS IN THWARTING HIM**

THE SHOCK OF THE NEW

Many of the top dogs in European football were being overhauled by rivals – Borussia Monchengladbach, Brugge, PSV and Torino all came good, but it was Liverpool the others had to look out for...

Another power shift was under way. In Germany, Bayern were being overtaken by Borussia Monchengladbach, where ex-Munich coach Udo Lattek had taken over from Hennes Weisweiler, whose insistence on team above stars was leading him to disaster at Barcelona.

In Holland, Ajax and Feyenoord had been pushed aside by PSV Eindhoven, while the most effective Dutch marksman of the era was Rob Rensenbrink, who was leading the Belgian club Anderlecht to two Cup-Winners' Cup triumphs in three seasons. Yet back in Belgium domestic command had been wrenched away by Anderlecht's northern rivals Brugge under Ernst Happel.

Even at Liverpool, a change of direction had occurred. Two years earlier, in July 1974, manager Bill Shankly had suddenly retired. Speculation on the reasons varied from Shankly's own wish to make up for lost time with his family to the value of his contract. The later consensus was that 'Shanks' had grown tired; he was human after all.

At first, it was impossible to imagine Liverpool without the Scot's passionate ferocity but, just as he had organized a perpetual regeneration of the team, so he had ensured a succession system out of the famed Boot Room.

Bob Paisley stepped up into Shankly's place. Although a virtual unknown to the fans, Paisley was so well schooled in 'the Liverpool way' that he would become the most successful manager in English football history.

In 15 years under Shankly, Liverpool had won three league titles, two FA Cups and one UEFA Cup, so Paisley inherited a superb team which he refined in his own way. Ray Clemence vied with Peter Shilton as England's No. 1 goalkeeper; Phil Neal was a rock-steady right-back and sure-fire penalty-taker; Emlyn Hughes, an England Under-23 left-back, had developed into an indomitable captain, first in midfield, then at the centre of defence; Ray Kennedy, a former double-winner at Arsenal who arrived on the day Shankly left, was aided by converted right-winger Ian Callaghan in the engine room; Kevin Keegan and John Toshack proved an ideal little-and-large partnership in attack.

Keegan was the finest English player of his generation.

He freely admitted to not possessing the greatest natural talent, but he made amends with his commitment. His talents had earned admirers on the continent, but he was content, for now, to conquer Europe on behalf of Liverpool.

They set out among a clutch of serious contenders including Borussia, Brugge, Benfica, PSV, Kiev, Real Madrid, Italy's newcomers Torino and the holders Bayern Munich.

Liverpool saw off Crusaders of Belfast 2–0, 5–0 in a first round which saw Benfica tumbled by Dynamo Dresden. Neal (penalty) and Toshack scored in the first leg; Keegan, David Johnson (two), Terry McDermott and Steve Heighway in the return.

114 | 1970s

In the second round, Liverpool returned from a tiring trek to Turkey to play Trabzonspor with a 1-0 defeat, but a salvo of three goals in the first 18 minutes from Heighway, Johnson and Keegan easily overcame the deficit back at Anfield. Elsewhere, conveniently, Madrid were removed from the equation by Brugge and Torino by Borussia.

Liverpool were matched with Saint-Etienne in the quarter-finals, where Bayern's reign came to an end. Their defeat by Kiev freed Franz Beckenbauer to fly off and share the brief fun and games of life with New York Cosmos in the North American Soccer League. Borussia edged out Brugge after hitting back from 2-0 down in the first, home leg in Dusseldorf. Little Dane Allan Simonsen struck the crucial equalizer which created a platform for the Germans to win 1-0 in Belgium and 3-2 overall. The other quarter-final saw Dresden surprisingly beaten by Zurich, who had seemed to be the weakest of the last eight but for whom striker Franco Cucinotta was enjoying the season of his life.

Liverpool's duel with Saint-Etienne was one of those stand-out ties which sealed the legend of the Kop.

The injured Keegan had missed the first leg in France, which Liverpool lost 1-0 to a late goal from Dominique Bathenay. However, England's captain was not only back for the return at Anfield but clipped the opening goal after barely two minutes.

Liverpool piled on the pressure, but Yvan Curkovic resisted acrobatically and it was still all-square on aggregate at the interval. The second half see-sawed thrillingly. Bathenay equalized on the night, Kennedy restored the balance, but now the French led on away goals. With the clock ticking down, Paisley sent on flame-haired 'super-sub' David Fairclough with a quarter of an hour to go. The trick worked again and to perfection: a 45-yard dash crowned by a fierce drive proved too much even for Curkovic, and Liverpool were into the semi-finals to a mocking Kop chorus of 'Allez, les Rouges!'

Zurich folded up both home and away. Neal scored two goals, one a penalty, in the first leg, and hard-working Jimmy Case struck twice at Anfield. Liverpool cruised in 6-1 on aggregate to face Borussia in Rome.

LEFT: **KEVIN KEEGAN MISSED THE FIRST LEG IN SAINT-ETIENNE BUT WAS BACK TO SCORE FOR THE REDS IN THEIR FAMOUS 3-1 VICTORY AT ANFIELD WHEN 'SUPERSUB' DAVID FAIRCLOUGH STRUCK THE WINNING GOAL**

LIVERPOOL WIN IT FOR BILL SHANKLY

Liverpool and Borussia Monchengladbach were old foes. They had met in the 1973 UEFA Cup Final, when the first leg was abandoned because of torrential rain, handing manager Bill Shankly the chance to revise his team and tactics decisively for the replay.

Contrastingly, two of the smallest men on the pitch also boasted the two largest profiles. England's Kevin Keegan and Denmark's Allan Simonsen were both destined to become European Footballer of the Year – Simonsen in 1977, Keegan in 1978 and 1979 – but both were also developing itchy feet.

This was Keegan's last competitive appearance for Liverpool before his £500,000 transfer to Hamburg, while Simonsen would wait just a year longer before flying off to Barcelona. (Ironically Borussia team-mate Uli Stielike would enjoy far greater success in Spain, with Real Madrid.)

The difference, as far as the future of both clubs was concerned, was that Liverpool would replace Keegan audaciously and magnificently with Kenny Dalglish from Celtic, whereas Borussia would never replace Simonsen effectively. Still, these were issues for the future.

Liverpool had been riding the crest of wave which had swept them to the brink of a fabulous treble. On 14 May they had secured their 10th league title with a goalless draw against West Ham; but a week later they lost 2–1 to Manchester United in the FA Cup Final. They had four days in which to pick themselves up again for the European showdown in Rome's Stadio Olimpico.

Both Liverpool and Borussia carried the insurance that, by virtue of domestic success, they would be back in the Champions Cup next season whatever the outcome. More than 30,000 Liverpool fans made the trip and turned the stadium into a Kop-from-home.

In the circumstances Borussia should have seized control from the start and sought to hit Liverpool while they were mentally down. Instead, the Germans looked the more nervous and it was Liverpool who were quicker into their stride. Before the half hour they had glided into the lead. Steve Heighway, the university graduate who later became master of the Liverpool academy, opened the way to goal for midfielder Terry McDermott.

At last Borussia came to life and levelled through Simonsen. Only the reflexes of Ray Clemence and the mental and physical resilience developed down the years saved the Reds as Borussia besieged Liverpool's goal

immediately after half-time. Then, midway through the half, Liverpool broke away down the left and the powerful Tommy Smith, scattering German defenders right and left in his path, headed Liverpool back in front.

Eight minutes from time Borussia's captain, Berti Vogts, tripped Keegan and the reliable Neal slotted home the

RIGHT: LIVERPOOL'S PHIL NEAL, EMLYN HUGHES AND JIMMY CASE PARADE THE EUROPEAN CUP BEFORE SOME 30,000 ECSTATIC SUPPORTERS

COPPA-EUROPEA
EUROPEAN CUP

final

BORUSSIA MOENCHENGLADBACH
v
LIVERPOOL

penalty. Liverpool were champions of Europe. It was a second Roman triumph for Paisley, who had previously entered the city with the invading Allied forces in the Second World War.

Not usually one for the limelight, he beamed broadly and proudly out at the assembled media as the flashlights exploded at the post-match press conference. Watching from the back of the media scrum, dignified but largely ignored in the commotion, stood Bill Shankly.

ABOVE: **FULL-BACK PHIL NEAL EXPERTLY LANDS HIS PENALTY BEYOND WOLFGANG KNEIB IN THE BORUSSIA GOAL TO SECURE THE EUROPEAN CUP FOR LIVERPOOL**

WEDNESDAY 25 MAY 1977
OLIMPICO, ROME

LIVERPOOL	**3**

MCDERMOTT 27, SMITH 65, NEAL 82 PEN

B. MONCHENGLADBACH	**1**

SIMONSEN 51

HT: 1-0. ATT: 57,000. REF: WURTZ (FR)

LIVERPOOL:
CLEMENCE - NEAL, SMITH, E. HUGHES*, JONES - CALLAGHAN, CASE, R. KENNEDY, MCDERMOTT - KEEGAN, HEIGHWAY.
MANAGER: PAISLEY.

MONCHENGLADBACH:
KNEIB - VOGTS*, WITTKAMP, WOHLERS (HANNES 79), KLINKHAMMER - BONHOF, WIMMER (KULIK 24), STIELIKE, SCHAFER - SIMONSEN, HEYNCKES.
COACH: LATTEK.

*CAPTAIN.

A BHOY'S OWN STORY

Kenny Dalglish replaced Kevin Keegan as the star striker in Liverpool's line-up, while Juve president Gianni Agnelli promised his Number 1 the pick of the production line for services rendered

When Kenneth Mathieson Dalglish signed for Liverpool from Celtic for £440,000 in the summer of 1977, he was the perfect successor to Kevin Keegan. He had joined the Bhoys at the time of their Lisbon triumph and would manage the singular achievement of scoring 100 league goals in both Scotland and England.

He would become Scotland's record international with 102 caps as well as the only player-manager to lead a club to the English league and cup double.

He was also a comparative rarity in being brought straight into Liverpool's first team rather than schooled in the reserves according to the usual Shankly/Paisley tradition. But then, when a club boasts the crowns of both England and Europe, a slow start to the following season is not an option.

Liverpool decided to live without the World Club Cup mayhem, instead contenting themselves with thrashing Keegan and his new club Hamburg 1-1, 6-0 in the European Supercup.

RIGHT: **BOB PAISLEY WAS THE MOST SUCCESSFUL MANAGER IN LIVERPOOL'S HISTORY AFTER HE WAS ELEVATED FROM THE SHADOWS OF THE BOOT ROOM AS BILL SHANKLY'S SUCCESSOR**

Real Madrid and Feyenoord, of the European grandees, were missing from the first-round draw of the Champions Cup. The significance, in Madrid's case, was immense. For the first time since they had beaten Servette in the inaugural Champions Cup in 1955, the six-times champions had not qualified for Europe at all.

The odds on West Germany regaining ground had lengthened. In the previous two years, both Bayern Munich (as holders) and Borussia Monchengladbach (as Bundesliga champions) had competed. Now it was down 'only' to Borussia. They were among eight contenders who had retained their domestic title: the others were Liverpool, Dresden, Benfica, Jeunesse d'Esch (Luxembourg), Trabzonspor (Turkey), Omonia (Cyprus) and Brugge (Belgium).

Brugge were breaking out of the shadow of Anderlecht, though the Brussels club were dominating the Cup-Winners' Cup. Brugge had reached one European final of their own in 1976, when they lost to Liverpool in the UEFA Cup after leading the first leg 2-0 at half-time at Anfield. Now Brugge had Liverpool in their sights, with revenge the spur.

Seeding secured a comparatively balanced opening round, from which Liverpool were exempt. A few ties slipped through the net. Benfica beat Moscow Torpedo on penalties after a goalless 210 minutes, Nantes edged Dukla Prague on away goals, and Atletico Madrid beat Dinamo Bucharest 3-2 overall with a late goal from Spain striker Ruben Cano.

When Liverpool joined the fray it appeared that the luck of the draw was not with them. Dresden were standing in the way. Not for long. Dalglish's European Cup debut for Liverpool was marked by a 5-1 win at Anfield which included a rare goal from another newcomer in central defender Alan Hansen. In mid-season, they would be joined by a third new Scot in aggressive midfielder Graeme Souness. The former Tottenham and Middlesbrough man once joked that Liverpool had signed him 'as Dalglish's interpreter', but he had many more significant qualities than the ability to translate Glasgow patter into Scouse.

Liverpool progressed 6-3 on aggregate while Brugge, 9-2 first-round winners against KPs of Finland, came through 2-1 against Panathinaikos. Brugge's English centre-forward Roger Davies, a 27-year-old 'veteran' of Derby's semi-final run in 1973, followed up his treble against the Finns with the home opener against the Greeks.

A Dalglish-less Celtic, Nantes and Red Star were other second-round losers, while interest ended at the quarter-final stage for Benfica, Ajax, Atletico Madrid and Celtic's surprise conquerors, Innsbruck. Ajax lost on penalties to Juventus, for whom Dino Zoff saved two spot-kicks. 'Tell him to come and see me and choose any car he wants,' said the Juventus (and Fiat) owner, Gianni Agnelli. For the first time since 1960, not one eastern European club reached the last eight.

Benfica faced Liverpool in the Estadio da Luz off the back of a 46-game unbeaten run. Nene gave them a 13th-minute lead, but Liverpool proved happily at home in the rain. Goals from Jimmy Case and Emlyn Hughes punctured both Benfica's record and their confidence. Dalglish broke

his European goal-scoring duck for Liverpool in the 4-1 return stroll.

Meanwhile, English referee Pat Partridge was keeping a lid on tempers in Spain, where Atletico Madrid beat Brugge 3-2 but lost 4-3 on aggregate. Seasoned Julien Cools and centre-forward Raoul Lambert scored decisive goals in the last half-hour as the Spanish revival burned itself out.

Brugge then needed extra time, punctuated by the expulsion of rugged Claudio Gentile, to edge out Juventus 2-1 in the semi-finals. Their reward was the longed-for repeat against Liverpool, who had overcome Borussia yet again: this time 4-2 on aggregate. Crucially, a muscle strain robbed Borussia of Allan Simonsen in both games. He was the competition's top scorer with five goals, and without him Borussia's attack stuttered to near standstill.

Dalglish scored Liverpool's second goal, his 29th of a rewarding first season. There was still one left in his armoury.

BELOW: **LIVERPOOL PLAYERS COME RUNNING FROM EVERY CORNER OF THE PITCH TO CONGRATULATE RAY KENNEDY (5TH FROM LEFT) ON SCORING AGAINST BORUSSIA IN THE SEMI-FINAL SECOND LEG**

LIVERPOOL GRIND OUT THEIR VICTORY

Udo Lattek, coach of Borussia, had no doubts about the outcome of the final after seeing his team torn apart in the semi-final second leg at Anfield. 'Liverpool are different class,' he said. 'The cup is theirs again without a problem.'

But there was a problem: Ernst Happel, Brugge's Austrian coach. He had plotted Feyenoord's 1970 victory over Celtic down to the last meticulous detail, and now he went about his return to the final with the same thoroughness. Not that this was anything like as simple.

In the first place, the venue was Wembley which, in spite of Brugge's 25,000 ticket allowance, would be coloured red for danger – just as it had been for Manchester United's home-from-home trouncing of Benfica a decade earlier.

In the second place, Happel's Feyenoord had boasted superb forwards in Ove Kindvall and Coen Moulijn. Brugge brought no one comparable to the party. Veteran striker Lambert was injured, as was midfielder Paul Courant. Happel, down to the bare bones, gambled on Hungary's Olympic silver medallist Lajos Ku playing wide out of midfield.

That left Jan Simoen alone up front. In essence, Brugge's intention appeared to be little more ambitious than smothering Liverpool in midfield, catching them repeatedly with an offside trap and dragging the match through 120 goalless minutes to a penalty shoot-out. This was bad news for Liverpool who, for all their European and domestic league expertise, struggled to score goals at Wembley. Their two previous visits – against Manchester United in the 1977 FA Cup Final and against Nottingham Forest in the current season's League Cup Final – had brought just the one goal.

Goalkeeper Birger Jensen proved the hero of a long evening for Brugge, after being forced into action within the first 20 seconds by Dalglish. As time went on the Dane proved similarly defiant in the face of a variety of other efforts, while his opposite number, Ray Clemence, had

next to nothing to do until five minutes before half-time.

The second half was as relentlessly uninspiring as the first, though Liverpool's pressure left gaps at the back which Jan Sorensen, once, and later Simoen, came close to exploiting. Almost at the mid point, however, Graeme Souness finally unhinged the Brugge defence and Dalglish stabbed home the winner from close range. The goal was long overdue, hard-earned and thoroughly deserved. To Liverpool, it brought a second successive Champions Cup; to Brugge, their just desserts.

Victory provided welcome consolation for English football after an otherwise depressing international season which had brought a second consecutive failure to qualify for the World Cup finals. Instead it was Italy who topped the preliminary group and headed off to Argentina. As in the previous World Cup, British hopes were to be vested – in vain as it turned out – in a Scotland for whom Dalglish and Souness never touched the heights they had scaled that season for Liverpool.

At club level, however, England reigned supreme in Europe, having overtaken Spain's aggregate of trophies. Of the 60 European club finals thus far, English teams had won 14, Spain 13, Italy nine, West Germany seven, Holland six, Portugal three, Scotland and Belgium two apiece.

Both Belgian victories were in the Cup-Winners' Cup, courtesy not of Brugge but of Anderlecht.

WEDNESDAY 10 MAY 1978
WEMBLEY, LONDON

LIVERPOOL   1
DALGLISH 64

CLUB BRUGGE   0

HT: 0-0. ATT: 92,000.
REF: CORVER (HOL)

LIVERPOOL:
CLEMENCE – NEAL, THOMPSON, HANSEN, E. HUGHES* – CASE (HEIGHWAY 63), R. KENNEDY, SOUNESS, MCDERMOTT – DALGLISH, FAIRCLOUGH.
MANAGER: PAISLEY.

BRUGGE:
JENSEN – BASTIJNS*, KRIEGER, LEEKENS, MAES (VOLDERS 70) – SORENSEN, COOLS, DE CUBBER, VANDEREYCKEN, KU (SANDERS 60) – SIMOEN.
COACH: HAPPEL.

*CAPTAIN.

LEFT: **FREED BY GRAEME SOUNESS'S INCISIVE PASS, KENNY DALGLISH CALMLY STEADIES HIMSELF BEFORE CHIPPING THE BALL HOME**

FAR LEFT: **DALGLISH IS MOBBED AS THE EUROPEAN CUP HEADS FOR ANFIELD**

THE YEAR OF THE UNDERDOGS

Back in 1978, you didn't have to have money to run a successful team, even if it came in handy. Everything was possible if you had the right manager. Step forward, Brian Clough and Bob Houghton

'Old Big 'ead' was back. In January 1975, four months after being ignominiously forced out of Leeds, Brian Clough had returned to work, back in the east Midlands, at Nottingham Forest – just the other side of the M1 from Derby.

Time had offered Clough a refreshing perspective. He accepted that, in his headstrong way, he had approached the Leeds job in a way guaranteed to make ill-judged enemies. But the terms of his dismissal were gilded with long-term financial security. Clough may have been a conviction socialist but he enjoyed the personality lifestyle.

This, in turn, fuelled his idiosyncratic behaviour. He might turn up in the dressing room for a big match only 10 minutes before kick-off; he might miss a game in order to watch a non-league match, or he might give his players a four-day break on a whim.

His style appeared far removed from what fusty Forest needed, becalmed with their memories and in the lower half of the old second division. But Clough had his pride and his plan. One step was to drop all his television work; another – in the summer of 1976 – was to send for his old managerial sidekick Peter Taylor.

At the end of that first half-season under Clough, Forest finished 16th out of 22 clubs; in 1976 they were eighth; in 1977, when Derby tried in vain to lure Clough back, they were promoted from third place; and in 1978 they went straight through and won not only the First Division championship but the League Cup as well.

Significantly, they finished seven points clear of Liverpool in the league and beat Liverpool 1–0 in the League Cup Final replay. Scottish left-winger John Robertson settled it with a penalty. He was among the half a dozen who shared the fast-track ride from second-division obscurity to European glory.

Others included striker Tony Woodcock, midfielders John McGovern and Martin O'Neill (future Celtic manager), centre-forward John O'Hare and right-winger Ian Bowyer. McGovern and O'Hare had been Clough disciples at Derby who also followed him, unhappily, to Leeds.

Success generated the money to buy even better players, such as the England goalkeeper Peter Shilton, from

Stoke, and the controversial Scottish terrier, Kenny Burns, from Birmingham City. But Clough also fished successfully in non-league waters for the likes of Long Eaton's Garry Birtles, whom Clough and Taylor would turn into a million-pound England centre-forward.

UEFA's seeding system took no account of clubs with little or no European track record. Thus, in the first round, unseeded Forest were drawn against Liverpool, in Europe for the 15th successive season. Crucially, Liverpool misjudged the City Ground opener. A goal down to an early strike from Birtles, Liverpool refused to shut up shop and were chasing an equalizer when Birtles broke away and

RIGHT: TERRY MCDERMOTT VAINLY ATTEMPTS TO FIRE THE BALL PAST PETER SHILTON IN THE FOREST GOAL AT ANFIELD. LIVERPOOL COULD NOT PUT A DENT IN FOREST'S 2–0 LEAD FROM THE FIRST LEG

created a second for Colin Barrett. Holders' skipper Emlyn Hughes said later: 'We treated it like a league match rather than a European away match. We attacked too much.'

'Perhaps now you people will realize we are quite a good side,' Clough told the TV cameras after the goalless second leg. Complacency also cost the rest of Europe's cream dear – which assisted the Forest cause.

In the first round alone, Juventus lost to Rangers, Monaco lost to Sweden's Malmo with their English manager Bob Houghton, while Brugge lost to Wisla Krakow. In the second round Real Madrid were beaten by Grasshopper Zurich and the goals of shooting star Claudio Sulser, while Kiev Dynamo lost to Malmo and PSV Eindhoven lost to Rangers.

Forest progressed to the quarter-finals with a 7–2 aggregate destruction of AEK Athens, managed by Ferenc Puskas.

They now drew Grasshoppers, for whom Sulser had scored nine goals in four games, prompting talk of an assault on the European Cup record of 14 goals set by Jose Altafini in the 1962–63 season. It was only talk and was soon stilled. Forest won 4–1, 1–1. Sulser scored the opening goal in the first leg and converted a penalty in the second. But they were not enough.

Clough and Forest continued making headlines in every direction. In November Clough turned down the offer of manager's job at one of his old clubs, Sunderland; in February, before the victory over Grasshopper, he made Birmingham City's Trevor Francis Britain's first £1 million footballer; in March, in between squashing the Hoppers, Forest beat Southampton 3–2 to become the first club to retain the League Cup.

Eligibility rules forced Francis to sit out both the quarter-final and the dramatic semi-final defeat of Koln, in which Forest hit back to win 1–0 in Germany after being held 3–3 at home. Not even the promise of a 40,000-Mark bonus could force the Germans back into the game and the tie.

Awaiting Nottingham Forest in Munich were Sweden's Malmo with their mixture of full-time professionals and part-time travel agents, students and firemen.

BELOW: **BRIAN CLOUGH AND PETER TAYLOR WERE A FANTASTICALLY SUCCESSFUL MANAGERIAL DOUBLE ACT UNTIL THEY FELL OUT AND SPLIT UP**

FOREST SHOW MALMO HOW TO DO IT

Swedish football was split down the middle in the late 1970s. In the one corner were the traditionalists who admired German pragmatism; in the other were the modernizers who followed the quasi-English style which had brought success for Bob Houghton at Malmo and Roy Hodgson at Halmstadt.

Admirers of the English way included IFK Gothenburg's new young coach, Sven-Goran Eriksson. Later he recalled: 'Bob and Roy brought English organization to our game and a new way of playing. Instead of standing off and counter-attacking they pressed when the opposition had the ball. They introduced all the things I'd seen as a kid every Saturday when I watched English football on television.'

Houghton had reached Sweden and Malmo via English non-league football and South Africa. No Swedish club had ever previously reached the semi-finals of the Champions Cup, let alone the final. Malmo's Sky Blues had been assisted by the luck of the draw and the failings of the usual ruling class. But Houghton, apart from organization and a sharp offside trap, also benefited from the solidity of

goalkeeper Jan Moller and the experience of 1974 World Cup midfielders Bo Larsson and Staffan Tapper.

Unfortunately, Larsson was unfit for the final. A knee injury which he had suffered against Wisla Krakow would end his career. His absence was a serious blow for a Swedish team resigned to being outsiders with few realistic expectations of turning European football on its head. Worse was to follow when the long-striding Tapper had to be substituted after little more than half an hour.

Forest should already have been ahead. Garry Birtles shot just over the bar and Malmo midfielder Anders Ljungberg cleared in desperation after Moller dropped a John Robertson corner. Then the goalkeeper saved at the

second attempt after a shot from Ian Bowyer slipped out of his hands. Malmo had a single chance, and even that one, wasted by a surprised Jan-Olov Kinnvall, stemmed from a mishit clearance by Kenny Burns.

Just on half-time, Forest's pressure was rewarded. Bowyer sent Robertson down the left and his perfect cross was dive-headed home by Trevor Francis at the far post. With that one touch the England forward repaid all of his £1 million fee and more.

Francis was not the luckiest of players. He had learned as a teenager how to withstand off-the-field pressure after being labelled 'Superboy' for his initial explosion at Birmingham. Francis discovered all about Clough's quirky manner when he was handed his debut for the A team in the Midland Intermediate League. The match ended in a 2–2 draw, and Clough gave Francis a rocket for not wearing shinpads. Back at the City Ground, he was quickly dispatched to make the tea.

By contrast, he could also thank Clough for the chance, in May 1979, to score the goal which provided 'the greatest moment of my life'.

By the glorious standards of the Champions Cup, however, the 1979 final was anything but a great moment.

WEDNESDAY 30 MAY 1979
OLYMPIA, MUNICH

NOTTINGHAM FOREST 1
FRANCIS 44

MALMO 0

HT: 1–0. ATT: 57,500.
REF: LINEMAYR (AUS)

FOREST:
SHILTON – ANDERSON, LLOYD, BURNS, CLARK – MCGOVERN*, BOWYER, ROBERTSON – FRANCIS, BIRTLES, WOODCOCK.
MANAGER: CLOUGH.

MALMO:
MOLLER – R. ANDERSSON, JONSSON, M. ANDERSSON, ERLANDSSON – PRYTZ, TAPPER* (MALMBERG 34), LJUNGBERG – HANSSON (T. ANDERSSON 82), CERVIN, KINNVALL.
COACH: HOUGHTON.

*CAPTAIN.

LEFT: **IF THE CUP FITS, WEAR IT: TREVOR FRANCIS BASKS IN THE GLORY OF VICTORY**

1980s

THE DESCENT INTO CHAOS

Triumph and tragedy marked the 1980s, and European football's descent into hooligan chaos reached its nadir with the Heysel Stadium disaster in Brussels. Within weeks English clubs had been barred from European competition for what proved to be five years. The Hillsborough tragedy of 1989 would also contribute to major changes in the presentation and financing of top-level football. By the end of the decade, the balance of power out on the pitch had swung back towards Italy and Milan were revitalized. The club's ambitious president Silvio Berlusconi ended up making almost as many headlines as Milan's star players such as Marco Van Basten and Ruud Gullit.

RIGHT: **FLARES GO OFF AS LIVERPOOL AND ROMA PLAYERS LINE UP BEFORE THE 1984 CHAMPIONS CUP FINAL IN ROME**

IAN RUSH

Country: Wales

Position: Centre-forward

Born: 20 October, 1961

Clubs: Chester, Liverpool
(England), Juventus (Italy),
Liverpool, Leeds United,
Newcastle United (England)

IAN RUSH

Joining Liverpool, particularly when I did late in the 1979–80 season, had to be considered a dream in any footballer's language. They had twice been European champions as well as the dominant club in England for more than a decade. But the perspective from the outside can be deceptive. I have to admit that at first, on arriving from Chester, I found it all a real struggle.

The team had gone out of the European Cup in the first round twice in a row – following those back-to-back wins in 1977 and 1978 – with early knockouts by Nottingham Forest and Dinamo Tbilisi.

At the start of the 1980–81 campaign we still had many of the men who had triumphed a few years before, and as Oulu Palloseura, Aberdeen and CSKA Sofia were overcome I never had a look-in.

Then my luck turned. Bob Paisley picked me for the League Cup Final replay win over West Ham, and the boss then had me in the side for the first leg of the European semi-final against Bayern Munich. We drew 0–0 at Anfield, and I was back on the bench for the second leg in Germany. I did not get on the pitch, but we drew 1–1 thanks to an away goal from Ray Kennedy.

Before the final against Real Madrid in Paris I went off to play for Wales against England buoyed up by the fact that Bob had told me I would be in the squad. I thought he meant in the 16. Instead I was 17th man, which in those days meant that although I was on the bench I didn't get stripped.

How can I complain, looking back? That was a great Liverpool team, and we proved it by winning the cup for a third time, with Alan Kennedy hitting the late winner. But remember that I was a young kid. I wanted to play. I was happy for the club, but disappointed for myself.

I wanted to leave. I went to see Bob Paisley that summer and told him so. After that, when he sent me on as a substitute in the first round against Palloseura the next season, I honestly thought I was putting myself in the shop window. But I scored my first goal for the club in that game,

which we won 7–0 – and quickly everything changed for the better for me.

I must say that Kenny Dalglish was very good to me. He gave me the perfect piece of advice when he said: 'Don't worry about anything else – if you want to stay in the side, your job is to get goals. Then you can gradually add the other things to your play.'

You can never predict how everything will work out. David Johnson got injured, which was bad luck for him but good for me, because it meant I was in the side regularly. We beat AZ67 Alkmaar – and I scored again – then went out to CSKA Sofia.

It may sound strange as we still had so many players who had won the competition, but I felt the inexperience of newer boys like Bruce Grobbelaar, Mark Lawrenson, Ronnie

LEFT: **IAN RUSH SPENT THE 1987-88 SEASON WITH JUVENTUS**

Whelan and me in this kind of football cost us. We were all right back on home ground in the English Football League, but European football was completely different. Teams sat back and hit you on the break, and we kept getting caught out. We were not smart enough.

No matter how often it happened, we just did not seem to learn our lesson. The same thing happened again in 1982–83. We won comfortably against Dundalk and HJK Helsinki, then lost 4–3 on aggregate to Widzew Lodz in the quarter-finals.

But you cannot play all these matches in different conditions, in different countries, against different clubs and players and styles, without building up the 'knowledge'. So I felt different about our prospects when we launched our 1983–84 campaign. I felt at last we had the experience we needed to make an impact.

We beat Odense 6–0 over the two legs in the first round, then played Athletic Bilbao. They held us goalless at Anfield and thought they were through then. But we went to Spain and won 1–0. The goal was something of a collector's item. Alan Kennedy didn't have a right foot, but he crossed with that foot; I rarely scored with a header, but I headed this one in.

We were picking up momentum. In the quarter-finals we beat Benfica home and away and I scored for the 1–0 win at Anfield and again in the 4–1 win in Lisbon. Our class showed in the Stadium of Light. I still look back on that as one of our great performances in Europe.

In the semi-final there was another. We beat Dinamo Bucharest 1–0 in the match at Anfield, remembered for that infamous incident when Graeme Souness was accused of breaking the jaw of one of their players. That really stoked up the atmosphere for the return in Romania. The stadium in Bucharest that night was the most intimidating place we had ever been. But Graeme loved it! He just seemed to get bigger and better as the game went on. I scored twice and we went through to the final against Roma in their own Olympic Stadium.

Joe Fagan had taken over as manager from Bob Paisley the year before, but little had changed. He had Ronnie Moran and Roy Evans working with him as a team, and the approach to the final was typical Liverpool: keep your feet on the ground and treat it as another game.

Phil Neal gave us the lead, but even when Roberto Pruzzo equalized, we still felt we were the stronger team. We couldn't get the second goal, though, and it went to penalties. Joe said: 'Don't worry about it, you've done all you can,' and that helped us to relax.

Graeme Souness, Phil Neal and I all wanted to take the first kick, but then we saw Steve Nicol walking away from us with the ball. There was nothing we could do about it – and he missed.

Graeme and Phil were on target, and then, with the count at 2–2, it was my turn. I can tell you that was the longest walk I have ever taken in football, with 80,000 Italians whistling at me. But as I ran up, their keeper helped me by moving to the right. I saw him out of the corner of my eye, which meant it was 'just' a little matter of knocking the ball into the other corner.

Brucie then did his famous knee-shaking act on the line and Francesco Graziani shot over. Now it was down to Alan Kennedy. He had missed every one when we had practised penalties in training and, for the first time, their keeper went the right way... but the shot was perfectly placed, right in the corner, and he had no chance.

The feeling was fantastic. To go and win the European Cup in the backyard of the opposition was a tremendous feat. I don't think it will happen again.

Graeme Souness left in the summer for Sampdoria. That was a big blow because he had been a major influence, but we had more experience among us now and felt we could cope.

We started our defence by beating Lech Poznan 5–0 on aggregate. Then I got a hat-trick in the first leg against Benfica and, despite a 1–0 defeat in Lisbon, we went through. Then came FK Austria, and after a 1-1 draw in Vienna we won 4-1. I scored twice in the first leg of the semi-final against Panathinaikos, but as I was on a booking, Joe Fagan left me out of the return in Athens to avoid any risks. We won 1-0 anyway.

Of course, the final against Juventus at the Heysel Stadium in Brussels will never be remembered for the football, but for the tragedy that cost so many lives. Until the memories were revived last spring when the clubs were drawn together in the Champions League, I am not sure many people could have told you that Michel Platini scored the winner for Juventus in Heysel from a penalty. At that stage we knew something had happened, but we really did not know what. We just wanted to get it over with. The whole match was unreal. When I joined Juventus later on, many people there told me they had felt exactly the same way.

The two clubs have had a strong bond ever since then. For example, when I was transferred back to Liverpool, all the negotiations were done by telephone, which just shows how much trust there was between the clubs and the people.

In football terms, the ban which followed the Heysel tragedy hit English football hard. Everton had won the League title in 1985, and I honestly believe they could have gone on to win the European Cup the following season... if Liverpool had not done it again, of course. I still believe we were the two best teams in Europe at the time.

LEFT: IAN RUSH SCORED
A TOTAL OF 20 GOALS FOR
LIVERPOOL IN EUROPE:
HIS PARTNERSHIP WITH
KENNY DALGLISH MEANT
THE REDS REIGNED AS
EUROPE'S TOP CLUB IN
THE MID-1980S

MIGHTY MOUSE JOINS THE REVOLUTION

The varying number of foreign imports allowed in each league led to disparities between different European sides. After leaving Liverpool in 1977, Kevin Keegan was finally coming to terms with life in Hamburg

Two years of Liverpool, plus one year and possibly more of Nottingham Forest, stirred unrest across the continent. The issue, with huge irony considering what the future held in store, was foreign imports.

Real Madrid, beating Levski Sofia of Bulgaria 3–0 overall in the late summer of 1979, were permitted only two foreigners: German midfielder Uli Stielike and the black England winger Laurie Cunningham, who had sold himself to Madrid during his summer holiday on the strength of a decisive display for West Bromwich Albion against Valencia in the UEFA Cup.

Milan, barred from using foreign players altogether, fell immediately. They drew 0–0 in Porto, then lost 1–0 at home. New coach Massimo Giacomini complained: 'It's an uneven playing field. The Spanish clubs can have two foreigners from anywhere, the Germans and the Dutch have their Danes and Swedes, while the English can pick as many Scots and Irish as they like.'

Giacomini was wide of the mark in thinking that German clubs looked only to Scandinavia. Hamburg, back for the first time since their epic run to the 1961 semis, had looked both south-east and north-west. Linking defence and midfield was the Yugoslav Ivan Buljan, while the attacking sparkle was provided by England's Kevin Keegan.

'Mighty Mouse', as the Germans nicknamed him, did not enjoy the best of starts. Hamburg had appeared a sensible destination when he quit Liverpool in 1977, but player and club took time to adjust to each other. Not until a palace revolution brought in Gunter Netzer (once of Borussia Monchengladbach and Real Madrid) as general manager and Branko Zebec (ex-Partizan Belgrade) as coach did everything come together. Then Hamburg ended the 1978–79 season as champions and Keegan was their 17-goal top scorer. Such was his strength of character – not least in overcoming his team-mates' initial

RIGHT: LAURIE CUNNINGHAM IN ACTION FOR REAL MADRID AGAINST HAMBURG IN THE VOLKSPARKSTADION. THE FIRST BLACK PLAYER TO REPRESENT ENGLAND AT ANY LEVEL, HE SADLY DIED IN A CAR CRASH OUTSIDE MADRID IN 1989, SHORTLY AFTER HELPING RAYO VALLECANO BACK INTO SPAIN'S TOP FLIGHT

resentment – that Keegan was voted European Footballer of the Year in both 1978 and 1979.

Lofty Horst Hrubesch at centre-forward complemented Keegan as had John Toshack at Liverpool. On Hamburg's return to the Champions Cup, Hrubesch scored three times against Valur Reykjavik in the first round; Keegan then scored once in each leg in a victory over Dinamo Tbilisi.

This was indirect vengeance, since Tbilisi had beaten Liverpool in the first round. Liverpool blamed the night-long disturbance of a torchlit march around their hotel by Georgian fans. In truth Tbilisi, inspired by Murtaz Khurtsilava in defence, David Kipiani in midfield and Ramaz Shengelia in attack, were good enough not to need outside help.

By Christmas, the goalposts were shifting. Keegan had already decided to move on at the end of the season. He could have doubled his £120,000-a-year salary at Real Madrid or in Italy, where the borders were about to creak open, while Chelsea were English favourites. No one foresaw Keegan returning, instead, to Southampton. Ever the exemplary professional, Keegan did not allow any of this to distract him from his football as the Champions Cup reached the quarter-final stage.

Ajax, revived by Danish midfielders Frank Arnesen and Soren Lerby, had strolled in with nonchalant victories over HJK Helsinki and Omonia Nicosia. As for Madrid, an away goal by Cunningham had edged them past Porto.

Forest launched their defence comfortably against Osters and Arges Pitesti. But Dynamo Berlin were a different proposition. The East German police club had just embarked on a remarkable run of 10 successive league titles. Everything was tilted in their favour, from transfers to referees. They were as dominant as they were despised. Few tears were shed when the club later collapsed into amateur league anonymity after the reunification of Germany

On 5 March 1980, Dynamo made headlines round Europe by beating Forest 1-0 at the City Ground in the quarter-final opener. Hans-Jurgen Riediger marked his return after a broken ankle with the 63rd-minute winner. Many assumed that Forest had been weakened by the mid-season sale of striker Tony Woodcock to Koln The appearance proved to be deceptive, however, as Forest hit back 3-1 behind the Berlin Wall with a double from Trevor Francis. Similarly, Real Madrid recovered from 2-0 down in the first leg to overcome Celtic 3-0 in the return. Hamburg missed hepatitis victim Buljan against his old club Hajduk Split, but still managed an away goals win, while Arnesen and Lerby scored in Ajax's 4-0 win over Strasbourg.

Lerby added another in the semi-final against Forest, but this time Ajax lost 2-1. Madrid, anticipating staging the final, thought they were home and dry when two goals from Carlos Santillana beat Hamburg in the Bernabeu. But Keegan and co thrashed Madrid out of sight, 5-1, in the Volksparkstadion.

This time Cunningham's away goal was no use to a Madrid side who ended up with only 10 men. Their underrated, moustachioed playmaker, Vicente del Bosque, was sent off six minutes from time.

FOREST FIRE IS TOO MUCH FOR HAMBURG

A campaign which had started with too much fire and fury ended with not enough. The first tie of the season had been staged amid sectarian strife and confusion. The final was played out among whispers.

The previous summer, the draw for the preliminary round had matched the champions of the two Irelands for the first time. Dundalk of the Republic were to play Northern Ireland's Linfield. Two days before the first leg, at Dundalk's Oriel Park, Lord Mountbatten and three companions were blown up in their fishing boat by the IRA; later that same day 18 soldiers were killed in a border ambush.

Fans fought against each other and the police before, during and after the 1-1 draw. More than 30 police were among the hundred-plus casualties. Dundalk then won the return 2-0 in front of a crowd of 750 in neutral, peaceful Haarlem.

Some 61 matches later, the Bernabeu was only half-full when northern European giants Nottingham Forest and Hamburg met in Madrid with the Champions Cup at stake. Self-conscious cheers from German and English fans bounced around the rest of the largely empty terracing.

Hamburg had lost the German league title, and Keegan wanted to go out in glory against Forest manager Brian Clough.

The pair had been on opposite sides, notoriously, in the first official match of Clough's tempestuous 44 days at Leeds. Liverpool's Keegan and the Leeds captain Billy Bremner had been sent off together in the FA Charity Shield.

Both Keegan and Clough were full-blooded competitors and proud patriots. Just as Clough went to his grave believing he should have been England manager, so Keegan had ensured that his Hamburg contract guaranteed his release for every England game, including friendlies.

Clough and his assistant Peter Taylor were away spying on Hamburg when news filtered through of a major blow. Trevor Francis, scorer of two crucial goals in the semi-final defeat of Ajax, had torn an Achilles tendon in a league game against Crystal Palace. He would miss not only the Champions Cup Final but also the European Championship finals in Italy. To compound Clough's problems, the wayward Stan Bowles – a typical gamble of a signing from Queens Park Rangers – had walked out on the club a week earlier. Thus Forest lined up a squad of 15 in Madrid, one short of the permitted maximum.

Hamburg had their own problems. Coach Zebec, an alcoholic, had been taken ill just before the season's end; midfield general Jimmy Hartwig was missing with a

knee injury; and Hrubesch, nursing an ankle problem, would not even have been on the bench had this not been the European Cup Final.

Keegan worked himself into the ground to little effect. Hrubesch's deputy, Jurgen Milewski, bounced off defenders Larry Lloyd and Kenny Burns. When Hrubesch did appear, for the second half, he was so much a passenger that his presence was more hindrance than help. It was all over by then, anyway. In the 19th minute John Robertson drifted in from the left and surprised 'keeper Rudi Kargus with a right-foot shot which scuffed in off a post.

Clough and Taylor – to polite applause from those Madrid fans who had bothered to turn out – again paraded the prize which justified their new three-year contracts.

WEDNESDAY 28 MAY 1980
BERNABEU, MADRID

NOTTINGHAM FOREST   1
ROBERTSON 19

HAMBURG   0

HT: 1-0. ATT: 51,000.
REF: GARRIDO (POR)

FOREST:
SHILTON – V. ANDERSON, LLOYD, BURNS, F. GRAY (GUNN 84) – MCGOVERN*, O'NEILL, BOWYER – MILLS (O'HARE 68), BIRTLES, ROBERTSON.
MANAGER: CLOUGH.

HAMBURG:
KARGUS – KALTZ, JAKOBS, HIERONYMUS (HRUBESCH 46), NOGLY* – BULJAN, MEMERING, MAGATH – KEEGAN, MILEWSKI, REIMANN.
COACH: ZEBEC.

*CAPTAIN

MAIN: **JOHN MCGOVERN HOLDS ALOFT THE EUROPEAN CUP FOR THE SECOND TIME AS NOTTINGHAM FOREST CAPTAIN**

FAR LEFT: **WINGER JOHN ROBERTSON IS MOBBED BY TEAM-MATES AFTER SCORING THE WINNER IN THE 19TH MINUTE**

THE 1980 FINAL | 135

LOOKING TOWARDS THE FUTURE

Nottingham Forest took a busman's holiday in Japan. Meanwhile, Real Madrid began their relentless march towards the final, as mighty Liverpool set off in the same direction with a 10-goal spree

Nottingham Forest had prepared for their second Champions Cup triumph by flying off on a team holiday break to Mallorca. They followed it up with a working jaunt to Japan. The reason for this exemplified the increasing popularity of the professional game around the world.

Japan wanted to host the World Cup one day. Traditionalists in Europe and South America thought this ludicrous, but the idea had been planted years earlier by Sir Stanley Rous during his presidency of FIFA. Eventually, of course, that dream would come true: in 2002 Japan and South Korea would jointly host the World Cup and the Far East in general would be courted by Europe's major clubs.

Forest's role in the pre-history was to accept an invitation to revitalize the battle-scarred World Club Cup after Japanese sponsorship had taken it to Tokyo. An 18-hour flight – from London via Anchorage and then down to Japan – was the cost in terms of time. A 1–0 defeat by Nacional of Uruguay, the South American champions, was the result. Then came the 18-hour flight back.

Ironically, by the time Forest were playing for world domination – 11 February 1981 – their grip on the European crown had already been released. CSKA Sofia, having deposed Ajax in 1973, repeated the feat in the first round. Tzvetan Yonchev scored the lone goal in Sofia, and Rujdi Kerimov struck the lone goal at the City Ground.

Years later Forest manager Brian Clough, rejecting claims that he ruled by fear, said: 'We surprised people because we were unconventional.' So now, with Forest eliminated, it was back to convention.

Italy had reopened the borders to foreign players. Just one, at first. Internazionale's initial investment was in the Austrian playmaker, Herbert Prohaska. Meanwhile Liverpool paraded an Israeli defender, Avi Cohen, as they followed the trend set spectacularly in England by Tottenham with their 1978 'capture' of Argentine World Cup-winners Osvaldo Ardiles and Ricardo Villa. These, however, were still the exception rather than the rule.

RIGHT: LIVERPOOL'S TERRY MCDERMOTT (VISIBLE AT EXTREME RIGHT OF PICTURE) SCORES AGAINST ABERDEEN AT PITTODRIE, THE ONLY GOAL OF THE GAME

Ajax were in place again, led by Soren Lerby who had been the competition's 10-goal top scorer from midfield the previous season. Bayern Munich had Paul Breitner, once their left-back, now an idiosyncratic playmaker feeding Kalle Rummenigge and backed up by a workmanlike supporting cast – even if defenders Wolfgang Dremmler and Klaus Augenthaler bore no comparison with Franz Beckenbauer.

Real Madrid were little changed from the side who had collapsed dramatically in the 1980 semi-finals against Hamburg. Even Yugoslav coach Vujadin Boskov had survived the fall-out.

Liverpool set off against Oulu Palloseura of Finland with just two changes, remarkably, from the team who had won the 1978 final against Brugge. Skipper Emlyn Hughes, slowed by injury, had been sold to Wolverhampton Wanderers, but midfielder Jimmy Case was merely held back in reserve. Terry McDermott scored in the 1–1 draw in Finland and then a hat-trick in a goal spree back at Anfield. Liverpool's 10 goals were completed by Graeme Souness (also a hat-trick), David Fairclough (two), Sammy Lee and Ray Kennedy. Even Oulu's consolation goal was scored by Geordie Keith Armstrong, which kept the scoresheet British.

The British theme was maintained by the second-round draw which matched Liverpool against the Scottish champions Aberdeen and their up-and-coming young manager Alex Ferguson. His admiration of Liverpool's professionalism was no secret. Years earlier, while taking his first managerial steps at St Mirren, he had persuaded Liverpool to send their newly crowned European champions for the Paisley club's centenary

match. Much later, at Manchester United, Ferguson would put Liverpool in the domestic shade. But Aberdeen did not possess such weapons back in the autumn of 1980. They lost 1–0 at home – McDermott again – and 4–0 at Anfield. Perversely, Scots scored all but one of the goals: Willie Miller with an own goal, Kenny Dalglish and Allan Hansen. Phil Neal was the odd marksman out.

Liverpool were thus one of four former champions to reach the quarter-finals. Following them into the last eight were Real Madrid, Inter and Bayern Munich. The Germans had thoroughly enjoyed again thrashing their old rivals from Ajax 5–1 in the Olympic stadium: Rummenigge and Dieter Hoeness, brother of aspiring general manager Uli, both struck twice. Back in Amsterdam Ajax won 'only' 2–1. The identity of the scorer of their second goal, an 18-year-old named Frank Rijkaard, went comparatively unremarked. Bayern won home and away against Banik Ostrava to earn a semi-final against Liverpool while Madrid – missing the injured Laurie Cunningham – snuffed out Moscow Spartak to draw old enemy Inter.

Liverpool, having beaten CSKA easily enough in the quarter-finals, then teetered on the brink against Bayern. Anfield saw no goals and extra time was looming in Munich when Ray Kennedy struck with eight minutes to go. Rummenigge's equalizer was too little, too late.

Simultaneously Madrid and Inter fought out their now customary war of attrition in the other semi. Santillana and Juanito struck in Madrid; sweeper Graziano Bini got one back in Milan. Madrid, not for the first time against Inter, sneaked through 2–1.

LIVERPOOL COMMITTED TO VICTORY

The more time passes, and the more players and coaches fret about overheated fixture schedules, the more Liverpool's consistency across all competitions in the late 1970s and 1980s has come to be appreciated. The competitive spirit imbued by Bill Shankly and maintained by Bob Paisley delivered commitment in the league, League Cup, FA Cup and Champions Cup (as well as Cup-Winners' Cup and UEFA Cup).

Years later right-back Phil Neal was emphatic: 'When you're winning game after game, you can't wait for the next match to come along. You want to play. Also, it's much easier to play when you're winning than when you're losing.'

Liverpool arrived in the Parc des Princes knowing that victory was essential for them to return to the Champions Cup. In the league they had lost eight times, the same as new champions Aston Villa. But they had also drawn 17 matches and slipped down to fifth, their lowest placing since 1965. They had lost to Everton in the fourth round of the FA Cup but made amends by winning the League Cup for the first time.

RIGHT: **PHIL THOMPSON LIFTS THE EUROPEAN CUP AS LIVERPOOL BECOME THE FIRST BRITISH TEAM TO WIN THE TROPHY THREE TIMES**

Now the target was to emulate Ajax and Bayern and win the Champions Cup a third time. Real Madrid meanwhile were chasing a record-extending seventh cup, 15 years after their last appearance in the final.

Madrid coach Vujadin Boskov was undecided about Laurie Cunningham, the inspirational English winger who they had bought for £995,000 from West Bromwich Albion. Injury had sidelined him for half the season. Without him Madrid had reached the final and finished narrow runners-up in the Spanish league.

In the end Boskov gambled that the provocation of facing English opposition might spur Cunningham back into his form

of the previous season when he staged a match-winning display against Barcelona in the Nou Camp.

In the event, Boskov was disappointed. Cunningham looked ring-rusty and a stranger to his team-mates. Nor was he the only big name to fail the exam.

Liverpool had identified the tetchy German, Uli Stielike, as Madrid's main man in midfield. He acted as focus for the balls coming out of defence and appreciated the channels in which to thread the attacking passes for Carlos Santillana and the hot-tempered Juanito.

But Stielike had reckoned without Sammy Lee. The 22-year-old Scouser may not have been one of Liverpool's big-money signings, but he put in more work than any of them, forcing Stielike so deep that he lost all value to Madrid.

Not that Liverpool's attack fared much better. The pattern for a tight game was clear in the first five minutes, when Jose Camacho went in two-footed on Graeme Souness and Neal twice tagged Cunningham.

The next hour was played out largely in midfield, with few half-chances worthy of the name. In time, Liverpool's competitive strength began to tell as Real tired. Nine minutes from the end, buccaneering full-back Alan Kennedy chested down a throw-in, walked through a pitiful excuse for a tackle by Julio Garcia Cortes and rammed an angled winner low past goalkeeper Agustin from about eight yards. With this strike, Kennedy lifted the game out of its lethargy and ended the dreaded prospect of a shoot-out after extra time.

Bob Paisley summed it up: 'Real Madrid may be a great club, but we're the better team.' Victory had put Paisley into the history books as the first manager to win the most prestigious of all club competitions three times.

ABOVE: SEIZING THE INITIATIVE, DEFENDER ALAN KENNEDY BLASTS THE ONLY GOAL OF THE GAME PAST AGUSTIN IN THE REAL GOAL. SABIDO, ANGEL AND TERRY MCDERMOTT LOOK ON

WEDNESDAY 27 MAY 1981
PARC DES PRINCES, PARIS

LIVERPOOL	1
A. KENNEDY 82	
REAL MADRID	0

HT: 0-0. ATT: 48,360.
REF: PALOTAI (HUN)

LIVERPOOL:
CLEMENCE - NEAL, THOMPSON*, HANSEN, A. KENNEDY - LEE, R. KENNEDY, SOUNESS, MCDERMOTT - DALGLISH (CASE 87), JOHNSON. MANAGER: PAISLEY.

REAL:
AGUSTIN - GARCIA CORTES (PINEDA 87), SABIDO, GARCIA NAVAJAS, CAMACHO* - ANGEL, DEL BOSQUE, STIELIKE - JUANITO, SANTILLANA, CUNNINGHAM.
COACH: BOSKOV.

*CAPTAIN

FOOTBALL'S NEW COMMERCIALISM

More and more plans were afoot to squeeze profit out of the People's Game. A simplistic seeding system was inflicted upon the European Cup, leading to an early bath for some of the big boys

Twenty-five years had passed since the first Champions Cup Final. Across the world it had inspired a competitive revolution which had changed the face of the game. Domestic leagues and cups were no longer the only prizes. Players, coaches and fans were excited by the cross-continental glory nights which rewarded even clubs who finished in the wake of the title winners.

The Fairs Cup, taken over by the European federation in 1971 and converted into the UEFA Cup, had been running since the mid-1950s; the Cup-Winners' Cup since 1960; the European Supercup from 1971. Japanese sponsorship cash had breathed new life into the World Club Cup. Copycat champions' cups had sprung up all over the world, from Africa to the Americas.

Concerns stirred within FIFA Haus in Zurich. The world federation's Brazilian president, Joao Havelange, had moved quickly to capitalize on the commercial value of the World Cup. Simultaneously, UEFA was developing the European Championship. But national team competitions needed two-

RIGHT: **PAUL BREITNER SLOTS HOME A PENALTY FOR BAYERN MUNICH VERSUS CSKA SOFIA**

and four-year time spans: the Champions Cup now represented the day-by-day pinnacle of international football.

Restrictions on imports and the continuing overriding value of gate receipts ahead of sponsorship and TV income also guaranteed a breadth of competition. Aston Villa proved the point, spectacularly. They ranked among football's great traditionalists. Their own William McGregor had been a driving force behind the 1888 launch of the Football League. Since then they had won the league and FA Cup seven times each.

One-time manager Tommy Docherty famously commented that Villa fans would 'turn up to watch the shirts dry'. That supporting power was significant in driving them to Champions Cup glory. It was a success achieved remarkably against a background of internal turbulence whirling around the on-and-off chairmanship of the club by travel firm millionaire Doug Ellis.

Victims in the fall-out included Ron Saunders, the manager who had shrewdly guided Villa to the 1981 league title. Saunders, outwardly dour but with a laconic sense of humour, was forced out after a contract bust-up just before the Champions Cup quarter-finals. Thus it was his erstwhile chief scout, Tony Barton, who blinked his way into the glare of publicity while steering Villa towards the ultimate European spotlight.

Valur Reykjavik (7-0), Dynamo Berlin (2-2 with an away goal), Dynamo Kiev (2-0) and Anderlecht (1-0) were brushed aside on their march to the final. Here they met a Bayern Munich side including three players who would feature in the West German squad who would be runners-up at the imminent World Cup finals in Spain.

Villa were assisted by the failures of a simplistic seeding system which 'permitted' a first-round meeting of Juventus and Celtic and a second-round match-up between Bayern and Benfica. Thus half the contingent of eight quarter-finalists were ring-rusty eastern European clubs. Only one progressed, CSKA Sofia, who maintained their jinx over the European Cup-holders by defeating Liverpool 2-1 on aggregate.

The holders had thumped luckless Oulu again in the first round then edged past AZ Alkmaar by the odd goal in nine. Ahead of the quarter-final against CSKA they followed Nottingham Forest's flightpath to Tokyo for the World Club Cup. Here Zico's team Flamengo took them apart, putting three goals without reply past the Zimbabwean Bruce Grobbelaar – a remarkable and charismatic replacement in goal for Ray Clemence who had left, surprisingly, for Tottenham Hotspur.

Ian Rush had started his prolific reign in Liverpool's attack, but got nowhere against the Bulgarians. Midfielder Ronnie Whelan scored the only goal at Anfield but Stoicho Mladenov struck back in Sofia – once late on and then again in an extra-time period which also saw the expulsion of Mark Lawrenson.

Villa, however, rolled on with a mixture of home-grown talent and other clubs' cast-offs who found new purpose and confidence under the claret-and-blue banner. These included Jimmy Rimmer, who had come from Arsenal, full-back Kenny Swain from Chelsea, centre-back Ken McNaught from Everton, midfield general and skipper Dennis Mortimer from Coventry, and Peter Withe from Southport, South Africa and Newcastle.

Inside-forwards Gary Shaw and Gordon Cowans had sparkled up through Villa's own youth ranks, while shrewd scouting work unearthed defensive anchor Allan Evans at Dunfermline and left-winger Tony Morley at Burnley. Morley was an outside-left of the old-fashioned variety who, when on song, terrified continental full-backs unaccustomed to being attacked at pace.

Shaw and McNaught scored the goals which brought a legendary victory over Dynamo Kiev – Oleg Blokhin and all – in the quarter-finals. Morley then snapped the only goal of the semi-final triumph over Anderlecht, second-round conquerors of Juventus.

Bayern Munich, having put eight goals past CSKA in the two legs of their own semi-finals, were not unduly concerned to learn of Villa's progress. They had fretted at the likely prospect of meeting Anderlecht in the Rotterdam final. Villa, they thought dismissively, presented a far simpler option.

BELOW: RON SAUNDERS, ASTON VILLA'S DISCIPLINARIAN MANAGER, LEFT THE CLUB JUST BEFORE THEY WON THE EUROPEAN CUP

VILLA FLOURISH IN THE DEEP END

Bayern set up camp on the Dutch coast at Scheveningen. They were already counting chickens. Barcelona had just won the Cup-Winners' Cup, so the Supercup would pack out the Olympic stadium, and television channels would be queueing for the rights auction. Then the trip to Tokyo for the World Club Cup promised another £350,000. The Germans had heard of Aston Villa but nothing of their players. If they had come across the odd one or two at national team level, they had forgotten. 'The cup is ours,' said defender Wolfgang Dremmler. 'Anything else is too fantastic to believe.'

This was not, of course, Tony Barton's attitude. His promotion to manager had trebled his salary and one of his first toys was a Mercedes-Benz. But that did not affect his attitude to German engineering. 'Bayern have two terrific players in Breitner and Rummenigge,' he said, 'but we have the better team.'

Bayern smiled patronizingly. The odds against Villa even lengthened 10 minutes into the game when goalkeeper Jimmy Rimmer injured a shoulder and had to be substituted by Nigel Spink. 'My Mum will be pleased!' Spink was reported to

RIGHT: **STRIKER PETER WITHE KNOCKS IN THE WINNING GOAL. LATER HE USED TO ROLL UP HIS TROUSER LEG AND JOKE: 'THIS IS THE SHIN THAT WON THE EUROPEAN CUP.'**

have said as he quit the substitutes' bench. Bayern's Hungarian coach Pal Csernai certainly was. He said later: 'I knew the substitute goalkeeper had played only a few league games. I thought this was a good sign.'

Csernai was wrong on both counts. Spink, a 23-year-old from Chelmsford, had not even played 'a few' league games; he had only ever played once before in Villa's first team. However, being thrown in at the deep end proved to be the making of him. In due course he even played for England.

Veteran finals observers recall this one as one of the poorest. Flowing passing movements were absent, but much of that was due to Villa's success in shutting down Bayern's attack. Not completely. Even Barton did not expect that. As he

said later, 'If you want to be successful sometimes you have to live dangerously.' In the first minutes of the second half Klaus Augenthaler and Bernd Durnberger both missed badly, and Allan Evans cleared off the goal-line. 'Bayern had enough chances to have won three finals,' reported *Kicker*, the German sports magazine.

But creating chances is pointless if a team does not take them. Villa drove the point home forcibly in the 67th minute. Morley turned Dremmler inside out and crossed for Peter Withe to anticipate 'keeper Manfred Muller's lunge. Frighteningly, for Villa fans, the lanky centre-forward almost fell over the ball as he tried to apply the finishing touch from a few yards before somehow managing to propel it over the goal-line. Withe, ironically, had once been sold by Nottingham Forest because Brian Clough did not think he was the man to spearhead an assault on the Champions Cup.

As for Csernai, he was so shocked by defeat that he could not face the civic banquet prepared for Bayern back in Munich. His players and directors were not impressed.

It was a bad month for Bayern and their old heroes. Former coach Udo Lattek did steer Barcelona to victory in the Cup-Winners' Cup, but Franz Beckenbauer missed out on a clean sweep of European medals. Against all the odds, Hamburg, Beckenbauer's new and last club, lost to IFK Gothenburg in the UEFA Cup Final. IFK were coached by a young man named Sven-Goran Eriksson.

Not that this mattered to anyone at Villa Park.

WEDNESDAY 26 MAY 1982
DE KUIJP, ROTTERDAM

ASTON VILLA	**1**
WITHE 67	
BAYERN MUNICH	**0**

HT: 0-0. ATT: 45,000.
REF: KONRATH (FR)

VILLA:
RIMMER (SPINK 10) - SWAIN, EVANS, MCNAUGHT, WILLIAMS - BREMNER, MORTIMER*, COWANS - SHAW, WITHE, MORLEY.
MANAGER: BARTON.

BAYERN:
MULLER - DREMMLER, AUGENTHALER, WEINER, HORSMANN - DURNBERGER, KRAUS (NIEDERMAYER 79), BREITNER, MATHY (GUTTLER 52) - D. HOENESS, RUMMENIGGE.
COACH: CSERNAI.

*CAPTAIN

THE YEAR OF LIVING DANGEROUSLY

Hooliganism, terrorism and war were the background to a season in which the Champions Cup trophy went missing and Juventus strove hard to be the top club in Europe after Italy had won the World Cup

Both the football world and the world in general were becoming increasingly dangerous places. The lead-up to the World Cup in Spain in the summer of 1982 had been scarred abroad by the Falklands War and domestically by an ETA bomb which wrecked Madrid's main telephone exchange.

Italy had become the first European nation to win the World Cup three times, and their top scorer Paolo Rossi, a betting scandal villain turned hero, had now set his sights on winning the Champions Cup with Juventus.

Villa approached their defence – against Liverpool, among others – with concern about the increasing threat of hooliganism. Their semi-final resistance against Anderlecht in Brussels the previous season had been played out against a backdrop of fan violence. A smattering of Villa-following drunks had sprawled their way across Brussels, battled with local fans and police at the Parc Astrid and then scrapped their way back into the city centre after the game. At a time when continental police and clubs claimed to have sorted out their own hooligans – and when English clubs were taking a more disciplined and responsible attitude to their own fans' travel – events in Brussels had appeared ominous.

In the event, the final in Rotterdam had gone off peacefully under the watchful gaze of extra units of Dutch riot police and the problem appeared to have been laid to rest. Nevertheless Villa had to play their opening home game in 1982–83 against Besiktas behind closed doors.

RIGHT: **JUVENTUS STRIKER ZBIGNIEW BONIEK POWERS HIS WAY PAST TONY MORLEY OF ASTON VILLA. JUVE WON 5-2 ON AGGREGATE**

Further embarrassment landed on their doorstep when the Champions Cup trophy, loaned by Villa to a Midland pub function, was stolen. Fortunately the cup, insured for £750,000, was recovered later in Sheffield. But Villa did not hang on to it for much longer before losing their grip, in a more orthodox manner, to Juventus in the quarter-finals.

The writing was on the wall for Villa when Paolo Rossi headed Juventus in front after only 40 seconds of the first leg in Birmingham. The breathtaking skills of Frenchman Michel Platini allied to the pace of Poland's Zbigniew Boniek, the craft of Roberto Bettega and the steel of Marco Tardelli did the rest. Juve won 2–1 at Villa Park and 3–1 back in Turin, where Platini scored twice – the first time courtesy of a blunder by 'keeper Nigel Spink.

Platini was the man of the moment in European football. He had joined Juve after an outstanding World Cup, and took a prime role in beating Villa after just having created all France's goals in a 3–0 win over Portugal. He would go on to be Serie A's top scorer for each of his first three seasons in Turin.

Villa's exit focused attention back on the Champions Cup after a brief spell in which the Cup-Winners' Cup had stolen

much of the limelight. The reason was £3 million-worth of Argentine talent named Diego Armando Maradona, who had transferred after the World Cup finals from Argentinos Juniors to Barcelona.

Maradona had struck a hat-trick against Apollon of Cyprus on his European club debut and promised to conquer the old world just as he had conquered the new. In the event, a bout of hepatitis and then a horrendous ligament injury inflicted by Andoni Goikoetxea – known ever after as the Butcher of Bilbao – prevented him from fulfilling his potential in Catalonia.

Back in the Champions Cup, Juve's semi-final rivals were Widzew Lodz, who had seen off Liverpool 4–3 on aggregate to guarantee an end to England's six-year domination of the Champions Cup. Liverpool's season had collapsed dramatically. Weeks earlier they had been in the running for a fabulous quadruple. Now the English league was the only prize still within reach. Manager Bob Paisley raged against Widzew's gamesmanship at Anfield but, as Widzew coach Wladyslaw Zmuda said: 'We knew what we had to do – and we did it.'

Real Sociedad progressed to the semi-finals for the first time at the expense of Sporting of Portugal, while Hamburg came through 4–2 overall against Dynamo Kiev. They had walked into the last eight courtesy of the second-round withdrawal of Nendori Tirana. The champions of hard-line communist Albania accepted the option of a £1,000 fine rather than face the Marxist-Leninist revisionists from Ukraine.

Hamburg edged Real Sociedad 3–2 in the semi-finals and thus qualified for a final duel in the new Athens Olympic stadium with Juventus, who had reached their second final in 10 years by defeating Lodz 4–2 on aggregate. Juventus angrily denied that their players had used the muscle-strengthening drug carnitine, which was rumoured to have helped Italy at the World Cup. 'We would never get into that,' said coach Giovanni Trapattoni – much as Juve officials would deny any knowledge of the use in the mid-1990s of a mixture of concoctions which would earn their then club doctor Riccardo Agricola a suspended jail sentence.

ABOVE: **FULL-BACK ALAN KENNEDY GETS AWAY A SHOT AGAINST WIDZEW LODZ AT ANFIELD. LIVERPOOL WON 3–2 ON THE NIGHT BUT LOST 4–3 ON AGGREGATE**

FORTUNE SMILES ON HAPPEL'S HAMBURG

Any visitor to the post-match press conference would have supposed it an easy task to pick out the winning coach. The one sat calm and composed with a slight smile playing around the corners of his lips; the other slumped forward, shoulders hunched, lips pursed with his eyebrows tracing a frown above blank eyes. But the ghost of a smile belonged to Giovanni Trapattoni, coach of losing favourites Juventus, while the lugubrious glare belonged to Ernst Happel, coach of first-time winners Hamburg.

Happel had an excuse for being bored: he had seen it all before. He had played the big matches in the 1950s, guided Feyenoord to Cup glory in 1970 and pulled Hamburg together when the fans were bemoaning the failure to hang on to Kevin Keegan. 'My teams have always been successful against Italian clubs in Europe,' said Happel. 'There is no secret. Each match is different. We knew how Juventus would play and what we had to do. From the first minute until the last minute we played with discipline in all departments.'

If this was not exactly romantic, Happel's players were happier. Several had exorcized demons from the previous year's World Cup Final: Manni Kaltz had his revenge over

Paolo Rossi, while Horst Hrubesch had the rare privilege of turning the tables and mugging Claudio Gentile. Both Kaltz and Hrubesch were survivors of the Hamburg team beaten by Nottingham Forest three years earlier. Jimmy Hartwig being absent from midfield again – injured in 1980, suspended now – it was another survivor in Felix Magath who picked up the baton. He not only tied the loose ends together in midfield but scored the loney goal after nine minutes.

Seven years had passed since the Champions Cup had provided a final without a British presence. Any fears that this

RIGHT: **HOLGER HIERONYMUS AND JURGEN MILEWSKI ACCEPT THE ACCLAIM OF THE HAMBURG FANS**

would mean a cat-and-mouse exhibition soon vanished. Ditmar Jakobs advanced to head over the bar at one end, veteran Roberto Bettega saw a trademark header well saved by Uli Stein at the other. Then Hamburg struck the decisive blow.

Pre-match fuss had centred on the natural talents of Michel Platini and Zibi Boniek. But somewhere down the line, Juventus blundered into believing the hype. In midfield they left Magath far too much space so he could run at them, scuttle past Bettega and curl his shot beyond 41-year-old Dino Zoff.

Hamburg held the lead by imposing their tactical will on the Italians. Once, Boniek even had to turn up behind Zoff to clear off their goal-line.

Juventus had to come out to attack and, like so many Italian teams of that *catenaccio*-stifled, counter-attacking era, lacked the know-how. They could have used a perceptive playmaker such as the Irishman Liam Brady. He had guided Juve to two league titles, but had then been released to accommodate Boniek. Hamburg, at least, were grateful.

Bettega, having played his last game for Juve shortly after having scored the club's 3,000th goal in Serie A, left the stadium with a backward glance, a wave and a rueful smile.

As for Happel, the Austrian shuffled off back into seclusion with an Austrian journalist friend who was compiling his memoirs. Have you got a smile out of him? the journalist was asked. 'Oh yes,' came the reply, 'at least three times.'

LEFT: DITMAR JAKOBS RISES ABOVE A STATIC JUVENTUS DEFENCE BUT HIS HEADER FLIES OVER THE BAR

WEDNESDAY 25 MAY 1983
OLYMPIC, ATHENS

HAMBURG	1
MAGATH 9

JUVENTUS	0

HT: 1-0. ATT: 73,500.
REF: RAINEA (ROM)

HAMBURG:
STEIN - KALTZ, JAKOBS, HIERONYMUS, WEHMEYER - ROLFF, GROH, MAGATH - MILEWSKI, HRUBESCH*, BASTRUP (VON HEESEN 56).
COACH: HAPPEL.

JUVENTUS:
ZOFF - SCIREA* - GENTILE, BRIO, CABRINI - BONINI, PLATINI, TARDELLI - BONIEK, ROSSI (MAROCCHINO 56), BETTEGA.
COACH: TRAPATTONI.

*CAPTAIN

NORTHERN LIGHTS SHINE AGAIN

It was all change at many leading European clubs as major personalities jumped ship or moved on to pastures new. Elsewhere, minds were turning to new ways of turning a profit from the game

Success for northern European clubs represented the triumph of 1980s pragmatism over romance. Real Madrid and Benfica, the fading old guard, had both ended up as losers in the other two European finals of 1983. In the Cup-Winners' Cup Alfredo di Stefano was the Madrid coach who had to give best to Alex Ferguson and an Aberdeen side containing no fewer than five future British club managers in Gordon Strachan, Alex McLeish, Willie Miller, Eric Black and Mark McGhee. In the UEFA Cup, Benfica, guided by the Swede Sven-Goran Eriksson, had fallen to Belgium's Anderlecht.

Elsewhere, the veteran Johan Cruyff stalked out on Ajax, after a league-and-cup double, to join rivals Feyenoord; ex-captain Billy McNeill parted company with Celtic after guiding them to three league titles in five years; Andrea Rizzoli, president of Milan's 1963 European Champions, died at 69; UEFA's Italian president Artemio Franchi was killed in a road accident and Bob Paisley retired as manager of Liverpool after winning 13 trophies in nine years.

Joe Fagan stepped up from the Boot Room with a minimum of fuss, and his managerial debut in Europe was decisive enough: Liverpool beat OB Odense 1–0, 5–0. But there were groans from Germany. Hamburg were unhappy at being granted the holders' once traditional first-round bye. UEFA had tried to be generous in thus balancing the draw after Albania's Vllaznia Skoder were barred as punishment for Nendori's withdrawal the previous year. 'They forget football is also a business,' said Hamburg's general manager Gunter Netzer, who would later become the influential front man of the consortium handling FIFA's World Cup television rights.

Elsewhere, minds were turning to more profitable ways of organizing football. England's top clubs had driven through a crucial regulatory change by which sides would now keep all their home match income instead of splitting it with the visitors. As for the Champions Cup, Liverpool revived their

RIGHT: **LIVERPOOL GOALKEEPER BRUCE GROBBELAAR GATHERS THE BALL SAFELY AGAINST BENFICA AS DEFENDER ALAN HANSEN STANDS BY**

original 1978 discussion document suggesting that the first round be organized in mini leagues. That was perfectly feasible back before the fragmentation of the Soviet Union and Yugoslavia, and when no one envisaged the champions of minnows such as Andorra and San Marino joining in. Liverpool's proposals had stemmed from an imbalance in the first round which had seen Ajax go out to Olympiakos Piraeus, the former UEFA Cup winners IFK Gothenburg fall to Roma, and Nantes pipped by Rapid Vienna.

Hamburg's debut was thus against Dinamo Bucharest in round two, and for Happel history repeated itself. In 1970, his Feyenoord had followed up their triumph by falling at the first hurdle the following season against Romanians; now Hamburg went the same way, losing 0–3, 3–2 against a Dinamo side who would go all the way to the semi-finals.

Other second-round winners included Benfica, Liverpool – Ian Rush scoring the lone goal which beat Bilbao – Dundee United and Roma.

The Scots emulated the 1963 achievements of neighbours Dundee in reaching the last four. They conceded only two goals to Malta's Hamrun Spartans, Standard Liege and Rapid Vienna en route to a dramatic defeat by a Roma side who had snuffed out IFK, CSKA and Dynamo Berlin. Outstanding were the Brazilian midfielder Paulo Roberto Falcao, Italian World Cup-winning right-winger Bruno Conti and Roberto Pruzzo, the free-scoring centre-forward. Pruzzo netted twice in the Stadio Olimpico where Roma picked themselves up off the floor after losing 2–0 at Tannadice.

Benfica had seen off Olympiakos in the second round 3–1 overall. One of their three goals in the Estadio da Luz was scored by lanky Danish striker Michael Manniche. Foreign players were still a novelty to fans of Benfica who had ended their prohibition after the old talent mines of Angola and Mozambique had gained independence. Manniche's name – with one 'n' omitted – was duly adopted as a nickname by an admiring young fan who would make his own mark in the competition 20 years further on.

A quarter-final against Liverpool was the last draw Benfica coach Sven-Goran Eriksson wanted. 'I consider them the best team in Europe now,' he said, 'and possibly over the last decade. But we can't escape. So play them we will and we aren't going to be afraid of their reputation or ability.' Fine words, but that was all. Ian Rush scored in both legs. The difference was that he scored the only goal at Anfield but contributed to a magnificent 4–1 triumph in the Stadium of Light. Ronnie Whelan (two) and Craig Johnston scored the others.

Liverpool's semi-final defeat of Dinamo Bucharest went a similar way: a 1–0 home win followed by a decisive 2–1 success abroad. The unstoppable Rush scored twice more.

Liverpool would thus face Roma in... Rome.

LEFT: **ROMA VERSUS DUNDEE UNITED: ROBERTO PRUZZO HAS JUST SCORED AND TRIES TO GET THE BALL BACK INTO PLAY AS SOON AS POSSIBLE, WHILE BRUNO CONTI LOOKS ON**

ROMA WOBBLE IN THE SHOOT-OUT

When Roma hit a sticky patch in mid-season, Bruno Conti complained out loud that they lacked self-confidence while Roberto Pruzzo whined that they lacked courage. Those qualities – or, rather, their absence – proved crucial against Liverpool's rip-roaring resilience in Roma's own home.

For years Roma had been a byword for financial wastage. This was the club whose reward for paying a world record £250,000 for Angelo Sormani in 1963 had been one domestic cup. Eventually a more pragmatic president in Dino Viola brought in Nils Liedholm, Milan's 1958 Champions Cup Final captain, to stabilize the ship. At last Roma ended a 41-year drought by winning the 1983 *scudetto*. But then Liedholm and Conti no longer saw eye to eye, while midfield general Paulo Roberto Falcao, his contract expiring, started collecting offers for a summer auction. Even Liedholm was no longer secure. Roma had Benfica's Sven-Goran Eriksson primed and ready to move in.

Travelling to Rome presented Liverpool with surprisingly few problems.

All their decisive displays had been away from Anfield. Held at home by Bilbao, restricted to one goal at home by both Benfica and Dinamo Bucharest... still they had come through. Skipper Graeme Souness put it simply: 'We've no worries about going to Rome. When you're under pressure, it puts you on your toes.'

Souness had been sorely missed while out injured early in the season. But like all Liverpool's stars, he had a habit of coming good just when it mattered – like Kenny Dalglish, who had returned as a match-winning substitute against Benfica after a facial injury; like Ian Rush, whose first goal in the return against Dinamo Bucharest had been his 100th in Liverpool colours and his 40th of a remarkable season.

Liverpool had happy memories of the Olimpico from 1977.

RIGHT: **LIVERPOOL FANS CREATE A SEA OF RED IN THE OLYMPIC STADIUM IN ROME**

But the 1984 final was not a patch on the Monchengladbach victory. The two men who could have ignited the flames, Falcao and Dalglish, both disappointed. Falcao, latest emperor of Rome, wandered around midfield looking barely interested. Up front Francesco Graziani was hampered by age, and Pruzzo by a stomach complaint.

Phil Neal struck the opener after 13 minutes with the first goal attempt worthy of the name; Pruzzo back-headed an equalizer just before the break after enormous perseverance by Conti. Roma looked a different team for 20 minutes after the interval but then subsided, and Liverpool revived in the last quarter of an hour before Swedish referee Erik Fredriksson whistled up extra time. Roma created a handful of half-chances on the way to the penalty shoot-out in which, confronted by the wobbly knees of Bruce Grobbelaar, they lost their nerve.

Liverpool started badly, with Steve Nicol shooting over the bar, but Conti and Graziani did the same with Roma's second and fourth attempts. Alan Kennedy, the unlikely 1981 match-winner in Paris, stepped up to beat Franco Tancredi and secure Liverpool's fourth Champions Cup.

Falcao, having opted out of the penalty contest, went overnight from hero to scapegoat. Roma's fans saw him play only four more times.

BELOW: **ROMA'S FRANCESCO GRAZIANI BLAZES A VITAL PENALTY OVER THE BAR TO HAND THE EUROPEAN CUP TO LIVERPOOL FOR THE FOURTH TIME**

WEDNESDAY 30 MAY 1984
OLIMPICO, ROME

LIVERPOOL	1
NEAL 15	
ROMA	1
PRUZZO 38	

AFTER EXTRA TIME
LIVERPOOL WON 4-2 ON PENS
HT: 1-1. 90 MIN: 1-1. ATT: 69,693.
REF: FREDRIKSSON (SWE)

LIVERPOOL:
GROBBELAAR - NEAL, LAWRENSON, HANSEN, A. KENNEDY - WHELAN, LEE, SOUNESS*, JOHNSTON (NICOL 72) - DALGLISH (ROBINSON 94), RUSH. MANAGER: FAGAN.

ROMA:
TANCREDI - NAPPI, RIGHETTI, NELA, BONETTI - FALCAO, TONINHO CEREZO (STRUKELY 115), DI BARTOLOMEI* - CONTI, PRUZZO (CHIERICO 64), GRAZIANI. COACH: LIEDHOLM.

*CAPTAIN

DESPERATE TIMES FOR FOOTBALL

The season started off well but went downhill fast as hooliganism mired the game and a Leeds United fan came to be murdered. It all culminated in the Bradford City fire and tragedy at Heysel

Champions Cup football in 1984–85 remains largely irrelevant. The only statistic of concern is the figure 39: the death toll among Juventus fans in the Heysel Stadium in Brussels before the final against Liverpool.

Yet the season had begun amid enormous promise at both international and domestic levels. Ian Rush, with his 32 goals, had been awarded the Golden Boot as the leading league marksman in Europe; Diego Maradona had left Barcelona for Napoli for a world-record £5 million; Karl-Heinz Rummenigge had quit Bayern Munich for Internazionale; Barcelona had gambled on a bright young English coach in Terry Venables; and Spain's superstars went on strike for a period of three weeks to win better pay further down the league.

Liverpool began the season slowly. They took just 11 points from their first nine games in the Football League, lost 1–0 to Independiente of Argentina in the World Club Cup in Tokyo, and

fell 2–0 to Juventus in the European Supercup amid the snows of Turin. The departure of Graeme Souness for Sampdoria took its toll, and newcomers such as Denmark's Jan Molby in midfield and Paul Walsh in attack needed time to adjust.

In the Champions Cup, however, it was a different tale. Lech Poznan, Benfica (again), FK Austria and Panathinaikos failed to disturb Liverpool's progress back to the final. Juventus matched them with victories over Ilves Tampere of Finland, Grasshopper, Sparta Prague and Bordeaux.

Elsewhere in Europe, Real Madrid won the UEFA Cup 3–1 on aggregate against Videoton of Hungary despite missing a penalty, having two goals disallowed for contentious offside decisions and conceding a rare home defeat in the second leg of the final. In the Cup-Winners' Cup, Everton, from the other side of Liverpool's Stanley Park, did English football proud by defeating Rapid Vienna 3–1 in Rotterdam.

In all three competitions, however, the atmosphere surrounding matches was deteriorating fast. In the Cup-Winners' Cup, Celtic were ordered to replay their second-round tie against Rapid after a missile – it remains unclear whether it was a coin or a whisky bottle – appeared to fell one of the Austrian players during the Scots' 3–0 win at Celtic Park.

In the UEFA Cup, Internazionale's Giuseppe Bergomi was knocked to the ground by a marble thrown from the crowd during their semi-final defeat by Real in Madrid. Inter, unlike Rapid, failed to obtain a replay despite taking their case to appeal. It was, said the Italian weekly *Guerin Sportivo*, recalling Inter's contentious 1971–72 scrap with Borussia Monchengladbach, a case of 'long-range rough justice'.

On 11 May, a Leeds United fan was murdered in a fight between rival fans during their last game of the season at Birmingham City.

In separate incidents, hundreds of fans of both clubs swarmed menacingly over the touchlines and it took a Light Brigade-style charge down the pitch by mounted police to repel them. Policemen and women, trapped at the back of the Leeds end, were punched, kicked and battered with pieces of wood wrenched off the advertising hoardings.

The next day, however, the battle of Birmingham did not even make the front page. Instead, it was eclipsed in pain by the deadly fire which had raged through the 76-year-old wooden main stand at Valley Parade, in Bradford.

Tales of heroism were mixed with tales of horror. One of the Bradford players ran to the burning stand to rescue his four-year-old son. Other supporters were not so lucky. The exit doors had been locked to prevent late-comers gaining free entry. Fans at the back of the stand had nowhere to run, and 53 died.

It was the worst British football tragedy since 66 Rangers and Celtic fans had lost their lives at Ibrox Park, in Glasgow, in 1971.

ABOVE: **FULL-BACK JIM BEGLIN SCORES THE FOURTH GOAL FOR LIVERPOOL AS THEY RUN OUT 4-0 WINNERS AGAINST PANATHINAIKOS IN THE SEMI-FINAL FIRST LEG AT ANFIELD**

THE GAME THAT DIDN'T MATTER

Eighteen days after the Bradford fire – with football still numb – Liverpool, Juventus and their fans turned up in Brussels for the Champions Cup Final. With hooliganism rampant, Liverpool had already expressed misgivings at the decision of UEFA and the local federation to permit open ticket sales in the Belgian capital. This, they pointed out, undermined the pre-planned segregation arrangements and meant that English and Italian fans would end up on the same terracing.

Pre-match coverage on television and radio might have been taken up by discussion of Liverpool's shock appointment of Kenny Dalglish as player-manager to succeed retirement-bound Joe Fagan. Instead, to their increasing concern and then voice-altering shock, the world's commentators found themselves describing deadly mayhem.

Trouble began around an hour before the scheduled kick-off. Both in the centre of Brussels and around the Heysel the atmosphere had been good and the riot police had kept a low profile. But Sectors Y and Z, up behind the one goal, were recipes for disaster with Juventus and Liverpool fans separated only by a low chicken-wire fence and a mere scattering of police.

Someone threw a bottle. Quickly a regular exchange of missiles developed across the 20 yards dividing the fans. Those police on the terrace were too few in number to dive in. So, with no one to keep the peace, several hundred Liverpool fans charged across the terrace. And charged again.

The Juventus fans retreated both back and down the terracing, crushing those at the end against a free-standing wall which overlooked an exit route from the pitch area.

Then the wall gave way and bricks, concrete and fans all cascaded down on to the ground beneath.

To see death unleashed so suddenly in so dramatic a fashion caused some police to 'freeze' – as one senior officer put it later. It may only have taken seconds for medical help to begin to arrive, and minutes to launch the emergency drill, but for 39 fans, it was already too late.

Riot police drew their batons, ran up on to the terracing and began to flail away at the Liverpool followers. That prompted several hundred trouble-seeking Italian fans to spill out over the terracing at the other end of the stadium and advance, spoiling for a fight themselves. As more police erupted to deal with that incursion, Joe Fagan came out to appeal for calm; so did some of the Juventus players.

RIGHT: **A RIOT POLICEMAN AT HEYSEL CAN DO VERY LITTLE IN THE AFTERMATH OF DISASTER**

Word began to filter through to the crowd of the casualty estimates. Repeated pleas for calm were interspersed with an ominous stream of appeals for friends and relatives of named Italians to come to the stadium office.

Behind Sector Z and out in the car park, tents were hastily thrown up in order that the injured and the dying could be shielded and cared for. Police reinforcements circled the pitch and, one hour 28 minutes late, Liverpool kicked off.

The decision to play on remains controversial to this day. Grisly and offensive for some, playing on at least kept the remaining fans in the stadium, heading off the certainty of more violence outside the ground and averting traffic problems for the emergency services.

Back on the pitch Liverpool lost Mark Lawrenson after only three minutes to a shoulder injury. An even first half ended goalless, but Juventus won the game 12 minutes into the second half.

Michel Platini converted a penalty after substitute Gary Gillespie was judged to have brought down Zibi Boniek. Liverpool protested in vain that the foul had been committed outside the box. Juventus thus took the cup back to Turin, shame-faced that they had run to their fans in celebration at the final whistle.

The Belgian legal service eventually prosecuted UEFA, the Belgian federation and the stadium authorities for inadequate security and ticket distribution. The Football Association withdrew its clubs from European competition, a decision which was ultimately overtaken when UEFA instituted its own indefinite ban with three years extra for Liverpool (reduced to one year extra on appeal).

'I don't know what's happening to football supporters,' said Fagan in a state of deep depression the next day. 'It's certainly not a sport any more. What is a game of football when that number of people are dead?'

LEFT: **AS THE LIVERPOOL PLAYERS TRAIL ROUND THE TRACK LED BY MANAGER JOE FAGAN, THE EXPRESSIONS ON THEIR FACES TELL THEIR OWN STORY**

WEDNESDAY 29 MAY 1985
HEYSEL, BRUSSELS

JUVENTUS	1
PLATINI 57 PEN	
LIVERPOOL	**0**

HT: 0-0. ATT: 60,000.
REF: DAINA (SWZ)

JUVENTUS:
TACCONI - SCIREA* - FAVERO, BRIO, CABRINI - BONINI, PLATINI, TARDELLI - BRIASCHI (PRANDELLI 84), P. ROSSI (VIGNOLA 89), BONIEK.
COACH: TRAPATTONI.

LIVERPOOL:
GROBBELAAR - NEAL*, LAWRENSON (GILLESPIE 3), HANSEN, BEGLIN - WHELAN, NICOL, WARK - DALGLISH, RUSH, WALSH (JOHNSTON 46).
MANAGER: FAGAN.

* CAPTAIN

THE HEALING PROCESS BEGINS

In the wake of Heysel, English teams were banned from European competition, leaving the way open for the other nations. And Terry Venables moved to Barcelona just as Maradona left for Naples...

Football's own fallout from Heysel was nothing compared with the human tragedy, but it was extensive.

Bert Millichip, chairman of the Football Association, answered the public mood when he unilaterally withdrew English clubs from European competition, but the haste in which he acted later drew revisionist attack. Nowhere was the European exit felt more keenly than in Liverpool. Everton's finest team in years had just won both the Cup-Winners' Cup and the league championship. They could have gone a long way in the Champions Cup in 1985–86.

Millichip and the Football Association – which ratifies all European entries – volunteered the withdrawal not merely as a statement of regret but as the only practical way to protect villages, towns and cities across the continent from the marauding violence which so often accompanied English clubs.

UEFA, under Jacques Georges, a Frenchman who rarely evinced any sympathies for the English game, accepted Millichip's gesture... and extended it for an indefinite period. The ban was still in force in 1990 when illness forced Georges to give way to Sweden's Lennart Johansson, who wasted little time bringing England back into the fold.

The technical and tactical repercussions of the five-year absence hampered English football for a decade. Some English analysts considered the Champions Cup devalued by the ban. Few abroad thought so.

One consolation for English reporters, wishing to stay on the European trail themselves, was that they had a perfect excuse: his name was Terry Venables.

In spring 1984, Barcelona president Josep Lluis Nunez had needed a new coach. His target was Bobby Robson, then at Ipswich. Robson reigned at Portman Road, under the benign gaze of the Cobbold brewing family, much as Alf Ramsey had done 20 years earlier. Like Ramsey, Robson was bound for the England job and a knighthood. He was also a man of his word and refused to break his Ipswich contract for the Barcelona dream.

Nunez, hugely disappointed, asked Robson to recommend an alternative. Robson suggested 42-year-old Venables, then turning out a bright young team at Queen's Park Rangers in west London. It says everything about Nunez's respect for Robson that he did, indeed, gamble on a coach who was virtually unknown outside Britain.

Venables, from Bethnal Green in east London, had played for England at every possible level from youth, amateur, Under-23 and B to senior level. A mainstream club career with Chelsea and Tottenham was his springboard to management. Venables was cute and sharp. His public relations skills were as high class as his innovative coaching talents. Later the media would be split in their assessment of Venables, but that was not until after the complexities of his business life – his pubs and his clubs – spilled over into the football world.

In 1984, Venables was on the way up. As soon as he secured the Barcelona job, he took Spanish lessons and, with a small scrap of paper as cue, gave his opening address to the *cules* (Barcelona fans, known for historical reasons as 'backsides') in Spanish. That gesture alone won him thousands of sympathizers, but guiding Barcelona to the league title in his first season, 1984–85, turned them into worshippers.

Barcelona had sold Diego Maradona on to Napoli for £5 million. He went out of the revolving door just as Venables spun in. Venables was not involved in the deal but, clearly, there was no way the Argentine would have accepted orders from an Englishman so soon after the Falklands war. Barcelona had been growing more and more embarrassed by the antics around town of Maradona and his notorious 'Clan' and were relieved when Napoli, with the financial support of a local bank and the approval of the *camorra*, their equivalent of the mafia, came up with the fig leaf of a world-record fee.

Venables imported Scottish centre-forward Steve Archibald, many of whose goals were laid on by Bernd Schuster, a headstrong German. Schuster, his career guided by a Svengali-like wife, was free to concentrate on his club career after falling out with national coach Jupp Derwall and refusing to play for West Germany.

They finished 10 points clear of runners-up Atletico Madrid in the Spanish league, losing only two of their 34 games. Already the name of Barcelona appeared to be virtually engraved on the 1986 Champions Cup.

That impression was enhanced by the charmed life which bore the Catalans to the final. They beat Sparta Prague and FC Porto on away goals, squeezed Juventus 2–1, then hit back from 3–0 down in the semi-final to beat IFK Gothenburg on penalties. Even more luckily for Venables and Barcelona, the final was to be held in Spain.

LEFT: BERND SCHUSTER, THE TALENTED BUT TEMPERAMENTAL STAR WHO FELL OUT WITH SO MANY PEOPLE, ON THE BALL FOR BARCELONA AGAINST IFK GOTHENBURG. THE FOLLOWING YEAR, HE MOVED ON TO REAL MADRID

BARCELONA'S LUCK FINALLY RUNS OUT

The popular peak of Terry Venables's managerial career was leading hosts England to the semi-finals of the 1996 European Championship, where they lost on penalties after extra time to Germany. But England, that night, were not as strong favourites as were Barcelona in May 1986.

Turning up, it seemed, would be enough. It was not even as if they were playing one of the other giants of the European game. Opponents in the Estadio Sanchez Pizjuan were Steaua Bucharest, the Romanian army team.

Only once before in 30 years had an eastern European club even managed to reach the final: when Partizan Belgrade lost to aristocratic Spanish opposition, Real Madrid, in 1966.

Stage, history and omens all pointed to Barcelona. No attention was paid to doubters who pointed out that Barca had scored only nine goals in eight games en route. Steaua had put a superior 13 past Vejle, Honved, Kuusysi Lahti and Anderlecht.

Former champions had long since fallen by the wayside: Juventus to Barcelona, Ajax to Porto and Bayern Munich to Anderlecht. Only five small plane-loads of Romanian fans flew in to Seville. To a man, the remainder of the 70,000 crowd were all willing on Barcelona to claim, at long last, that elusive first Champions Cup.

FINAL DE LA COPA DE EUROPA DE CLUBS CAMPEONES

PROGRAMA OFICIAL

Miércoles, 7 Mayo 1986 - 8.15 de la tarde
Estadio Ramon Sanchez Pizjuan, Sevilla

F.C. BARCELONA
STEAUA DE BUCAREST

RIGHT: **STEAUA BUCHAREST HERO HELMUT DUCADAM TIPS THE BALL OVER THE BAR TO SAFETY**

FAR RIGHT: **STEAUA BUCHAREST WERE ONLY THE SECOND EASTERN EUROPEAN SIDE TO WIN THE CHAMPIONS CUP BUT THEY KNEW HOW TO CELEBRATE**

The pressures on Barcelona of past and present meant that a classic was too much to expect. Venables had counselled long and hard against complacency, but in vain. As his Romanian counterpart, Emerich Jenei, said, 'Barcelona had everything to lose, we had everything to win.'

It was no surprise that French referee Michel Vautrot showed his yellow card in quick succession to three Spaniards and one Romanian and was then minded to lecture both captains before brawn took over entirely from brain.

Barcelona commanded the early possession but found few gaps in a Steaua defence whose sweeper, Miodrag Belodedici, appeared to have been playing European finals all his life. Then, gradually, the Romanians began to gain in confidence and nerve. Even so, it was a surprise five minutes before the

end when Venables, trying to shake things up, took off Schuster. 'He looked tired,' said the manager later. Schuster disagreed. He stalked straight to the dressing rooms with never a glance at the dug-out.

In extra time, Venables replaced Archibald with Pichi Alonso, whose hat-trick had inspired the semi-final turnaround against IFK, but to no avail.

Thus the final turned on penalties – the worst sequence ever seen at such a level. Not until shot number five did anyone score, and it was Steaua's Marius Lacatus. Gavril Balint converted their next.

In the meantime, 'keeper Helmut Ducadam had saved from Alexanco, Pedraza and Alonso, and then, finally and decisively, he saved from Marcos. The winger thus missed the opportunity to become the first son to emulate his father and win the European Cup, father being Real Madrid defender Marquitos.

Family concerns of a different nature weighed on Barcelona captain Jose Sanchez, whose wife had given birth a few hours before kick-off. He said: 'This is both the happiest and saddest day of my life.'

The argumentative Schuster did not line up for Barcelona the next season; nor did 'keeper Urruti, since Barcelona had already agreed to buy fellow Basque Andoni Zubizarreta from Bilbao; Venables lasted a further 16 months.

And Steaua's hero Ducadam? On holiday a few weeks later, he suffered a thrombosis in his right arm which very nearly killed him. He never played again.

WEDNESDAY 7 MAY 1986
SANCHEZ PIZJUAN, SEVILLE

STEAUA BUCHAREST	0
BARCELONA	0

AFTER EXTRA TIME
STEAUA WON 2-0 ON PENS.
HT: 0-0. 90 MIN: 0-0. ATT: 75,000.
REF: VAUTROT (FR)

STEAUA:
DUCADAM - BELODEDICI - IOVAN*, BUMBESCU, BARBULESCU - BALINT, BALAN (IORDANESCU 72), BOLONI, MAJARU - LACATUS, PITURCA (RADU 107).
COACH: JENEI.

BARCELONA:
URRUTI - GERARDO, MIGUELI, ALEXANCO*, JULIO ALBERTO - MARCOS, VICTOR, SCHUSTER (MORATALLA 85), PEDRAZA - ARCHIBALD (PICHI ALONSO 106), CARRASCO.
COACH: VENABLES.

*CAPTAIN

THE ENGLISH ARE NOT MISSED

Barcelona added Lineker and Hughes to their ranks as they mounted a further attack on the supremacy of Real Madrid. Behind closed doors, new formats were being suggested for the future of the game

The summer of 1986 belonged to Diego Maradona, who excited Napoli's Italian dreams by the manner in which he inspired Argentina's World Cup triumph in Mexico. Napoli fans took almost as much pleasure as Argentine supporters in the malicious deception of the 'Hand of God' goal against England.

But Napoli had finished only third in Serie A. Juventus were back in the Champions Cup, strengthened by Denmark's Michael Laudrup as they pursued the twin target of achieving their European dream while staying ahead of the game in Italy – and of Milan refinanced by media tycoon Silvio Berlusconi.

Meanwhile the only way in which English league stars could now pursue their European dream was by moving abroad.

Thus England's Gary Lineker – six-goal top scorer in Mexico – and Wales's Mark Hughes quit Everton and Manchester United respectively to spearhead Barcelona's domestic pursuit of Real Madrid.

Certainly there was no immediate prospect of a return for English clubs. UEFA president Jacques Georges observed that the hooligan situation was growing worse, not better, after fans of West Ham and Manchester United caused problems en route to pre-season friendlies in Holland. Then, when Bradford hosted neighbours Leeds, a chip kiosk was set alight, missiles were hurled and fans, mindful of Valley Parade's recent tragedy, flooded on to the pitch in search of safety.

RIGHT: **THE BRILLIANT MICHEL PLATINI OF JUVENTUS TAKES ON REAL MADRID'S CENTRAL DEFENSIVE PAIRING**

Back in Europe, English clubs were not missed as Real Madrid returned to the Champions Cup after two seasons of success in the UEFA Cup. Dutch coach Leo Beenhakker looked for goals to Emilio Butragueno, who had scored four for Spain against Denmark at the World Cup.

Steaua apart, two other former champions set out in hope: Celtic and Bayern Munich. Bayern, having invested the £3-million Rummenigge fee wisely, had won the German double, pipping Werder Bremen on the last day of the league season then beating Stuttgart 5-2 in the cup final. Their dubious reward was a testing first-round start against PSV Eindhoven who had finally persuaded parent company Philips to invest in breaking the Ajax/Feyenoord stranglehold on Dutch football. Leading PSV's assault on Europe were Ruud Gullit, winger Gerald Vanenburg and Danish midfielder Frank Arnesen.

In the event, PSV did not manage even one goal over the two legs. Bayern won it in Eindhoven in the first game with strikes from Reinhold Mathy, and progressed past FK Austria and Anderlecht to a semi-final against Real Madrid. The Spanish champions, after an easy start against Young Boys Berne, had struggled to edge out Juventus and Red Star.

The second-round draw which matched Madrid against Juventus infuriated both clubs, while UEFA officials were none too pleased either. In the event, Madrid won on penalties after each club had won 1-0 at home. But that was not the point. The three European club competitions were showing a four per cent increase in attendances, and the financial benefits of a successful run were becoming more and more significant.

Behind closed doors in West Germany, UEFA leaders considered a blueprint for the future. The Champions Cup had a regular, convenient entry of 32 clubs. The favourite proposal was for eight to be seeded into groups of four clubs each. They could play each other home and away and the group winners could go on to the knockout quarter-finals.

Few dissenters raised their voices. UEFA had already created a hardship fund to reimburse the minnows, in the main from Scandinavia, Cyprus and Luxembourg, who found that travel costs on their (usually) single away leg outweighed their income from the return. Now everyone, giants and minnows alike, could be guaranteed three home games.

The idea was circulated to the national associations for further consideration.

In the meantime, another new name was breaking into European club consciousness: FC Porto. Europe, from a Portuguese perspective, had been almost exclusively the preserve of the Lisbon giants Benfica and Sporting. Porto, from the north, were the poor relations of the so-called 'big three'. Yet Porto had a longer European pedigree, having been Portugal's first competitors in the Champions Cup, albeit unsuccessful ones, falling at the very first hurdle to Bilbao in 1956-57.

In 1978-79 Porto went out in the first round again, and they lost in the second round both the following year and in 1985-86. So it was a matter of both surprise and rejoicing when victories over Rabat Ajax of Malta, Viktovice and Brondby lifted them into the last four in the spring of 1987.

The final would thus pit newcomers (Porto or Kiev) against former champions (Bayern or Madrid).

PORTO UPSTAGE BAYERN'S SUPERSTARS

Vienna's Prater stadium was a perverse choice of venue given that its 60,000 capacity contrasted starkly with the average 4,000 attendances at local league matches. But the choice was an acknowledgement of the three-year rebuilding of the Prater demanded after lumps of concrete and cladding began falling off the old façade.

Collapsing façade summed up the failures of Dynamo Kiev and Real Madrid to reach the final. In Kiev's case, doubling up as the Soviet national team had sapped even the scientifically applied resources of their coach Valeri Lobanovsky. They lost 2–1 both home and away against Porto.

Madrid's prospects were wrecked by a 4–1 defeat in a stormy first leg away to Bayern in Munich. Madrid finished with nine men after the expulsions of Juanito and Mino. 'Stupid' was what playmaker Michel said of Juanito, who had retaliated against Lothar Matthaeus by stamping on the German's head and back. Madrid won the return 1–0, a comparative failure which prompted a missile-throwing finale from Madrid's notorious *Ultrasur* supporters.

Bayern approached the final having studied videos of Porto's defeat by Juventus in the 1984 Cup-Winners' Cup Final. That was good news for the Portuguese, who had changed personnel significantly and were also weakened by injuries. They presented a cosmopolitan mixture: forwards Celso and

Juary were both Brazilian, goalkeeper Jozsef Mlynarczyk was Polish, and raiding winger Rabah Madjer an Algerian World Cup star. That was without counting home-grown favourites such as Paulo Futre, their brilliant attacking starlet, and the prolific Fernando Gomes, former winner of the European Golden Boot.

The spectre of crowd trouble haunted the run-up to the final. At the Cup-Winners' Cup Final the previous week, Ajax's 10,000 travelling fans behaved themselves perfectly after Marco Van Basten's winner against Lokomotive Leipzig in Athens, but thousands had run amok in Amsterdam.

RIGHT: LIKE SO MANY BEFORE HIM, JOAO PINTO CANNOT RESIST PUTTING THE CUP ON HIS HEAD. IN VIENNA, PORTO PLAYERS WERE SO EAGER TO RUN THE CUP OVER TO THEIR SUPPORTERS THAT THEY FORGOT TO COLLECT THEIR WINNERS' MEDALS BEFOREHAND

UEFA had apparently learned nothing from Heysel. In Vienna several thousand Bayern fans found themselves in the heart of the Porto section. Portuguese travel agencies had been unable to sell their ticket allocations. UEFA impounded some, but at least 1,300 were acquired by German agencies at three times face value.

On the night, happily, it all went off peacefully. This was due partly to the deployment of 1,100 police, partly to the good sense of both batches of fans, and partly to the most engrossing final since Liverpool's 1977 win over Borussia Monchengladbach.

Bayern scored first through left-winger Ludwig Kogl with the complicity of referee Alexis Ponnet. The Belgian had wrongly ordered Jaime Magalhaes not to stand in front of Hans Pflugler at the throw-in which led to the goal. The Germans then gave up all serious attempt to score again. Bayern had taken single-goal final victories over Rangers in the 1967 Cup-Winners' Cup and over Saint-Etienne in the 1976 Champions Cup. This time, however, in the last 13 minutes that defensive shield buckled.

First Madjer cheekily back-heeled an equalizer from Juary's short cross, and then he crossed from the left to the far post where the Brazilian substitute shot home. Porto's players were so delighted to see skipper Joao Pinto collect the Cup that in their haste to run the trophy to their delirious fans they forgot to collect their winners' medals.

LEFT: PAULO FUTRE, PORTO'S BRILLIANT YOUNG STARLET, MESMERISES THE BAYERN DEFENCE WITH HIS CLOSE CONTROL AS HE EMBARKS ON ANOTHER INCISIVE RUN

WEDNESDAY 27 MAY 1987
PRATER, VIENNA

FC PORTO   2
MADJER 77, JUARY 81

BAYERN MUNICH   1
KOGL 25

HT: 0-1. ATT: 62,000.
REF: PONNET (BEL).

PORTO:
MLYNARCZYK - JOAO PINTO*, EDUARDO LUIS, CELSO, IGNACIO (FRASCO 66) - QUIM (JUARY 46), JAIME MAGALHAES, SOUSA, ANDRE - FUTRE, MADJER.
COACH: JORGE.

BAYERN:
PFAFF - WINKELHOEFER, NACHTWEIH, EDER, PFLUGLER - FLICK (LUNDE 82), MATTHAEUS*, BREHME - M RUMMENIGGE, D. HOENESS, KOGL.
COACH: LATTEK.

*CAPTAIN

BUSINESS AS USUAL

Real Madrid took on Napoli amid eerie silence and before a crowd of 499, which didn't stop sparks from flying. Meanwhile Partizani of Albania were expelled for having four players sent off in one game

'Now for the Champions Cup,' bawled Diego Maradona after inspiring Napoli to their first Italian league title. Tens of thousands of Neapolitans, many of whom had probably never set foot within the Stadio San Paolo, ran out into the streets singing, chanting and dancing after the 1–1 draw with Fiorentina which sealed the title. It was a poor game but, together with Internazionale's 1–0 defeat by Atalanta – former Nottingham Forest hero Trevor Francis scoring the goal – was enough to secure Napoli's title with one game to go.

As Napoli awaited the first-round draw, their domestic rivals went into the transfer market. Juventus bought Ian Rush from Liverpool to replace Michel Platini, who had retired at just

RIGHT: **PSV'S RONALD KOEMAN, WHO COMBINED ELEGANCE ON THE BALL WITH A STEELY APPROACH OFF IT, BEATS THE CHALLENGE OF A BORDEAUX PLAYER**

32, while Milan put their faith in the Dutch pair of Marco van Basten from Ajax and Ruud Gullit from PSV.

Napoli were novices in terms of European experience and were thus unseeded in the draw... which was UEFA's only excuse for how they came to be matched against Real Madrid. Both clubs were shocked – Madrid because they would have to face Maradona and co without any support, the excesses of the *Ultrasur* against Bayern having earned Madrid a two-match closed-door order. (In the end, the second match was opened up on appeal, but played in a stadium 350 kilometres from the Spanish capital.)

Napoli had strengthened their attack by signing the fine Brazilian centre-forward Careca, but Maradona's preparations for Madrid were characteristically turbulent. First he was involved in a will he/won't he saga over his appearance in the English Football League centenary match. Next came caustic comments about Madrid's Hugo Sanchez and Emilio Butragueno, followed by a row with Napoli's own fans, who jeered him when he missed a penalty in a friendly against Argentine champions Rosario Central.

What should have been one of the biggest European club occasions was thus played out in front of 499 staff, officials and media in the Estadio Bernabeu, which was nevertheless surrounded by riot police with water cannon on account of unrealized fears that the *Ultrasur* might try to storm the gates.

Out on the pitch the mood was bad-tempered and the quality patchy. Madrid attacked down the wings, forcing Maradona deep to assist Italian resistance. Playmaker Michel converted a penalty in the first half and defender Miguel Tendillo bludgeoned another goal in the second. The players kicked and snapped as they left the pitch at the final whistle in an eerie silence.

Naples, for the return, was the exact opposite. Even a cacophonous 82,231 crowd, however, paying Italian record receipts of £2.2 million, could not prevent Madrid, for the 12th time, seeing off Italian opposition. Defender Giovanni Francini shot Napoli ahead on nine minutes, Careca missed an open goal on 40, and Butragueno punished him and Napoli with an equalizer three minutes later. Napoli faded under the mental pressure of needing to score three times to win the tie. Not even Maradona could generate a spark of inspiration. His solitary European club trophy would thus be the UEFA Cup, in 1989.

Madrid–Napoli was not the only tie which provided first-round heat. Partizani of Albania were expelled from European competition and banned for four years after having four players sent off in a 4–0 defeat by Benfica in Lisbon. Ironically, Partizani had been assisted to their Albanian title win by

points penalties imposed on domestic rivals Dinamo, Nentori and Flamurtari for poor disciplinary records.

The remainder of the competition proceeded comparatively peacefully. Madrid believed their name was on the trophy when they beat holders Porto, then took revenge over Bayern Munich, only to slip up on away goals against PSV in the semi-finals. They took defeat badly. Michel and Hugo Sanchez were banned for nine and three matches respectively for jostling referee Bruno Galler (bans reduced on appeals to three matches and one match).

PSV were carrying all before them both at home and abroad. In Holland they had set a national record with 17 consecutive wins. Ironically, the directors remained doubtful as to whether coach Guus Hiddink had the requisite experience for the job.

Benfica followed up the Partizani scrap by knocking out Aarhus, Anderlecht – avenging their 1983 UEFA Cup Final defeat – and Steaua in the semi-finals. They reached the final under their third coach in a year.

Englishman John Mortimore had been replaced after winning the 1987 league title, and his Danish successor, Ebbe Skovdahl, had been sacked by a newly elected board after guiding Benfica into the Champions Cup quarter-finals. Antonio Oliveira, better known as Toni, completed the job of driving them on to Stuttgart.

ABOVE: **GRAEME SOUNESS, THE VOLUBLE PLAYER-MANAGER OF RANGERS, PROTESTS HIS INNOCENCE AFTER A GROIN-HIGH CHALLENGE ON A STEAUA BUCHAREST PLAYER**

PSV HIT BENFICA FOR SIX IN SHOOT-OUT

Ronald Koeman trotted out for the Champions Cup Final bearing the label of the most controversial player in Europe. This was not because of his iron tackling in the heart of the PSV defence, nor because of the power of his free-kicks and penalties. His notoriety owed everything to the force of his alleged words.

Koeman was reported in a Dutch magazine as praising a team-mate for putting French playmaker Jean Tigana out of PSV's quarter-final against Bordeaux. The article caused a furore, and Koeman was fined and suspended briefly by PSV. Koeman was also then banned for three matches by UEFA.

This meant that he would miss both legs of the semi-final against Real Madrid as well as the final, if PSV qualified.

Koeman promptly denied the remarks, the magazine admitted misquoting him and the president of the Dutch federation endorsed PSV's appeal.

UEFA originally proposed hearing it in May, but now PSV complained that speed was of the essence and the European federation duly brought it forward to the morning of the second leg against Madrid. Koeman's ban was cut to that night's game only, freeing him to play in the final if PSV qualified without him – which they did.

PSV managed it just the same way they had beaten Bordeaux in the quarter-finals, on the away-goals rule. This was hardly surprising. PSV turned up in Stuttgart having scored nine goals in eight games, while Benfica had scored

nine in seven, having been spared a second leg against Partizani by virtue of that first-round walkover.

Not until the 34th minute of the final did right-winger Gerald Vanenburg produce the first shot of the game, forcing a diving save from Silvino – the same Silvino who later turned up at Porto and then Chelsea as goalkeeper-coach.

At half-time it was goalless, and spectacle was notable for its absence. Koeman shot over the top from a touched free-kick before Benfica's lone attacking threat, Rui Aguas, was forced out of the game by a hamstring injury. With him went most of Benfica's hopes of emulating the cup-winning achievements of his father, Jose Aguas.

Extra time came and went with little more to entertain the crowd, and thus the final went to penalties for the second time in three years. Koeman rammed home PSV's first and everyone followed suit in the 10-kick sequence. When the score reached 5–5, it went to sudden death. Then Anton Janssen scored before Hans Van Breukelen crowned an outstanding season by stopping Veloso's underpowered kick.

PSV coach Guus Hiddink had every reason to be satisfied. His team had already won the Dutch league and cup, and now they had completed the treble. As he said, 'I don't like penalties, but justice was done.' Prophetically, he also tipped Holland, with its nucleus of PSV players, to do well in the European Championship finals back in West Germany.

Benfica coach Toni thought his team 'lost with dignity'. He added, 'Tonight we have written another golden page in Benfica's history.'

'Do you call three goal efforts in 120 minutes golden?' he was asked. Toni did not answer.

WEDNESDAY 25 MAY 1988
NECKAR, STUTTGART

PSV EINDHOVEN	**0**
BENFICA	**0**

AFTER EXTRA TIME
PSV WON 6-5 ON PENS.
HT: 0-0. 90 MINS: 0-0. ATT: 68,000.
REF: AGNOLIN (IT).

PSV:
VAN BREUKELEN - GERETS*, NIELSEN, R. KOEMAN, HEINTZE - VANENBURG, LERBY, VAN AERLE, LINSKENS - KIEFT, GILLHAUS (JANSSEN 107).
COACH: HIDDINK.

BENFICA:
SILVINO - VELOSO, DITO, MOZER, ALVARO - CHIQUINHO, SHEU*, ELZO, PACHECO - M. MAGNUSSON (HAJRI 112), RUI AGUAS (VALDO 56).
COACH: TONI.

*CAPTAIN

THE BENEFITS OF HORSE SENSE

Johan Cruyff returned to Barca as manager but it was in Italy that football caught a glimpse of its new money-making future as Silvio Berlusconi took over the reins at Milan and went to work on his side

Two diverse events in the summer of 1988 – quite apart from Johan Cruyff's return to Barcelona as coach and Holland's European Championship victory – appeared to be setting the agenda for the next two decades. The first was the Italian league triumph of Milan, powered by the aggressive, acquisitive Silvio Berlusconi. The second was UEFA's imposition of a limit of four foreigners per team in European competition, 'to protect the clubs, the competitions, and encourage the development of home-grown talent', as president Jacques Georges put it.

These restrictions in fact had a minimal effect, because most countries imposed even more rigorous controls. Worst affected – though not until after their return in 1990 – would be the English clubs, for whom Northern Irish, Scottish and Welsh players counted as foreigners. In any case, the whole artificial farrago would be swept away in the mid-1990s.

Berlusconi was a different story, because of who he was and because of what he represented; this was nothing more nor less than the aggressive commercialism which would swiftly revolutionize the face of European football.

RIGHT: **BRILLIANT ORANGE: MILAN'S FABULOUS DUTCH TRIUMVERATE OF RUUD GULLIT, MARCO VAN BASTEN AND FRANK RIJKAARD, WHO HELPED MAKE UP ONE OF THE GREATEST ITALIAN TEAMS EVER**

A long-time Milan fan, Berlusconi had built a millionaire's empire through a media conglomeration based on regional commercial television channels. They provided a light entertainment diet of game shows, pop music and football which shattered the grip of state broadcaster RAI. They also generated profits which propelled Berlusconi on into publishing, insurance, grocery chains and, ultimately, politics.

Berlusconi made no secret of his strategy of winning friends and influencing votes through football. He even named his political party 'Forza Italia', the traditional chant of encouragement for the national team.

Milan were in a sorry state when Berlusconi swooped, in the nick of the time. One of the European Cup's original giants had been relegated twice in quick succession – once as punishment for match-fixing – and were £20 million in debt.

Berlusconi, setting a pattern that Roman Abramovich would emulate at Chelsea, paid off the debts and provided the cash to buy Marco van Basten, the finest centre-forward of his era, from Ajax and Ruud Gullit from PSV Eindhoven for a then world-record £6 million. After Milan won the Serie A *scudetto* for the first time in nine years, Berlusconi financed the acquisition of a third key Dutchman in Frank Rijkaard.

Turning stars into winners takes a top-class coach. Berlusconi found him in Arrigo Sacchi. The shoemaker from Fusignano had never played at professional level, but, as Sacchi said, 'you don't have to have been a horse to be a successful jockey'. Sacchi's horse sense produced a winning thoroughbred by mixing Dutch fluidity with Italian backbone as represented by the likes of stopper 'Billy' Costacurta, Sacchi's pupil and playmaker Carlo Ancelotti, sweeper and skipper Franco Baresi and the magnificent young left-back Paolo Maldini.

Milan were favourites from the outset in the 1988–89 Champions Cup. Serious opposition was represented by Real Madrid, Werder Bremen, Red Star Belgrade and a Steaua team reinforced by the intuitive and sharp-tempered Gheorghe Hagi. It said everything about the state of Romanian football that Steaua – commanded by dictator's son Nicu Ceausescu – signed Hagi from Sportul Studentesc and then brazenly refused to pay a fee.

Milan had to prove their mettle in Europe almost from the start and long before the Italian season opened. The start of Serie A was delayed until October after the conclusion of the Olympic Games. Still, even ring-rusty Milan found the initial task easy against Vitosha Sofia. Pietro Paolo Virdis, a journeyman Italian forward, and Gullit made it 2–0 in Bulgaria. Van Basten – having signed off the previous season with Holland's wonderful European title-winner against the Soviet Union – rattled home four goals in a 5–2 win back in Milan.

Berlusconi's edifice shook next time out against Red Star. The Yugoslavs took the lead in Milan, only for Virdis to level. He was then sent off in Belgrade when Milan, a goal down to a strike from Dejan Savicevic, were rescued by the fog. German referee Dieter Pauly abandoned the game after just under an hour. Next day, the teams played out another 1–1 draw, and the tie thus went to penalties. Goalkeeper Giovanni Galli saved from both Savicevic – ironically, given his later transfer to Milan – and Mitar Mrkela before Frank Rijkaard put away the decisive kick.

It was hardly easier in the quarter-finals. Milan's tie with Bremen produced just one goal, scored from a second-leg penalty by the lethal Van Basten.

In the semi-final, Madrid, reinforced by Bernd Schuster's arrival in midfield, could not hold Van Basten either. Milan followed up their 1–1 draw in the Bernabeu with a 5–0 romp back in the Stadio Meazza at San Siro. Van Basten, naturally, was again among the scorers. Madrid had never taken a worse beating in Europe.

BELOW: THE ENIGMATIC ARRIGO SACCHI, WHO NOT ONLY BUILT A SUPREME MILAN SIDE BUT ALSO HELPED REVOLUTIONIZE THE ITALIAN GAME TACTICALLY

MILAN BRUSH ASIDE FEEBLE STEAUA

On 11 April 1989, UEFA's executive agreed to readmit English clubs in 1990–91, 'dependent upon the support of the British government'.

Delight was guarded – and short-lived. Just four days later some 94 Liverpool fans were killed and 170 injured at Sheffield Wednesday's Hillsborough before an FA Cup semi-final against Nottingham Forest. Fans were crushed to death against the very fences supposed to protect them from each other.

Lord Taylor's subsequent report prompted the move to all-

seater stadia which was taken up by FIFA for the World Cup and UEFA for all its competitions. That demanded massive new investment in the game's infrastructure and, by chance, the demand was perfectly timed to suit the multinationals and their marketeers on the back of the imminent broadcasting expansion fired by satellite television. In the driving seat sat Silvio Berlusconi.

No wonder he was furious to learn – on the eve of what he fully expected to be Milan's demonstration of his power – of a

WEDNESDAY 24 MAY 1989
NOU CAMP, BARCELONA

MILAN   **4**
GULLIT 18, 38, VAN BASTEN 27, 46

STEAUA BUCHAREST   **0**

HT: 3-0. ATT: 100,000.
REF: TRITSCHLER (WG)

MILAN:
G. GALLI - TASSOTTI, COSTACURTA (F. GALLI 74), F. BARESI*, P. MALDINI - DONADONI, COLOMBO, RIJKAARD, ANCELOTTI - GULLIT (VIRDIS 60), VAN BASTEN.
COACH: SACCHI.

STEAUA:
LUNG - PETRESCU, UNGUREANU, BUMBESCU, IOVAN - STOICA*, MINEA, HAGI, ROTARIU (BALINT 46) - LACATUS, PITURCA.
COACH: IORDANESCU.

*CAPTAIN

strike by Spanish TV engineers. The prospects of a blackout prompted Berlusconi to pull strings in all directions. His own technicians and extra cameras flew to Barcelona in a military plane on the morning of the game. Thus 300 million telespectators around the football world saw Milan win the Champions Cup for the third time (ironically the only one of more than 80 contracted nations not see the final was Spain).

Along the way, Paolo Maldini became the first son to emulate his father, Cesare, as a European Cup-winner. Victory also elevated Ruud Gullit and Marco van Basten, each the scorer of two goals, to rivalry with Diego Maradona for the status of the world's greatest player. Maradona was winning

the UEFA Cup with Napoli. But he was no longer as persistently effective a force as either of the Dutchmen.

Milan were brilliant. Before Gullit hobbled off on the hour, they had provided the smartest footballing exhibition since Ajax's initial blur against Juventus in 1973. Gullit – playing his first match since keyhole surgery after the semi-final win over Real Madrid – not only scored twice but also hit a post and created one of Van Basten's goals.

Coach Arrigo Sacchi had set up his team to play with 100 per cent physical commitment, a high level of technical invention and rare football intelligence. Afterwards Milan's skipper and anchor Franco Baresi said, 'It's difficult to play football like that, but when we do I think we can beat anybody.'

The only lingering doubt over the quality of Milan's performance had to do with the inadequacy of the opposition. Steaua presented an old-fashioned Italian *catenaccio* with little spirit or attacking intent. Coach Anghel Iordanescu, a winner as a player in 1986, blamed the pressure of 11 games in 32 days, including domestic league and cup and World Cup ties. Since both Romania's government and football were riddled with corruption, whispers were soon circulating about the team's motivation or lack of it.

Not that Berlusconi let such questions spoil his delight as he took over the presentation ceremony – although he had more in mind than 'merely' winning a cup. Berlusconi was set on changing the face of European football.

LEFT: RUUD GULLIT KNOCKS THE BALL BEYOND GOALKEEPER SILVIU LUNG FOR MILAN'S THIRD

BELOW: MILAN – AND SILVIO BERLUSCONI – BASK IN THE WARM GLOW OF VICTORY AT THE NOU CAMP

1990S

TEN YEARS THAT SHOOK FOOTBALL

The 1990s were the most turbulent years in European club history. England returned to the Champions Cup after a six-year absence, while Marseille took the trophy to France for the first time and were then kicked out for match-fixing. Real Madrid regained winners' status, but it was Manchester United who served up the most dramatic success in the cup's history. Off the pitch, the communist collapse brought 18 more nations into UEFA with their eyes on a share of the profits generated by the commercially driven introduction of the mini-league format. Simultaneously, a little-known Belgian footballer rocked the foundations of not only the European but the world game.

RIGHT: **BARCELONA PLAY HOSTS TO MANCHESTER UNITED IN THE WORLD-FAMOUS NOU CAMP, NOVEMBER 1994**

PAOLO MALDINI

Country: Italy

Position: Left-back,
central defender

Born: 26 June, 1968

Club: AC Milan

PAOLO MALDINI

I have been extremely lucky. Not only because I have won the Champions Cup four times and played in seven finals, but because, when I look back over my career, I realise how fortunate I was to play in the particular era I did.

Of course, I did not always understand this at the time. But in the 1980s and early 1990s, it was easier for young players to break through even at Serie A level. For example, I made my debut for Milan at 16 because, when a couple of players were injured, there was always the chance the coach would turn to you. Today, all the big clubs have 25 or more players in their squad – a majority of them foreigners – and that makes it tough for a youngster to get a break.

My first match was against Udinese in 1985 and, just four years later, there I was winning my first Champions League final against Steaua Bucharest. It's a game, oddly enough, about which I can recall very little – though it has assumed legendary status for many of Milan's fans because that victory launched a great new era in our history.

What I do remember is that our victory was achieved in circumstances which will probably never be repeated, given that the entire Nou Camp stadium in Barcelona was packed full of our own fans.

Nowadays, UEFA's rules and regulations would not allow one club to buy up all the tickets but that is what Milan did that night. I remember sitting on the team bus as we made our way into the ground, surrounded on all sides by Milan fans. It was like sailing in through a red-and-black sea of humanity.

Looking back, I am sure those scenes had as much of a positive effect on us as they had a negative effect on the Romanian players.

The next year, against Benfica at the Prater stadium in Vienna, was entirely different. We were sure we would beat the Portuguese again – as my father's team had done in 1963 – but we went into that game very tired. We had to summon up every last spark of energy, so it was not surprising that we struggled a bit. It was a Champions Cup

that we won much more with our heads than with our legs.

Every final, you see, is different. The third I played is proof enough. Now I can smile, thinking back about the way we played against Marseille in Munich, especially in the first half. It was incredible that we managed to lose to them. It was also a painful defeat at the time because there was no way we deserved to lose – and that is talking about only the match itself, not about other issues which emerged later.

When you are lucky enough to take home so many prizes, it sometimes happens that you do not remember exactly what you have won or how you won it. That is not to dismiss the value of each occasion, more a reflection on the relentless pace of today's football: no sooner have you taken home one medal than you are back at the beginning of the pursuit for another.

LEFT: **PAOLO MALDINI CELEBRATES THE WINNING GOAL IN THE DERBY AGAINST INTER IN SERIE A, FEBRUARY 2005**

One exception to that rule, though, was our 1994 Champions League final win over Barcelona. The press, especially the foreign media, gave us no hope. Barcelona were certainly a good side, but we knew they had weaknesses and how to exploit them and we went for it, ruthlessly.

We did miss Franco Baresi and Alessandro Costacurta through suspensions but we had the advantage of having wrapped up the Italian League *scudetto* long before the final. Barcelona, by contrast, had won the Spanish title just days before the match, so they had been fighting, mentally, on two fronts.

Of course, success in any match depends on your overall, comprehensive approach and not only on your physical readiness. But I must say that at no stage – for all that they had forwards like Romario and Hristo Stoichkov – did we feel that they were a better team than us.

My memory of that night in Athens is that we played an almost perfect game. We completely stifled difficult opponents and gave them absolutely nothing.

In football you must accept that you can lose. We did it not only against Marseille but against Ajax in 1995 and, of course, Liverpool in 2005. For years, after we lost to Ajax in Vienna, I thought that perhaps that was destined to have been my last final. And then, eight years later, I had the unforgettable experience of raising the Champions Cup after we beat Juventus at Old Trafford in 2003.

People may think it strange that this match means so much to me – a final we won only in a penalty shoot-out. But there was a very special family connection. That was not only my first time as Champions Cup-winning captain but it was back in England where, 40 years earlier, Milan had won their first cup... with my father as captain.

LEFT: MALDINI BECAME
THE OLDEST AS WELL AS
THE QUICKEST SCORER IN
A CHAMPIONS LEAGUE
FINAL IN 2005 WHEN HE
VOLLEYED THE BALL INTO
THE NET AFTER 53
SECONDS AGAINST
LIVERPOOL, BUT HE
STILL FINISHED UP ON
THE LOSING SIDE

THE RISE OF THE MEDIA MOGULS

Where Italy had Berlusconi, France had Bernard Tapie, a man with a supreme talent for making and losing money. Marseille were on the up, but Zinedine Zidane left the city, taking his talents elsewhere

The 1980s had produced social and political turbulence around the globe and football felt the 'trickle-down' fallout. Opportunities to access the televisual and commercial riches likely to be generated in the 1990s attracted a new breed of would-be club owners: men who saw only the potential millions and whose knowledge of the game was often disruptively scanty.

At least Milan's owner and president Silvio Berlusconi had long been a fan. In fact, he had bought the club against the advice of father Luigi, who feared 'all the bad publicity it brings its presidents'. Silvio responded that the likes of Felice Riva in the early 1960s and Felice Colombo 20 years later had lacked his business rigour.

Further afield, eastern Europe's communist rock-face had crumbled, just like the Berlin Wall, amid the aftershocks of the self-destructive reforms launched in the Soviet Union by Mikhail

Gorbachev. In due course, Russia would produce its own self-made millionaires with a yearning for football club toys.

Of course the West remained far ahead. The era which raised Berlusconi in Italy produced similar men elsewhere with driving ambitions and ruthless streaks. The French media, for example, could hardly believe their good luck when France threw up its own apparent Berlusconi in Bernard Tapie.

The 'rags to riches, back to rags and back again to comparative riches' story of Tapie would one day be turned into a feature film by the director Marina Zenovich. Tapie was a small-time singer turned actor turned businessman turned asset-stripping multi-millionaire. At one stage he owned the Marseille docks and a television channel, was a socialist MP and even attained junior ministerial rank under President François Mitterrand.

But above all else Tapie will be remembered for his role in

RIGHT: **BERNARD TAPIE, WHO WAS RESPONSIBLE FOR REVIVING MARSEILLE'S FORTUNES AND THEN FOR CAUSING THEM TO PLUNGE DURING THE CLUB'S PERIOD OF DISGRACE**

the most dramatic of the many rises and falls in the history of Olympique Marseille – because this was the stage on which he finally over-reached himself.

Marseille's fans are the most passionate in France. In the late 1980s, they included a young son of Algerian immigrant parents whose name was Zinedine Zidane. He idolized both the club and their Uruguayan forward Enzo Francescoli, and he was mortified to be overlooked as a teenager.

But Marseille's football club also possessed a reputation for living on the edge. They had won the league in 1971 and 1972, then collapsed into relegation and bankruptcy under the weight of debt run up under the controversial reign of Marcel Leduc, who had already once lifted the club out of the second division in the mid-1960s.

In 1986 Tapie bought control on a whim, following a suggestion made during a dinner at the Soviet Embassy by the wife of mayor Gaston Defferre. He splashed out on outstanding players, including Francescoli, Germany's Rudi Voller and Klaus Allofs, France's own Jean Tigana, Manuel Amoros and Jean-Pierre Papin and England's Chris Waddle. The former Tottenham winger became the fourth-most-expensive player in the world when he signed for £4.25 million.

Five times in a row from 1989 Marseille won the French league title. Tapie, who never hesitated to breach the privacy of the dressing room to issue a reprimand or a call to arms, demanded the lion's share of the credit.

But winning leagues and cups in France was not enough. Tapie envisaged jousting with Berlusconi on the international stage. Their weapons were going to be their football clubs.

Marseille's initial salvo fell short. Milan progressed towards the 1990 final by disposing of Finland's HJK Helsinki in the first round by 5–0 overall and of John Toshack's Real Madrid 2–1 in the second round. But, lacking the injured Ruud Gullit for almost all the season, they needed extra time against both Belgium's Mechelen in the quarter-finals and Bayern Munich in the semi-finals. That secured a second successive final appearance, this time against Benfica.

The Portuguese club's presence in Vienna infuriated Tapie, because it was achieved at the expense of Marseille in the most unfortunate circumstances.

Tapie, impatiently, really did believe that Marseille, that season, would win the European Cup. As it turned out they came within a hand's breadth of reaching the final.

Victories over Brondby, AEK Athens and CSKA Sofia earned the semi-final against Benfica, with the first leg in the intense atmosphere of the Stade Velodrome. Strikes from Franck Sauzee and Papin brought a 2–1 win which threatened to be enough when the second leg in Libson remained scoreless heading into the final stages.

Then, in the 83rd minute, Belgian referee Marcel van Langenhove and his linesman were unsighted as substitute Vata Garcia controlled a pass with his hand before shooting the deadlock-breaking goal. Marseille's players – including Vata's marker Eric Di Meco who had stopped playing, awaiting the whistle – mobbed Van Langenhove, but all to no avail. The goal stood. Benfica, and not Marseille, were in the final.

MILAN GO DUTCH AGAINST BENFICA

Frank Rijkaard was a popular target for the media in the build-up to the final between Milan and Benfica in Vienna – the second staging in the Prater in four years. The Dutchman who earned his living in Italy should really have been doing so in Portugal instead.

When Rijkaard left Ajax in the middle of the 1987–88 season after falling out with coach Johan Cruyff, he was bought by Sporting Clube of Lisbon. But someone in Sporting's office failed to send off the registration forms within the required period, and the Portuguese federation barred his mid-term arrival as out of time.

Sporting wanted Rijkaard to sit out the season, but he knew that would cost him his place in Holland's team who would soon be heading for the European Championship finals in West Germany. He persuaded Sporting to loan him to Spanish club Zaragoza and then played so well at the European finals

that he generated an offer from Milan which even reluctant Sporting dared not refuse.

Now he could strike a blow for his old club – for whom he had never played – by putting one over on their local rivals.

Victory for Milan would be significant on several levels. They wanted to repeat the 1963 triumph over Benfica, but they also needed victory to return to the Champions Cup the next season. Diego Maradona's Napoli had snatched the Serie A *scudetto* from them on the back of a match at Atalanta awarded to them controversially by the league disciplinary committee. A coin had apparently floored Napoli's Brazilian midfielder Alemao. Years later it emerged that Alemao was cynically told by Napoli physios to stay down in order to achieve just that end. Finally, Milan needed to win to justify Berlusconi's self-appointed stance as the would-be revolutionary leader who was in the process of promoting a

self-selected, self-perpetuating 'European Television League'.

The spectacle from the Prater for a worldwide TV audience was hardly enthralling. Milan won, deservedly, but thanks only to the class of Marco van Basten and the winning strike from Rijkaard past 'keeper Silvino Louro. The decider climaxed an end-to-end move involving Milan 'keeper Giovanni Galli, Billy Costacurta and the inevitable Van Basten.

Oddly, Milan's flow was not helped by the return to the starting line-up of Ruud Gullit. He had played just 97 minutes of football up to the final, after injury ruled him out of most of the season. Even Van Basten referred to this disturbance: 'It was not so easy to start playing alongside Gullit again. We've had to change things. Maybe it wasn't so easy for him either.'

Benfica coach Sven-Goran Eriksson, intriguingly, blamed defeat on excessive planning and defensive drills. 'We were so busy trying to play Gullit and Van Basten offside that we forgot about Rijkaard and let him come through on his own.'

Naturally, Europe's sports headlines the next morning were devoted to the extended reign of Milan and their big-money superstars. By contrast, no such publicity was granted to the transfer of a journeyman Belgian pro from FC Liege to French second division club Dunkerque. As time went on, however, Jean-Marc Bosman would prove more influential than Gullit, Van Basten and Rijkaard all put together.

LEFT: JAIME PACHECO, CAPTAIN OF BENFICA, CHASES AFTER ANGELO COLOMBO OF MILAN

FAR LEFT: MARCO VAN BASTEN HOLDS UP THE EUROPEAN CUP. THE DUTCH MASTER SET A EUROPEAN CUP RECORD OF 18 GOALS IN 23 MATCHES FOR MILAN AND WAS EUROPEAN FOOTBALLER OF THE YEAR THREE TIMES – IN 1988, 1989 AND 1992

WEDNESDAY 23 MAY 1990
PRATER, VIENNA

MILAN	1
RIJKAARD 67	
BENFICA	0

HT: 0-0. ATT: 58,000. REF: KOHL (AUS)

MILAN:
G. GALLI – TASSOTTI, COSTACURTA, F. BARESI*, MALDINI – ANCELOTTI (MASSARO 67), COLOMBO (F. GALLI 89), RIJKAARD, EVANI – VAN BASTEN, GULLIT.
COACH: SACCHI.

BENFICA:
SILVINO – JOSE CARLOS, RICARDO, SAMUEL, ALDAIR – THERN, VITOR PANEIRA (VATA 78), JAIME PACHECO* (CESAR BRITO 59), VALDO – HERNANI, M. MAGNUSSON.
COACH: ERIKSSON.

*CAPTAIN

DAWN OF THE BOSMAN ERA

In Belgium, a footballing nobody's transfer passed virtually unnoticed but was later to have a seismic effect on the game worldwide. Diego Maradona scored his only European Cup goals

Jean-Marc Bosman's transfer from Liege to Dunkerque was one event among many in the soccer summer of 1990. Above all, Germany – 'West' for the last time before football caught up with reunification – won the World Cup in Italy against Diego Maradona's grumpy Argentina.

England fell to the Germans in the semi-finals after a penalty shoot-out but gained international consolation: UEFA, pushed by new president Lennart Johansson, agreed to readmit English clubs to European competition. In fact, English champions Liverpool's extra season of banishment meant they were still barred from the Champions Cup, which thus went ahead again without English representation. But Manchester United would make amends by not only entering but winning the Cup-Winners' Cup.

As for Bosman, he was bitterly upset when his Belgian club Liege refused to ratify his transfer, since Dunkerque were unable to come up with the necessary paltry fee of around £4,000. Bosman was out of contract with Liege but was frozen

out of the game by the anachronistic Belgian regulations. Liege cut his wages by 60 per cent.

A local court ruled that Bosman was free to join Dunkerque, but the Belgian federation, fearing the wider consequences of its loss of authority, appealed. Ironically, such an impasse simply could not have arisen under the more sophisticated rules of Belgium's neighbours.

Out on the pitch, the early rounds went according to the form book. Sebastian Losada scored a hat-trick in Real Madrid's 10-1 overall thrashing of Odense, while Rabah Madjer grabbed four in the second leg of Porto's 13-1 aggregate dismissal of Portadown. The convention-busting Roman Catholic signing Mo Johnston scored five in all in Rangers' 10-0 drubbing of Valletta, as did Peter Pacult in Innsbruck's 7-1 crushing of Kuusysi Lahti.

Diego Maradona scored his first – and last – two Champions Cup goals in Napoli's 3-0 first-leg defeat of Hungary's Ujpest. His team-mate Alemao, who had helped

them trick their way to the Italian title, scored one of Napoli's brace in the return.

Marseille opened up with a 5-1, 0-0 defeat of Dinamo Tirana. Jean-Pierre Papin scored a first-leg hat-trick supported by strikes from Philippe Vercruysse and a tempestuous new signing named Eric Cantona. On the bench sat none other than Franz Beckenbauer, West Germany's World Cup-winning manager of a few months earlier.

Tapie had met Beckenbauer after buying a controlling stake in adidas, with which 'Der Kaiser' had long-time promotional links. From there it was a short step to the Stade Velodrome. Beckenbauer said, 'Tapie is a dynamic personality who knows exactly what he wants.' Later he changed his mind.

Unwanted was coach Gerard Gili, who was demoted on Beckenbauer's arrival and quit the morning after the second leg against Tirana.

In the second round, Real Madrid thrashed Innsbruck 9-1 in the Bernabeu with three goals from Emilio Butragueno and four from Hugo Sanchez; Vercruysse scored a hat-trick in Marseille's 8-4 overall defeat of Lech Poznan; Rangers, managed by Graeme Souness, had to give best to Red Star Belgrade; Scottish interest was thus maintained only by Alan McInally, who scored a goal as a substitute in Bayern Munich's 7-0 aggregate thrashing of CSKA Sofia.

As for the Italians, Napoli drew 0-0 home and away against Moscow Spartak and thus went to a shoot-out. 'El Diego' put away his kick, but Marco Baroni missed and Napoli lost 5-3. Maradona lasted only another two months at Naples before quitting Italian football under a dope-test cloud.

Holders Milan, awarded a first-round bye, opened up with a narrow win over Brugge. Coach Arrigo Sacchi fretted over a goalless draw at home before Milan won 1-0 in Belgium despite having Marco van Basten sent off.

That red card and ensuing suspension proved crucial against Marseille in the quarter-finals. Milan, misfiring badly in the Dutchman's absence, could only draw 1-1 at home, Ruud Gullit and Papin matching strikes. In the return, Chris Waddle scored on 75 minutes and Milan appeared to be heading out. Then, with two minutes remaining, referee Bo Karlsson awarded a free-kick and Marseille fans, thinking the match was over, overflowed on to the pitch. As the players waited for police to clear away the fans, so one of the floodlights failed.

Milan's players, fearing for their safety, walked off and subsequently refused Karlsson's instruction to return to complete the game. Karlsson counted down to the 90 minutes, declared the match abandoned and Marseille the winners. Milan, blaming Marseille incompetence for both the floodlight failure and the security issue, demanded a replay. UEFA

refused and Marseille thus progressed to a semi-final against Moscow Spartak.

The Russians had been surprise quarter-final winners against Madrid, but proved short of surprises against Marseille, who won 3-1 in Moscow and 2-1 at home. Ghanaian Abedi Pele scored the first goal in each game.

The other semi matched Red Star against Bayern Munich. It proved a disastrous tie for Bayern's Klaus Augenthaler. Bayern lost 2-1 at home but were 2-1 ahead in the return in Belgrade, and heading for extra time, when the luckless sweeper put through his own goal in the last minute. Red Star went on to the final, Bayern merely went home.

ABOVE: RUUD GULLIT ATTEMPTS TO CALL HIS MILAN TEAM-MATES OFF THE PITCH AT MARSEILLE'S VELODROME STADIUM

BELOW: CHAIRMAN, DAVID MURRAY (TOP CENTRE) AND MANAGER GRAEME SOUNESS (TOP RIGHT) NERVOUSLY WATCH AS RANGERS CRASH OUT AT IBROX AGAINST RED STAR BELGRADE

RED STAR MAKE MARSEILLE PAY PENALTY

Marseille's motto '*Droit au But*' means 'Straight to goal', but their players forgot all that in the final against a similarly unadventurous Red Star. The previous summer the law-making International Board had amended the offside law: now it was enough for an attacking player to be level with the penultimate defender. At Bari neither side showed the slightest interest in taking avantage of the relaxation.

Red Star were only the third eastern European club to reach a final after Partizan Belgrade in 1966 and Steaua Bucharest in 1986 and 1989. They played against the backdrop of increasing domestic tension and in the sure knowledge that their team was about to fall apart. Fine performances on the way to Bari had prompted bids for midfielders Robert Prosinecki and Sinisa Mihajlovic and forwards Dejan Savicevic and Darko Pancev. National boss Miljan Miljanic had repeatedly blocked Prosinecki's attempts to move abroad, but both FIFA and UEFA had come out in the player's favour and Red Star could not hold him.

Marseille's most significant change had been on the bench. Franz Beckenbauer, a fish out of water in both Marseille the city and Marseille the club, had been kept on the payroll but replaced as coach by the veteran Raymond Goethals. This was Goethals's second stint in charge; he had already guided Marseille to the semi-finals in 1989. With his trademark white, wide-belted coat and permanent cigarette dangling from a corner of his mouth, Goethals looked the archetypal French football coach, except for one vital thing: he was Belgian.

Goethals had managed the Belgian national team and guided Anderlecht to Cup-Winners' Cup success. But his reputation was haunted by a match-fixing scandal while at Standard Liege in 1983. Standard were convicted of trying to bribe members of the opposing Waterschei team before the last game of the season to ensure they won the league title – which they did. Goethals was banned for life, but the sentence was subsequently commuted.

Years later, seeking to play it all down, Goethals remarked, 'It was nothing to do with me at all, but of course, as coach, you must always know what is going on in the dressing room...'

Goethals's tactic now, in Bari's flying saucer-like World Cup stadium, was to deploy his midfielders to protect defence rather than support attack; similarly Red Star's Ljubko Petrovic left Pancev isolated upfield. Hardly surprisingly, it was 0-0 at the end of extra time and went to penalties – the fourth Champions Cup Final to be decided in this manner.

Manuel Amoros, an experienced World Cup veteran, missed Marseille's first kick, and Red Star converted all theirs to win 5-3. Chris Waddle thus suffered his second shoot-out defeat in Italy inside 12 months, after his – and England's - Turin failure against West Germany in the World Cup.

On the other side of the coin, Red Star's sweeper Miodrag Belodedici became the first player to land the cup with two different clubs, having been a winner in 1986 with Steaua.

RIGHT: **RED STAR CELEBRATE BEFORE THE INEVITABLE BREAK-UP OF THEIR SIDE AFTER THE BIG EUROPEAN CLUBS MOVED IN FOR THEIR STARS**

WEDNESDAY 29 MAY 1991
SAN NICOLA, BARI

RED STAR BELGRADE   **0**

MARSEILLE   **0**

AFTER EXTRA TIME
RED STAR WON 5-3 ON PENS.
HT: 0-0. 90 MIN: 0-0. ATT: 58,000.
REF: LANESE (IT)

RED STAR:
STOJANOVIC* - JUGOVIC, BELODEDICI,
NAJDOVSKI, MAROVIC -
SABANADZOVIC, MIHAJLOVIC,
PROSINECKI, BINIC - SAVICEVIC
(DODIC 84), PANCEV.
COACH: PETROVIC.

MARSEILLE:
OLMETA - AMOROS, BOLI, MOZER, DI
MECO (STOJKOVIC 112) - GERMAIN,
CASONI, FOURNIER (VERCRUYSSE 75)
- WADDLE, PAPIN*, PELE.
COACH: GOETHALS.

*CAPTAIN

ABOVE: **STRIKER DARKO PANCEV
WHEELS AWAY IN DELIGHT AFTER
CONVERTING HIS PENALTY**

LEFT: **RED STAR'S FANS FLOOD
THE SAN NICOLA STADIUM WITH
COLOUR AND SMOKE**

FOOTBALL DANCES TO TV'S TUNE

After much political toing and froing, the Champions Cup now had a format to suit it to the brave new world of televised football. Johan Cruyff was back driving Barcelona to success as coach

In the late 1970s Liverpool had fronted up a proposal to turn the initial rounds of the Champions Cup into a mini-league system. In the late 1980s, far more threateningly, Milan president Silvio Berlusconi had produced his own blueprint for a European Television League.

A balancing act had to be achieved. UEFA needed the big clubs, but the big clubs also needed the European federation, which legitimized their presence within the football family. The players likewise needed to remain within that family to participate in the World Cup and European Championship.

UEFA thus moved diplomatically forwards by deciding to replace the quarter-final and semi-final rounds with a group structure comprising two mini-leagues of four clubs each, playing each other home and away and with the winners heading direct into the Wembley final – the Empire Stadium's selection being another welcome-back gesture towards English football.

What UEFA did not recognize, however, was the pace of political change driven by the European Union. President Lennart Johansson and long-serving general secretary Gerd Aigner even swam against the tide by restricting clubs to a maximum of four non-national players (players not qualified to play for the club's national association). UEFA said it wanted to protect grass-roots development, but an instant anomaly was the effect on returning English clubs, who found that their Scots, Welsh and Irish players were suddenly 'foreigners'.

UEFA's attitude to the law was disgracefully expressed in a decision to prohibit Belgium from hosting European finals after its appeal court rejected UEFA's appeal against a suspended jail term imposed on former general secretary Hans Bangerter; he had been charged as UEFA's representative responsible for the Heysel disaster. The European federation was clinging firmly to the arrogant mantra dictated by former president Jacques Georges: 'We are a Swiss-based organization and the laws of the European Community are nothing to do with us.'

Other people thought differently. Jean-Marc Bosman had seen his action against the Belgian football authorities referred to the European Court of Justice in Luxembourg. Belgian courts considered that, in the light of European law, they lacked juridical competence. As Bosman, increasingly

impoverished by his legal battle, set up a temporary home in the garage adjoining his parents' home, the rich and famous played on. For him, a decision was still some way away.

Red Star defended their crown with a transfer-torn team; the only other previous winners in the draw were PSV Eindhoven and Benfica; Marseille were there again, while Barcelona returned for the first time in six years.

Barca's coach now was Johan Cruyff. Ironically, he would prove far more successful at the Nou Camp as manager than he

had been as a player. He remained, however, as innovative as ever. He was the first coach to use a TV monitor in his dug-out, and he believed in using the full length and breadth of the pitch. The technical virtuosity of his Spanish players, mixed with hand-picked imports, allowed Barcelona to circulate the ball with a speed, control and accuracy which had their opponents chasing shadows. Versatility was also a Cruyff watchword. England's Gary Lineker, in Cruyff's early days, had been pushed away to the right wing. To English fans it looked bizarre. But that was how Barcelona had won the 1989 Cup-Winners' Cup, so Cruyff could point to results.

Success came at a heavy price. Chain-smoker Cruyff had needed emergency heart surgery during the 1990–91 season and was still convalescing while assistant and former winger Charly Rexach took the team on to the league title. Now was surely the time to end that Champions Cup jinx.

Barca opened up by defeating Hansa Rostock, last champions of the now-defunct East Germany. Cruyff was back in the dug-out to see his team, inspired in attack by the hot-tempered Hristo Stoichkov and two-goal Michael Laudrup, win 3–0 at home and lose by an inconsequential 1–0 away. It nearly went wrong in the second round, however. Barcelona won 2–0 at home to Germany's Kaiserslautern with two goals from future sports director Txiki Beguiristain, but they were losing 3–0 in Germany, heading into stoppage time, before Jose Bakero popped up with the tie-turning last-kick away goal.

Barcelona were accompanied into Group B by Dynamo Kiev, by a Sparta Prague side who had surprisingly ousted Marseille, and by a Benfica outfit who had not only outwitted but even ultimately outrun Arsenal. Barcelona topped the group ahead of Sparta with a game to spare.

Group A matched Sampdoria, Red Star, Anderlecht and Panathinaikos. Sampdoria set the pattern by defeating Red Star 2–0 on the opening match day. They never looked back and ended two points clear of the fading holders.

With instability increasing in the Balkans, Red Star had been forced by UEFA to play their home matches in Hungary and Bulgaria. Their sole consolation for a collapsing season was a World Club Cup victory over Chile's Colo-Colo.

BELOW: JOHAN CRUYFF, THE BARCA MANAGER, PREACHES WHAT HE PRACTISED AS THE OUTSTANDING PLAYER OF HIS GENERATION

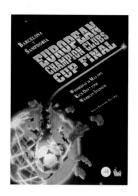

HISTORY REPEATS ITSELF FOR BARCA

Barcelona coach Johan Cruyff did not pull any punches after his ghostbusters finally laid the hoodoo of those Champions Cup Final defeats in 1961 and 1986.

'It's been a great night,' he said deep in the bowels of Wembley Stadium, 'because it's been such a long time coming. Winning the cup as a player was very special, but winning it as a coach is fantastic as well. Ronald Koeman is a coach's dream: he can create a goal out of nothing at any time of the game.' In fact only nine minutes remained of extra time when

Koeman thundered home the winner from a tapped free-kick.

Sampdoria kept their own feelings to themselves. Their players and coach Vujadin Boskov, a loser also with Real Madrid in 1991, skipped the post-match press conferences. The Brazilian perception of Toninho Cerezo in midfield and the lethal understanding of 'twins' Roberto Mancini and Gianluca Vialli up in attack had proved insufficient.

This was history repeating itself. Four years earlier Barcelona had beaten Sampdoria in the final of the Cup-

Winners' Cup. But then the Genoa club financed by oil tycoon Paolo Mantovani had been on the up. Defeat at Wembley was the end of an era. Sampdoria had finished sixth in Serie A and the ambitious Vialli would head off within weeks for Juventus.

Not that Barcelona cared. They had choreographed the greatest moment in their history down to the finest detail. Just before the decisive free-kick, Cruyff had been preparing to bring on Miguel Angel Nadal in midfield for the tiring youngster, Josep Guardiola. When the kick was whistled, Cruyff held Nadal back. As soon as the ball flew beyond Gianluca Pagliuca, Cruyff sent on not Nadal but Jose Ramon Alexanko. Thus the veteran club captain was there in place to lead his team up the 39 steps and collect the prize that mattered most. Not only that, but Barcelona, forced to play the game in orange, had brought their 'real' maroon-and-blue shirts for their players to wear as they collected their medals.

Barcelona thus became only the second Spanish club to

win the Champions Cup (after Real Madrid) and the third club (after Juventus and Ajax) to have collected all three main European club trophies at one time or another. Koeman not only collected the official man of the match award but became the second player (after Miodrag Belodedici) to win the Champions Cup with different clubs, having been a winner in 1988 with PSV Eindhoven.

Of course, Cruyff also joined the history-makers as the second cup-winning captain-cum-coach (after Real Madrid's Miguel Munoz) and only the third cup-winning player-turned coach (after Munoz and Italian Giovanni Trapattoni).

Koeman, goalkeeper Andoni Zubizarreta, Michael Laudrup and Hristo Stoichkov thus secured their place in Barcelona's player pantheon alongside old heroes such as Ladislav Kubala, Luiz Suarez, Sandor Kocsis and co. They were still celebrating long after Sampdoria had slunk away, their players throwing their shirts to their fans more in tantrum than tribute.

WEDNESDAY 20 MAY 1992
WEMBLEY, LONDON

BARCELONA 1
KOEMAN 111

SAMPDORIA 0

AFTER EXTRA TIME
HT: 0-0. 90 MIN; 0-0. ATT: 70,827.
REF: SCHMIDHUBER (GER)

BARCELONA:
ZUBIZARRETA* – NANDO, R. KOEMAN, JUAN CARLOS, FERRER – GUARDIOLA (ALEXANKO 113), BAKERO – EUSEBIO, M. LAUDRUP, STOICHKOV – SALINAS (GOIKOETXEA 64).
COACH: CRUYFF.

SAMPDORIA:
PAGLIUCA – MANNINI, PARI, VIERCHOWOD, LANNA – LOMBARDO, KATANEC, TONINHO CEREZO, BONETTI (INVERNIZZI 72) – VIALLI (BUSO 100), MANCINI*.
COACH: BOSKOV.

*CAPTAIN

THE FOOTBALL MONEY-GO-ROUND

Some called it 'a break with tradition', others 'a betrayal', but a new format for the Champions Cup arrived shaped by the wishes of TV broadcasters and Silvio Berlusconi's vision for the future

KNOCK-OUT STAGE

In the autumn of 1991 UEFA had summoned an extraordinary congress at which the 35-strong membership granted it full control of all television and commercial rights to the new mini-league system. The experiment was now formalized in the officially branded UEFA Champions League – note, no apostrophe – and a young, Lucerne-based marketing company named TEAM was contracted to package it and sell it.

TEAM could trace its history back to the Brazilian Joao Havelange's victory over Sir Stanley Rous in the 1974 FIFA presidential elections. Votes for Havelange, from Africa in particular, were swung by Horst Dassler, the influential adidas director. Dassler's reward was to be granted commercial control of the World Cup, first in partnership with English sport's super salesman Patrick Nally and then in his own right, from 1982 onwards, through Dassler's specialist company ISL. Bosses of ISL were Dassler's former aide Klaus Hempel and Jurgen Lenz. After Dassler's premature death in 1987, Hempel and Lenz were

RIGHT: **JOSEP GUARDIOLA OF BARCELONA REACHES THE BALL JUST AHEAD OF CSKA MOSCOW'S DIMITRI KORSAKOV**

FAR RIGHT: **ERIC CANTONA IN HIS DAYS AS A LEEDS PLAYER GETS THE BETTER OF STUTTGART'S UWE SCHNEIDER**

ousted by the rest of the family. They set up a new office around the corner in Lucerne, used their top-level contacts to perfect effect and thus won for their new agency – TEAM – the most lucrative ongoing contract in football's commercial history.

It was with TEAM's guidance that UEFA set up the Champions League parameters: a small pool of multinational sponsors were signed up and guaranteed match broadcast exposure on every Champions League programme worldwide. In each country exclusive rights were sold, virtually at auction, to one single broadcaster.

That, in the United Kingdom, was initially ITV. Later, after pressure from the European commission, single-broadcasting restrictions were varied. Not that this reduced the value of the TV contracts, because cable and satellite channels were by then falling over themselves to buy into the action.

The commercial complexity applied only to the league stage which made up, initially, the second half of the season. The first half was taken up with the opening knock-out rounds. In 1992–93 that spelled failure for, among others, holders Barcelona at the hands of CSKA Moscow, and Leeds United at the hands of Scotland's Rangers.

Leeds, last winners of the Football League championship ahead of the launch of the Premier League, had only just scrambled through the first round. UEFA had amended its foreign players rule in the face of continuing pressure from the European commission.

Now clubs could field a maximum of five foreign-born players, but at least two must have lived in the club's country of origin for at least five years. The so-called 'three and two' rule would haunt Stuttgart coach Christoph Daum for years after.

In the first round Stuttgart beat Leeds 3–0 at home and thought they had progressed on the away-goals rule after losing 'only' 4–1 at Elland Road. However, Daum had miscounted in introducing foreign substitute Jovica Simanic for the last eight minutes. Leeds protested, UEFA ordered a single-leg replay in neutral Barcelona, and goals from Gordon Strachan and substitute Carl Shutt – on in place of the ineffective Eric Cantona – brought a 2–1 win.

It was Leeds's last hurrah. In the second round, they lost 2–1 both away and home to Rangers. Top-scoring Ally McCoist struck decisively both at Ibrox Park and at Elland Road.

GROUP STAGE

Bernard Tapie's European ambition was burning stronger than ever. When Marseille slithered out against Red Star Belgrade in the second round the previous season, Tapie had stormed into the dressing room afterwards promising the most explosive

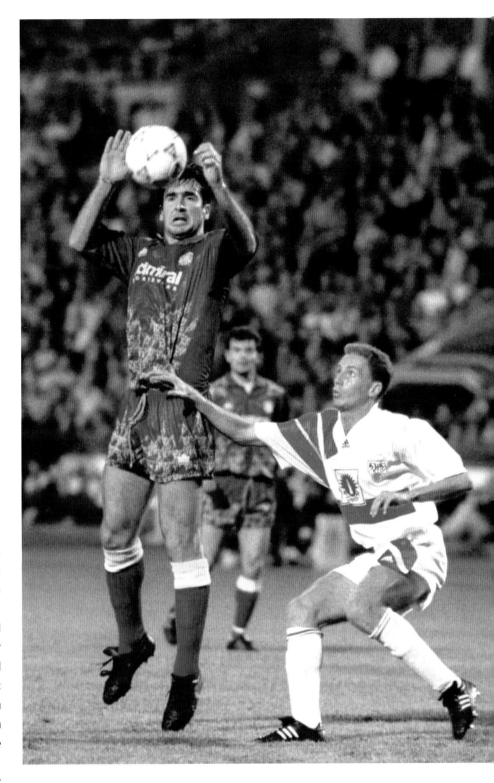

clear-out in the history of even this most turbulent club.

Wherever Marseille went they were pursued by scandal, controversy and worse. In 1991, Tapie had been suspended for a year by the French football authorities for 'injuring sporting morale' with his furious tirades at referees; his players, led by star striker Jean-Pierre Papin, had threatened to strike in support of 'BT'.

Amid all the controversy they had strode on to win the

SILVIO BERLUSCONI

In the autumn of 1991, Milan's president Silvio Berlusconi, interviewed by this author for *World Soccer* magazine, set out a vision for the future of European club football which becomes more prescient with every season that passes.

'Gradually the concept of the national team will become less and less important. It is the clubs with which fans associate. A European championship for clubs is inevitable. The new format is a step in the right direction, but only a step.

'The European cups, as they have organized, have become a historical anachronism. It's economic nonsense that a club such as Milan might be eliminated in the first round. A European cup that lasts the whole season is what Europe wants.

'After all, Europe wanted an economic community with monetary union and a customs union. It's inevitable it should want a football union too. And the clubs will lead the way – each playing around 80 games a season.

'In my six years as president I have never seen our best team play – except in my head. Someone is always injured or ill or suspended. So we need many quality players and the players themselves accept this.

'Milan are my laboratory for the future. We have to reach an audience beyond the stadium. That means television, the theatre of the global village.

'Football is currently ignoring part of its support. First are the fans in the stadium, but that means only 50,000 or 60,000. Then there are the fans who watch bits and pieces of soccer on the state channels. But the third audience, which we are not yet reaching, is to be found through pay-TV. Through cable and satellite you must be able to reach the committed fan who wants to watch our games.

'Milan must be a part of that. We would like to be the best, of course. But at the highest level winning or losing is often a matter of luck. What is important is that we are among the main actors in this theatre.'

league title, and might have won the double as well. But then Marseille were drawn against Bastia in the semi-finals of the French cup. It was the biggest match in Corsica for more than 20 years, and Bastia put up a massive temporary stand to more than double the 8,500 capacity of the old Furiani stadium.

Tragically, around 15 minutes before the scheduled kick-off, the new stand started to collapse. Fans plunged more than 60 feet into a tangle of seats and scaffolding.

Players, including Marseille's Englishman Trevor Steven, ran to help the rescuers. Amazingly, only 14 people were killed, although more than a thousand were hurt.

The French federation decided to abandon the cup.

Marseille were not to blame, of course. Rather the incident exemplified the passion and allure which attached to Tapie's team. Living up to that pressure was by no means always easy for the players; they were forever under the spotlight. However, they progressed unbeaten through their Group One campaign, winning three and drawing three of their six matches on the way to topping the table and reaching the final.

Rangers finished one point adrift, to their frustration and disbelief. Succeeding years proved this narrow failure to have been perhaps the most costly in the Light Blues' long and proud history.

Milan, as expected, topped Group Two by following up on an intimidating opening display which saw Marco van Basten score all their goals in a 4-0 thrashing of IFK Gothenburg.

ABOVE: **MARCO VAN BASTEN SCORES THE THIRD GOAL FOR MILAN IN THEIR 4-0 ANNIHILATION OF GOTHENBURG**

MARSEILLE WIN BATTLE BUT LOSE WAR

Marseille's delight in becoming the first French club to win the Champions Cup lasted only days. Even on the night of the final in Munich, whispers told of a gathering storm to dwarf anything else in the club's history.

The story of the match is simple. Coach Fabio Capello had steered Milan through a record sequence of 58 unbeaten league matches and victories in all six Champions League ties on the road to Munich. He was thus the man who got it right for the best part of two years but wrong on the night which mattered.

Milan had their best team out, including £13-million, world-record signing Gianluigi Lentini in midfield. In attack, Capello gambled on Marco van Basten at centre-forward. He had scored six goals in the Champions League and 13 in 15 Serie A matches, but was struggling to overcome recurring ankle

trouble. All this meant only a place on the substitutes' bench for the former Marseille favourite, Jean-Pierre Papin.

Milan had the class but Marseille the commitment. Two minutes before half-time Basile Boli powered through a crowded penalty box to head home Abedi Pele's corner for the only goal. An hour later Bernard Tapie was joining his players on their lap of honour.

In truth it was a lap of dishonour. Six days earlier, back in France, Marseille had beaten struggling Valenciennes 1–0 to secure the league once more and clear their heads for Munich. But at half-time in Valenciennes the home club had protested to the referee that Marseille had tried to bribe three of their players – forward Christophe Robert, Argentine World Cup-winner Jorge Burruchaga and midfielder Jacques Glassmann – successfully in two cases.

38. FINALE UM DEN POKAL DER EUROPÄISCHEN MEISTERVEREINE

OLYMPIQUE MARSEILLE – AC MAILAND
Mittwoch, 26. Mai 1993 · 20.15 Uhr

RIGHT: AS MARCEL DESAILLY AND CHRIS WADDLE QUEUE UP FOR THEIR SHARE OF THE GLORY, MIDFIELDER FRANCK SAUZEE HOLDS ON TO THE TROPHY

WEDNESDAY 26 MAY 1993
OLYMPIA, MUNICH

MARSEILLE 1
BOLI 43
MILAN 0

HT: 1-0. ATT: 64,400. REF:
ROTHLISBERGER (SWZ)

MARSEILLE:
BARTHEZ - ANGLOMA (DURAND 64),
BOLI, DESAILLY, EYDELIE - SAUZEE,
DESCHAMPS*, DI MECO - BOKSIC,
VOELLER (THOMAS 78), PELE.
COACH: GOETHALS.

MILAN:
S. ROSSI - TASSOTTI, COSTACURTA, F.
BARESI*, P. MALDINI - DONADONI
(PAPIN 56), ALBERTINI, RIJKAARD,
LENTINI - VAN BASTEN (ERANIO 85),
MASSARO.
COACH: CAPELLO.

*CAPTAIN

Later it emerged that before the game Robert's wife had been handed £30,000 in cash at the Marseille team hotel by defender Jean-Jacques Eydelie. She had then buried it in her mother's garden. When Robert tried to draw his team-mates into the scandal, Glassmann blew the whistle. Nine days after Marseille's Munich triumph, the French league called in the public prosecutor.

In time it emerged that Marseille had fixed far, far more than just the infamous match with Valenciennes. Tapie's lieutenants had siphoned off cash into various anonymous bank accounts in Switzerland and Liechtenstein. With the help of a small army of agents, this cash was used to swing transfer deals and influence referees.

Tapie eventually – though not until 1997 – went to jail for match-fixing. Eydelie, Burruchaga, Robert and Marseille general manager Jean-Pierre Bernes all received indefinite bans.

Marseille were stripped of their 1993 league title and relegated as punishment. They had to sell all their best players to stay afloat financially and were barred from the following season's Champions Cup after being initially drawn against AEK Athens.

Glassmann was rewarded with FIFA's fair play award but, such being the perversity of the French game, was jeered wherever he played. Many fans blamed him for destroying the Marseille dream, and also for breaking an unwritten code of loyalty. Glassmann was not the only innocent victim. Van Basten aggravated his ankle injury in Milan's losing cause in Munich. He never played again.

As for Tapie, a decade later he returned to his beloved Marseille... as general manager.

ABOVE: **PURSUED BY RUDI VOLLER, BASILE BOLI RACES TOWARDS THE MARSEILLE FANS AFTER SCORING PAST GOAL-KEEPER SEBASTIANO ROSSI**

THE GREAT DASH FOR CASH

As football's brave new world began to offer greater financial rewards, Arsene Wenger's Monaco replaced disgraced Marseille and gave several of Europe's bigger clubs a run for their money

KNOCK-OUT STAGE

Manchester United, in 1993, had become the first winners of the new FA Premier League. The top division of the historic Football League, increasingly frustrated at having to share so much of their income with the lower-division minnows, had conived with the Football Association to break away. Negotiations had taken around 18 months and the timing was perfect. Manchester United had led the restructuring race to the Stock Exchange in 1991 and had been best placed to take commercial advantage of both the Premier League

RIGHT: **MANCHESTER UNITED'S ERIC CANTONA IS SENT OFF AGAINST GALATASARAY IN THE INTIMIDATING ATMOSPHERE OF THE ALI SAMI YEN STADIUM**

power game and, very soon, the BSkyB satellite buy-out of the competition's TV rights.

Over the next decade, hundreds of clubs around the world sent inquiry teams to Old Trafford to wonder at the Megastore and English football's financial miracle. Even officials from Germany, Italy and Spain pondered whether similar restructuring was the answer. In fact, the English game had moved only to copy the continental system by which the leagues operated as direct subsidiaries of the national association. The brilliance of the Premier League revolution was in the branding and marketing.

In the autumn of 1993, of course, the jury remained out on whether the Premier League's dash for (comparative) self-

control would work. Similarly, the credibility of the Champions League and/or Cup was on the line. It was not only the Marseille scandal. Georgian club Dinamo Tbilisi, previous winners of the Cup-Winners' Cup, were expelled from the competition and fined after trying to bribe the referee of their preliminary-round home leg against Northern Ireland's Linfield.

The scope of the competition had been extended as political and military events in eastern Europe brought more new nations into the UEFA fold. Thus 20 clubs competed in the preliminary round and were joined by a further 22 clubs in the first round. Two knock-out rounds followed, with the surviving eight clubs entering the two-group Champions League. Beyond that UEFA had decided to reintroduce semi-finals to reduce the number of dead matches towards the end of the group stage. Thus the group-winners would play off against the 'opposite' runners-up in single-match semi-finals. The group-winners were deemed to deserve home advantage.

British interest did not reach that far. Rangers, anxious to make up for their near-miss in 1993, lost on away goals to Levsky Sofia in the first round. Manchester United, having finally cracked the domestic title challenge after 26 impatient years in the wilderness, fell by the same sword, but in the second round and against Galatasaray of Turkey.

Manager Alex Ferguson was a frustrated man. United had led 2–0 within 13 minutes of the kick-off in the first leg at Old Trafford, with a third-minute strike from inspirational skipper Bryan Robson and an own goal by Hakan Sukur. But the Turks hit back fearlessly through Arif Erdem and Swiss international Kubilay Turkyilmaz (two). Only a late equalizer from Eric Cantona saved United's pride and unbeaten home European record.

A goalless draw in the intimidating atmosphere of the Ali Sami Yen stadium in Istanbul sent United out on the away-goals rule. Galatasaray went on into the group stages. They would not win a match, as it turned out, but they celebrated all the way to the bank.

ABOVE: **ONE OF THE MOST FEARSOME SIGHTS IN FOOTBALL, RANGERS' DUNCAN FERGUSON LEAPS ABOVE LEVSKI SOFIA'S ALEXANDER MARKOV TO PUT A HEADER IN ON GOAL**

1993-94

MAIN: **ARSENE WENGER ON THE SIDELINES OF THE SAN SIRO, WATCHING HIS TEAM, MONACO, IN ACTION AGAINST AC MILAN**

GROUP STAGE

The most surprised entrants into the group stage were Monaco. They had finished third in France the previous season behind Marseille and Paris Saint-Germain and had expected to be playing European football in the UEFA Cup.

Then Marseille were expelled from the Champions League and Monaco, because they had yet to open their UEFA Cup campaign, were propelled up among the nouveaux riches.

At least they had the players for it, headed by Jurgen Klinsmann, the West German World Cup-winning striker. Klinsmann enjoyed talented support from Belgian playmaker Enzo Scifo and future French World Cup-winners in Lilian Thuram, Manu Petit and Youri Djorkaeff. Bringing the best out

of them was an up-and-coming young coach from Alsace named Arsene Wenger.

First-round opponents AEK Athens were initially reluctant to play Monaco. They had been drawn originally against Marseille and pleaded to UEFA in vain for a walkover into the second round. They never got there. Monaco beat them 2–1 overall and then former holders Steaua Bucharest 4–2 to reach the group stage.

Here they were matched in Group A with Moscow Spartak, Galatasaray and favourites Barcelona, still under the command of Johan Cruyff. The decisive matches saw Barcelona beat Monaco both home and away. Txiki Beguiristain scored both goals in Barca's 2–0 win in the Nou Camp, and Hristo

Five minutes before half-time Costacurta was sent off for tripping Klinsmann. He was not the only Milan player who would miss the final. Captain and sweeper Franco Baresi was shown a yellow card and, because it was his third of the campaign, he too was automatically condemned to missing Milan's seventh appearance in the final.

Despite their handicap, Milan dominated the second half. Demetrio Albertini scored with a superb long-range shot after a free-kick, and Daniele Massaro volleyed a magnificent third after a defence-splitting, cross-field pass from Christian Panucci.

As Milan coach Fabio Capello said: 'It was an extraordinary performance to win such an important game so decisively with only 10 men.'

In the other semi-final, Barcelona had to wait only 10 minutes before the path to the final opened up before them. That was how long it took for Stoichkov to open the scoring against Porto from close range after an attack organized by Romario and raiding left-back Sergi. The same three players were involved in the second goal after 35 minutes. The Brazilian striker found Sergi in space on the left and once more the lethal Stoichkov pounced in front of goal. Porto lost all hope of recovery when captain Joao Pinto was sent off on the hour. Dutchman Ronald Koeman scored Barcelona's third goal in the 72nd minute – unusually for him from open play. Later Sergi said: 'This was probably our best game of the season.'

BELOW: **PORTO'S BULGARIAN STRIKER EMIL KOSTADINOV TAKES ON TOUGH-TACKLING RONALD KOEMAN OF BARCELONA**

Stoichkov scored the winner in the Stade Louis II. Outclassed, Spartak and Galatasaray managed a meagre one win and seven goals between them.

Like Barcelona, Milan came through Group B unbeaten, a point ahead of FC Porto. That produced a semi-final line-up of Milan at home to Monaco and Barcelona at home to the Portuguese.

Milan won comfortably by 3–0, despite playing more than half the match with only 10 men after the first-half expulsion of central defender Alessandro Costacurta. They took the lead after 14 minutes when Monaco failed to mark up at a left-wing corner from Zvonimir Boban. French international Marcel Desailly rose to head past 'keeper Jean-Luc Ettori.

MIGHTY MILAN

In the words of the clichéd old football report, Milan kicked off with a rush... and were soon out of sight against a Barcelona side who had been many neutrals' favourites. After all, Barcelona boasted the one-touch, perpetual motion style instilled by Johan Cruyff, while Milan had selection problems. Suspension had cost them central defenders Alessandro Costacurta and Franco Baresi, while the requirements of UEFA's restrictions on foreigners left Romania centre-forward Florin Raducioiu and Denmark forward Brian Laudrup in the stand.

Barcelona's attack was spearheaded by a fearsome partnership in Bulgaria's Hristo Stoichkov and the Brazilian Romario, who was about to inspire his country's record fourth World Cup triumph in the United States. However, they saw very little of the ball. Instead, Milan took the game by the scruff of the neck, with Frenchman Marcel Desailly providing the power and Yugoslav Dejan Savicevic all the skill and inspiration. Desailly, signed the previous autumn from Marseille, thus became the first man to win the Champions Cup with two different clubs in successive seasons.

Ironically, coach Fabio Capello had considered Savicevic, the former Red Star man, a talented luxury who lacked the temperament either to sit patiently in the stand or to slot comfortably into the team pattern on the odd occasions when injuries demanded his services. The exiled Slav had been saved only – and repeatedly – by a one-man fan club comprising Silvio Berlusconi. But that was nothing in power terms. Milan's president had by now used his football springboard to become prime minister. Shamelessly he had adopted the fans' chant of 'Forza Italia' as his party's name.

No one doubted his Midas touch, least of all Milan fans. Now Savicevic scored one goal and was involved in creating the other three. Christian Panucci also had a ninth-minute 'goal' disallowed by English referee Philip Don for offside. Don had been appointed at short notice after death threats to the original referee, Dutchman John Blankenstein. Given the presence of his compatriot Johan Cruyff on the Barcelona bench, Blankenstein's appointment by UEFA had always been unwise.

Five years earlier Milan had also won the Champions Cup Final 4–0. But Steaua had offered mere token resistance. This was very different. Barcelona were on top of their game, but Milan were simply on a different footballing planet. Cruyff sat impassively back on the Barca bench, apparently resigned to the fact that Milan were in unstoppable mood. Goalkeeper Andoni Zubizarreta would later become the Catalan scapegoat but, in fairness, while the Basque icon may not have been

at his best, he was exposed by his defence's inability to withstand Milan's skill and pace.

Milan had threatened already through Panucci, Massaro and Desailly before Savicevic glided around Miguel Angel Nadal and chipped to the far post for Massaro to open

Final 1994

WEDNESDAY 18 MAY 1994
OLYMPIC, ATHENS

MILAN 4
MASSARO 22, 45, SAVICEVIC 47,
DESAILLY 59
BARCELONA 0

HT: 2-0. ATT: 70,000. REF: DON (ENG)

MILAN:
S. ROSSI - TASSOTTI*, F. GALLI, P.
MALDINI (NAVA 84), PANUCCI -
DONADONI, DESAILLY, ALBERTINI,
BOBAN - SAVICEVIC, MASSARO.
COACH: CAPELLO.

BARCELONA:
ZUBIZARRETA* - FERRER, R. KOEMAN,
NADAL, SERGI (QUIQUE 73) -
GUARDIOLA - BEGUIRISTAIN (EUSEBIO
51), AMOR, BAKERO, STOICHKOV -
ROMARIO.
COACH: CRUYFF.

*CAPTAIN

LEFT: **THE VICTORIOUS MILAN SIDE CELEBRATE IN THE OLYMPIC STADIUM, IN ATHENS**

the scoring. Then Savicevic and the Croat, Zvonimir Boban, combined with Panucci and Roberto Donadoni to build a second for Massaro on half-time.

Two minutes after the interval Savicevic himself scored after dancing past Nadal. He hit the post on 58 minutes,

Barcelona failed to clear and Demetrio Albertini put in Desailly for goal number four. Six minutes from time the irrepressible Savicevic again hit an upright.

As the shattered Zubizarreta said, 'Milan played to 100 per cent of their potential – perfect.'

RESCHEDULING THE FIXTURES

Everything was being done to ensure the progress of the top dogs to produce viewing figures for the television companies. Meanwhile, a young Ajax side went into battle with all the confidence of youth

GROUP STAGE

This was the watershed season when a cup competition was converted into the foundation stone for the long-awaited European superleague envisaged by Berlusconi. Stability had been the key to success down the years for domestic competitions, but the Champions League was bucking the rules.

Now four groups of four teams played in the first half of the season after a preliminary knock-out round. In the spring, competition stepped back into knock-out mode in line with the Cup-Winners' Cup and the UEFA Cup. One short-lived by-product was that champion clubs outside the top 24 nations were removed from the Champions League set-up altogether and dumped into the expanded dustbin of the UEFA Cup.

The pace of expansion owed much to television pressure. Competing clubs were guaranteed the income from three home matches on top of set appearance money and bonuses per point. But UEFA benefited the most. The lucrative exclusive TV and sponsorship deals provided an annual income from which all the junior competitions plus various development agencies could be funded.

TV channels gained the virtual security of an ongoing national interest through the legitimate fixing of entry procedures. The UEFA coefficient (a ranking based on a computation of match results over the preceding five years) was used to seed top-nation clubs direct into the mini-leagues.

UEFA also cleared Wednesday nights for the Champions League. Tuesday became the designated night for the UEFA Cup, Thursday for the Cup-Winners' Cup. Later, after the 1999 scrapping of the Cup-Winners' Cup, the UEFA Cup switched to Thursdays, with the expanding Champions League taking over Tuesdays.

However, results out on the pitch showed that not all the

RIGHT: **HRISTO STOICHKOV** CELEBRATES ONE OF HIS TWO STRIKES FOR BARCELONA AGAINST MANCHESTER UNITED IN THE NOU CAMP

FAR RIGHT: **GEORGE WEAH GIVES** OLIVER KAHN 'THE EYES' AS HE PLACES THE BALL BEYOND THE BAYERN GOALKEEPER self-obsessed giants of the European club game were as good as they thought.

In Group A, IFK Gothenburg were surprise winners ahead of the 1994 finalists Barcelona, with Manchester United the most notable of failures. They finished level on points with Barcelona but failed in the head-to-head contest against the Spanish champions. Johan Cruyff's men drew 2–2 at Old Trafford, then thrashed United 4–0 at home with one superb goal from Romario and two equally adept from Hristo Stoichkov. United fretted over the import restrictions which cost them the presence of Danish goalkeeper Peter Schmeichel between the sticks and the four-game suspension which barred French inspiration Eric Cantona.

In Group B, Paris Saint-Germain were the only team to end the mini-league stage with a 100 per cent record. Bayern Munich, with Lothar Matthaeus reverting from sweeper to midfield, followed them thanks to a decisive 4–1 win over Dynamo Kiev on the last match day. French striker Jean-Pierre Papin, completely fit just briefly, scored twice.

Group C saw Benfica and Hajduk Split qualify. Hajduk were one of three quarter-finalists to progress all the way through from the preliminary round. Argentina's Claudio Caniggia starred for Benfica, scoring twice in a crucial 3–1 win over Anderlecht. He also missed a penalty.

In Group D, Ajax Amsterdam dominated the keynote confrontation with holders Milan. The Dutch champions won both home and away to establish themselves as cup favourites. Milan squeezed through courtesy of a 1–0 victory over Casino Salzburg in Vienna on the last match day. The clubs had finished level on points, and Milan, like Barcelona, qualified on head-to-head results.

The first Italo-Austrian duel had proved stormy. Salzburg goalkeeper Otto Konrad was struck on the head by a bottle in the Stadio Meazza. Konrad played on after treatment but was later substituted after Milan went 2–0 ahead. Konrad spent the night in hospital after Salzburg, without him, lost 3–0.

KNOCK-OUT STAGE

The fixture pressure developed by the Champions League forced cuts in many leagues' winter break. But three of the eight 1995 quarter-finalists were still hampered: Hajduk Split, IFK and rivals Bayern Munchen.

The Swedes wandered around Europe playing friendlies to regain fitness after their close-season. Their confidence was strengthened when Lothar Matthaeus fell awkwardly during one of Bayern's own friendlies and was ruled out for the season. Hajduk used the winter break to contract several new players, but Barcelona were weakened by homesick Romario's exit to Flamengo of Rio de Janeiro, while Milan 'lost' veteran Dutchman Ruud Gullit back to Sampdoria.

Thus it was not one of Milan's foreign superstars who made all the difference against Benfica but home-grown Italian Marco Simone. He scored twice in a 12-minute spell midway through the second half of the first leg. Milan might even have won the goalless return against Benfica had not both Simone and Zvonimir Boban been foiled by the posts.

Ajax, with an average age of 23 despite the presence of 32-year-old Frank Rijkaard, had no problems with Hajduk. They drew 0–0 away and won 3–0 at home. Two-goal defender Frank de Boer outscored his attacking twin Ronald for once.

The normal pattern of draw away, win at home was upset in Munich and Gothenburg. Bayern were held 0–0 by IFK in the Olympic stadium, and their prospects in the return dipped further after 22 minutes when goalkeeper Sven Scheuer was sent off. Their Italian coach Giovanni Trapattoni pulled out all the tactical stops and Bayern seized a two-goal lead through Alex Zickler and Christian Nerlinger. The eventual 2–2 draw secured qualification on the away-goals rule.

Finally, the 'tie of the round' saw Barcelona held 1–1 in the Nou Camp by a goal from George Weah, the newly crowned African Footballer of the Year. Back in Paris, it seemed as if the fates were with Barcelona. PSG hit the posts five times, and just after the break Barcelona snatched the lead through Jose Bakero. Catalan hopes faded in the closing 18 minutes, however, when Paris gained overdue reward for their near-misses through Rai and Vincent Guerin. Paris were through to their third consecutive European semi-final; Barcelona, beaten in the Champions Cup Final the previous year, had this time fallen two rounds short.

In the semi-finals, Ajax and Bayern had old scores to settle. Memories of the great old days of Cruyff, Keizer and Krol came flooding back. Not so much in the goalless first leg in Munich but rather in the return in Amsterdam, when Ajax secured their place in the final with a runaway 5–2 victory. One goal for Jari Litmanen, another for the Nigerian Finidi George

and a third for Ronald de Boer, provided Ajax with a 3–1 interval lead. Only one brief incident in the second half worried the Dutch: that was when defender Danny Blind handled in the penalty box. Hungarian referee Sandor Puhl, to Dutch relief,

awarded a yellow card rather than a red and not only did Ajax qualify for the final – so did their skipper.

The other semi-final possessed an intriguing element in Milan's thinly disguised admiration for PSG's attacking leader, Weah. In the event, he never got a look in as Zvonimir Boban stole away in the last minute to convert a cross from Dejan Savicevic. The former Red Star man was Milan's hero in the return, scoring both Milan's goals in a 2-0 victory.

LEFT: **FORMER RED STAR MIDFIELDER ZVONIMIR BOBAN CELEBRATES HIS 91ST MINUTE STRIKE AGAINST PSG WITH MARCEL DESAILLY AND FRANCO BARESI: MILAN WON 2-0**

FRANK RETURNS TO HAUNT OLD FRIENDS

Triumph in Vienna was, with hindsight, Ajax's last hurrah. The financial landslip prompted by the Champions League would see the Amsterdam club's much-admired development system turn into a nursery not so much for them as for richer neighbours in Spain, Italy and England.

Within little more than two years, their entire winning team – apart from retirement-bound Frank Rijkaard – had been lured abroad. In the meantime they left a proud legacy in the form of players, none more promising than 18-year-old substitute Patrick Kluivert, whose late winner earned the Dutch a fourth Champions Cup.

Rijkaard's contribution was a perfect farewell to international football. The 32-year-old midfielder had scored Milan's winner in the 1990 final against Portugese side Benfica in the same Viennese stadium. This time Rijkaard, who had already announced his end-of-season retirement, created the decisive goal. Rijkaard said later: 'I feel sorry for my Italian friends, but sometimes football is like that.

Kluivert was not the only 18-year-old substitute who tormented Milan in the climactic last few minutes of the 1994–95 UEFA Champions League campaign. He had entered soon after the Nigerian, Nkankwo Kanu, had joined the action to disturb Milan's defensive control. The plan was for their young legs to wear down the Italian club's elder statesmen.

Van Gaal explained: 'Milan were more experienced than us. That's why I put two 18-year-old boys on the field in the second half and they won it for us.'

Milan, with only one player aged under 25 and missing the injured Dejan Savicevic, came close to a goal only in the 44th minute, when Marco Simone's volley was fisted away by 'keeper Edwin van der Sar.

Victory for Ajax avenged their defeat by Milan in the 1969 final and guaranteed them the honour of being top seeds, as holders, the following season. For Milan, defeat prevented them equalling Real Madrid's record of six wins in European football's most prestigious club event. Having lost their domestic league title to Juventus, Silvio Berlusconi's irritated giants were not destined to return for several years.

RIGHT: **FRANK RIJKAARD IN ACTION AGAINST HIS FORMER CLUB, MILAN. RIJKAARD'S 32 YEARS RAISED THE AVERAGE AGE OF HIS TEAM TO 23, WHICH SHOWS HOW YOUTHFUL THE OTHERS WERE**

Back in Holland, the city of Amsterdam erupted into a jubilant mass of red and white as thousands of fans poured into the city centre to celebrate. They danced on tram stop shelters, waving red banners and scarves. Some wore T-shirts emblazoned 'Louis for president' – referring to Ajax coach Louis van Gaal.

Having beaten the Italian side twice at the group stage, Ajax thus boasted a hat-trick of victories against Milan over the season. As Italian coach Fabio Capello said, 'Any team who can beat the holders three times in one season deserve to win the cup.'

UEFA and its sponsors could not have been happier. A survey by the marketing managers from TEAM revealed that 3.64 billion viewers across Europe had watched its Champions League broadcasts. That represented a staggering 61 per cent increase of 1.4 billion viewers in a year.

Back in Belgium, however, Jean-Marc Bosman barely noticed. He was focused solely on the imminent trial of his case before the European Court of Justice in Luxembourg. UEFA's hierarchy remained unconcerned. After all, what did European law matter to the newly enriched European football federation?

WEDNESDAY 24 MAY 1995
ERNST-HAPPEL-STADION, VIENNA

AJAX 1
KLUIVERT 83

MILAN 0

HT: 0-0. ATT: 49,500.
REF: CRACIUNESCU (ROM).

AJAX:
VAN DER SAR – REIZIGER, BLIND*, F. DE BOER – R. DE BOER, SEEDORF (KANU 52), RIJKAARD, DAVIDS – GEORGE, LITMANEN (KLUIVERT 65), OVERMARS.
COACH: VAN GAAL.

MILAN:
S. ROSSI – PANUCCI, COSTACURTA, F. BARESI*, P. MALDINI – DONADONI, ALBERTINI, DESAILLY, BOBAN (LENTINI 83) – SIMONE, MASSARO (ERANIO 89).
COACH: CAPELLO.

*CAPTAIN

ABOVE: **ON THE EVE OF HIS RETIREMENT AS A PLAYER, FRANK RIJKAARD FINDS THAT A SHINY PIECE OF SILVERWARE IS INFINITELY PREFERABLE TO THE USUAL GOLD WATCH**

LEFT: **MANAGER LOUIS VAN GAAL HOLDS UP THE CHAMPIONS CUP SEIZED BY HIS TALENTED YOUNG AJAX SIDE AS THE CROWD GOES CRAZY AND PHOTOGRAPHERS SNAP AWAY FOR TOMORROW'S BACK PAGES**

The Bosman ruling went further than anyone had expected and opened up a fabulous new world of wealth to top-flight footballers. But Dynamo Kiev were expelled for a scandal involving fur coats

GROUP STAGE

The European Court published its judgement on 15 December 1995, and it was an historic victory for Jean-Marc Bosman against his club Liege. The Court went even further than Bosman had expected. Not only did it rule that all European Union professionals could move fee-free between member states on the expiry of their contracts, but it also ruled illegal, as a consequence, all regulations restricting the employment of EU citizen footballers within other member states.

Bosman's victory opened up a fabulously wealthy new

RIGHT: JUVENTUS STRIKER GIANLUCA VIALLI ATTEMPTS TO SHOW BORUSSIA DORTMUND DEFENDER JURGEN KOHLER A CLEAN PAIR OF HEELS

world for his fellow professionals, but in winning it he lost everything. Fighting the European and Belgian authorities cost him his home, two marriages, his playing career and the prospect of any further employment within the game.

Although in addition to winning the case advocate Jean-Louis Dupont won Bosman a million euros in compensation, much of that went in legal fees even before the Belgian taxman demanded a cut.

Like Jacques Glassman, the whistle-blower who brought down Marseille, Bosman became *persona non grata* within the football family because he stood up for what he believed to be right. His supporters included FIFpro, the international players' union to which the English Professional Footballers'

Association is affiliated. But, with the exception of contributions from the Dutch national squad and a few individuals in gratitude for the service he had done his fellow professionals, Bosman received no financial recognition.

FIFpro duly organized a benefit match, but even that was tainted because various federations scandalously refused permission for its staging within their territories.

The Bosman ruling was published just after the completion of the Champions League group stage, which featured a preliminary knock-out round, followed by four groups of four clubs. Domestic champions seeded 25 and below had been hived off into the UEFA Cup.

Dynamo Kiev were one of eight clubs 'promoted' from the preliminaries. They were then expelled from Group A after their opening 1-0 home win over Panathinaikos. It came to light that the Spanish referee Antonio Lopez Nieto and his assistants were offered expensive fur coats by Kiev's directors on the eve of the match. Danish club Aalborg, Kiev's qualifying victims, took over their Group A slot. Kiev were banned for three seasons, although the ban was later commuted.

Group A saw Panathinaikos and Nantes reach the quarter-finals, surprisingly edging out FC Porto, while the only club with a 100 per cent record proved to be Moscow Spartak in Group B. They invested their Champions League

LEFT: WITH HIS DAZZLING RUNS AND INCH-PERFECT FREE-KICKS, ALESSANDRO DEL PIERO WAS THE OUTSTANDING PLAYER IN THE JUVENTUS SIDE WHICH REACHED THE FINAL IN 1996. HE WAS THE PERFECT REPLACEMENT FOR ROBERTO BAGGIO

cash wisely in bringing home internationals such as striker Sergei Yuran, midfielder Vasili Kulkov and goalkeeper Stanislav Cherchesov. But English champions Blackburn Rovers, for all steel magnate Jack Walker's millions, proved a disappointment. A misjudgement by England goalkeeper Tim Flowers presented Yuran with the only goal of their home opener against the Russians. From that point, Spartak never looked back and Blackburn never looked like qualifying. Legia Warsaw finished runners-up.

Juventus topped Group C. The pre-season sale of Italy's 1994 World Cup hero Roberto Baggio to Milan was compensated by the emergence of Alex del Piero. He inspired the early victories which lifted Juve into the last eight ahead of Dortmund with two match days remaining.

Ajax began their title defence in Group D as they ended

1994-95 – with a 1-0 win. This time Real Madrid were the victims of Marc Overmars's 14th-minute goal. The Dutch champions thus shot straight to the top of the table and never lost command of a group in which Madrid finished runners-up. Teenage striker Raul Gonzalez became the youngest player to score a Champions League hat-trick in Real's 6-1 thrashing of Ferencvaros.

KNOCK-OUT STAGE
Lennart Johansson announced that he had been left quite unimpressed by the Bosman judgement. 'Nothing has changed,' he said. 'We cannot allow the law to interfere with our game.' That was rich coming from the president of a European federation whose legal, commercial and marketing expertise had nailed into financial submission

the continent's most powerful sponsors and broadcasters.

In fact, Johansson could not have been more wrong. Sitting on its Swiss sidelines, UEFA had ignored the reality that its clubs had to abide by the laws of other lands. Its restrictions still worked for Switzerland, but were illegal throughout the rest of western Europe. Within weeks the European Union federations had lifted controls on EU players and, going beyond Bosman, had extended the principle of no-fee transfers on expiry of contracts to national as well as international transfers.

The remainder of the Champions League season was governed by UEFA's outmoded regulations, but only by gentleman's agreement. Behind the scenes feverish activity was under way as the giants planned how to invest their Champions League cash in the best players western Europe now had to offer. On the pitch, the group winners did not have everything their own way in the quarter-finals. Panathinaikos, Juventus and Ajax all progressed, but Spartak fell to French champions Nantes. The first leg in France saw Japhet N'Doram and Nicolas Ouedec provide a 2–0 victory over a ring-rusty Russian team who were further weakened by the sales of 'keeper Stanislav Cherchesov, skipper Viktor Onopko, midfielder Vasili Kulkov and striker Sergei Yuran to Austria, Spain and England. The Russians quickly levelled the aggregate score in Moscow, but eventually lost 4–2 overall.

There were no such problems for Ajax against Borussia Dortmund. The tie was virtually decided by the first leg in Germany and a goal in each half from Edgar Davids and Patrick Kluivert.

Dortmund's hopes of a second-leg surprise were wrecked when skipper and sweeper Matthias Sammer was sent off. Ajax also won the return by 1–0 through a goal from teenager Kiki Musampa.

A clash of outsiders matched Legia Warsaw against Panathinaikos. The first leg, in icy Warsaw, was dominated by Polish goalkeeper Jozef Wandzik – playing against his fellow-countrymen.

His saves secured a goalless draw for Panathinaikos, who won 3–0 back in Athens, where two goals fell to another Polish export in striker Krzysztof Warzycha.

The outstanding quarter-final saw Real Madrid and Juventus renew a 34-year rivalry. Madrid had been disturbed by the coaching replacement of Jorge Valdano by Arsenio Iglesias. But he had brief cause to celebrate after Raul's first-half goal brought victory in the Bernabeu. Outstanding for Madrid was Denmark's Michael Laudrup, once of Juventus. But his inside knowledge proved of no avail in Turin: Juve won 2–0 and 2–1 overall.

The semi-finals, with a pre-ordained draw, matched Ajax

against Panathinaikos and Juventus against Nantes. Ajax suffered a major setback when they marked their last European tie in the old Olympic stadium with a 1–0 defeat to an 87th-minute goal from the prolific Warzycha.

But Ajax coach Louis van Gaal was being prophetic rather than arrogant when he warned: 'We are not beaten yet.' Within four minutes of the kick-off in Athens, Jari Litmanen silenced 75,000 noisy Greek fans by levelling the aggregate score. He struck again 13 minutes from the end and Panathinaikos, throwing caution to the wind, were punished further on the break by Nordin Wooter.

Juventus won their home leg against Nantes by 2–0 with second-half goals from captain Gianluca Vialli and Vladimir Jugovic. Vialli's goal, surprisingly, was his first European goal of the season, but he followed up with another in France as Juve went through 4–3 on aggregate.

BELOW: **LENNART JOHANSSON** WAS UNIMPRESSED BY THE BOSMAN RULING: 'NOTHING HAS CHANGED' WAS HIS RESPONSE, WHICH WAS SIMPLY FLYING IN THE FACE OF FACTS

JUVENTUS CELEBRATE BELATED GLORY

When Juventus won the Champions League they celebrated as if for the first time. Their previous victory, in 1985, had been in the shadow of the Heysel disaster. As chief executive and former striker Roberto Bettega said, 'This is for real. We could never celebrate winning in 1985. We have waited a long time for this.'

But even the achievement of squeezing past outgoing holders Ajax on penalties would prove to be tarnished glory. Four years later, outspoken comments about the muscle-bound nature of various Juve players by Zdenek Zeman, an Italian-based Czech coach, turned out to be their undoing. Zeman's comments prompted a criminal investigation by a Turin public prosecutor, Raffaele Guariniello, himself ironically a Juve fan.

Guariniello had long been concerned about rumours of doping in Italian football. Zeman's comments gave him the excuse to home in on Juventus.

An inquiry team removed more than one hundred medicines and potions from the club's premises and this ultimately – in November 2004 – led to a suspended jail sentence for club doctor Riccardo Agricola for 'sporting fraud' between 1994 and 1998.

In the spring of 2005, Dick Pound, head of the World Anti Doping Agency, demanded that Juventus be stripped of the titles they had won in those years which included three Serie A titles, one Italian cup, one World Club Cup, one European Supercup and... this 1996 Champions' crown. Victory, even if claimed only by virtue of a shoot-out, was deserved on the day. Juventus out-shot Ajax by 13-6 and out-scored them on corners by 10 to six. Afterwards ,coach Marcello Lippi hailed the way his players – intriguingly, with hindsight – had maintained the pace of their game throughout the 120 minutes.

Juventus could have won it early on. First Alex del Piero needed just a little too long in front of goal, then Fabrizio Ravanelli, the grey-haired 'Silver Fox', fired hastily high and wide. Finally Ajax 'keeper Edwin van der Sar and Frank de Boer allowed Ravanelli to steal the ball from between them and shoot home from the narrowest of angles.

One goal was less than Juve deserved but allowed Ajax to

RIGHT: (L TO R) GIANLUCA VIALLI, MICHAEL REIZIGER, PATRICK KLUIVERT AND MORENO TORRICELLI ARE INVOLVED IN BALLETIC ACTION

FAR RIGHT: SKIPPER GIANLUCA VIALLI WITH THE TROPHY. BEHIND HIM IS GOALSCORER FABRIZIO RAVANELLI

equalize four minutes before half-time. De Boer, making up for his blunder, surprised Angelo Peruzzi with a free-kick and, when the ball was pushed out to Jari Litmanen, the Finn scored to become the competition's top marksman with nine goals. Gianluca Vialli hit the bar and was foiled brilliantly on three occasions by Van der Sar as Ajax survived into extra time.

Surviving penalties, however, turned out to be beyond them. Juve succeeded in Rome where Olimpico hosts Roma had failed against Liverpool in 1984. Ajax coach Louis van Gaal was disappointed but not surprised. He said, 'You can tell, at the start of the penalties, who is going to win. When you have only a few players volunteering, then you know you have lost.'

WEDNESDAY 22 MAY 1996
OLIMPICO, ROME

JUVENTUS   1
RAVANELLI 12

AJAX   1
LITMANEN 40

AFTER EXTRA TIME
JUVENTUS WON 4-2 ON PENS.
HT: 1-1. 90 MIN: 1-1. ATT: 70,000.
REF: DIAZ VEGA (SP)

JUVENTUS:
PERUZZI - TORRICELLI, FERRARA,
VIERCHOWOD, PESSOTTO - CONTE
(JUGOVIC 43), PAULO SOUSA (DI LIVIO
56), DESCHAMPS - RAVANELLI
(PADOVANO 76), VIALLI*, DEL PIERO.
COACH: LIPPI.

AJAX:
VAN DER SAR - SILOOY, BLIND*, F. DE
BOER (SCHOLTEN 67), BOGARDE - R.
DE BOER (WOOTER 91), LITMANEN,
DAVIDS - GEORGE, KANU, MUSAMPA
(KLUIVERT 46).
COACH: VAN GAAL.

*CAPTAIN

NEW FACES IN THE DRESSING ROOM

It was all change at the summit of European football as the old restrictions on nationality disappeared. Rosenborg of Norway defeated Milan and Zinedine Zidane became a Juventus player

GROUP STAGE

Squad statistics tell the tale of the instant effect of Bosman. Juventus had played out 1995-96 with four foreigners but now boasted six, including new star Zinedine Zidane. Borussia Dortmund increased their import quota from six to 10, Milan from six to eight and Manchester United from three to seven (discounting the UK and Irish contingents). Over subsequent seasons the foreigner count exploded, also handing national

RIGHT: **AJAX'S NIGERIAN FORWARD TIJANI BABANGIDA AGAINST AUXERRE**

coaches a convenient excuse for disappointments in World Cups and European Championships.

Simultaneously, the élite clubs moved towards a joint strategy vis-à-vis UEFA and the Champions League. This would eventually lead to the creation of G-14, with its secretariat in Brussels, because the clubs at least recognized the central significance of the European Union to world football.

Perversely, the 1996–97 group stages saw the end of the Milan era. Their dreams of winning the cup for a record-equalling sixth time were blown away in unlikely fashion on the last match-day of Group A, when the Norwegians of Rosenborg Trondheim went to the Stadio Meazza needing nothing less than victory... and achieved it by 2–1. FC Porto won the group.

Rosenborg were a prime example of everything which was both good and bad about the Champions League. Having once reached the group stages, they used the income to buy their domestic rivals' top players, thus simultaneously strengthening their own domestic position while undermining their opponents.

The Norwegians had no need of a place in the semis or the final to balance their budget, as did the Italians, Spanish and English. Merely taking part was enough. By 2005 they had capitalized on that financial trick so effectively that they had carried off the Norwegian league title 13 years in a row.

That victory over Milan remained the high point of their exploits. Milan had just reappointed Arrigo Sacchi as coach, after his resignation as Italy boss the previous Sunday, and needed only one point. But they fell behind to Harald Brattbakk after 29 minutes and lost to a 69th-minute winner from Vegard Heggem after French striker Christophe Dugarry had equalized on the stroke of half-time.

Milan's astonishing collapse deprived the competition of an all-Italian quarter-final against the newly crowned world club champions Juventus. Silvio Berlusconi, Milan's millionaire owner, described the defeat as 'the lowest point in our luck and in the league since I have been at Milan'.

While Milan were sinking, European pedigree was being roused elsewhere on the continent. Ajax, bidding to reach their third consecutive final but needing an away win from their last Group A tie to qualify, rose to the challenge and beat Grasshopper 1–0 in Zurich. Patrick Kluivert's goal kept alive the Dutch champions' remarkable record of not having lost an away tie for three seasons. Ajax thus finished second behind Auxerre, who clinched their quarter-final place with a 2–1 win over Rangers in France.

In Group C, Manchester United, third before their last group game, defeated Rapid Vienna 2–0 in Austria and had

Juventus to thank for snuffing out Fenerbahce's quarter-final hopes by the same score in Turin. Ryan Giggs and Eric Cantona scored for United, whose fans spent as much time listening out for the score from Turin as watching their own side's level-headed performance in sub-zero temperatures.

Atletico Madrid beat Widzew Lodz 1–0 in their final fixture to win Group B ahead of Dortmund, who finished runners-up after winning their final match 4–3 against the faded glories of Steaua Bucharest.

KNOCK-OUT STAGE

Nigeria had struck a major blow for African football in 1996 by winning the Olympic Games football gold in Sydney. The legacy of confidence invested in their players quickly made itself felt across the European game. No one felt it more strongly than Ajax Amsterdam and Atletico in the Champions League quarter-finals.

Ajax, Juventus, Manchester United and Borussia Dortmund were favourites heading into the last eight and justified their status by progressing. But Ajax very nearly did not make it.

ABOVE: **PAUL GASCOIGNE OF RANGERS HITS THE TURF AFTER A CHALLENGE FROM BERNARD DIOMEDE OF AUXERRE**

BELOW: **JEAN-MARC BOSMAN WRAPS HIMSELF IN THE FLAG OF THE EUROPEAN COMMUNITY AFTER THE JUDGE RULED IN HIS FAVOUR AND SIMULTANEOUSLY TRANSFORMED THE ENTIRE WORLD OF FOOTBALL**

RIGHT: **ALESSIO TACCHINARDI OF JUVENTUS BEATS AJAX'S RONALD DE BOER TO THE BALL**

It took Nigerian forward Tijani Babangida to score one minute from the end of extra time to set the seal on a 4-3 aggregate victory over luckless Atletico.

Holders Juventus reached the last four by beating Rosenborg 2-0 in the second, home leg and 3-1 overall. French midfielder Zinedine Zidane had led the way by taking inadvertent advantage of a blunder by Rosenborg 'keeper Jorn Jamtfall in the 29th minute. Jamtfall's clearance struck the surprised Juventus playmaker and rebounded into the net. It was one of Zidane's luckiest goals, but he had deserved a change of international fortune.

The previous summer Zidane's colourless performances for France at Euro 96 in England had rung alarm bells in Turin. Happily, Zidane's lethargy was due merely to the combined effects of a car accident shortly before the finals and an extra-long season. His previous club, Bordeaux, had played the

summertime Intertoto Cup in 1995 and then gone all the way through to the following year's UEFA Cup Final.

Manchester United became the first English semi-finalists for 12 years when they beat FC Porto 4-0 at home and forced a 0-0 draw away. United withstood a barrage of early pressure from the Portuguese champions, unaware of problems outside the ground where 20 fans were injured after clashes with police amid security chaos.

In the other quarter-final, Borussia Dortmund beat Auxerre 4-1 on aggregate in a duel between two of Europe's most venerable coaches in German Ottmar Hitzfeld and Frenchman Guy Roux.

The semi-final repeat between Juventus and Ajax generated none of the nail-biting tension of the 1996 final. First-half goals from Nicola Amoruso and the giant Christian Vieri earned a 2-1 win for Juve in Amsterdam, and they ran

away 4-1 with the second leg. A 70,000 crowd in the Delle Alpi saw veteran Attilio Lombardo head in a corner in the 34th minute and then set up Vieri in the 36th. Mario Melchiot replied for the Dutch with 15 minutes to go before Amoruso and Zidane struck twice more for Juve in quick succession.

The other tie saw Borussia Dortmund achieve the rare feat of winning both home and away against Manchester United. An own goal from Gary Pallister provided the first victory in Dortmund, a strike from Lars Ricken the second at Old Trafford. With veteran Jurgen Kohler in brilliant form at the heart of the defence and goalkeeper Stefan Klos making stunning stops from Andy Cole and substitute Ryan Giggs, the Germans survived relentless pressure. 'Losing the goal so early in the game was a bit of a handicap, but we could have overcome that if we had taken any of the chances,' said United's manager Alex Ferguson, before adding: 'Next season we will be back.'

ABOVE: OLE-GUNNAR SOLSKJAER PUTS THE BALL IN THE BACK OF THE NET FOR MANCHESTER UNITED AGAINST BORUSSIA DORTMUND, BUT THE GOAL IS RULED OUT BY THE REFEREE

DORTMUND UPSET THE OLD LADY

The sight of Portuguese midfielder Paulo Sousa hobbling around the Olympic stadium's athletics track in triumph said everything about Borussia Dortmund's surprise dethroning of holders Juventus.

Dortmund had been outsiders from the moment the two clubs emerged from their semi-finals, and the fact that the final was in the back yard of fierce domestic rivals Bayern was expected to be of little assistance. Juventus were clear favourites and Dortmund were there to make up the numbers.

But Dortmund coach Ottmar Hitzfeld, due to retire 'upstairs' after the final by his own choice, had other ideas. So did back-to-fitness Matthias Sammer in the heart of defence; so did Dortmund's two former Juventus midfielders Sousa and German Andreas Moller.

Sousa did not want only victory: he wanted revenge. Juve had transfer-listed him at the end of the previous season while he was still convalescing from a knee injury. Dortmund had taken the gamble and Sousa wanted to repay both clubs in contrasting ways. In the closing minutes of the final he had to be carried off, nursing a badly bruised leg. But not even a

RIGHT: **KARLHEINZ RIEDLE**
SCORES FOR DORTMUND

fracture would have prevented him limping back out for the presentations and the opportunity to celebrate a Juventus defeat just a year after he had been celebrating their victory.

Dortmund's success enhanced German domination of European football. The national team were European champions, Schalke had just won the UEFA Cup – also against Italian opposition in Internazionale – and Sammer was the reigning European Footballer of the Year.

History was against Dortmund. Juve had beaten them in a UEFA Cup Final, in the UEFA Cup semi-finals and on aggregate in a previous Champions League tie. But they possessed an inner knowledge of the Italian team's organization, not only through Moller and Sousa but through two more Juve old boys in defenders Stefan Reuter and Jurgen Kohler.

Dortmund took the lead with their first shot after 29 minutes. Juve failed to clear Moller's corner, Scot Paul Lambert centred and Karlheinz Riedle chested down before shooting home. Four minutes later, Riedle rose unmarked to head home another Moller corner. Central defenders Ciro Ferrara and Paulo Montero stood and stared at each other in recrimination while Riedle skipped away, ecstatic. On the day before the final he had told his team-mates of his dream that he would score twice. Dortmund held their advantage to half-time despite a spirited Juventus fightback. Zinedine Zidane shot against a post and Christian Vieri had a 'goal' disallowed for handball.

Lippi rang the changes at half-time to bring the barely fit Alex del Piero into the action. The switch paid off when Del Piero's close-range shot climaxed a move engineered by Croatia striker Alen Boksic.

Six minutes later, however, Hitzfeld countered with a match-winning substitution of his own. Lars Ricken had been on the pitch only 16 seconds when he pursued a slide-rule pass from Moller and lobbed out-of-position 'keeper Angelo Peruzzi from 30 yards.

Peruzzi had missed the previous day's training session to fly home and visit his wife and new baby daughter. Doubtless he wished he had stayed there.

WEDNESDAY 28 MAY 1997
OLYMPIA, MUNICH

BORUSSIA DORTMUND 3
RIEDLE 29, 34, RICKEN 71

JUVENTUS 1
DEL PIERO 64

HT: 2–0. ATT: 65,000. REF: PUHL (HUN)

DORTMUND:
KLOS – REUTER, KOHLER, SAMMER*, KREE – HEINRICH, LAMBERT, PAULO SOUSA, MOLLER (ZORC 88) – RIEDLE, CHAPUISAT (RICKEN 70).
COACH: HITZFELD.

JUVENTUS:
PERUZZI – PORRINI (DEL PIERO 46), FERRARA, MONTERO, IULIANO – DI LIVIO, DESCHAMPS, ZIDANE, JUGOVIC – VIERI (AMORUSO 73), BOKSIC (TACCHINARDI 87).
COACH: LIPPI.

*CAPTAIN

LEFT: **THE OUTSTANDING ANDREAS MOLLER IN HIS TEAM'S MOMENT OF TRIUMPH**

THE TRIUMPH OF PRAGMATISM

The Champions League rules continued to be adapted to suit all interested parties as the European Cup grew away from its roots. In Madrid, fans found another way of moving the goalposts

GROUP STAGE

Champions League? Not from 1997 onwards. The trophy with which revived Real Madrid flew home at the season's end had been turned into a hybrid by UEFA's controversial expansion to admit runners-up from the nations ranked as Europe's top eight. That meant expanding the first round proper from four to six groups, with the group winners plus the two runners-up with the best records reaching the quarter-finals.

To do that UEFA had to attract the support of the minnow nations. This was gained by recalling their downgraded champions from the UEFA Cup and putting them into the Champions League preliminaries. Bringing runners-up into the Champions Cup was not new. Several of the launch clubs in 1955–56 had not been champions because the competition had been organized, initially, by invitation. Then Real Madrid's

subsequent domination persuaded UEFA to allow the Spanish runners-up to enter in 1956–57 (Bilbao), 1957–58 (Sevilla) and 1958–59 (Atletico Madrid).

The runners-up who kicked off a new era in the second qualifying round for the 1997–98 Champions League were Barcelona (Spain), Newcastle United (England), Feyenoord (Holland), Bayer Leverkusen (Germany), Paris Saint-Germain (France), Parma (Italy), Sporting (Portugal) and Besiktas (Turkey). The one anomaly was the presence in the preliminary draw of both Turkish champions Galatasaray and runners-up Besiktas. UEFA's eight top-seeded countries had all been promised two Champions League places, but the award of a direct seeding to holders Dortmund meant pushing Turkey back in the pecking order. Happily both Galatasaray and Besiktas won through to the group stage.

RIGHT: **DAVOR SUKER OF REAL MADRID SCORES AGAINST ROSENBORG**

Intriguingly, only one of the domestic runners-up progressed to the quarter-finals: Germany's Leverkusen.

In effect the groups were decided over two match-days. Borussia Dortmund, Manchester United, Dynamo Kiev and Bayern Munich had a comparatively easy ride – all four sewing up their own group leadership with one game to play and a fortnight remaining. But that still left an abundance of drama for the sixth and last match day.

Juventus had a close call in Group B. They qualified as one of the two group runners-up with best records because, while they were beating group winners Manchester United 1-0, Rosenborg Trondheim could only draw 2-2 with Olympiakos in Group D. Juventus owed their victory to a late goal from Filippo Inzaghi. However, it would not have been enough if Olympiakos's Predrag Djordjevic had not scored two minutes from time to salvage a 2-2 draw for the Greeks and eliminate Rosenborg.

Had the Norwegians held on for a 2-1 victory, they would have gone through to the quarter-finals with 13 points as one of the two best second-place teams.

Instead, they finished with 11 and went out. Juventus went through with 12 points, and Leverkusen got in with 13 as the other 'best runners-up' (the deciding factors being points scored, mutual results, goal difference and goals scored).

Juve hero Inzaghi said: 'I didn't realize we had qualified until I saw my team-mates jumping up and down on the touchlines. This must be the most important goal of my career.'

Real Madrid waited until the last match to win Group D by thrashing FC Porto 4-0. Croatia's Davor Suker scored twice, with the other two coming from Fernando Hierro and Brazilian left-back Roberto Carlos. Leverkusen and Monaco, in Group F, played out a 2-2 draw which was good enough to see both through.

BELOW: **MANCHESTER UNITED'S TEDDY SHERINGHAM GETS HOT UNDER THE COLLAR AGAINST JUVENTUS**

KNOCK-OUT STAGE

Germany had three sides in the quarter-finals: Leverkusen, holders Borussia Dortmund and Bayern Munich. Yet, remarkably, within six months all the talk would be about a German crisis after the national team collapsed in the World Cup quarter-finals in France.

Leverkusen were now out of their depth. Real Madrid proved it by beating them 4-1 on aggregate. The margin would have been greater but for Leverkusen goalkeeper Dirk Heinen in the second leg in Spain. He pulled off two superb first-half saves from Raul but had no answer when French international Christian Karembeu scored four minutes into the second half.

Karembeu had only just joined Madrid after a long battle to quit Sampdoria, but was proving worth the wait since he had also scored Madrid's goal in the first leg. New striking hero Fernando Morientes and veteran defender Fernando Hierro (penalty) extended the lead.

Dortmund needed an extra-time goal from Swiss veteran Stephane Chapuisat to lift them into the semi-finals at the expense of Bayern. His goal, after 109 minutes, was the only one either side managed in the two legs.

Juventus slipped through eventually against Dynamo Kiev but, again, did not make life easy for themselves. Held 1–1 at home, Juve had to go and win 4–1 in the Ukraine capital for a 5–2 aggregate success.

Pippo Inzaghi scored a hat-trick. As coach Marcello Lippi commented: 'When this team have to rise to the occasion, they always manage it.'

Completing the semi-final line-up were Monaco at the expense of Manchester United. After forcing a 0–0 draw in the principality, United fell behind at Old Trafford to an early strike by David Trezeguet. Ultimately, they went out on the away-goals rule despite a second-half effort from Norway striker Ole-Gunnar Solskjaer. Manager Alex Ferguson complained that Monaco 'only had one shot and that was the goal'.

Monaco coach Jean Tigana said: 'The highest point in my career as a player was when France beat Brazil in the 1986 World Cup in Mexico. This is the highest point as a coach.' It was also the end of road for Tigana, as Monaco then fell 6–4 on aggregate to Juventus in the semi-finals. Juventus dominated the first leg to win 4–1 thanks to a hat-trick, including two penalties, from Del Piero and a late goal from Zinedine Zidane. A 3–2 defeat in Monte Carlo changed nothing.

Chaos theory turned into reality in the other semi-final, between Real Madrid and Dortmund, after probably the most embarrassing incident in the Estadio Bernabeu's history. Minutes before kick-off a group of notorious *Ultrasur* supporters brought down the ball-catch netting behind one of the goals. One post fell on to the goal frame, smashing the cross-bar and uprooting the frame. Dutch referee Mario van der Ende took both teams off the pitch and the kick-off was delayed by 45 minutes. No spare goal could be found in the Bernabeu, so groundstaff had to break into Madrid's training ground three miles away for a replacement.

When the match did get under way, goals from Fernando Morientes and Christian Karembeu earned Madrid a 2–0 win, but they also collected a massive fine from UEFA for their security failures. By comparison, the second leg was a tame goalless draw, so Madrid's overall victory set up what Juve coach Marcello Lippi described as 'the dream final'.

LEFT: **FABIEN BARTHEZ EMBRACES HIS TEAM-MATES AFTER MONACO'S 1–0 VICTORY AT OLD TRAFFORD, TO WHICH HE SOON RETURNED AS MANCHESTER UNITED'S 'KEEPER**

REAL GO BACK WHERE THEY BELONG

'This,' said Alfredo Di Stefano, 'is what European cup finals should be all about.' While Juventus coach Marcello Lippi had called it 'the dream final', the occasion would turn out, of course, to be a delight for the one team and a nightmare for the other.

The match-up in Amsterdam's Arena was a throwback to another era, when Europe's Latin aristocrats ruled the football world, buying the best players and paying them the biggest wages, building – and filling – the largest stadia in Europe, and lifting the game into a new dimension.

Not all the commercial and professional millions in play could equate to the value of the tradition represented by the two clubs. Hence *Marca*, the Spanish sports daily, had left its entire front page blank white the morning after Madrid had qualified for their first Champions Cup Final since 1981; hence Italy's *Gazzetta dello Sport* cleared six pages to recount the events of Juve's semi-final triumph and look towards the final.

Closer to the big day, trouble set in when Dutch air traffic controllers refused to accept charter flights bringing not only Spanish and Italian fans but even the Juventus team. UEFA gave the Dutch federation 24 hours to sort it out, and eventually the government declared a temporary lifting of flight restrictions to avert a public relations disaster.

In goal there appeared little to choose between a happily secure Angelo Peruzzi and Madrid's grumpy German, Bodo Illgner.

In defence, Juve missed the solidity of the injured Ciro Ferrara, while illness denied Madrid the services of Aitor Karanka. Compensation for Juve had been in the progress of Mark Iuliano, whereas Madrid leaned even more heavily on the aggressive leadership of Fernando Hierro.

Juventus possessed both skill and direction in midfield through the contrasting French duo of Didier Deschamps and

Zinedine Zidane, but Madrid had been galvanized by the mid-term arrival of Christian Karembeu alongside the perceptive Fernando Redondo.

In attack, Pippo Inzaghi had wiped away Juve's concerns over the sale of Christian Vieri to Atletico Madrid. For Madrid, Fernando Morientes had made such rapid progress that Davor Suker was no longer first-choice partner for the trickily naughty Pedrag Mijatovic.

As in 1997, Juventus were favourites. As in 1997, they ended up with losers' medals. A technically engrossing game played at remarkable pace saw the Italians seize early control, only for Madrid – with ex-Ajax man Clarence Seedorf tireless in midfield and Hierro a tower of strength – to 'think' their way back into the match.

Madrid had lost form so badly in the Spanish league that they had finished outside the top two places which would have guaranteed a Champions League return the following season. It was almost unthinkable for the aristocrats from the Spanish capital. Juventus, crowned Italian champions once again, did not have that worry.

Yet, in the second half, Madrid cast off the pressure and began to play their football. In the 66th minute, Yugoslav striker Mijatovic seized on a loose ball on the edge of the six-yard box, stepped wide of Peruzzi and clipped the ball home. It was the only goal.

After 32 years Real Madrid, original champions of Europe, were back where they knew they always belonged.

Two days later, Jupp Heynckes, their German coach, quit.

LEFT: **ZINEDINE ZIDANE HAS A SHOT BLOCKED BY THE REAL MADRID WALL**

WEDNESDAY 20 MAY 1998
ARENA, AMSTERDAM

REAL MADRID 1
MIJATOVIC 66
JUVENTUS 0

HT: 0-0. ATT: 50,000. REF: KRUG (GER)

MADRID:
ILLGNER - PANUCCI, HIERRO, SANCHIS*, ROBERTO CARLOS - KAREMBEU, REDONDO, SEEDORF - RAUL (AMAVISCA 90), MIJATOVIC (SUKER 89), MORIENTES (JAIME 81). COACH: HEYNCKES.

JUVENTUS:
PERUZZI* - TORRICELLI, IULIANO, MONTERO, PESSOTTO (FONSECA 71) - DI LIVIO (TACCHINARDI 46), DESCHAMPS (CONTE 77), DAVIDS, ZIDANE - INZAGHI, DEL PIERO. COACH: LIPPI.

*CAPTAIN

PIONEERS MARCH BACK TO THE FRONT

Threatened with a breakaway league, UEFA offered more prize money and managed to persuade Europe's top clubs to keep things in the family. On the pitch, Manchester United were at their peak

1998-99

GROUP STAGE

The brave new commercial and televisual world depended heavily on traditional 'names' to sell the products – whether cars, tyres or satellite dishes.

Conveniently, then, the age of the Champions League had been dominated by Milan, Ajax, Juventus, Borussia Dortmund and Real Madrid – all original European pioneers. It was appropriate that in 1999 Manchester United joined them on

the podium after defeating Bayern Munich 2–1 in one of the most dramatic of finals.

Such an explosive ending was a fitting climax to a tumultuous year which started with UEFA's representative Lennart Johansson being trounced by Sepp Blatter in FIFA's presidential election on the eve of a World Cup won in some style by the French hosts.

Zinedine Zidane scored two goals in the concluding victory

RIGHT: **INTER MILAN GOALKEEPER GIANLUCA PAGLIUCA TIPS THE BALL OVER THE BAR AGAINST REAL MADRID AT THE BERNABEU**

FAR RIGHT: **SERGIY REBROV SCORES FOR DYNAMO KIEV AGAINST ARSENAL AT HIGHBURY**

over Brazil to wipe the floor with critics of his displays in Juve's cup final defeats by Dortmund and Madrid.

Behind the scenes, UEFA was working flat-out to keep the big clubs on board. Media Partners, a Milan-based marketing agency working with the blessing of Silvio Berlusconi, had generated proposals for a breakaway superleague. To be played in midweek with no promotion or relegation, the ties would be screened worldwide on sponsored pay-per-view.

This time, at least, UEFA saw the danger signs. Johansson and chief executive Gerd Aigner knew the clubs preferred the convenience of remaining within the family, but recognized the economic realities and the danger to their own competitions and income. Also, UEFA would not be thanked by the rest of the game for allowing a handful of greedy clubs to carve up the structure of world football.

Halfway through the new season's group stage, UEFA

brokered a peace deal with the 12 rebel clubs (Ajax, Barcelona, Bayern Munich, Borussia Dortmund, Internazionale, Juventus, Liverpool, Manchester United, Marseille, Milan, Porto and Real Madrid). Adriano Galliani, Berlusconi's right-hand man at Milan and future president of the Italian league, said, 'The clubs have affirmed their wish to work with UEFA. We must make concessions but so must UEFA.'

The clubs agreed to let UEFA control the purse strings, while the European federation responded with a sharp increase in the clubs' income share via match fees and points bonuses. Winning the Champions League had been worth £8 million to Real Madrid in 1998. Four years later, Madrid would earn double the money for winning the same prize.

Two of the 12, Manchester United and Bayern Munich, had been drawn together in Group D. The Germans finished with their noses in front, pipping United by one point. Even so, United progressed to the quarter-finals courtesy of the complex qualifying system: the winner of each of the six groups went through to the last eight, plus the two runners-up with the best records. At least United were in good company in qualifying via the back door. So did holders Real Madrid from Group C, which was won by old rivals Internazionale.

Olympiakos Piraeus qualified as winners of Group A, along with Juventus from Group B – though the Italians were not sure of reaching the quarter-finals until after the final whistle of their last group match. UEFA undertook a detailed study of the rules and regulations before confirming that Juve placed ahead of Turkey's Galatasaray and Norway's Rosenborg. All three clubs had finished on eight points.

There were no such problems in Groups E and F for Dynamo Kiev and Kaiserslautern. The attacking power of Kiev's young

strikers Andriy Shevchenko and Sergiy Rebrov lifted them three points clear of Lens and Arsenal, while Kaiserslautern finished five points clear of Benfica.

KNOCK-OUT STAGE

A flurry of drama marked the quarter-finals which saw the new improved Manchester United march on and holders Real Madrid tumble out.

United were proving unstoppable in all directions. They were on their way to winning the English league and FA Cup double with a team perfectly balanced between youth and experience, home-grown players and imports.

Peter Schmeichel was arguably the best goalkeeper in the world, organizing defence with a ferocity which Roy Keane matched with his leadership in midfield. David Beckham was emerging as a major personality on the right of midfield, his crossing talents superbly complemented by the pace and skill of Ryan Giggs on the left.

Opponents' efforts to defend the flanks left gaps in the centre which were ruthlessly exploited by strikers Dwight Yorke and Andy Cole. Few clubs had the supporting luxury of quality forwards such as England's Teddy Sheringham and the Norwegian Ole-Gunnar Solskjaer to bring off the substitutes' bench. Yorke had cost £12 million from Aston Villa the previous autumn and was in the midst of a golden thread of form which brought him 52 goals in 89 starts over four years for United.

Two of the most important of those goals earned United a 2–0 home win over Internazionale in the quarter-finals which the Italians could not overturn back in Milan.

Madrid shot themselves in the foot ahead of their tie against Kiev Dynamo by replacing Dutch coach Guus Hiddink. Hiddink had guided Holland to the World Cup semi-finals the previous year and then steered Madrid to victory in the World Club Cup. But the internal politics of the Bernabeu dressing room proved too much and he was abruptly 'thanked' with a short-lived replacement by John Toshack. The tie with Kiev was a personal triumph for Andriy Shevchenko, who scored in the 1–1 draw in Spain and both goals in the Ukrainians' 2–0 home win.

RIGHT: **REAL MADRID'S GUTI GOES FLYING AFTER A CHALLENGE FROM DYNAMO KIEV'S VLADYSLAV VASCHUK**

Juventus squeaked through against Olympiakos, an 85th-minute away goal from Antonio Conte in the second leg handing them the away-goals advantage. As for the all-German clash, Bayern had fewer problems than they feared seeing off Kaiserslautern - winning 2-0 at home and by a masterful 4-0 away. Nerves got the better of Kaiserslautern in front of their own fans; they never recovered after the eighth-minute expulsion of their Hungarian central defender, Janos Hrutka.

United appeared to be on their way out after being held 1-1 by Juventus at Old Trafford in the first leg of the semi-final. But manager Alex Ferguson said he was confident that United would score in Turin. Not only did they score but they secured a sensational 3-2 win after Juventus had seized an early 2-0

lead with goals from Filippo Inzaghi. United's goals were scored by Keane, Cole and Yorke. Keane's satisfaction at playing the game of his life was marred by the second yellow card which would bar him from leading United out in the final.

'After that performance I can say only that Manchester deserve to win the cup itself,' said Juventus coach Carlo Ancelotti, generous in defeat.

Bayern, of course, had other ideas after beating Kiev 3-3, 1-0. The Germans had goalkeeper Oliver Kahn to thank for a string of superb saves in the second leg in Munich. He held Shevchenko and co at bay just long enough for Mario Basler to snatch a breakaway goal for Bayern at the other end. After that 36th-minute strike, Kiev faded and Bayern strode into the final.

LEFT: **ROY KEANE SCORES AGAINST JUVE IN THE SEMI-FINAL BUT A SECOND YELLOW CARD KEPT HIM OUT OF THE FINAL**

MANCHESTER UNITED PULL OFF A MIRACLE

'You know, this would have been Sir Matt Busby's 90th birthday today. Well, perhaps he was up there kicking a lot for us tonight,' said manager Alex Ferguson, basking in the barely credible euphoria of United's final glory.

The climax of the world's greatest international club competition had never seen anything like it as United won with two stoppage-time goals. United's achievement of the treble of UEFA Champions League, domestic league and FA Cup – emulating the feats of Celtic, Ajax and PSV Eindhoven – was matched by the amazing concluding drama.

Just as United and their fans – and even manager Ferguson – could barely believe it, neither could Bayern. In the moments which followed referee Pierluigi Collina's final whistle Ferguson looked almost as dazed and shell-shocked as Bayern boss Ottmar Hitzfeld. The difference was that Hitzfeld continued to look shell-shocked as the cup presentation took place.

Ferguson quickly emerged from his stupor. 'I didn't like most of the match,' he said, 'but the most important thing it showed was that you can never deny our people's spirit and will to win. That's what did it for us. In the closing minutes I had been preparing myself mentally for defeat – thinking that maybe it wasn't our year and I would need to keep my dignity. Then, well... at the final whistle I was just stunned. I didn't say anything to the players. I just hugged and kissed them –

slavered all over them. It was the greatest moment of my life.'

Both finalists were below strength. United missed suspended skipper Roy Keane plus Paul Scholes from midfield, while Bayern lacked injured top scorer Giovane Elber and French World Cup-winning left-back Bixente Lizarazu. Ferguson adjusted by moving David Beckham inside from the wing and switching Ryan Giggs from left to right.

United were the more nervy in the opening exchanges, especially goalkeeper Peter Schmeichel in his last game for the club. A couple of fluffed clearances encouraged Bayern,

RIGHT: **IN HIS REGULATION CLUB SUIT, MANAGER ALEX FERGUSON ACKNOWLEDGES UNITED'S AMAZING TURNAROUND WITH A BIG SMILE AND TWO CLENCHED FISTS**

who went ahead in the sixth minute. Mario Basler's low, curling free-kick eluded Schmeichel after Ronny Johnsen had tripped Carsten Jancker.

As time ticked on down, so United threw on substitute strikers Teddy Sheringham and Ole-Gunnar Solskjaer and left gaps at the back in an increasingly desperate pursuit of an equalizer. Bayern nearly capitalized. Substitute Mehmet Scholl hit a post on 79 minutes, and then Carsten Jancker's overhead effort struck the bar. Bayern were still leading 1–0 when fourth official Fiorenzo Treossi held up the illuminated board signalling three minutes of added time.

The numbers stood out red for danger, but Bayern failed to notice. In the last minute of the 90 United forced a corner.

Schmeichel charged upfield, exacerbating the penalty box chaos. Stefan Effenberg hooked out the loose ball, Giggs drilled it back in and Sheringham turned the equalizer inside Oliver Kahn's right-hand post.

It seemed, agonizingly for the Germans, that United had won a last-minute reprieve. It was going to extra time. But worse was to come for Bayern's distraught defenders. United forced Sami Kuffour into conceding another corner. Beckham curled it in, Sheringham headed on and Solskjaer stabbed the ball up into the roof of the net.

Bedlam erupted all around the ground. For the second time in their history, Manchester United were kings of Europe – and the treble turned Alex Ferguson into a knight to remember.

LEFT: **IT'S NOT OVER UNTIL IT'S OVER: OLE-GUNNAR SOLSKJAER EMPHASIZES THIS ANCIENT TRUTH WITH HIS LAST-MINUTE GOAL AS MANCHESTER UNITED COMPLETE ONE OF FOOTBALL'S MOST AMAZING COMEBACKS**

WEDNESDAY 26 MAY 1999
NOU CAMP, BARCELONA

MANCHESTER UNITED	**2**
SHERINGHAM 90, SOLSKJAER 90	
BAYERN MUNICH	**1**
BASLER 6	

HT: 0–1. ATT: 90,000.
REF: COLLINA (IT)

UNITED:
SCHMEICHEL* – G. NEVILLE, STAM, JOHNSEN, IRWIN – GIGGS, BECKHAM, BUTT, BLOMQVIST (SHERINGHAM 66) – YORKE, COLE (SOLSKJAER 80). MANAGER: FERGUSON.

BAYERN:
KAHN* – BABBEL, MATTHAEUS (FINK 80), KUFFOUR, LINKE – BASLER (SALIHAMIDZIC 89), JEREMIES, EFFENBERG, TARNAT – JANCKER, ZICKLER (SCHOLL 71). COACH: HITZFELD.

* CAPTAIN

2000S

NO LONGER THE PEOPLE'S GAME?

The new millennium saw the advent of a brave, if less romantic, new order within European football. The Bosman ruling had ushered in commercial conformity along with set dates for international competitions and even fixed pan-European transfer deadlines. Money now ruled more than ever before. The 'Galactico' scale of Real Madrid's achievements in the Champions League was trumped by the billionaire potential of Chelsea's new Russian owner, Roman Abramovich. But the trophy-winning efforts of Porto in the Champions League and Greece in the European Championship proved that even the best-paid plans of football's ruling class could not guarantee results on the pitch.

RIGHT: **AC MILAN VERSUS JUVENTUS AT 'THE THEATRE OF DREAMS', AKA OLD TRAFFORD, IN MAY 2003**

ZINEDINE ZIDANE

Country: France

Position: Midfielder

Born: 23 June, 1972

Clubs: Cannes, Bordeaux
(France), Juventus (Italy),
Real Madrid (Spain)

ZINEDINE ZIDANE

Zidane

I was aware of the European Cup when I was growing up, but not from a really, really young age. I think the first European Cup final I remember clearly, my first sense of the trophy being different from the other games, was the Heysel tragedy final of 1985, with Michel Platini playing for Juventus against Liverpool.

Obviously, that was not a pleasant final to have as your first genuine memory of the European Cup, but it does remain the earliest I can recall. You see, whatever Platini did for Juventus had a huge impact on everyone in France. He was a fantastic player.

Not that I was a Juventus fan – I supported Olympique de Marseille. I used to go regularly to watch them play at the Stade Velodrome in the 1990s. I remember Chris Waddle, Jean-Pierre Papin and Basile Boli. I liked Waddle, but my hero was always Enzo Francescoli, the Uruguayan. He was amazing – I named my son after him. He remains my idol, one of the all-time greats, and the player who most inspired me. I consider myself fortunate to have met him since.

I did not attend either of Olympique's two European finals, 1991 or 1993, but I remember watching them with

LEFT: ZINEDINE ZIDANE SUCCEEDED LUIS FIGO AS THE WORLD'S MOST EXPENSIVE PLAYER WHEN HE WENT FROM JUVENTUS TO REAL MADRID FOR £45 MILLION IN 2001. HE WAS FIFA WORLD PLAYER OF THE YEAR IN 1998, 2000 AND 2003

friends; a whole load of us gathered round the television. I did go to a lot of their home games, though. I think you enjoy the matches more from the stands than on the pitch. I certainly did. That is not to say I do not enjoy playing, of course. Football is still more a hobby than a job for me. I have always seen it like that and I am proud of being a footballer. But I remember watching games from the stands in Marseille so fondly. It is a great stadium with a unique atmosphere.

When they finally won the European Cup, Marseille was an incredible place to be, the party atmosphere was indescribable. It's a very special city, one that loves football. People have told me it's like Liverpool, and I can

understand that; Marseille is a tough city, a port which has its problems but also one that has a soul, a real sense of community and identity. The place went crazy in 1993: a French team winning the European cup, a team that was not from a capital city - and against Milan, of all people.

I had to wait for my own debut in the European Cup until I was at Juventus. They had won it the season before, in 1996, and we reached the final again, but lost to Borussia Dortmund, which was so disappointing. Then the next year we lost to Real Madrid. Thank goodness I was part of the France team who won the World Cup a few weeks later! But honestly, I went into that World Cup final thinking: 'Oh, dear, here we go again.' I had to win that one, because I'd lost three finals in a row: a UEFA Cup Final with Bordeaux against Bayern Munich in 1996, then the Champions finals against Borussia in 1997 and Madrid in 1998. I was starting to think I would never win anything, so it was vital to win the World Cup.

Not that winning the World Cup diminishes the importance of the European Cup, and it certainly did not spoil my appetite. I still wanted to win it one day - perhaps more than most because of those lost finals. Luckily, I was able to win it in my first season with Madrid.

I went to Spain because I wanted to try something new. I was feeling a little tired of Italy. It was difficult playing there, much harder than it is in Spain for players like me, and Real Madrid were the perfect opportunity. People have asked me about the napkin story from Monte Carlo and, yes, it is true that, during a meal, the Real Madrid president Florentino Perez passed a napkin down to me asking if I wanted to play for Madrid. But, no, he did not write the message in English: it was me who wrote in English: 'Yes.' I don't really know why. His message to me was in French, I think, maybe Spanish. I can't remember exactly, but it wasn't in English!

The expectation at Real Madrid is probably greater than anywhere else - although the pressure at Juventus was pretty intense. At Madrid, I started enjoying my football again, because the attitude to the game in Spain is different. Also, I found that the style of play suited me better. There are complications playing for Real Madrid, but you know about that when you sign for them. You expect that intensity. Real Madrid are the biggest club there is, from a huge capital city, with lots of fans and loads of attention from all the media.

All the more so in the European Cup. To be honest, I try to approach all matches and competitions in the same way, but you feel something different about Madrid when it comes to the European Cup. It's a sense that this is 'Madrid's competition'.

I'm glad to say that finally, with Madrid, I won the trophy, against Bayer Leverkusen in Glasgow. People talk about my winning volley, but nine times out of ten that would have flown into the crowd.

I was lucky: I caught it just right, quickly and cleanly, but I had to strike it like that because the ball came down from so high. I'm not saying it was a bad cross from Roberto Carlos, though. As it turned out it was quite the opposite: the perfect cross. After all, it ended up a goal, didn't it?

I could not sleep that night, and I admit I watched the goal a few times on video. That was the perfect image of what Real Madrid is all about: the club which always has to win.

LEFT: **ZIDANE'S WONDERFUL VOLLEY WHICH WON REAL THEIR RECORD NINTH EUROPEAN CUP AT HAMPDEN PARK, GLASGOW, AGAINST BAYER LEVERKUSEN**

GETTING THE BALANCE RIGHT

The format of the competition continued to evolve, although it wasn't totally successful to judge by the number of dull games. Still, Real Madrid versus Manchester United was a cracker...

GROUP STAGE

UEFA's approach to the Champions League was Olympian. But instead of *Citius, Altius, Fortius* – swifter, higher, stronger – the European federation's motto would have read: bigger, longer, richer.

The major clubs were demanding a permanent right of access. Their cause, to bend and expand the qualification formula, was supported by television channels from the Big Five (England, France, Germany, Italy and Spain) which needed the guaranteed presence of 'their' clubs to justify their enormous outlay.

Thus the Champions League expanded again in 1999–2000. Now it comprised a weirder concoction than ever, with two qualifying rounds, a first group phase of eight groups of four teams, then a second phase of four groups of four teams... before the knock-out stages.

This prompted a rethink about the other two European cup competitions. Admitting non-champions into the Champions League lowered the quality of the UEFA Cup, whose credibility was further compromised by the decision to relegate into it the third-placed clubs from the first-round groups of the Champions League. The Cup-Winners' Cup had been wound up altogether after Lazio's 1999 victory over Mallorca. Domestic cup-winners were added to the flotsam and jetsam of the UEFA Cup.

The first group stage of the revamped Champions League, as critics had feared, produced dull matches with too great a disparity between the likes of Manchester United, Barcelona, Lazio and Real Madrid and minnows such as Slovenia's Maribor and Austria's Sturm Graz.

Not that the giants had matters all their own way. The qualifying rounds had removed the reviving CSKA Moscow,

RIGHT: **BAYERN MUNICH'S PAULO SERGIO HEADS HOME HIS SIDE'S FOURTH GOAL AGAINST REAL MADRID**

Dinamo Tbilisi, the fast-rising French champions Lyon, Partizan Belgrade and Rapid Vienna. Joining those embarrassed failures were former UEFA and Cup-Winners' Cup holders Parma. They were dispatched by a Rangers team under Dutch coach Dick Advocaat who, courtesy of Bosman, saw only one Scot start both legs: midfielder Barry Ferguson.

Further Italian depression followed in the first group stage. Although Fiorentina and Lazio, coached by the Swede Sven-Goran Eriksson (formerly of IFK, Benfica and Roma), progressed, Milan blundered by losing their last Group H game 3–2 to Galatasaray. Milan thus finished bottom of the table and dropped out of Europe altogether, while Galatasaray finished third.

The Turks' fine team, featuring home-grown centre-forward Hakan Sukur, Romanian playmaker Gica Hagi and Brazil's World Cup-winning 'keeper Claudio Taffarel, slipped down into the UEFA Cup. Their consolation was going on to win it – on penalties in Copenhagen – against fellow Champions League exiles Arsenal.

Lazio, Barcelona, Valencia and Sparta Prague all topped their groups undefeated, while one defeat apiece was the acceptable return for other winners such as Rosenborg, Real Madrid, Chelsea and holders Manchester United.

Barcelona remained undefeated in the second group stage as well, while United again lost just the once by 2–0 in Florence against Fiorentina, whose goals came from the Argentinians Gabriel Batistuta and Abel Balbo. Valencia followed United through.

A Spanish trio in the quarters was completed by Real Madrid, who finished second to Bayern Munich in Group C and pipped Dynamo Kiev – with whom they finished level on points – by courtesy of their superior head-to-head record. The veteran Ukrainian coach Valeriy Lobanovskiy was furious because Kiev had the better goal difference.

KNOCK-OUT STAGE

Real Madrid and Manchester United, the two venerable 'old boys' among the last eight, set the competition alight with their quarter-final.

Madrid had proved so erratic in the Spanish league that they had sacked coach John Toshack in mid-season and then suspended the £23-million French striker Nicolas Anelka when he dared question the tactical preferences of caretaker Vicente del Bosque. The avuncular manner of Del Bosque, a runner-up as a player against Liverpool in 1981, was deceptive (so deceptive that it would ultimately cost him his job, though not for several more highly successful years).

Madrid were held goalless at home by United in the first

BELOW: **IN MURKY CONDITIONS CREATED BY FLARES THROWN ON TO THE SAN SIRO PITCH BY FANS, CHELSEA'S ALBERT FERRER SWINGS OVER A CROSS DESPITE THE ATTENTIONS OF MILAN'S ANDRIY SHEVCHENKO**

leg, then raced into a 3-0 lead after 52 minutes of a sensational return at Old Trafford. United skipper Roy Keane scored an own goal and Raul added two more. Fernando Redondo was the colossus in midfield who helped snap United's grip on the cup. David Beckham and Paul Scholes (penalty) struck late on, but this time around substitutes Teddy Sheringham and Ole-Gunnar Solskjaer could not fashion a repeat of the miracle of Barcelona.

Madrid's heroes included centre-back Ivan Campo, who would later star with nearby Bolton, and the England winger Steve McManaman, who had run down his Liverpool contract so that he could join Madrid on a free transfer.

The other ties saw Bayern Munich squeeze out FC Porto, Valencia thrash prospective Italian champions Lazio – winning 5-2 in Spain with a highly memorable hat-trick from midfield tyro Gerard – and Barcelona needing extra

be officiating when Barcelona and Chelsea met in even more controversial circumstances.

Victory over United fired Madrid's confidence against Bayern Munich, their old nemesis, in the semi-finals. Anelka, who had forced his way out of Arsenal controversially the previous summer to join Madrid, had now made his peace with Del Bosque. The coach duly restored him to the attack and the Frenchman expressed his thanks by scoring both home and away in the 3–2 overall defeat of the Germans.

Barcelona were favourites to beat Valencia in the other semi-final. But Valencia's Argentine coach Hector Cuper had other ideas. Cuper had been appointed by Valencia on the strength of taking Mallorca to the Cup-Winners' Cup Final the previous season. He built hard-working, compact teams, but Valencia also benefited from the skilful leavening provided by the likes of Gaizka Mendieta in midfield and Argentine forwards in winger Christian 'Kily' Gonzalez and striker Claudio Lopez, nicknamed The Louse.

Mendieta was outstanding against Barcelona, scoring in both legs which Valencia won, with surprising ease, 4–1, 2–1. He not only dispatched Barcelona but also fatally undermined Barcelona's long-serving president Josep Lluis Nunez and their former Ajax coach, Louis van Gaal.

BELOW: **BARCELONA'S RIVALDO AND AMEDEO CARBONI OF VALENCIA TUSSLE FOR THE BALL**

time to get the better of Chelsea in a topsy-turvy thriller.

Chelsea won 3–1 at Stamford Bridge, then lost 5–1 in Barcelona after extra time. The nail-biting drama in the Nou Camp included a potentially crucial penalty miss by Brazilian World Player of the Year Rivaldo. The referee responsible both for awarding that spot-kick and for sending off Chelsea's Nigerian left-back Celestine Babayaro on 98 minutes was Sweden's Anders Frisk – who one day would again

REAL USE LOCAL KNOWLEDGE TO WIN

Champions Cup history was made in the magnificent Stade de France, with two clubs from the same country contesting the final for the first time. Madrid were favourites to foreigners, while debutants Valencia were favoured by a majority of Spaniards. But Madrid, the men in black, knew them too well.

Manchester United were being lauded as the richest club in Europe, but football grandeur was still about more than money, and Madrid moved way out into a class all their own as they won *La Octava* – their eighth Champions Cup.

Madrid had made a habit of drawing the best out of their old retainers. Alfredo di Stefano and Ferenc Puskas were winning European cups deep into their 30s; team-mate Luis Molowny became the backroom master par excellence, emerging every now and then as caretaker to win one trophy or another; now his mantle had fallen on the modest Vicente del Bosque.

Both teams quickly fell into a pattern of play possible only between teams who knew each other well, although even half-

Final 2000

chances were few and far between in the opening exchanges. Steve McManaman busily covered the length and breadth of the pitch in attack and very nearly gained a reward on the half-hour when a deflected cross from Fernando Morientes ricocheted off his shin and forced a sharp reflex save from Jose Santiago Canizares.

Morientes was playing only because of injury to Brazil winger Savio, but he was a perpetual, lurking danger and, six minutes before half-time, he headed the opening goal from a short right-wing cross by right-back Michel Salgado, son-in-law of president Lorenzo Sanz.

Valencia pressed strongly in the minutes before the interval but failed to pull the goal back, and this proved decisive as second half drew on. The more they threw men forward, the more they were at the mercy of the pace of Nicolas Anelka, Raul and McManaman on the break.

Two goals in a five-minute spell midway through the second half killed them off. First Valencia only half-cleared a long throw from Brazilian left-back Roberto Carlos and

McManaman volleyed Madrid's second. Then, five minutes later, with Valencia encamped in the Madrid penalty box, the ball was hammered clear and Raul ran unchallenged from half-way before rounding Canizares and sliding in goal number three. It was a breathtaking slalom which reminded old-timers of how Puskas had run similarly from half-way to score against Benfica in the 1962 final. Then, of course, Madrid lost. This time, as Raul had said, 'Losing has not crossed my mind. I have thought only of winning, winning and winning'.

Three goals ahead, Madrid could afford the sentimental gesture of bringing on 35-year-old club captain Manuel Sanchis to lift the trophy for the second time in three years on the night he equalled Paco Gento's record of 97 European appearances. Placards around the Stade de France proclaimed the message: 'Welcome Home!' They referred to the final's return to its first host city (although the inaugural final in 1956 had been played in the old Parc des Princes). Real Madrid fans screamed much the same thing when their heroes paraded the trophy back in the Spanish capital's Cibeles square.

LEFT: **AITOR KARANKA EMBRACES FERNANDO MORIENTES AFTER THE STRIKER GRABBED THE FIRST GOAL FOR REAL MADRID**

OPPOSITE: **CHRISTIAN KAREMBEU AND NICOLAS ANELKA BRAVE THE CELEBRATORY DOWNPOUR TO CLING ON TO THE CUP**

WEDNESDAY 24 MAY 2000
STADE DE FRANCE, SAINT-DENIS

REAL MADRID	**3**

MORIENTES 39, MCMANAMAN 67, RAUL 75

VALENCIA	**0**

HT: 1-0. ATT: 78,000.
REF: BRASCHI (IT)

MADRID:
CASILLAS - MICHEL SALGADO (HIERRO 84), IVAN CAMPO, KARANKA, ROBERTO CARLOS - RAUL*, REDONDO, IVAN HELGUERA, MCMANAMAN - ANELKA (SANCHIS 79), MORIENTES (SAVIO 71). COACH: DEL BOSQUE.

VALENCIA:
CANIZARES - ANGLOMA, PELLEGRINO, DJUKIC, GERARDO (ILIE 68) - MENDIETA*, FARINOS, GERARD, KILY GONZALEZ - ANGULO, CLAUDIO LOPEZ. COACH: CUPER.

*CAPTAIN

FIGO'S HOMAGE FROM CATALONIA

Florentino Perez became president of Real Madrid and signed Luis Figo from Barcelona as English and Spanish clubs dominated the competition. Ominously, Bayern Munich were still in the hunt...

2000-01

GROUP STAGE

France had lit up European football in the summer of 2000 by winning the European Championship with a golden goal against Italy in Rotterdam. But as the tournament reached its climax, a remarkable battle was being waged simultaneously off the pitch.

Defeated hero of the semi-finals had been the Portuguese winger-turned-playmaker Luis Figo. Although a last-kick golden goal penalty by Zinedine Zidane brought France victory over Portugal, Barcelona's Figo was the outstanding player. Admiring fans of co-hosts Holland and Belgium were not the only observers who thought so. Their opinion was shared by a Spanish millionaire property developer.

Florentino Perez had grown increasingly concerned at what he saw as profligate management of Real Madrid by president Lorenzo Sanz. In the summer of 2000, and despite Madrid's Champions Cup triumph, Perez not only challenged Sanz in the

RIGHT: **THE LEAST POPULAR MAN IN CATALONIA, LUIS FIGO IN ACTION AGAINST LAZIO**

club's presidential election but beat him. His trump card was the promise to sign Figo from... Barcelona. Perez kept his word, as did Figo, although the transfer made him a figure of hate throughout Catalonia. Missiles were hurled at him on his annual returns to the Nou Camp, including, on one occasion, a pig's head.

Even more remarkably, Perez wiped out Madrid's astronomical £350-million debt by selling land around the Estadio Bernabeu after the city council – at his persuasive behest – reclassified it for development. Not that this did Madrid a lot of good on the pitch in 2000–01, even if they began well enough. They topped their table in the first group stage, as did Arsenal, Valencia, Sturm Graz, Bayern Munich, Anderlecht, Milan and Deportivo La Coruna.

The presence at the top table of 'Super Depor' was further evidence of the benefits generated by a combination of the Bosman ruling and a television explosion in western Europe. Depor had always been a modest yo-yo club, sliding up and down between Spain's top divisions. Suddenly, they had the money to invest – wisely and successfully – in a solid squad in which Spanish pride was mixed with Brazilian technique and Argentine know-how. Depor, agreed the experts, were one of Europe's outstanding teams in the full sense of the word.

First-round failures included most notably Juventus – who did not even secure the consolation of a UEFA Cup slot – and Barcelona. Other former winners who failed to advance included PSV Eindhoven and Hamburg. Portugal's Sporting Clube were the sole team not to register a victory. Only three teams managed to complete their programme undefeated: Valencia, Manchester United and Deportivo.

English and Spanish clubs dominated the second group stage, with both nations providing three quarter-finalists. Bayern Munich and Turkey's Galatasaray were the interlopers to the party organized by Arsenal, Leeds United and Manchester United from England and Madrid, Deportivo and Valencia from Spain.

Leeds were back for the first time in almost a decade. They had been runners-up to Milan in Group H in the first stage and runners-up to Madrid in Group D in the second round. Qualification for the quarter-finals was secured by a concluding 3-3 draw against a Lazio side depressed by the knowledge that coach Sven-Goran Eriksson had already agreed to quit and make history as England's first foreign manager.

Peter Ridsdale, the Leeds chairman, had made available every penny he could raise in building a team intended to be a permanent, self-financing presence in the Champions League. 'Living the dream,' he called it, never for a moment envisaging the nightmare to come.

KNOCK-OUT STAGE

Racist abuse of players had long been a sorry vocal feature of football crowds. But it had also long been tolerated by directors, officials and players. From the early 1970s English league matches had been marked by the 'monkey chants' and fruit missiles aimed at a rapidly increasing number of black players, initially of immigrant West Indian background.

BELOW: JUVENTUS STAR EDGAR 'THE PIT BULL' DAVIDS AND DEPORTIVO LA CORUNA'S CESAR SAMPAIO BATTLE FOR POSSESSION

The issue had been highlighted by the game's successful attraction of a wealthier audience following the creation of all-seater stadia. Simultaneously, television producers realized that the technology which was bringing all the action and all the noise into the nation's homes was picking up the bad with the good.

The English players' union, the Professional Footballers' Association, was among the initial leaders in a number of anti-racism campaigns.

Progress was slow but at least it was progress of a sort, and it drew attention to the problem. The reality – that education was needed throughout Europe – was thrown into ever sharper focus.

Ajax Amsterdam had threatened to pull out of European competition after one racist-fuelled visit to the Hungarian capital Budapest to play Ferencvaros. Arsenal then fell foul of the most high-profile racist chanting incident yet noted in the Champions League in the 2000–01 quarter-finals.

Drawn against Valencia, manager Arsene Wenger's men hit back in the first leg at Highbury from 1–0 down to win 2–1 with second-half strikes from Thierry Henry and Ray Parlour. They then lost 1–0 in Mestalla to a 76th-minute goal from Valencia's Norway striker John Carew and were eliminated by the away goal conceded at Highbury.

Bitterness at such a narrow defeat was exacerbated by the racist abuse aimed at Arsenal defenders Ashley Cole and

Lauren, skipper Patrick Vieira and forwards Henry, Sylvain Wiltord and substitute Nwankwo Kanu. At one stage the game was interrupted as Carew – himself black – tried to calm the fans, but all to no avail.

Valencia were fined £9,250 by UEFA, which was a derisory fistful of small change to the club, as Vieira pointed out. UEFA, demonstrating a breathtaking ignorance of the issue, then disgracefully fined Vieira £2,300 for daring to criticize the sum.

Arsenal were not the only English losers. Manchester United went out in the quarters for the second year in succession. This season, as in the previous one, their conquerors would go on to win the competition. Bayern Munich coach Ottmar Hitzfeld had the satisfaction of getting the better of his old friend and rival Sir Alex Ferguson both at Old Trafford (1–0) and in Munich's increasingly outdated Olympiastadion (2–1). Holders Real Madrid lost 3–2 in Turkey against Galatasaray but enjoyed a comfortable 3–0 ride back at the Bernabeu courtesy of two more goals from Raul. However, Spanish champions-elect Deportivo left themselves too much to do against Leeds and came up just short – losing 3–2 on aggregate after a 3–0 loss at Elland Road.

In the semi-finals, Bayern avenged their defeat of the previous year by winning home and away to dethrone Madrid, while Valencia reached a second straight final after holding Leeds goalless at Elland Road and running out easy 3–0 winners at the Mestalla, where Alan Smith was shown an academic red card in the last minute.

Leeds manager David O'Leary, positive in defeat, praised the season-long progress achieved by his 'babies'. In football terms, as it turned out, his team would never grow up. In little more than a year O'Leary himself would be gone, and even the £30-million sale of defender Rio Ferdinand to Manchester United could not bring Leeds out of the financial tail-spin plunging them towards relegation and the verge of bankruptcy.

LEFT: **ZINEDINE ZIDANE, REAL'S WORLD RECORD SUMMER SIGNING**

FAR LEFT: **LEEDS UNITED'S RIO FERDINAND AND NIGEL MARTYN CAN NOT BELIEVE THE REFEREE IS ALLOWING JUAN SANCHEZ'S STRIKE TO STAND DURING THEIR SIDE'S SEMI-FINAL WITH VALENCIA**

BECKENBAUER STILL HAS MIDAS TOUCH

Franz Beckenbauer was back. By now Bayern Munich's former sweeper, skipper and coach was club president, and his Midas touch continued to work as Bayern defeated Valencia in a penalty shoot-out.

Not that the 46th European Cup final will be remembered for its quality. Until golden goal extra time neither goalkeeper was ever seriously tested from open play.

Italian observers, pondering their own clubs' European failures, were left even more perplexed and depressed by the inability of Juventus and the rest to make a stronger impression.

Valencia duly created an unwanted piece of history as the first club to lose two successive finals. But it could have been different. The Spaniards, battle-hardened for the final by their 2000 defeat at the hands of Real Madrid, set off in style, scoring in the second minute. Norway striker John Carew rounded Ghanaian defender Sami Kuffour out on the left, and Swedish defender Patrik Andersson handled the ball after falling in the ensuing goalmouth scramble. Valencia

RIGHT: **MAN OF THE MATCH OLIVER KAHN STOPS SLOVENE FORWARD ZLATKO ZAHOVIC'S PENALTY IN THE SHOOT-OUT**

skipper Gaizka Mendieta fired low past goalkeeper Oliver Kahn's right hand.

The explosive pace was maintained, and four minutes later Bayern were awarded a penalty of their own after Jocelyn Angloma tripped Stefan Effenberg in full flight. However Mehmet Scholl's kick ricocheted over the bar off the legs of 'keeper Jose Santiago Canizares and Valencia survived. Six minutes into the second half, Bayern were awarded a second penalty. This time it was skipper Effenberg who took the responsibility. He made no mistake and the teams were back on level terms.

Neither side could find a winning goal, either during the rest of normal time or in the extra 30 minutes, which meant the agony and ecstasy of the shoot-out.

It all came down to the ultimate gladiatorial drama between goalkeepers Kahn and Canizares.

Up in the VIP box among kings and prime ministers, Pele, Michel Platini and Jorge Valdano looked on, hypnotized, as Kahn saved victoriously from Zlatko Zahovic, Amedeo Carboni and Mauricio Pellegrino.

Victory rounded off a magnificent four days for Bayern, who had retained their German domestic championship the previous weekend. UEFA also breathed a corporate sigh of relief that the Champions League had been won by a club who were, indeed, formal champions back home.

Bayern thus carried off the cup for the fourth time in what was their eighth final. No wonder that their players, after the lap of honour, did not want to leave the pitch.

Valencia coach Hector Cuper admitted that he could not watch the penalties. Not so Beckenbauer, who said: 'You have to be lucky to win in a shoot-out, but I think this team deserved it. Kahn has been fantastic in the Champions League. He is the main reason we won.'

LEFT: OUTSTANDING SKIPPER STEFAN EFFENBERG – OR 'EFFING STEFFENBERG' AS ONE ENGLISH PLAYER MEMORABLY CALLED HIM – HOLDS UP THE TROPHY FOR ALL TO SEE

WEDNESDAY 23 MAY 2001
GIUSEPPE MEAZZA, MILAN

BAYERN MUNICH   **1**
EFFENBERG 50 PEN

VALENCIA   **1**
MENDIETA 2 PEN

AFTER EXTRA TIME
BAYERN WON 5-4 ON PENS.
HT: 0-1. 90 MIN: 1-1. ATT: 70,000.
REF: JOL (HOL)

BAYERN:
KAHN – SAGNOL (JANCKER 46),
KUFFOUR, P. ANDERSSON, LIZARAZU –
SCHOLL (PAULO SERGIO 108),
EFFENBERG*, HARGREAVES, LINKE –
SALIHAMIDZIC, ELBER (ZICKLER 100).
COACH: HITZFELD.

VALENCIA:
CANIZARES – ANGLOMA, AYALA
(DJUKIC 90), PELLEGRINO, CARBONI –
MENDIETA, SANCHEZ (ZAHOVIC 67),
AIMAR (ALBELDA 46), BARAJA, KILY
GONZALEZ – CAREW. COACH: CUPER.

*CAPTAIN

REAL MADRID GO GALACTIC

Real Madrid had a formidable line-up featuring some of the world's most expensive talent. It seemed Sir Alex Ferguson had a major appointment with destiny but he wasn't happy with David Beckham

GROUP STAGE

The events of 9/11 cast their pall over the Champions League. The opening Tuesday night of the 2001-02 campaign was the very day of the terrorist attacks on New York and Washington. UEFA, characteristically slow to respond to the real world, ordered Tuesday's matches to go ahead before bowing to outraged sentiment and postponing the Wednesday schedule.

Appeals against the results of the first games, however, were rejected. Borussia Dortmund's Matthias Sammer was one of several coaches who claimed that news of the events had upset their players – leading, in Borussia's case, to a 2-2 draw away to Dynamo Kiev.

'We had to force ourselves to go out for the match,' said Sammer, 'because of the tragedy in America. It's no surprise we played really badly.'

Real Madrid, when they did join the action, signalled their intentions for their centenary season by emerging as 2-1 winners from a testing opener away to Roma. It was only the third time Madrid had won in Italy and, ironically, they did so in the absence of Zinedine Zidane. Their world record £45-million signing had been ruled out by a suspension held over from his days with Juventus.

Luis Figo, Zidane's predecessor as the world's costliest player, moved into the Frenchman's playmaking role and not only scored one goal but created the other for Guti. Madrid, revelling in their new 'Galacticos' nickname,

RIGHT: **FINNISH MIDFIELDER JARI LITMANEN SCORES FROM THE SPOT FOR LIVERPOOL AGAINST ROMA**

duly became the first team to reach the second round.

They were accompanied by group runners-up Roma and, from the other groups, Liverpool and Boavista, Panathinaikos and Arsenal, Nantes and Galatasaray, Juventus and Porto, Barcelona and Bayer Leverkusen, Deportivo La Coruna and Manchester United, plus holders Bayern Munich and Sparta Prague.

Third-place finishes and consolation places in the UEFA Cup were the lot of Lokomotiv Moscow, Borussia Dortmund, PSV Eindhoven, Celtic, Lyon, Lille and Feyenoord, the UEFA Cup's ultimate victors.

Among those eliminated were Lazio. The Italians, who replaced coach Dino Zoff with Alberto Zaccheroni in mid-campaign, paid a heavy price for the summer sales of stars such as Juan Veron and Pavel Nedved and the depressing form of strikers Hernan Crespo and Claudio Lopez. In eight Serie A outings and six Champions League games, the Argentines managed two goals between them.

English media excitement grew in the second stage. While old rivals Manchester United and Bayern Munich qualified from Group A, Barcelona and Liverpool progressed

from Group B thanks to Roma's collapse. The Italians led the group with two matches remaining after a superb 3–0 win over Barcelona through goals from Emerson, Vincenzo Montella and Damiano Tommasi, but then slipped up against both Galatasaray and Liverpool.

In Group C, Real Madrid became the first certain qualifiers with two matches to spare after winning 2–1 away to FC Porto in Portugal thanks to early strikes from Santiago Solari and Ivan Helguera. Panathinaikos followed.

Group D ended in bad-tempered confusion with Leverkusen and Deportivo qualifying at the expense of Arsenal and Juventus. UEFA's decision to use head-to-head results before goal difference to separate teams level on points was the cause of English and Italian last-day depression. Deportivo, already sure of qualifying through that system, put out a weakened team at home to Leverkusen and lost. That effectively eliminated Arsenal, who had beaten Leverkusen 4–1 only a few weeks earlier. The Gunners finished third in the group, with Juve bottom.

KNOCK-OUT STAGE

Sir Alex Ferguson, in the eyes of the media, was on something akin to a divine mission. He had decided that this would be his last season as manager of Manchester United and, by friendly accident, the Champions League Final was to be staged at Hampden Park, in his home city of Glasgow.

ABOVE: BAYER LEVERKUSEN'S BRAZILIAN DEFENDER LUCIO STRETCHES IN A BID TO BLOCK ARSENAL STRIKER THIERRY HENRY'S SHOT

The plans for Ferguson's retirement – specifically, into what role at United, if any, he would be moving – had yet to be settled. But United's chief executive Peter Kenyon had been so convinced of the need to find a new manager that he had reached an informal agreement with Sven-Goran Eriksson.

Whispers that United were poised to steal England's manager were circulating freely in the game, while confirmations and denials were notable by their absence. United's players, however, remained unaffected.

In the previous nine years under Ferguson they had won seven league championships and three FA Cups – including three doubles – in addition to that magnificent 1999 Champions League triumph.

United had strengthened their attack with the forceful Dutchman Ruud van Nistelrooy, who fed greedily on the wing assists from David Beckham and Ryan Giggs.

But concern was increasing over the rising tension in Ferguson's relationship with Beckham, whose pop star cult status had been enhanced by his marriage to 'Posh' Victoria Adams of the Spice Girls.

Out on the pitch, the tension weighed only on opposing defenders. United were drawn against Deportivo in the quarter-finals. They won 2-0 in north-west Spain, with goals from Beckham and Van Nistelrooy, and 3-2 back at Old Trafford.

Depor had defenders Lionel Scaloni and Aldo Duscher sent off – Duscher for inflicting the injury which would deprive Beckham of full fitness at the World Cup finals that summer. The injured Manchester United superstar became the object of constant media speculation in his home country: would he/wouldn't he be available to captain Sven-Goran Eriksson's promising side in the summer and the broken metatarsal

RIGHT: **WITH SAMI HYYPIA GROUNDED, LUCIO BEATS JERZY DUDEK TO SCORE FOR BAYER LEVERKUSEN AGAINST LIVERPOOL**

bone in his foot seemed to take a veritable eternity to heal.

The semi-finals matched United, without the injured Beckham, against the unfashionable Bayer Leverkusen.

Coach Klaus Toppmoller had welded an effective unit out of disparate elements who included penalty-taking goalkeeper Hans-Jorg Butt, Brazilians in central defender Lucio and playmaker Ze Roberto, injury-prone sweeper Jens Nowotny and attacking midfielder Michael Ballack.

Ballack had scored twice as the Germans beat Liverpool 4–3 on aggregate in the quarter-finals, and he struck his sixth of the campaign in helping end Ferguson's dream. Bayer edged United on the away goals rule: 2–2 at Old Trafford, 1–1 at the BayArena. In both matches United led 1–0; in both matches Oliver Neuville grabbed the decisive equalizer.

Ferguson, denied his dream departure, decided to stay on as manager after all; Eriksson stuck with England.

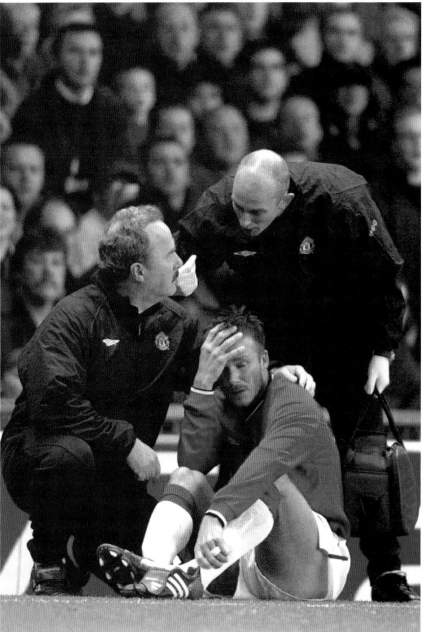

In the other half of the draw, Madrid had proved unstoppable. They took revenge over Bayern Munich for the previous season's defeat and then faced old Spanish enemies Barcelona in the semis.

For the Spanish media it was the Tie of the Century. Madrid had beaten Barcelona in the 1960 semis but had been eliminated – for the first time in the European Cup's history – by the Catalans the following autumn. On top of that, it was 20 years since Madrid had won in the Nou Camp, where the first leg was to be staged.

So much for history. Zinedine Zidane and Steve McManaman scored the second-half goals which provided Madrid with a 2–0 success. A 1–1 draw back in the Estadio Bernabeu saw them return to Hampden on a 3–1 aggregate.

ABOVE: **DAVID BECKHAM LOOKS DISTINCTLY DAZED AFTER THE CHALLENGE FROM DEPORTIVO'S ALDO DUSCHER WHICH THREATENED TO PUT HIM OUT OF THE WORLD CUP FINALS**

REAL CLINCH CUP FOR THE NINTH TIME

Destiny decided it: not only did Real Madrid's world-record signing Zinedine Zidane score a magnificent winning goal, but victory was saved by a home-grown substitute 'keeper in Iker Casillas, who accomplished a remarkable triple-save sequence four minutes into extra time.

Between them, they secured Madrid's record-extending ninth European Cup as a glittering climax to their centenary season. Coincidentally, Zidane also walked away with his first winner's medal.

Hampden had seen Madrid first lay claim to legendary status back in 1960 with the 7–3 trouncing of Eintracht Frankfurt. Now once again the victims were German.

Everything seemed to conspire against Bayer Leverkusen, right down to the suspension which denied them the creative services of Ze Roberto and the ligament injury which sidelined skipper and defensive anchor Jens Nowotny.

Madrid's toughest opposition was not, perhaps, Leverkusen but the weight of expectation created by the realization that this was their last chance of a trophy in their centenary season. They had finished third in the league and runners-up in the Spanish cup, and a further failure would have been a grievous 'reward' for all those world-record millions invested in Zidane and Luis Figo, not to mention Raul's golden handcuffs.

Oddly, Leverkusen confronted a similar nightmare after finishing runners-up in the German league and runners-up in their own cup. For them, too, the treble had been there, and they too had let it slip, piece by painful piece.

Leverkusen's bid to become the fourth German winners appeared lost when Raul struck in Madrid's first serious attack in the ninth minute. Roberto Carlos, preparing a throw-in, spotted Raul drifting behind the Leverkusen defence and popped the ball into his stride. Raul claimed his 34th Champions League goal by pushing the ball ever so gently past Hans-Jorg Butt's left hand.

In 1960, Frankfurt had scored first and Madrid had saved the day by snapping back. Now history was turned on its head as Leverkusen squared within five minutes. Bernd Schneider curled in a free-kick from the left and Lucio rocketed into the penalty box to rise above the Madrid defence and head the equalizer.

Leverkusen, who had been aggressively chasing shadows in midfield in the early minutes, now found new confidence and direction. But it was Madrid who struck next with the class expected of the world's number one footballer.

Zidane had coasted quietly around Hampden until the 44th minute. Then Santiago Solari sliced a gap on the left, Roberto Carlos swung in a looping cross and Zidane uncoiled just

RIGHT: **HAMPDEN PARK HAS SELDOM SEEN A BETTER GOAL THAN ZINEDINE ZIDANE'S EXPLOSIVE VOLLEY**

FAR RIGHT: **REAL'S PLAYERS FULLY ENJOY THEIR NINTH EUROPEAN CUP WIN**

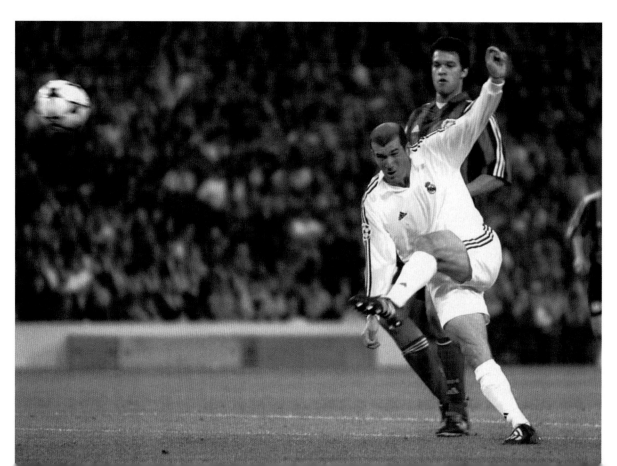

WEDNESDAY 15 MAY 2002
HAMPDEN PARK, GLASGOW

REAL MADRID   **2**
RAUL 9, ZIDANE 45

BAYER LEVERKUSEN   **1**
LUCIO 14

HT: 2-1. ATT: 52,000. REF: MEIER (SWZ)

MADRID:
CESAR (CASILLAS 68) - MICHEL
SALGADO, HIERRRO*, IVAN HELGUERA,
ROBERTO CARLOS - FIGO
(MCMANAMAN 61), MAKELELE (FLAVIO
CONCEICAO 73), ZIDANE, SOLARI -
RAUL, MORIENTES. COACH: DEL
BOSQUE.

LEVERKUSEN:
BUTT - ZIVKOVIC, LUCIO (BABIC 90),
PLACENTE - SCHNEIDER, SEBESCEN
(KIRSTEN 65), RAMELOW*, BALLACK -
NEUVILLE, BASTURK, BRDARIC
(BERBATOV 38). COACH: TOPPMOELLER.

*CAPTAIN

outside the penalty box to explode a left-foot volley high beyond Butt's right hand. It was a goal to grace the greatest of occasions and would have honoured any one of the Madrid greats who had gone before.

The longer the match went on, the more physical it became. Injury-hobbled Luis Figo was substituted by Steve McManaman, and goalkeeper Cesar, injured in falling under pressure, had to be replaced by Casillas.

Referee Urs Meier then signalled seven minutes of overtime, which proved sensational. First 'keeper Butt joined the Leverkusen attack at a free-kick, only to glance his header inches wide, then Casillas produced that stunning hat-trick of last-ditch stops from Yildiray Basturk, Ulf Kirsten and Bernd Schneider.

No wonder that it was Casillas, rather than Zidane, that the Madrid reserves hoisted shoulder-high at the final whistle.

LIKE FATHER, LIKE SON

As Italian sides made a comeback, Paolo Maldini made history by following his father as the captain of a European Cup-winning side. Once more Real Madrid versus Manchester United was a classic...

GROUP STAGE

Statistics reigned supreme amid Milan's resurgence to claim their fifth Champions Cup. Skipper Paolo Maldini finished the tournament not only emulating father Cesare – winning captain in neutral England back in 1963 – but with a European club record 123 appearances.

Along the way he had overtaken Barcelona and former Ajax defender Frank de Boer, who was left on 121. Also surpassed was Maldini's compatriot, the former Internazionale defender Giuseppe Bergomi, who played a grand total of 117 European club games between 1980 and 1999.

The first group stage saw Arsenal and Borussia Dortmund qualify from Group A with a game to spare. Arsenal secured progress despite losing twice in a row, by 2–1 to home to

RIGHT: ALEX DEL PIERO LINES UP A FREE-KICK AGAINST NEWCASTLE UNITED WITH A LITTLE HELP FROM FRIENDS SUCH AS EDGAR DAVIDS

Auxerre – an unhappy 53rd birthday for manager Arsene Wenger – then 2–1 in Dortmund despite Thierry Henry's free-kick. Dortmund's Czech playmaker Tomas Rosicky scored from a deflected free-kick of his own and a controversial penalty awarded against 'keeper David Seaman.

Group B saw Valencia qualify on the back of a 1–0 win in Liverpool. That left Gerard Houllier's men needing a win in Basel on the last match day. A topsy-turvy tie saw them fight back to 3–3 from 3–0 down but Michael Owen's equalizer was not enough. Liverpool ended third, one point behind Christian Gross's Swiss champions.

Holders Real Madrid qualified from Group C despite going off the boil. First they dropped a 2–0 lead at home to AEK Athens – AEK coach Dusan Bajevic described the 2–2 draw as a 'historic' result – then they lost 1–0 in the Bernabeu to Roma. Francesco Totti scored the decisive goal. Victory delighted

Roma coach Fabio Capello, who had laid the foundations of this Madrid side five years earlier.

The Italian revival was maintained in Group D by Internazionale despite a surprise home defeat by Lyon, and in Group E by Juventus despite a 1–0 defeat away to Sir Bobby Robson's Newcastle United. Manchester United booked their place in the second stage from Group F after a mere four match days, followed by the 2002 runners-up Bayer Leverkusen. Their German rivals Bayern Munich were embarrassed to finish bottom of Group G without a win in six games. 'FC Hollywood' and coach Ottmar Hitzfeld were savaged by the media after losing home and away to group-winners Milan.

Barcelona, in Group H, were the only club to win all six games and came close to a repeat in the second phase. Only a goalless away draw against runners-up Inter spoiled a record which made a nonsense of erratic domestic form which saw coach Louis van Gaal replaced by Radomir Antic.

Inter shattered Newcastle's dreams by winning 4–1 at St James's Park. Newcastle had to play most of the match with 10 men after Craig Bellamy's early expulsion for throwing a punch at Marco Materazzi. Bellamy had already missed three first-phase matches through suspension for a TV-spotted head-butt against Dynamo Kiev.

Leverkusen responded to finishing bottom of the group by sacking coach Klaus Toppmoller, their hero eight months

BELOW: **CHRISTIAN GROSS'S FC BASEL WALK OFF THE OLD TRAFFORD PITCH AFTER LOSING 3-1 TO MANCHESTER UNITED**

earlier. Arsenal snatched initial leadership of Group B by winning 3–1 in Rome with a hat-trick from Henry but ultimately had to give best to Ajax and Roma.

Milan and Real Madrid led the way from Group C, followed by Manchester United and Juventus from Group D. United floored Juve twice in a week, winning 2–1 at Old Trafford and then 3–0 in Turin, where Juve shamed Italian clubs' reputation for disciplined defending. The Old Lady of Turin still squeezed through a statistical minefield after they, Basel and Deportivo all finished on seven points.

KNOCK-OUT STAGE

Three years earlier Manchester United and Real Madrid, meeting in the quarter-finals, had provided the tie of the round. Now they repeated the explosive magic, although this time neither went on to ultimate glory.

Madrid had added Ronaldo, Brazil's nine-goal World Cup-winning leader the previous summer, to their 'Galactico' squad. He failed to score in the first leg in Spain, which Madrid won 3–1, but struck a memorable hat-trick inside the first hour

at Old Trafford. When coach Vicente del Bosque substituted him, the Old Trafford crowd – who included an obscure young Russian businessman named Roman Abramovich – rose for a sporting standing ovation.

But the drama was not over. At the time Madrid led 3–2 with United having replied through Ruud van Nistelrooy's 14th goal of the European campaign and an own goal off Ivan Helguera.

Around the time Ronaldo went off, United manager Sir Alex Ferguson brought on David Beckham, who had been relegated to the deep-freeze of the substitutes' bench by a breakdown in the relationship between manager and player. Tangled emotions must have gone through both men's minds as Beckham struck twice to salve United's pride with a 4–3 win.

Elsewhere, another embattled coach was winning his important battle. Milan's Carlo Ancelotti, sacked two years earlier by Juventus, had not always been at one with owner/prime minister Silvio Berlusconi and executive Adriano Galliani over tactics and selection.

But the man who had been Milan's midfield anchor when

they won the cup in 1989 and 1990 under Arrigo Sacchi masterminded a 0-0, 3-2 win over Ajax which lifted the Italians into their first semi-final in eight years.

They were joined by neighbours Internazionale, who beat Valencia on away goals. Juventus provided Italy with a third semi-finalist by outlasting Barcelona.

After a 1-1 draw in Turin, Juventus resisted magnificently in the Nou Camp, despite the 79th-minute expulsion by English referee Graham Poll of midfielder Edgar Davids, the so-called 'Pit Bull'. Once more, the score was 1-1 at 90 minutes, but Barcelona struggled to keep up the pace in extra time and substitute Marcelo Zalayeta struck Juve's winner with six minutes remaining.

One of the semi-finals – as with the infamous quarter-final of April 2005 – paired Milan with neighbours Inter. This 'Euro-derby' was more cautious than classic.

Although the San Siro stadium is home to both clubs, Milan were nominally home in the goalless opener and thus won through courtesy of the away-goals rule after a 1-1 draw in the return. Andriy Shevchenko scored in first-half stoppage time. Inter levelled only shortly before the end through Nigerian substitute Obafemi Martins.

Juventus came through against Real Madrid in the other semi-final to secure the first all-Italian final. Czech playmaker Pavel Nedved was outstanding in the first leg, which Real won 2-1 in Madrid, and even better in the return, which Juve turned around 3-1. Unfortunately, Nedved also collected his second yellow card of the competition, and celebrations of his decisive third goal were muted by the knowledge that he would miss the final.

Madrid, for whom Juve old boy Zinedine Zidane struck a last-minute consolation goal, appeared to lack conviction right from the start. They badly missed the leadership of talismanic nine-goal Raul, ruled out of the tie by appendicitis.

Final 2003

MILAN STAY COOL AS JUVE CRACK UP

MAIN: **ANDRIY SHEVCHENKO SENDS GIANLUIGI BUFFON THE WRONG WAY IN THE PENALTY SHOOT-OUT AND MILAN ARE HOME AND DRY**

It was nerve which decided the 2003 final after 120 minutes and a penalty shoot-out. Milan, shored up by veteran know-how, held theirs; Juventus, five of whose multi-millionaires refused point blank to take a spot-kick, lost theirs – and with it the first all-Italian final.

Unique places in European football were thus secured by Paolo Maldini and Clarence Seedorf. Skipper Maldini followed in the footsteps of 'Papa Cesare', who had raised the first of Milan's five cups 40 years earlier in England.

Dutch midfielder Seedorf became the first man to win the prize with three different clubs after his triumphs with Ajax in 1995 and Real Madrid in 1998. The fact that he missed one of the penalties was forgotten in the happy aftermath.

Juventus, significantly, were lacking Czech playmaker Pavel Nedved through suspension, while Milan had everyone available after veteran defender Billy Costacurta passed a late fitness test. Milan also possessed, in Carlo Ancelotti, a coach with recent and invaluable insight into the Juve psyche.

'new Rivera' or the 'new Baggio'. But his creative contribution was fitful and his shooting poor.

Milan thought they had the lead after only eight minutes. Pippo Inzaghi crossed from the left and Shevchenko fired low past Gianluigi Buffon. Unfortunately, Manuel Rui Costa's supporting momentum had run him in front of Buffon into an offside position.

Juventus made a tactical switch at half-time, rearranging their midfield with the replacement of Mauro Camoranesi by Antonio Conte. The veteran substitute nearly made a decisive impact within a minute, heading against the Milan bar from Del Piero's cross, and Milan were thankful to concede 'only' a corner.

At the other end Maldini, diving, headed wide a right-wing free-kick by Andrea Pirlo. That was on the hour and was the last significant chance as both teams shadow-boxed their way to 'silver goal' extra time.

This was a short-lived experiment by UEFA, intended to provide a less extreme alternative to golden goal sudden death which had turned out to be less than totally successful. Now teams entering extra time played the full first 15 minutes of it whether or not a goal was scored. If the scores were level at that stage, they then played the full second 15 minutes. This was meant to dispel overcautious play.

A week earlier an FC Porto team under Jose Mourinho, coaching's rising star, had come through that same test to beat Celtic and win the UEFA Cup. In the event the International Board declared the system illegal the following spring.

Milan and Juve duly failed to produce a goal of any shade or colour and stumbled to a shoot-out. Juve first had problems finding enough willing shooters, and then David Trezeguet, Marcelo Zalayeta and Paolo Montero all misfired.

After the game, Juve coach Marcello Lippi summed up, with masterful understatement: 'When four or five players refuse to take a penalty, it's difficult.'

WEDNESDAY 28 MAY 2003
OLD TRAFFORD, MANCHESTER

**MILAN 0
JUVENTUS 0**

AFTER EXTRA TIME
MILAN WON 3-2 ON PENS.
HT: 0-0. ATT: 63,215. REF: MERK (GER)

MILAN:
DIDA - NESTA, COSTACURTA (ROQUE JUNIOR 66), MALDINI*, KALADZE - GATTUSO, PIRLO (SERGINHO 71), RUI COSTA (AMBROSINI 87), SEEDORF - SHEVCHENKO, F. INZAGHI. COACH: ANCELOTTI.

JUVENTUS:
BUFFON - THURAM, FERRARA, PAULO MONTERO, TUDOR (BIRINDELLI 42) - CAMORANESI (CONTE 46), TACCHINARDI, DAVIDS (ZALAYETA 65), ZAMBROTTA - DEL PIERO*, TREZEGUET. COACH: LIPPI.

*CAPTAIN

He sent out Milan to seize the initiative from the start. They failed to score but at least they took so much out of Juve's legs that, even when Milan had been reduced to 10 effective men in extra time with Roque Junior a passenger, Juve lacked the energy to capitalize.

The match was a classic only in chessboard terms. Few chances were created, although Milan's Ukrainian striker Andriy Shevchenko was man of the match. He rounded off a mixed season by climaxing a performance of pace and physical commitment by converting the decisive penalty.

Nedved's absence offered Alex del Piero an opportunity to express the skills which once earned him labels as the

LEFT: **FOLLOWING IN HIS FATHER'S FOOTSTEPS TO WIN THE EUROPEAN CUP, SKIPPER PAOLO MALDINI EMBRACES CESARE MALDINI**

FOOTBALL'S RUSSIAN REVOLUTION

Just when football had developed prudent housekeeping habits, along came Roman Abramovich to buy Chelsea and take transfer fees sky high. Meanwhile, Jose Mourinho's Porto were on a roll

GROUP STAGE

Just when it seemed as if football was getting a grip on its chaotic finances, with UEFA laying down an accountancy standard, along came Roman Abramovich to blast financial logic out of the water.

Chelsea had qualified for the Champions League by finishing fourth in the Premiership under the leadership off the pitch of the irascible Ken Bates and the guidance on it of the idiosyncratic Italian Claudio Ranieri. Then, on 26 June 2003, came the 'Russian Revolution' sparked by a 37-year-old son of Saratov, a southern Russian city on the banks of the Volga.

Initially, it was whispered that Abramovich had bought

RIGHT: **HENRIK LARSSON** DEMONSTRATES THE THIN LINE BETWEEN SUCCESS AND FAILURE BY HEADING JUST WIDE OF OLIVER KAHN'S GOAL DURING THE CELTIC V BAYERN MUNICH GAME AT CELTIC PARK

Chelsea by accident, having spotted Stamford Bridge only on the drive back to Heathrow after a visit to Tottenham. He was painted as a man who had thrown millions at the club on an instant, ignorant whim. But inquiries into the murky world of post-communist Russia revealed that a businessman who courted Europe's most influential politicians and power-brokers never acted on the spur of the moment.

Orphaned before the age of three, brought up by uncles, schooled in the ruthless, fast-changing world of the collapsing communist empire, Abramovich had amassed a fortune which sent him straight to the top of the *Sunday Times* Rich List.

For a matter of small change, some £140 million, he bought the west London club and immediately paid off its crippling debts. Then, over the next 15 months, he splashed

out £210 million on some of Europe's finest footballers.

Nor did he spend only on players. Within months he had lured Peter Kenyon from Manchester United as chief executive and was pursuing England manager Sven-Goran Eriksson, whose guidance was obvious behind a number of the signings.

Ranieri, as the Italian himself acknowledged, was a 'dead man walking'. But the Tinkerman – initially a derisory label but one he liked – scampered endearingly down his cul-de-sac. Chelsea beat Zilina of Slovakia 2-0, 3-0 in the qualifying round, then topped group G ahead of Sparta Prague, conceding only three goals in their six games.

UEFA had changed formats again. President Lennart Johansson, alarmed by European players' evident fatigue at the 2002 World Cup, had enforced a revisionist switch. This saw the second group stage replaced by a knock-out round. The G-14 elite was opposed to the plan on financial grounds, but for once the greater good prevailed.

Group A saw French champions Lyon surprisingly finish

ABOVE: ROMAN ABRAMOVICH AT THE STADE LOUIS II STADIUM BEFORE CHELSEA'S SEMI-FINAL FIRST LEG WITH MONACO. WATCHING IN THE BACKGROUND IS FORMER CHAIRMAN KEN BATES

2003-04

ahead of Bayern Munich, who overtook Celtic on the last match day by defeating Anderlecht 1-0 with a penalty from their new Dutch spearhead Roy Makaay.

Arsenal recovered from the shock of an opening 3-0 beating at Highbury by Internazionale to top Group B. Arsene Wenger's men came back from the dead after taking just one point from their first three games. Thierry Henry struck twice in their 5-1 revenge triumph away to Inter.

Even more remarkable was the progress of Monaco in Group C on the back of an 8-3 thrashing of Deportivo La Coruna. Before the match Depor goalkeeper Jose Molina had told coach Jabo Irureta that he was feeling a little unwell but was OK to play.

By half-time, when Molina was substituted, Depor were 5-2 down. Monaco's reserve striker, the Croat Dado Prso, built himself an international reputation overnight with four goals. Remarkably, Depor still managed to qualify for the second round as group runners-up.

Juventus, seeking amends for the Old Trafford penalties fiasco, topped Group D ahead of Real Sociedad, followed by Manchester United and Stuttgart (Group E), Real Madrid and Porto (Group F) plus Milan and, surprisingly, Celta Vigo (Group H).

Madrid, having plundered Manchester United for David Beckham and coach Carlos Queiroz, strolled easily onwards. They won 3-1 away to Porto and patronizingly gave some of the youngsters a run-out for the concluding group game against the Portuguese runners-up. It ended 1-1, but Porto coach Jose Mourinho would have the last laugh.

KNOCK-OUT STAGE

Monaco were also to have a laugh at Madrid's expense. Coach Didier Deschamps had seen his plans for the season thrown into confusion by serious injury the previous summer to their top-scoring striker Shabani Nonda. In a panic, and just before the 31 August transfer deadline, Monaco went to Real Madrid to arrange the one-season loan of Fernando Morientes.

The Spanish World Cup centre-forward had been relegated to the subs' bench in Madrid by Ronaldo. Ironically, despite having missed the eight-goal thrashing of Deportivo, he would still emerge as the tournament's nine-goal leading marksman. One of those nine goals was the crucial away strike which pulled Monaco back to 'only' 2-1 down away to Lokomotiv Moscow in the Russian capital in the first leg of their second-round knock-out tie.

French football took further pride in Lyon's defeat of Real Sociedad. Surprisingly, to outsiders, Monaco's progress was not universally welcomed in France. Domestic rivals such as Marseille, Paris Saint-Germain and even Lyon resented the way Monaco used the principality's tax-haven status to attract the likes of Morientes, who were beyond the others' reach because of high 'mainland' tax rates.

Deschamps snapped back: 'If we weren't successful in Europe the French ranking would drop and these other clubs wouldn't have so many European places available. They're jealous.'

In the quarter-finals Monaco, with right-winger Ludovic Giuly hampered by injury, were drawn against a Real Madrid buoyed by victory over Bayern Munich. Deschamps's fears that

ABOVE: THIERRY HENRY CELEBRATES HIS SECOND GOAL - AND ARSENAL'S THIRD - IN THE SAN SIRO AGAINST INTER MILAN

this was a step too far appeared well-founded when Madrid led 4–1 in Spain with nine minutes to go. Then up stepped the exiled Morientes with another priceless late goal, this time against his own club.

The return became French football legend. Raul extended Madrid's overall lead and Giuly's equalizer in first-half stoppage time appeared of minimal importance. But, as Giuly walked off at half-time, Zinedine Zidane muttered: 'Haven't you worked it out – we're absolutely shattered.' Morientes headed Monaco's second shortly after the restart. Giuly flicked home a second. At 5–5 on aggregate, Monaco had triumphed courtesy of the away-goals rule.

'Now we don't need to fear anyone,' said Giuly. Not even Chelsea, who had seen off Arsenal – suffering their usual Champions League stage fright – in the quarter-finals. In the first leg Monaco hit back from 1–0 down at home, despite having Alekos Zikos sent off, to beat west London's big spenders 3–1.

Chelsea manager Claudio Ranieri was blamed for misjudging his use of substitutes and, unbelievably, back at Stamford Bridge he repeated the mistake.

Chelsea went 2–0 up, only to concede a controversial and morale-sapping goal to Ibarra on half-time. Morientes, roaming freely around Stamford Bridge, drove in a superb equalizer for the 2–2 draw.

Monaco, against all the odds, had forged their way through to a final joust with another bunch of outsiders from Porto.

The second-round tie against Manchester United could hardly have begun worse for Porto coach Jose Mourinho. For the home leg striker Derlei was injured, while midfield anchor Costinha was suspended, and United went ahead on 14 minutes through Quinton Fortune.

But United had problems of their own, with Rio Ferdinand ruled out by an eight-month ban for failing to take a dope test. South African Benni McCarthy capitalized with a volley in the 29th minute and a header in the 78th. United suffered further when skipper Roy Keane was sent off for treading on keeper Vitor Baia.

After 32 minutes at Old Trafford, Paul Scholes put United level on aggregate and ahead on away goals, but it was not enough. In the last minute, Costinha disobeyed orders not to drift forward and scored from close range after Tim Howard only parried McCarthy's free-kick.

Mourinho jigged in delight down the Old Trafford touchline and Porto duly danced past Lyon in the quarter-finals and Deportivo in the semis.

LEFT: TIM HOWARD CAN NOT HOLD BENNI MCCARTHY'S FREE-KICK AND PORTO'S COSTINHA PUTS THE REBOUND BEYOND HIS REACH. MANCHESTER UNITED ARE OUT...

MOURINHO OUTSWIMS HIS FELLOW SHARKS

The previous year, after Porto's UEFA Cup Final victory, coach Jose Mourinho had been asked about rumours that he was planning to move on. He responded that he had worked hard at Porto, wanted to see how far he could go in the Champions League, and would then consider his options.

Reaching the Champions' final had not been among his calculations back then. He had said: 'We can do quite well but we cannot expect to live with the sharks.' Yet now Mourinho was about to become a shark himself: before the final in the heart of the Ruhr, it was an open secret that he would be replacing Claudio Ranieri at Chelsea.

That was the quirk about this final. Monaco and Porto were not approaching it as empire-builders. Quite the reverse. Both were about to sell off the family silver.

Porto were to lose playmaker Deco to Barcelona, while defenders Paulo Ferreira and Ricardo Carvalho would follow Mourinho to west London. As for Monaco, Dado Prso was joining Rangers, loanee Luis Ibarra was heading back to Porto, Fernando Morientes was returning to the Real Madrid auction room, Edouard Cisse and Jerome Rothen were off to Paris Saint-Germain, and Ludovic Giuly would join Barcelona.

Porto started favourites, if only on account of the UEFA Cup-winning experience. Only one French club had emerged victorious from five previous tilts at the crown, and even that success – Marseille's in 1993 – had been tarnished by charges of corruption.

Deschamps had been the captain who raised the cup for Marseille that day. But he had added a 'legitimate' victory with Juventus three years later and thus now stood one match from becoming the youngest winning coach: at 35 he was 10 months younger than Real Madrid's Jose Villalonga in 1956.

The first half saw little goalmouth action. Porto used their anchor Costinha to stifle Fernando Morientes, while Monaco lost luckless Giuly to injury after a mere 22 minutes. At one stage, Monaco – spurred on by Rothen down the left – began to take the upper hand. Yet it was Porto who opened the scoring against the run of play through Carlos Alberto.

Given Monaco's attacking failure, Deschamps should have made changes at half-time. Instead he persisted for more than a quarter of an hour with the team whose touch and

RIGHT: **PORTO'S DECO PICKS HIS SPOT FOR THE SECOND GOAL AGAINST MONACO**

confidence faded a little further every time they fell victim to Porto's disciplined offside trap. Thus Monaco were eventually punished twice by substitute Dmitri Alenitchev on the break. First he helped set up Deco for goal number two, then he strode clear himself to thump home Derlei's assist.

Porto were not pretty, and much of their passing was below their own deft standard. Yet their second Champions Cup – 17 years after the first – meant that they had at last emulated the achievement of Benfica, twice victorious over 40 years earlier.

When it came time to celebrate, however, Mourinho had vanished into the crowd. He had bigger sharks to fry.

LEFT: **PORTO'S COLOURFUL SUPPORTERS IN FULL FORCE**

BELOW: **AS HIS PORTO PLAYERS CELEBRATE, THE BROODING FIGURE OF JOSE MOURINHO STANDS FRESHLY BEMEDALLED IN THE BACKGROUND**

WEDNESDAY 26 MAY 2004
AUFSCHALKE, GELSENKIRCHEN

FC PORTO   3
CARLOS ALBERTO 39, DECO 71, ALENITCHEV 75

MONACO   0

HT: 1-0. ATT: 53,053.
REF: MILTON NIELSEN (DEN)

PORTO:
VITOR BAIA* – PAULO FERREIRA, RICARDO CARVALHO, JORGE COSTA, NUNO VALENTE – COSTINHA – PEDRO MENDES, DECO (PEDRO EMANUEL 85), MANICHE – DERLEI (MCCARTHY 79), CARLOS ALBERTO (ALENITCHEV 60). COACH: MOURINHO.

MONACO:
ROMA – IBARRA, RODRIGUEZ, GIVET (SQUILLACI 72), EVRA – CISSE (NONDA 64), BERNARDI, ZIKOS, ROTHEN – GIULY* (PRSO 68), MORIENTES. COACH: DESCHAMPS.

*CAPTAIN

REDS SNEAK UP ON THE INSIDE RAIL

Football has changed over the years but it has never been able to banish controversy. There was more than ever this term as unfancied Liverpool went from zeroes to heroes in a very short space of time

GROUP STAGE

The term which climaxed with Liverpool winning one of the most sensational of finals began just like the initial campaign back in 1955.

Many basic elements remained the same as they had been when the competition started. The destiny of the grand silver cup was still contested between two teams of 11 players. The goals separating victory from defeat were still approved in an instant by a lone referee.

But much else had changed.

Sharp eyesight was demanded to interpret the flickering black-and-white images recorded by primitive TV coverage of the first final. Now more than two dozen cameras claim almost every angle in colour.

In 1955, the players wore only numbers and club badges on their shirts. There were no sportswear logos, no shirt adverts, no subliminal assortment of stripes and swirls. Beyond that, there were no high-tech footballs or boots fashioned to swerve the ball in and around the goalmouth. Nor were there all-seater stadia, while protection against the elements was minimal for spectators.

The referee wore only black. No trendy colours. No further assistance beyond his two linesmen. Life was simpler. There were no extra complications from the away-goals rule or penalty shootouts. Nor did you need a fourth official to check the substitutes; there was no need, there were no substitutes.

As Alfredo Di Stefano observed: 'Today's footballers only appear to play more than us; it's not true when you consider

RIGHT: **PHILLIP COCU CELEBRATES AFTER SCORING FOR PSV AGAINST MILAN IN THE SEMI-FINAL. MILAN HIT BACK IMMEDIATELY THROUGH AMBROSINI TO TAKE THE WIND OUT OF THE DUTCH CLUB'S SAILS**

today's substitutions and rotation. We used to play the full 90 minutes of every game – even if we were injured.'

Attitudes quickly changed with the worldwide spread of professionalism. In the 1950s, football was still in touch with its sporting roots. Di Stefano again: 'We never celebrated a goal like today's players. We had too much respect for our opponents.'

There were no tabloid storms about footballers' failure as role models. The age of the angry young man lacked anyone to compare with the scowling youth of a Wayne Rooney or Antonio Cassano. England captain Billy Wright marrying Joy Beverley was a world away from the wedded life of the Beckhams.

The money had changed. Di Stefano, Paco Gento and Jose Maria Zarraga each collected a £1,250 bonus in 1960 for having won all five European Cups with Real Madrid. While English footballers were nailed to a £20 weekly maximum wage, it seemed astronomical. Yet Michael Owen, on joining Madrid from Liverpool in the summer of 2004, turned over as much every couple of hours.

Still a dozen of the 1950s pioneers were among the 32 clubs contesting the 2004–05 groups. Six 'old boys' were among the 16 who progressed: Madrid despite the short, turbulent coaching reigns of Jose Camacho and Mariano Garcia Remon, Juventus, Manchester United, Milan, Barcelona and

holders Porto – who sacked new Italian coach Gigi Del Neri before the season had even begun for 'poor timekeeping'.

Accompanying them were old faces in new places. Liverpool demanded a major rebuilding job of Rafa Benitez (ex-Valencia); Leverkusen and Bayern Munich had been shaken up by former Cup-winning players in Klaus Augenthaler and Felix Magath; PSV Eindhoven had gone back to the future with successful 1988 coach Guus Hiddink; Internazionale leaned on Roberto Mancini (ex-Sampdoria); Chelsea powered in greedy pursuit of everything in sight under a self-proclaimed 'special one' in Jose Mourinho. Stability was a rare boast for Didier Deschamps (Monaco), Thomas Schaaf (Werder Bremen) and Paul Le Guen (Lyon) – and Le Guen quit as soon as Lyon, the next May, had secured their fourth successive French league title.

Qualifying failures included CSKA Moscow. They finished third in Chelsea's group, the draw having raised eyebrows since the Brazilian-sprinkled Muscovites were sponsored by the Sibneft oil corporation owned by... Roman Abramovich. Ironically, it was CSKA who went on to European glory, winning the UEFA Cup into which they had been relegated by Chelsea and Porto.

And Liverpool? They sneaked through thanks to a magnificent goal from Steven Gerrard, three minutes from the end of their concluding group game against Olympiakos.

BELOW: **LIVERPOOL AND JUVENTUS PLAYERS OBSERVE A MINUTE'S SILENCE AT ANFIELD IN MEMORY OF THE HEYSEL STADIUM VICTIMS**

2004-2005

KNOCK-OUT STAGE

A frown flitted across the face of Sepp Blatter. The setting was a country house hotel in South Wales and the date was Saturday, 26 February. The annual meeting of the law-making International Board had just approved experiments with goal-line technology.

The FIFA president believed in the universality of the game: that it should be played under the same conditions from World Cup Final to pub league. Now the one body on which England still commanded a decisive say in the worldwide game had defiantly opened the door to technological assistance.

Anders Frisk might have wished for video support at half-time in Barcelona. Chelsea's 2-1 defeat in a second-round first leg was followed by claims that home coach Frank Rijkaard had breached the sanctity of the referee's dressing room at half-time and thus influenced the subsequent expulsion of striker Didier Drogba.

Chelsea manager Jose Mourinho had refused to attend the obligatory post-match press conference. His behaviour and subsequent comments earned a two-match touchline ban. But the intimidatory atmosphere assisted Chelsea to a 4-2 turnaround win at Stamford Bridge.

Controversy was nothing new for Frisk. He had abandoned a group match in Rome after being struck by a missile following his sending-off of Philippe Mexes. But this time the consequences were extreme. His telephones, email and home were inundated with threats to himself and his family.

Frisk's response was immediate retirement, a dramatic gesture consistent with his theatrical style of refereeing.

Of course, the Champions League coped without him. Arsenal, crucially below par in Munich, slipped out 3-2 on aggregate to Bayern. Real Madrid, lacking in conviction under a third coach in Brazilian Vanderlei Luxemburgo, lost in extra time to Juventus. Michael Owen's rise in stature could not compensate for the fading of Luis Figo.

Liverpool won home and away against Bayer Leverkusen; PSV saw off Monaco; Milan edged stuttering Manchester United; Inter saw off Porto and Lyon thrashed Werder Bremen 3-0 away and 7-2 in France where Sylvain Wiltord scored a hat-trick.

In the quarter-finals, the Arsenal discard scored his sixth goal of the term to earn a shootout against PSV, but here Lyon came unstuck.

Bayern, meanwhile, were no match for a second English challenge. Frank Lampard scored two superb goals at Stamford Bridge and Chelsea flowed on despite losing 3-2 in the last European tie to be played in Munich's iconic Olympiastadion. Milan repeated their 2003 win over Inter to the fury of their neighbours' fans. The second leg had to be abandoned by German referee Markus Merk after a firework-flecked hail of missiles - one felling Milan goalkeeper Dida - halted play 16 minutes from time.

Further Italian losers were Juventus. For the first time in the 20 years since Heysel they had been drawn against Liverpool. A highly charged emotional occasion at Anfield, when an unforgiving band of Juve fans turned their backs on a memorial gesture, ended in a 2-1 home win. Surprisingly, that sufficed back in goalless Turin.

Liverpool thus flew home knowing Chelsea came next.

ABOVE: ROMA'S BRAZILIAN STRIKER MANCINI FIRES THE BALL INTO THE REAL MADRID WALL DURING A GAME THAT WAS PLAYED BEHIND CLOSED DOORS AFTER REFEREE ANDERS FRISK HAD BEEN STRUCK BY A MISSILE FROM THE CROWD AT AN EARLIER MATCH

Europe was consumed by a tie which far overshadowed Milan's scrappy scuttling of PSV.

Mourinho and Chelsea were heading for the club's first league title in 50 years, but Liverpool had learned vital lessons from their earlier defeat by Mourinho's men in the League Cup Final. Assisted by injuries which denied Chelsea the starting commitment of wingers Arjen Robben and Damien Duff, Liverpool emerged goalless from Stamford Bridge. Back at Anfield, manager Rafa Benitez ordered another cautious start. His perverse reward was a disputed fourth-minute goal for Luis Garcia which – backed by the defensive inspiration of Jamie Carragher – proved decisive.

Chelsea claimed William Gallas had hooked the ball back into play before it crossed the line but Slovak referee Lubos Michels would have none of it.

A 9-million-strong audience quickly registered the fact that even slow-motion TV replays could not resolve the mystery. Blatter must have smiled at that.

LIVERPOOL'S AMAZING COMEBACK

Liverpool made more money out of the 2004–05 Champions League than Milan. Their share of UEFA's pot added up to £20.5 million, while Milan coined 'only' £17.5 million. But victory in Istanbul, as it turned out, was not about the money but the glory.

The momentous recovery which sent a fifth European Cup into a permanent place of honour at Anfield ensured this final a legendary slot in not only the European Cup but international and club football in general.

Three billion TV viewers in 200 countries were transfixed by Liverpool's record-beating comeback from 3-0 down at half-time. Even captain Steve Gerrard, man-of-the-match scorer of Liverpool's first goal and fouled for the penalty which led to their equaliser, appeared in a trance afterwards.

He said: 'Milan deserved to be three-up at half-time. They were some heads down in the dressing room at the interval and I was afraid it was going to be tears at 90 minutes. But the manager made some changes and put a bit of belief back into the players. The important thing was to get a bit of respect back for the fans.'

Tactically, the days of the WM formation, of *catenaccio* and 4-2-4 had long gone. Both teams began with sophisticated variations of 4-4-2. But whereas Milan, initially, had the right men to express themselves perfectly on that stage Liverpool did not. Milan began with their 'gala' line-up, while Benitez gambled on the fragile fitness of Australian Harry Kewell to

assist Milan Baros up front. The ploy meant leaving a chasm in midfield for which Liverpool were duly punished.

After just 53 seconds Kaka was fouled by Djimi Traore and Andrea Pirlo's right-wing free kick was hooked home by skipper Paolo Maldini. Ironically, his records in becoming both the fastest scorer in a Champions' Final and the oldest, at 36, would be forgotten in defeat.

The injured Kewell was substituted by midfielder Vladimir Smicer to little effect. Andriy Shevchenko was wrongly judged offside as he 'scored' on 29 minutes but it hardly mattered as Kaka twice helped set up Chelsea loanee Hernan Crespo in the seven minutes before half-time.

What happened next is hotly disputed by the separate camps. Traore claimed that the celebratory sounds coming from the Milan players at the break inspired Liverpool's revival; Benitez said switching to three at the back was crucial; others saw the injury to full-back Steve Finnan which prompted Didi Hamann's arrival in central midfield as decisive.

The sum total, at least, contributed to Liverpool pulling level after what Milan coach Carlo Ancelotti later described as 'six inexplicable minutes of madness'.

Gerrard headed the first from John Arne Riise's left-wing cross; Smicer thundered the second off goalkeeper Dida's hands; and Xabi Alonso stabbed home a rebound after Dida parried his initial penalty following Gattuso's trip on Gerrard.

Milan could have regained all that lost ground three

RIGHT: **STEVEN GERRARD SETS LIVERPOOL ON THE COMEBACK TRAIL AS HE HEADS HOME JOHN ARNE RIISE'S CROSS**

minutes from the end of extra time. But Jerzy Dudek made a remarkable double save from Shevchenko before the Polish goalkeeper defied the Ukrainian again, to permanent effect, in the shoot-out.

Liverpool were not the only winners. UEFA, having generated £30 million in the first year of the Champions League, was now coining in around £1.5 billion: big business.

For Gabriel Hanot, editor of *L'Equipe* and founding father of the competition, of course, sporting merit had been all that mattered... and so it was on the night in Istanbul.

LEFT: AFTER HIS CLOWNISH ANTICS IN THE SHOOT-OUT, JERZY DUDEK STOPS SHEVCHENKO'S POORLY STRUCK PENALTY TO BRING A FIFTH EUROPEAN CUP TO LIVERPOOL

BELOW: STEVEN GERRARD HOLDS UP THE EUROPEAN CUP, A SCENE WHICH NOT EVEN LIVERPOOL'S MOST ARDENT FANS COULD HAVE ENVISAGED WHEN THEIR SIDE WERE 3-0 DOWN

WEDNESDAY 25 MAY 2005
THE ATATURK STADIUM, ISTANBUL

LIVERPOOL	**3**

(GERRARD 53, SMICER 55, ALONSO 59)

MILAN	**3**

(MALDINI 53SEC, CRESPO 38, 43)

3-2 ON PENALTIES AFTER EXTRA TIME
HT: 0-3. 90MIN: 3-3. ATT: 69,000
REF: MEJUTO GONZALEZ (SP)

LIVERPOOL:
DUDEK · FINNAN (HAMANN 46), CARRAGHER, HYYPIA, TRAORE · LUIS GARCIA, GERRARD*, ALONSO, RIISE · BAROS (CISSE 83), KEWELL (SMICER 22). MANAGER: BENITEZ

MILAN:
DIDA · CAFU, NESTA, STAM, MALDINI* · KAKA, PIRLO, GATTUSO (RUI COSTA 111), SEEDORF (SERGINHO 83) · CRESPO (TOMASSON 83), SHEVCHENKO. MANAGER: ANCELOTTI

PENALTIES (MILAN FIRST): SERGINHO OVER 0-0, HAMANN 0-1; PIRLO SAVED 0-1; CISSE 0-2; TOMASSON 1-2, RIISE SAVED 1-2; KAKA 2-2, SMICER 2-3; SHEVCHENKO SAVED 2-3.

*CAPTAIN

BARÇA DO A EUROPEAN DOUBLE

Arsenal defeated an unlikely list of fancied sides to reach their first Champions League final, against Barcelona, while holders Liverpool were forced to work their way through mid-summer pre-qualifying

GROUP STAGE

Valdebibas sits on the northward-spreading fringe of Madrid, near Barajas airport. There, in May, 2006 – 50 years after the first European Cup Final – Real Madrid played Reims once more.

This anniversary celebration marked the official opening of the Estadio Alfredo Di Stefano, which is as far as fans may progress inside Madrid's new sports city. The great man, recovered from heart surgery, was guest of honour. Old foe-turned-team-mate, Raymond Kopa, sent apologies from a retirement home in Corsica after surgery of his own.

Eight days later, Paris was host – as it had been in 1956 – to the real thing between Barcelona and Arsenal. In 1956, the venue was the old Parc des Princes; now it was the Stade de France, officially within Saint-Denis, but "Paris" in football parlance.

The Madrid re-run was history on display, with all the club's trophies from the Di Stefano era being brought under guard from the Bernabeu and displayed in front of the main stand.

But Paris was also a history lesson between Barcelona, historic under-achievers in Europe, against Arsenal, whose legend had been honoured by the copying of the club's name worldwide.

RIGHT: LIVERPOOL SKIPPER STEVEN GERRARD ESCAPES THE ATTENTIONS OF CHELSEA'S NEW GHANAIAN MIDFIELDER MICHAEL ESSIEN IN THE GROUP G TIE BETWEEN THE CUP HOLDERS AND THE PREMIERSHIP CHAMPIONS AT ANFIELD

Two Frenchmen were looking further ahead. The one week saw Zinedine Zidane playing his last game in Madrid before heading for the World Cup and retirement; the next week saw Thierry Henry pondering whether to leave Arsenal for Barcelona. Thus history repeated itself again: in 1956 the see-sawing Frenchman had been Kopa, balanced between Reims and Madrid.

At least in 1956 the holders returned automatically the next season to defend their crown. This time, initially, that same opportunity was denied to Liverpool, despite the drama of their recovery to beat Milan in Istanbul. UEFA, in redrafting the rules for the Champions League, had omitted the right of defence. Liverpool, in finishing fifth in the Premiership, had failed to guarantee automatic re-entry to the competition. The Football Association and Premier League had to lobby hard before UEFA acquiesced with bad grace, obliging Liverpool to begin their defence of the trophy in the first qualifying round.

Hence, on July 12 – a mere 48 days after partying in Istanbul – manager Rafael Benitez and Co. found themselves heading back to square one. The draw had been kind: Liverpool faced only the short trip to see off TNS of Wales, before despatching Kaunas of Lithuania and then CSKA Sofia to regain entry to the group stages and a renewal of their rivalry with Chelsea.

Both meetings in Group G, at Anfield and then Stamford Bridge, ended goalless, but the return was hardly peaceable after a clumsy tackle by Chelsea's new Ghanaian, Michael Essien, on Dietmar Hamann. Liverpool's veteran German said it was the worst tackle he had ever suffered, and the incident sparked a touchline spat between Benitez and his Chelsea counterpart, Jose Mourinho – who later accused the Liverpool bench of "crying" throughout the game.

By then, both clubs had made sure of qualifying with a game to spare – as had Juventus and Bayern Munich, Arsenal and Ajax, Barcelona, Lyon and Real Madrid plus Internazionale.

This was fortunate for Madrid, whose hasty dismissal of Brazilian coach Wanderley Luxemburgo after less than a year was rewarded with a pride-pricking 2-1 defeat in their last group match by bottom club Olympiakos Piraeus. Rosenborg Trondheim, whose 13-year league-championship-winning reign in Norway had just come to an end, finished third and claimed the consolation of a UEFA Cup fade-out.

Milan had to wait until the last matchday before topping Group E, while Rangers scraped out of Group H after drawing 1-1 with Internazionale, and Artmedia Bratislava simultaneously failed to beat Porto. Peter Lovenkrands's goal kept manager Alex McLeish in his job for the rest of the season.

Artmedia were already popular with Rangers: in the third qualifying round, they had eliminated 'old firm' rivals Celtic. Artmedia won the first leg in Bratislava 5-0, the worst possible start for new Celtic manager Gordon Strachan.

He would have the last laugh, however. Celtic went on to win the Scottish league, while Hearts – revived by a Lithuanian transplant from banker Vladimir Romanov – ultimately pipped Rangers to the second Champions League slot.

The one blow to English pride was Manchester United's failure to progress for the first time in eleven years. A 2-1 defeat away to Benfica on the last matchday – despite an early lead provided by Paul Scholes – was a worrying introduction to European football for Malcolm Glazer and his sons, United's much-derided new American owners.

Goals from Geovanni and Beto left United bottom of the group, so they missed even the consolation of a place in the UEFA Cup. Those goals also provided United with a depressing return to the city in which George Best had risen to world fame back in 1965. The Northern Irishman, who had just died at the age of 59, after a long battle against illnesses brought on by the lifestyle he enjoyed in his earlier days, would not have recognised this United.

BELOW: **CRISTIANO RONALDO HOLDS HIS HEAD IN FRUSTRATION AS EVERYTHING GOES WRONG FOR MANCHESTER UNITED EN ROUTE TO THE 2-1 DEFEAT BY BENFICA IN LISBON WHICH KNOCKED THEM OUT OF THE CHAMPIONS LEAGUE**

KNOCK-OUT STAGE

No-one had any doubts that when Roman Abramovich bought Chelsea and their debts, his ambitions stretched way beyond winning merely the League Cup and the Premiership. Jose Mourinho and £200m-worth of players had achieved those targets in the Portuguese coach's initial season. Next step up was the Champions League.

Semi-finals defeats by Monaco in 2004 and by Liverpool in 2005 had established Chelsea's European potential. Mourinho appeared supremely confident in the fact.

Chelsea had already left Manchester United and Arsenal trailing in the Premiership title race, and Mourinho had blithely expressed a lack of concern over whether Chelsea finished first or second in their first-round group, because he assessed all the potential opponents as top quality.

Finishing second, on the 'wrong' side of the seeded second round draw, proved to be a costly misjudgement. After UEFA's assortment of plastic lottery balls had been spun around the goldfish bowls, Chelsea found themselves having been drawn once more, as in the previous season's quarter-finals, to face Barcelona.

But this was not the previous term's fragile Barcelona, concentrated most intently on winning their first Spanish league title for six years. This was a more mature team, strengthened by the addition of a remarkable Argentine teenager.

Leo Messi was such a talented kid that Barcelona brought him to Spain aged 13. In the summer of 2005 he had captained Argentina to victory in the World Youth Cup in Holland. An eligibility dispute had restricted his appearances for Barcelona in the first half of the Spanish season, and thus he now had something to prove.

Barcelona also had something to prove in general. They felt they had been 'psyched out' of it by Chelsea in the row over referee Anders Frisk the previous season. Coach Frank Rijkaard was quietly determined that they would not fall into the same trap twice – and they did not.

Barcelona won 2-1 at Stamford Bridge, where Chelsea's left-back Asier Del Horno nonsensically left Norwegian referee Terje Hauge with no option but to show him the red card for ignoring the ball and blundering through on Messi.

The Catalans could have won more easily. Messi hit the bar and John Terry – who had earlier put though his own goal – twice cleared off the line before Samuel Eto'o struck a late winner.

A 1-1 draw back in Barcelona, where Mourinho was still taunted as "the translator" after his initial spells there under Bobby Robson and Louis Van Gaal, was not enough as Chelsea paid the price for overconfidence. One trophy – the Premiership again – was all Abramovich would have to show for his investment.

Chelsea would have considered it poor consolation that holders Liverpool, having headed them by one point in the group, succumbed to a surprising 3-0 aggregate defeat by Benfica.

Barcelona went on to reach the final by defeating Benfica and Milan and, in the process, establishing themselves as Europe's form team. In terms of quality, Arsenal, after

ABOVE: **SKIPPER THIERRY HENRY CELEBRATES SCORING ARSENAL'S SECOND GOAL IN THE 2-0 VICTORY OVER JUVENTUS IN THE QUARTER-FINALS WHICH WAS ALSO ONE OF THE GUNNERS' LAST HOME MATCHES AT HIGHBURY**

overcoming both the surprise pre-season sale of captain Patrick Vieira to Juventus and then a string of injuries, were not far behind. They proved the point by defeating imploding Real Madrid, bad-tempered Juventus and then the disciplined newcomers Villarreal.

Oddly, Villarreal were the most awkward of the three. Madrid and Juventus went out complacently to play their own football and proved vulnerable to Cesc Fabregas's work ethic in midfield and Thierry Henry's electric pace in attack. Only against Villarreal, who paid pragmatically close-marking attention, did Arsenal struggle.

Argentine playmaker Juan Roman Riquelme, outstanding throughout the Champions' campaign, should have taken the tie into extra time with a last-minute penalty in front of the "Yellow Submarine's" own supporters. But Arsenal goalkeeper Jens Lehmann dived left to save, propelling himself into the number-one slot with World Cup hosts Germany and launching the Gunners into their first Champions' final.

ABOVE: FRENCH RIGHT WINGER LUDOVIC GIULY ANTICIPATES KAKHA KALADZE'S TACKLE TO STRIKE BARCELONA'S CRUCIAL GOAL AWAY TO MILAN IN THE SPANISH CHAMPIONS' SEMI-FINAL TRIUMPH IN THE STADIO MEAZZA

LEFT: JENS LEHMANN IS ARSENAL'S PENALTY HERO AFTER DIVING TO SAVE JUAN ROMAN RIQUELME'S LAST-MINUTE PENALTY AND THUS SECURE THE 1-0 AGGREGATE VICTORY OVER VILLARREAL WHICH SENT THEM ON INTO THE FINAL

BARÇA VANQUISH VALIANT ARSENAL

'Ronaldinho v. Thierry Henry' was the billing for the final, overshadowing the team contest between two great European under-achievers. Barcelona had won the Champions' crown just once, while Arsenal had never previously progressed beyond the quarter-finals.

Barcelona were acknowledged as the finest footballing side in Europe, just ahead of Arsenal – once manager Arsene Wenger had begun to guide his squad beyond a lengthy injury crisis. The Catalans' ultimate victory was thus logical in perspective but controversial in nature, and short of the footballing style and craft for which the neutrals longed.

At least the final contained a built-in consolation prize. Both teams were assured of a return ticket for next season, Barcelona as champions of Spain and Arsenal through a fourth-place finish secured on the last day of the season through Thierry Henry's hat-trick against Wigan.

Neither side had lost any of their 12 matches on the road to the city with dual connections. Ronaldinho, current World and European Footballer of the Year, had spent two seasons with Paris Saint-Germain, while Henry had been born and brought up in the capital. An additional twist of intrigue was the possibility of Henry leading Arsenal for the last time before switching sides.

Coaches Frank Rijkaard and Arsene Wenger caused few ripples with their line-ups. Arsenal preferred the experience of revived Sol Campbell to Swiss youngster Philippe Senderos in

defence, while Ashley Cole had regained his fitness just in time to play at left-back.

The absences of Campbell and Cole earlier in the season had prompted a critical storm when Wenger picked a first-ever Premiership squad without a single Englishman for a 5-1 win over Crystal Palace in February. Wenger had been caught off guard by the fuss, protesting: "When I pick my team I look at players, not passports."

Barcelona had Rafael Marquez fit to take his place in the heart of defence, the first Mexican to appear in a Champions' final. But both he and skipper Carles Puyol were caught asleep in the second minute when Henry skipped in front of them to reach a low short cross from Emmanuel Eboue, and was foiled only by the alert Victor Valdes. The ball bounced away for a corner, and Valdes was immediately in superb action again, this time beating away Henry's powerful angled drive.

If Arsenal had started with Jose Antonio Reyes or Robin Van Persie, or even the retiring veteran Dennis Bergkamp to partner Henry in attack, they might have pressed home that early advantage decisively. Instead, foregoing a second striker for the sake of five men strung cautiously across midfield, they lacked the essential weaponry.

Barcelona's initial tactics were doubtless a delight to Wenger. Ronaldinho sat far up front like an orthodox centre forward, which simplified Arsenal's task of controlling him. Ludovic Giuly played wide right and Samuel Eto'o wide left.

RIGHT: **JENS LEHMANN IS CAST IN THE ROLE OF SCAPEGOAT AS HE IS SENT OFF BY REFEREE TERJE HAUGE FOR BRINGING DOWN BARCELONA STRIKER SAMUEL ETO'O IN THE OPENING STAGES OF THE FINAL**

LEFT: BARCELONA'S ECSTATIC
PLAYERS CELEBRATE THE
CLUB'S SECOND EUROPEAN CUP
SUCCESS AS SKIPPER CARLOS
PUYOL HOISTS THE TROPHY
AFTER ITS PRESENTATION BY
UEFA PRESIDENT LENNART
JOHANSSON

The first time the Cameroonian moved into the centre proved disastrous for Arsenal. The Cameroon striker exchanged passes with Ronaldinho and was arrowing towards goal when fast-advancing keeper Jens Lehmann sent him tumbling. Referee Terje Hauge immediately blew for the foul – infuriating Barcelona, since Giuly had whipped the loose ball into the net.

Hauge disallowed the goal, awarded Barcelona a free kick on the edge of the penalty box and sent off Lehmann. It was not the exit the German had wanted on his last Arsenal appearance before taking up his newly-won number-one spot with Germany for the World Cup finals.

Wenger and Rijkaard agreed later that the offence deserved a red card, but Wenger would have preferred a delay on the whistle. That way Arsenal would have conceded the goal in the likelihood that Lehmann would have been shown "only" a yellow card and they would have retained eleven men. As it was, the sending-off killed the game for which the purists had hoped.

Barcelona, it seemed, now needed only play their football and – maybe not sooner, but surely later – the goals would come. Arsenal's panic was evidenced by the manner in which the rattled Eboue took off Gio van Bronckhorst at the knee.

Ironically, it was Arsenal who took the lead. More perversely, the goal stemmed from a dive by Eboue, which gained an undeserved free kick at the expense of Barcelona captain Puyol. Henry floated in a perfect, fading free kick and Campbell headed gloriously home. "I was sure there was a goal in this match for Sol," said Wenger, "because Barcelona are poor in the air at defending set pieces."

Barcelona's bemused team went in at half-time haunted by their previous disaster finals: the luckless 3-2 defeat by Benfica in 1961, the penalty shocker against Steaua in 1976 and the humiliation by Milan in 1994.

Fate then teased them again. When Ronaldinho sliced Arsenal open and Eto'o turned Campbell, the striker saw Manuel Almunia's despairing right hand deflect the ball against a post. At the other end, Henry wasted a clear run-in on goal and Barcelona punished him conclusively.

First, Henrik Larsson touched a through-ball delicately to the left and Eto'o darted in to beat substitute keeper Almunia on the near post, as Arsenal appealed in vain for offside. If the goal were illegal, it only balanced out the Gunners' own in the first half. The record sequence of ten clean sheets had thus ended five minutes short of the thousand.

Almost immediately, it was all over. Juliano Belletti charged forward from right back, Larsson turned the ball brilliantly back into his path and the Brazilian rocketed an angled shot through Almunia.

Andreas Iniesta, on appearing for the second half, had brought new zest to Barcelona's midfield, Larsson had laid on both goals while and Belletti struck the winner. Arsenal had been sunk by the subs.

WEDNESDAY MAY 17 2006
STADE DE FRANCE, PARIS

BARCELONA   2
(ETO'O 76, BELLETTI 80)

ARSENAL   1
(CAMPBELL 36)

HT: 0-1. ATT: 85,000
REF: HAUGE (NOR)

BARCELONA:
VALDES - OLEGUER (BELLETTI 70),
MARQUEZ, PUYOL*, VAN BRONCK-
HORST - VAN BOMMEL (LARSSON 60),
EDMILSON (INIESTA 46), DECO - GIULY,
RONALDINHO, ETO'O.
COACH: RIJKAARD

ARSENAL:
LEHMANN - EBOUE, TOURE, CAMP-
BELL, COLE - HLEB (REYES 84), FAB-
REGAS (FLAMINI 73), GILBERTO SILVA,
PIRES (ALMUNIA 19), LJUNGBERG -
HENRY*.
MANAGER: WENGER
SENT OFF: LEHMANN (18)

*CAPTAIN

EUROPEAN CUP RECORDS (1955-2006)

1955-56

Semi-finals:

Real Madrid bt Milan 4-2, 1-2 (5-4 on agg)

Reims bt Hibernian 2-0, 1-0 (3-0 on agg)

Final: Real Madrid bt Reims 4-3

Top scorer: Milos Milutinovic (Partizan Belgrade), 8 goals

1956-67

Semi-finals:

Real Madrid bt Manchester United 3-1, 2-2 (5-3 on agg)

Fiorentina bt Red Star Belgrade 1-0, 0-0 (1-0 on agg)

Final: Real Madrid bt Fiorentina 2-0

Top scorer: Dennis Viollet (Manchester United), 9 goals

1957-58

Semi-finals:

Real Madrid bt Sevilla 8-0, 2-2 (10-2 on agg)

Milan bt Manchester United 1-2, 4-0 (5-2 on agg)

Final: Real Madrid bt Milan 3-2 aet

Top scorer: Alfredo Di Stefano (Real Madrid), 10 goals

1958-59

Semi-finals:

Real Madrid bt Atletico Madrid 2-1, 0-1, 2-1 (playoff, after 2-2 on agg)

Reims bt Young Boys 1-0, 0-3 (3-1 on agg)

Final: Real Madrid bt Reims 2-0

Top scorer: Just Fontaine (Reims), 10 goals

1959-60

Semi-finals:

Real Madrid bt Barcelona 3-1, 3-1 (6-2 on agg)

Eintracht Frankfurt bt Rangers 6-1, 6-3 (12-4 on agg)

Final: Real Madrid bt Eintracht Frankfurt 7-3

Top scorer: Ferenc Puskas (Real Madrid), 12 goals

1960-61

Semi-finals:

Benfica bt Rapid Vienna 3-0, 1-1 (4-1 on agg)

Barcelona bt Hamburg 1-0, 1-2, 1-0 (playoff, after 2-2 on agg)

Final: Benfica bt Barcelona 3-2

Top scorer: Jose Aguas (Benfica), 10 goals

1961-62

Semi-finals:

Benfica bt Tottenham Hotspur 3-1, 1-2 (4-3 on agg)

Real Madrid bt Standard Liege 4-0, 2-0 (6-0 on agg)

Final: Benfica bt Real Madrid 5-3

Top scorer: Heinz Strehl (Nurnberg), 8 goals

1962-63

Semi-finals:

Milan bt Dundee 5-1, 0-1 (5-2 on agg)

Benfica bt Feyenoord 0-0, 3-1 (3-1 on agg)

Final: Milan bt Benfica 2-1

Top scorer: Jose Altafini (Milan), 14 goals

1963-64

Semi-finals:

Internazionale bt Borussia Dortmund 2-2, 2-0 (4-2 on agg)

Real Madrid bt FC Zurich 2-1, 6-0 (8-1 on agg)

Final: Internazionale bt Real Madrid 3-1

Top scorers: Vladimir Kovacevic (Partizan), Sandro Mazzola (Inter), Ferenc Puskas (Real Madrid), 7 goals each

1964-65

Semi-finals:

Internazionale bt Liverpool 1-3, 3-0 (4-3 on agg)

Benfica bt Vasas Gyor 1-0, 4-0 (5-0 on agg)

Final: Internazionale bt Benfica 1-0

Top scorers: Eusebio (Benfica), Jose Torres (Benfica), 9 goals each

1965-66

Semi-finals:

Real Madrid bt Internazionale 1-0, 1-1 (2-1 on agg)

Partizan Belgrade bt Manchester United 2-0, 0-1 (2-1 on agg)

Final: Real Madrid bt Partizan Belgrade 2-1

Top scorers: Florian Albert (Ferencvaros), Eusebio (Benfica), 7 goals each

1966-67

Semi-finals:

Celtic bt Dukla Prague 3-1, 0-0 (3-1 on agg)

Internazionale bt CSKA Sofia 1-1, 1-1, 1-0 (playoff, after 2-2 on agg)

Final: Celtic bt Internazionale 2-1

Top scorers: Jurgen Piepenburg (Vorwarts), Paul Van Himst (Anderlecht), 6 goals each

1967-68

Semi-finals:

Manchester United bt Real Madrid 1-0, 3-3 (4-3 on agg)

Benfica bt Juventus 2-0, 1-0 (3-0 on agg)

Final: Manchester United bt Benfica 4-1 aet

Top scorer: Eusebio (Benfica), 6 goals

1968-69

Semi-finals:

Milan bt Manchester United 2-0, 0-1 (2-1 on agg)

Ajax bt Spartak Trnava 3-0, 0-2 (3-2 on agg)

Final: Milan bt Ajax 4-1

Top scorer: Denis Law (Manchester United), 9 goals

1969-70

Semi-finals:

Feyenoord bt Legia Warsaw 0-0, 2-0 (2-0 on agg)

Celtic bt Leeds United 1-0, 2-1 (3-1 on agg)

Final: Feyenoord bt Celtic 2-1 aet

Top scorers: Mick Jones (Leeds United), Ove Kindvall (Feyenoord), 7 goals each

1970-71

Semi-finals:

Ajax bt Atletico Madrid 0-1, 3-0 (3-1 on agg)

Panathinaikos bt Red Star Belgrade 1-4, 3-0 (away goals, agg 4-4)

Final: Ajax bt Panathinaikos 2-0

Top scorers: Antonis Antoniadis (Panathinaikos), 10 goals

1971-72

Semi-finals:

Ajax bt Benfica 1-0, 0-0 (1-0 on agg)

Internazionale bt Celtic 0-0, 0-0 (5-4 on pens, agg 0-0)

Final: Ajax bt Internazionale 2-0

Top scorers: Johan Cruyff (Ajax), Antal Dunai (Ujpest Dozsa), Lou Macari (Celtic), Sylvester Takac (Standard Liege), 5 goals each

1972-73

Semi-finals:

Ajax bt Real Madrid 2-1, 1-0 (3-1 on agg)

Juventus bt Derby County 3-1, 0-0 (3-1 on agg)

Final: Ajax bt Juventus 1-0

Top scorer: Gerd Muller (Bayern Munich), 12 goals

1973-74

Semi-finals:

Bayern Munich bt Ujpest Dozsa 1-1, 3-0 (4-1 on agg)

Atletico Madrid bt Celtic 0-0, 2-0 (2-0 on agg)

Final: Bayern Munich bt Atletico 4-0 (replay after 1-1 aet)

Top scorers: Gerd Muller (Bayern Munich), 8 goals

1974-75

Semi-finals:

Bayern Munich bt Saint-Etienne 0-0, 2-0 (2-0 on agg)

Leeds United bt Barcelona 2-1, 1-1 (3-2 on agg)

Final: Bayern Munich bt Leeds United 2-0

Top scorers: Eduard Markarov (Ararat Yerevan), Gerd Muller (Bayern Munich), 5 goals each

1975-76

Semi-finals:

Bayern Munich bt Real Madrid 1-1, 2-0 (3-1 on agg)

Saint-Etienne bt PSV Eindhoven 1-0, 0-0 (1-0 on agg)

Final: Bayern Munich bt Saint-Etienne 1-0

Top scorer: Jupp Heynckes (Borussia Mg), 6 goals

1976-77

Semi-finals:

Liverpool bt FC Zurich 3-1, 3-0 (6-1 on agg)

Borussia Moenchengladbach bt Kiev Dynamo 0-1, 2-0 (2-1 on agg)

Final: Liverpool bt Borussia Moenchengladbach 3-1

Top scorers: Franco Cucinotta (Zurich), Gerd Muller (Bayern Munich), 5 goals each

1977-78

Semi-finals:

Liverpool bt Borussia Moenchengladbach 1-2, 3-0 (4-2 on agg)

Club Brugge bt Juventus 0-1, 2-0 (2-1 on agg)

Final: Liverpool bt Club Brugge 1-0

Top scorer: Allan Simonsen (Borussia Mg), 5 goals

1978-79

Semi-finals:

Nottingham Forest bt FC Koln 3-3, 1-0, (4-3 on agg)

Malmo bt FK Austria 0-0, 1-0 (1-0 on agg)

Final: Nottingham Forest bt Malmo 1-0

Top scorer: Claudio Sulser (Grasshopper), 11 goals

1979-80

Semi-finals:

Nottingham Forest bt Ajax 2-0, 0-1 (2-1 on agg)

Hamburg bt Real Madrid 0-2, 5-1 (5-3 on agg)

Final: Nottingham Forest bt Hamburg 1-0

Top scorer: Soren Lerby (Ajax), 10 goals

1980-81

Semi-finals:

Liverpool bt Bayern Munich 0-0, 1-1 (away goals, agg 1-1)

Real Madrid bt Internazionale 2-0, 0-1 (2-1 on agg)

Final: Liverpool bt Real Madrid 1-0

Top scorers: Terry McDermott (Liverpool), Karl-Heinz Rummenigge (Bayern Munich), Graeme Souness (Liverpool), 6 goals each

1981-82

Semi-finals:

Aston Villa bt Anderlecht 1-0, 0-0 (1-0 on agg)

Bayern Munich bt CSKA Sofia 3-4, 4-0 (7-4 on agg)

Final: Aston Villa bt Bayern Munich 1-0

Top scorer: Dieter Hoeness (Bayern Munich), 7 goals

1982-83

Semi-finals:

Hamburg bt Real Sociedad 1-1, 2-1 (3-2 on agg)

Juventus bt Widzew Lodz 2-0, 2-2 (4-2 on agg)

Final: Hamburg bt Juventus 1-0

Top scorer: Paolo Rossi (Juventus), 6 goals

1983-84

Semi-finals:

Liverpool bt Dinamo Bucharest 1-0, 2-1 (3-1 on agg)

Roma bt Dundee United 0-2, 3-0 (3-2 on agg)

Final: Liverpool bt Roma 1-1 aet, 4-2 on pens

Top scorer: Viktor Sokol (Minsk Dinamo), 6 goals

Records

1984-85

Semi-finals:

Juventus bt Bordeaux 3-0, 0-2 (3-2 on agg)

Liverpool bt Panathinaikos 4-0, 1-0 (5-0 on agg)

Final: Juventus bt Liverpool 1-0

Top scorers: Torbjorn Nilsson (IFK), Michel Platini (Juventus), 7 goals each

1985-86

Semi-finals:

Steaua Bucharest bt Anderlecht 0-1, 3-0 (3-1 on agg)

Barcelona bt IFK Gothenburg 0-3, 3-0 (5-4 on pens, agg 3-3)

Final: Steaua Bucharest bt Barcelona 0-0 aet, 2-0 on pens

Top scorer: Torbjorn Nilsson (IFK), 7 goals

1986-87

Semi-finals:

FC Porto bt Dynamo Kiev 2-1, 2-1 (4-2 on agg)

Bayern Munich bt Real Madrid 4-1, 0-1 (4-2 on agg)

Final: FC Porto bt Bayern Munich 2-1

Top scorer: Borislav Cvetkovic (Red Star), 7 goals

1987-88

Semi-finals:

PSV Eindhoven bt Real Madrid 1-1, 0-0 (away goals agg 1-1)

Benfica bt Steaua Bucharest 0-0, 2-0 (2-0 on agg)

Final: PSV Eindhoven bt Benfica 0-0 aet, 6-5 on pens

Top scorers: Jean-Marc Ferreri (Bordeaux), Gheorghe Hagi (Steaua), Rabah Madjer (Porto), Ally McCoist (Rangers), Michel (Real Madrid), Jose Rui Aguas (Benfica), 4 goals each

1988-89

Semi-finals:

Milan bt Real Madrid 1-1, 5-0 (6-1 on agg)

Steaua Bucharest bt Galatasaray 4-0, 1-1 (5-1 on agg)

Final: Milan bt Steaua Bucharest 4-0

Top scorer: Marco Van Basten (Milan), 9 goals

1989-90

Semi-finals:

Milan bt Bayern Munich 1-0, 1-2 (away goals agg 2-2)

Benfica bt Marseille 1-2, 1-0 (away goals agg 2-2)

Final: Milan bt Benfica 1-0

Top scorers: Jean-Pierre Papin (Marseille), Romario (PSV), 6 goals each

1990-91

Semi-finals:

Red Star Belgrade bt Bayern Munich 2-1, 2-2 (4-3 on agg)

Marseille bt Moscow Spartak 3-1, 2-1 (5-2 on agg)

Final: Red Star Belgrade bt Marseille 0-0, 5-3 on pens

Top scorers: Peter Pacult (Tirol), Jean-Pierre Papin (Marseille), 6 goals each

1991-92

Semi-finals – group-winners were deemed to be winning semi-finalists this term:

Group I: Sampdoria 8pts, Red Star 6, Anderlecht 6, Panathinaikos 4

Group II: Barcelona 9pts, Sparta Prague 6, Benfica 5, Kiev Dynamo 4

Final: Barcelona bt Sampdoria 1-0 aet

Top scorers: Jean-Pierre Papin (Marseille), Sergei Yuran (Benfica), 7 goals each

1992-93

Semi-finals – group-winners were deemed to be winning semi-finalists this term:

Group I: Marseille 9pts, Rangers 8, Club Brugge 5, CSKA Moscow 2

Group II: Milan 12pts, IFK Gothenburg 6, FC Porto 5, PSV Eindhoven 1

Final: Marseille bt Milan 1

Top scorer: Romario (PSV), 7 goals

1993-94

Semi-finals:

Milan bt Monaco 3-0 (single match)

Barcelona bt FC Porto 3-0 (single match)

Final: Milan bt Barcelona 4-0

Top scorers: Ronald Koeman (Barcelona), Wynton Rufer (Werder Bremen), 8 goals each

1994-95

Semi-finals:

Ajax bt Bayern Munich 0-0, 5-2 (5-2 on agg)

Milan bt Paris Saint-Germain 2-0, 1-0 (3-0 on agg)

Final: Ajax Amsterdam bt Milan 1-0

Top scorer: George Weah (Paris Saint-Germain), 8 goals

1995-96

Semi-finals:

Juventus bt Nantes 2-0, 2-3 (4-3 on agg)

Ajax bt Panathinaikos 0-1, 3-0 (3-1 on agg)

Final: Juventus bt Ajax 1-0

Top scorer: Jari Litmanen (Ajax), 9 goals

1996-97

Semi-finals:

Juventus bt Ajax 2-1, 4-1 (6-2 on agg)

Borussia Dortmund bt Manchester United 1-0, 1-0 (2-0 on agg)

Final: Borussia Dortmund bt Juventus 3-1

Top scorer: Ally McCoist (Rangers), 6 goals

1997-98

Semi-finals:

Juventus bt Monaco 4-1, 2-3 (6-4 on agg)

Real Madrid bt Borussia Dortmund 2-0, 0-0 (2-0 on agg)

Final: Real Madrid bt Juventus 1-0

Top scorer: Alessandro Del Piero (Juventus), 10 goals

1998-99

Semi-finals:

Manchester United bt Juventus 1-1, 3-2 (4-3 on agg)

Bayern Munich bt Kiev Dynamo 3-3, 1-0
(4-3 on agg)

Final: Manchester United bt Bayern Munich
2-1

Top scorer: Andriy Shevchenko (Kiev
Dynamo), 10 goals

1999-2000
Semi-finals:

Valencia bt Barcelona 4-1, 1-2 (5-3 on agg)

Real Madrid bt Bayern Munich 2-0, 1-2 (3-2
on agg)

Final: Real Madrid bt Valencia 3-0

Top scorers: Mateja Kezman (Partizan
Belgrade), Mikhail Mikholap (Skonto
Riga), 6 goals each

2000-01
Semi-finals:

Bayern Munich bt Real Madrid 1-0, 2-1 (3-1
on agg)

Valencia bt Leeds 0-0, 3-0 (3-0 on agg)

Final: Bayern Munich bt Valencia 1-1 aet,
5-4 on pens

Top scorer: Raul (Real Madrid), 7 goals

2001-02
Semi-finals:

Real Madrid bt Barcelona 2-0, 1-1 (3-1 on
agg)

Bayer Leverkusen bt Manchester United 2-
2, 1-1 (away goals, agg 3-3)

Final: Real Madrid bt Bayer Leverkusen 2-1

Top scorer: Ruud Van Nistelrooy
(Manchester United), 10 goals

2002-03
Semi-finals:

Juventus bt Real Madrid 1-2, 3-1 (4-3
on agg)

Milan bt Internazionale 0-0, 1-1 (away
goals, agg 1-1)

Final: Milan bt Juventus 0-0 aet, 3-2
on pens

Top scorer: Ruud Van Nistelrooy
(Manchester United), 14 goals

2003-04
Semi-finals:

Monaco bt Chelsea 3-1, 2-2 (5-3 on agg)

Porto bt Deportivo La Coruna 0-0, 1-0 (1-0
on agg)

Final: FC Porto bt Monaco 3-0

Top scorer: Fernando Morientes (Monaco),
9 goals

2004-05
Semi-finals:

Liverpool bt Chelsea 0-0, 1-0 (1-0 on agg)

Milan bt PSV Eindhoven 2-0, 1-3 (away
goals, agg 3-3)

Final: Liverpool bt Milan 3-3 aet (3-2 pens)

Top scorer: Ruud Van Nistelrooy
(Manchester United), 8 goals

2005-06
Semi-finals:

Arsenal bt Villareal 1-0, 0-0 (1-0 on agg)

Barcelona bt Milan 1-0, 0-0 (1-0 on agg)

Final: Barcelona bt Arsenal 2-1

Top scorer: Andriy Shevchenko (Milan),
9 goals

WINNERS (BY CLUB)
UEFA Champions League/European Cup:

Real Madrid	9	Porto	2
Milan	6	Aston Villa	1
Liverpool	5	Borussia Dortmund	1
Ajax	4	Celtic	1
Bayern Munich	4	Feyenoord	1
Barcelona	2	Hamburg	1
Benfica	2	Marseille	1
Internazionale	2	PSV Eindhoven	1
Juventus	2	Red Star Belgrade	1
Manchester United	2	Steaua Bucharest	1
Nottingham Forest	2		

WINNERS (BY COUNTRY)
UEFA Champions League/European Cup:

Country		Country	
Spain	11	Portugal	4
England	10	France	1
Italy	10	Romania	1
Germany	6	Scotland	1
Holland	6	Yugoslavia	1

All-time top scorers (Champions Lge/Cup):

Raul (Real Madrid)	51
Alfredo Di Stefano (Real Madrid)	49
Andriy Shevchenko (Kiev, Milan)	43
R. Van Nistelrooy (PSV, Manchester Utd)	43

Single-season Top Scorers:

Jose Altafini (Milan, 1962-63)	14
Ruud Van Nistelrooy (Man Utd, 2002-03)	14

**Most Appearances (European Cup/
UEFA Champions League):**

Paolo Maldini (Milan)	126
Raul (Real Madrid)	95

Most Winners Medals:

Francisco Gento (Real Madrid)	6
Alfredo Di Stefano (Real Madrid)	5
Jose Maria Zarraga (Real Madrid)	5

Wins With Three Different Clubs:

Clarence Seedorf (Ajax 1995, Real Madrid
1998, Milan 2003)

Winners As Player and Coach:

Miguel Munoz (Real Madrid)

Giovanni Trapattoni (Milan/Juventus)

Johan Cruyff (Ajax/Barcelona)

Carlo Ancelotti (Milan)

Frank Rijkaard (Milan, Ajax/Barcelona)

Most Goals (Player) in One Tie:

Jose Altafini (Milan v US Luxembourg,
1962-63), 8 goals (5 home, 3 away)

Highest aggregate win:

18-0, Benfica v Stade Dudelange (1965-66)

All page numbers in *italics* refer to illustrations

A

Aalborg 209
Aarhus 45
Aberdeen 137
Abramovich, Roman 258, 262-3, *263*, 276
AC Milan 15, 18, 19, 20, 26, 27, 28-9, 38, 40, 44, 48, 52, 53, 54-5, 57, 64, 76, 77, 78-9, 84, 86-7, 88, 90, 132, 168-9, 170-1, 175-6, 178, 180-1, 183, 194-5, 199, 200-1, 203, 206-7, 214, 215, 238, 258, 260-1, 270, 272, 275, 276, *277*, 279
Adelardo, Sanchez 103, *103*
AEK Athens 77, 123, 195, 257
Aguas, Jose 45, *47*, 49, *49*, 51, 52, 54, 167
Aguas, Rui 167
Ajax Amsterdam 26, 27, 52, 69, 73, 76, 77, 78-9, *80-1*, 84, 86, 88, 90, 91, 92-3, 95, 96, *97*, 99, 100-1, 102, 105, 110, 114, 119, 133, 136, 137, 148, 180, 203, 206-7, 210, 211, 212, 215, 217, 246, 275
Albert, Florian 65
Aldair 179
Alessandria 55
Alexanko, Jose Ramon 189
Allison, Malcolm 76
Allodi, Italo 100
Almunia, Manuel 279
Alonso, Juanito 19, 20, 28, 32
Alonso, Pichi 159
Alonso, Xabi 272
Altafini, Jose 53, 54, *54*, 55, 78, 99, 123
Amancio, Amaro Varela 57, 59, 61, 65, 73
Amarildo, Tavares Silveira 57
Amoros, Manuel 184
Anderlecht 18, 22, 37, 53, 61, 65, 73, 76, 107, 114, 118, 144, 161, 187, 264
Andersson, Bjorn 109
Anelka, Nicolas 239, *242*
Angelillo, Valentin 57
Antoniadis, Antonis 91, 93
Antwerp 26
Aragones, Luis 105
Araquistain, Jose 50, 51, 66
Archibald, Steve 157, 159
Ards 31
Ardiles, Osvaldo 136
Arges Pitesti 133
Arsenal 95, 246, 251, 256, 258, 264, 270, 274, 275, 276-7, *276*, 278-9, *278*

Artmedia Bratislava 275
Ashton, John 73, 74
Aston Villa 138, 141-3, 144, 145
Athletic Bilbao 130
Atletico Madrid 31, 32, 65, 83, 91, 98, 99, 103, 104-5, 119, 215
Atvidaberg 83, 104
Augenthaler, Klaus 183
Augusto, Jose 44, 46, 49, 74
Auld, Bertie 88
Auxerre 216, 217, 257
Avenir 86
Ayala, Ruben 103
AZ Alkmaar 141, 129

B

Babangida, Tidjani *214*, 216
Baggio, Roberto 58, 209, *209*
Bakhramov, Tofik 47
Ball, Alan 91
Barcelona 15, 18, 32, 40, 41, 44, 45, 46-7, 56, 84, 91, 102, 107, 156-7, 158-9, 168, 176, 186, 187, 188-9, 199, 200-1, 202, 204, 240, 241, 251, 253, 257, 270, 274, 276, 278-9, *278*, *279*
Baresi, Franco 171, 199, 200
Barison, Paolo 28, 53, 55
Baroni, Marco 183
Barthez, Fabien *222*
Barton, Tony 142, 143
Basel 86, 91, 103, 258
Basten, Marco Van *168*, 169, *180*, 181, 193, *193*, 194, 195
Bastia 192-3
Bathenay, Dominique 115
Batteux, Albert 21, 32
Bayer Leverkusen 220, 222, 223, 237, 252-3, 254
Bayern Munich 98, 99, 102, 103, 104-5, 106, 107, 108-9, 112-13, 114, 137, 141, 142-3, 161, 162-3, 165, 179, 183, 203, 227, 229, 230-1, 239, 240, 247, 248-9, 251, 264, 270, 275
Beckham, David 228, 252, 253, *253*, 258
Bedin, Gianfranco 65, 95
Beguirstain, Txiki 198
Belletti, Juliano 279
Bello, Concetto Lo 74, 89
Belodedici, Miodrag 159
Benfica 26, 37, 38, 44-5, 46-7, 48, 49, 50-1, 52, 53, 54-5, 56, 57, 61, 62-3, 65, 73, 74-5, 76, 77, 96, 103, 114, 118, 119, 130-1, 149, 165, 166-7, 175, 179, 180-1, 203, 204, 275, *275*, 276, 279
Benitez, Rafa 271, 275

Benitez, Victor 55
Bent, Geoff 27
Bergkamp, Dennis 278
Bergomi, Giuseppe 153
Berlusconi, Silvio 168-9, 170, 178, 181, 186, 192, 215, 227
Bernabeu, Santiago 15, 18, 19, 32, 42, 49, 61
Bernardini, Fulvio 23, 25
Berry, John 22
Besiktas 31, 144, 220
Best, George 65, *72*, 73, 77, 275
Beto 275
Bettega, Roberto 147
Bilbao 22-3
Bini, Graziano 137
Birmingham City 72, 106
Birtles, Garry 122-3, 125
BK Copenhagen 31
BK1913 Odense 49, 130
Blackburn Rovers 210
Blanchflower, Danny 48
Blankenburg, Horst *94*
Bliard, Rene 32
Blind, Danny 204
Blokhin, Oleg 110-11
Boban, Zvonimir 205, *205*
Boer, Frank De 212
Boli, Basile 194, 195, *195*
Bologna 9, 57, 61
Boniek, Zbigniew *144*, 147, 155
Boninsegna, Roberto 94, 95, 96
Bordon, Ivano 96
Borussia Dortmund 22, 27, 57, 62, 102, 209, 211, 215, 217, 218-19, 223, 250, 256
Borussia Monchengladbach 91, 94, 95, 96, 112, 113, 116-17, 118, 119, 120
Boskov, Vujadin 139, 188
Bosman, Jean-Marc 181, 182, 186, 207, 208-9, 214, *215*
Bosque, Vicente Del 239-40, 242, 258
Bradford 153
Braine, Raymond 9
Breitner, Paul 108-9, *140*
Bremen, Werder 65
Bremner, Billy 87, *87*, 106, 108
Brennan, Shay 65, 74
Broadbent, Peter 31, 40
Brocic, Ljubisa 46
Bronckhorst, Gio van 279
Brown, Bill *49*
Brungs, Franz 57
Buckingham, Vic 90
Buffon, Gianluigi 76
Buffon, Lorenzo 28, 76
Burgnich, Tarcisio 59, *59*, 95
Burnley 44, 45
Burns, Kenny 122, 125, *133*, 135
Busby, Matt 21, 22, *22*, 24, *34-5*, 64-5, 72, 73, 74, *75*

Byrne, Roger 22, 27, *27*, 61

C

Cagliari 91
Cajkovski, Tschik 108
Callaghan, Ian 61
Campbell, Kevin *186-7*
Campbell, Sol 278, 279
Caniggia, Claudio 203
Canizares, Jose 243, 249
Cantona, Eric 183, 191, *191*, *196*, 197, 215
Capellini, Renato 69, 71
Capello, Fabio 100, 194, 199, 200, 207
Careca 165
Carew, John 246, 248
Carlos, Jose 179
Carniglia, Luis 28, 32, 57
Casado, Pedro 51
Case, Jimmy 119, 137
Casillas, Iker, 254
Casino Salzburg 203
Cavem, Domiciano 46, 47, 50, 51
Celtic 68-9, 70-1, 73, 76, 77, 86, 87, 88-9, 91, 95, 99, 103, 133, 153, 161, 261, 264, 275
Chalmers, Steve 69, 71
Charles, John 31, 48, 52
Charlton, Bobby *6*, 7, *7*, 22, 27, 65, *72*, 73, 74, *74*, 75, 77
Chelsea 18, 48, 240-1, 262-3, 265, 270, 271, *274*, 275, 276
Clarke, Allan 87, 106
Clemence, Ray 116, 120-1
Clough, Brian 99, 100, 106, 122, 123, *123*, 125, 134, 136
Club Brugge 114, 118-19, 120-1, 183
Cocu, Philip *268*
Coen, Avi 136
Cole, Andy 217, 228
Cole, Ashley 278
Coleraine 106
Collar, Enrique 31
Colman, Eddie 22, 27, *27*
Colonna, Dominique 32
Coluna, Mario 44, 45, 47, 51, 53, 55, *63*, 74
Combin, Nestor 86
Connelly, George 87
Connelly, John 65
Conti, Bruno 150
Cools, Julien 119
Corso, Mariolino 59, 61, 63, 65, 95, 96
Costacurta, Alessandro 199, 200
Crahay, Jose *57*
Craig, Jim 71
Cramer, Dettmar 106, *107*, 109
Crawford, Ray 53
Crerand, Paddy 65, 74
Crespo, Hernan 272
Crossan, Johnny 48

Cruyff, Johan 69, 77, *78*, 84, 90, 91, 93, *94*, 95, 96, *98*, 99, 102, 106, 148, 168, 180, 186, *187*, 188, 198, 200, 203
Crusaders 114
Csernai, Pal 143
CSKA Moscow 191
CSKA Sofia 40, 69, 99, 102, 105, 129, 137, 141, 275
Cucchiaroni, Tito 26, 28
Cudicini, Fabio 76, 77, 78
Cullis, Stan 10, *11*, 40
Cunningham, Laurie 132, *132*, 139
Cuper, Hector 241
Curkovic, Yvan 110, 111, 115
Czibor, Zoltan 22, 30, 40, 46, 47

D

Dalglish, Kenny 95, 116, 118, 119, *120*, 121, 129, 150p
Dassler, Horst 190
Daucik, Ferdinand 22
Daum, Christoph 191
Davies, Roger 100, 119
Deans, 'Dixie' 95
Debattista, Lolly 52
Del Horno, Asier 276
Del Sol, Luis 43, 48
Deportivo 247, 251, 258, 264
Derby County 99, 106, 112-13
Desailly, Marcel 200
Deschamps, Didier 264, *266*
Diaz, 'Panadero' 103
Didi 30, 42, 43
Dienst, Gottfried 47
Dijk, Dick Van 93
Dinamo Bucharest 61, 65, 103, 130, 149, 150
Dinamo Tiblisi 133, 197, 239
Dinamo Tirana 73, 182
Djurgarden 19
Domazos, Mimis 93
Domenghini, Angelo 65
Dominguez, Rogelio 32
Dorfel, Gert 45
Ducadam, Helmut 159
Dudek, Jerzy 273, *273*
Duivendobe, Wim Van 86
Dukla Prague 26, 40, 48, 53, 61, 69
Dunfermline Athletic 69
Dundee United 52, 53, 149
Dunne, Tony 74
Durnberger, Bernd 84
Duscher, Aldo 252
Dynamo Berlin 133
Dynamo Dresden 83, 103, 105, 114, 118
Dynamo Kiev 73, 99, 100, 110-11, 141, 162, 187, 203, 209, 227, 229

E

Eboue, Emmanuel 278, 279
Edwards, Duncan 22, 23, 27, *27*

Effenberg, Stefan 231, 249, *249*
Eintracht Braunschweig 73
Eintracht Frankfurt 15, 41, 42-3, 50, 66
Ellis, Arthur 22
Emmerich, Lothar 57
Eriksson, Sven-Goran 124, 149, 181, 239, 244, 252
Espanol 61
Essien, Michael *274*, 275
Eto'o, Samuel 276, 278, *278*, 279
Eusebio *36*, 37-9, *37*, *39*, 47, *48*, 49, 50, 51, *51*, 53, *53*, 54, 55, *62*, 63, 73, 74, 75
Everton 57, 60, 91, 138, 153

F

Fabregas, Cesc 277
Facchetti, Giancinto 59, *59*, 61, 69, *83*, 84, 95
Fagan, Joe 130, 155, *155*
Fairclough, David 115
Farago, Lajos 22
Fazekas, Arpad 53
FC Porto 132, 161, 162-3, 165, 182, 209, 217, 240, 251, 261, 265, 266-7, 275
FC Zurich 69, 106, 115
Fenerbahce 76, 112, 216
Ferdinand, Rio 247
Ferencvaros 19, 79, 84, 65, 246
Ferguson, Alex 137, 197, 217, 229, 230, *230*, 247, 251
Ferran, Jacques 18
Ferrer, Albert *239*
Fevre, Ulrich Le 95
Feyenoord 48, 52, 53, 79, 86, 87, 88-9, 91, 96, 106, 114, 118, 120, 149
Figo, Luis 244, *244*, 250, 255
Finnan, Steve 272
Fiorentina 23, 25, 52, 59, 78, 87, 164, 238
Fitzpatrick, John 77
FK Austria 9, 49, 53, 131, 161
Floriana 53
Flowers, Ron *40*
Flowers, Tim 209
Fontaine, Just 30, 31, *32*, 44, 45, 53, 110
Foulkes, Bill 65, 73, 74
Francescoli, Enzo 179
Francini, Giovanni 165
Francis, Trevor 123, *124*,125, *125*, 133, 164
Frisk, Anders 270, 276
Futre, Paulo 162, *163*

G

Gaal, Louis Van 207, *207*, 211, 213, 241
Galatarasay 53, 99, 197, 198, 220, 239, 247

Galic, Milan 66
Galli, Giovanni 169
Gascoigne, Paul *215*
Gaspart, Joan 15
Gemmell, Tommy 86, 88
Gemmill, Archie 71
Genoa 28
Gensana, Enrique 46
Gentile, Claudio 119
Gento, Francisco 15, 20, 21, 25, 28, 32, 44, 48, 59, 66, 73, 86
George, Charlie 113
Georgescu, Dudu 103
Geovanni 275
Germano, Luis 46, 63
Gerrard, Steven 269, 272, *273*, 274
Ghezzi, Giorgio 76
Giacomini, Massimo 132
Giggs, Ryan 215, 228, 231
Giles, Johnny 87, 106
Gilzean, Alan 53
Giresse, Alain *152*
Giuly, Ludovic *277*, 278, 279
Glassmann, Jacques 194
Glentoran 73
Gloria, Otto 44, 74
Goddet, Jacques 18
Goethals, Raymond 184
Gonzalez, Raul 210
Gormlie, Bill 22
Gornik 48, 61
Graca, Jaime 74, 75
Graham, George 95
Grasshoppers 123, 216
Greaves, Jimmy 48, 54
Gregg, Harry 27, 65
Gren, Gunnar 26
Grillo, Ernesto 26, 27, 28
Grobbelaar, Bruce 130
Groot, Henk 77
Grosso, Ramon Moreno 65, 66
Guardiola, Josep *190*
Guarneri, Aristide 59
Gudjohnsen, Eidur *271*
Gullit, Ruud *168*, 169, 171, 179, 181, *183*
Guttmann, Bela 37, 38, 44, 47, *51*, 52, 54
Gyor, Vasas 61

H

Haan, Arie 93, 96, 99, *99*
Hajduk Split 203, 204
Haller, Helmut 61, 100
Hammann, Didi 272, 275
Hamburg 45, 132-3, 134-5, 145, 146-7, 148-9
Hammerl, Josef 31
Hamrin, Kurt 77, 78
Hanegem, Wim Van 87, 88
Hanot, Gabriel 10, 18, 25, 32, 273
Hansa Rostock 187

Hansen, Johnny 107
Happel, Ernst 23, 86, *86*, 88, 89, 120, 146
Hasil, Franz 88
Hauge, Terje 276, *278*, 279
Haynes, Johnny 48, 76
Heart of Midlothian 276
Hearts of Oak 31
Hector, Kevin 99
Heighway, Steve 116
Henrique, Jose *74*
Henry, Thierry 246, 257, 264, *264*, 275, *276*, 277, 278, 279
Heredia, Juan Carlos 105
Herrara, Chus 50
Herrera, Helenio 32, 41, 44, 46, 56-7, *56*, 59, 63, 65, 69, 71
Heynckes, Jupp 94
Hibernian 19, 20, 31
Hidalgo, Michel 21
Hiddink, Guus 167, 228
Hidegkuti, Nandor 61
Himst, Paul Van 53
Hinton, Alan 100
Hitchens, Gerry 48
Hitzfeld, Ottmar 103, 218
HJK Helsinki 179
Hoeness, Uli 83, *104*, 105, 108, 112
Hogan, Jimmy 9
Honved 10, 22
Hood, Harry 91
Horn, Leo 25, 51
Houghton, Bob 124-5
Howard, Peter 27
Hrubesch, Horst 133, 135, 146
Hughes, Emlyn 119, 123, 137
Hughes, John 87, 88
Hughes, Mark 160
Hulshoff, Barry *91*
Hungaria 9
Hunt, Roger 61, *61*, 69
Hunter, Norman 87
Hvidovre 73
Hyypia, Sami *252-3*

I

IFK Gothenburg 193, 202, 204
Iniesta, Andreas 279
Innsbruck 182, 183
Internazionale/Inter Milan 44, 46, 48, 56-7, 58-9, 61, 62-3, 65, 69, 72, 84, 94, 95, 96, 136, 137, 227, 257, 258, 263, 275
Invernizzi, Gianni 96
Inzaghi, Filippo 221, 229
Ipswich Town 52, 53, 106
Israel, Rinus 88, *89*

J

Jacquet, Aime *21*
Jair 57, 59, 63, 65, 71, 95
Jakobs, Ditmar 147, *147*

Jansen, Wim 87, 88
Janssen, Anton 167
Jenei, Emerich 159
Jensen, Birgir 120
Johansson, Lennart *279*
Johnstone, Jimmy *69*, 71, 76, 88, *91*
Johnston, Mo 182
Jones, Cliff 48
Jones, Mark 26, 27, *27*
Jones, Mick 86, 87
Jonquet, Robert 32
Jordan, Joe 106
Juanito 162
Jugovic, Vladimir 211
Jurion, Jef 53
Jusufi, Fahrudin 66
Juventus 9, 15, 31, 44, 45, 48, 49, 50, 52, 57, 73, 98, 99, 100-1, 103, 119, 131, 144, 146-7, 154-5, 162, 209, 211, 212, 214, 215, 217, 218-19, 221, 222-3, 224-5, 229, 236, 258, 259, 260-1, 264, *269*, 275, *276*, 277

K

Kahn, Oliver 229, 230, *248-9*
Kaladze, Khaka 277
Kaltz, Manni 146
Kanu, Nkankwo 206, 247
Kapellmann, Jupp 84
Kapsis, Anthomis 93
Karembeu, Christian 223, 225
Kaunas 275
Keane, Roy 229, *229*
Keegan, Kevin 114, 115, *115*, 116, 132-3, 134
Keflavik 99
Keizer, Piet 69, 77, 79, 91, 93, 96
Kendall, Howard 93
Kennedy, Alan 139, *139*, 145
Kennedy, Ray 137
Kewell, Harry 272
Kidd, Brian 74, *77*
Kilmarnock 65
Kindvall, Ove 86, 88, 89, 120
Kinvall, Jan-Olav 125
Kitabdjan, Michel 108
Klinsmann, Jurgen 198
Klodt, Berni 31
Kluivert, Patrick 206, 215
Kocsis, Sandor 10, 30, 40, 41, 44, 45, 46
Koeman, Ronald *164*, 166, 167, 188, 189, *189*, 199, *199*
Kogl, Ludwig 163
Kohler, Jurgen 217
Konrad, Otto 203
Kopa, Raymond *18*, 20, 21, 23, 25, 30, *30*, 31, 32, 42, 44, 45, 53, 110, 274, 275
Korsakov, Dimitri *190*
Kostadinov, Emil 199

Kostic, Bora 27
Kovacs, Stefan 95, 110
Kovacevic, Vladimir 66
KPV Kokkolan 91
KR Reykjavik 86
Kreitlein, Rudolf 66
Kreyermaat, Reiner 52, 53
Kress, Richard 43
Krol, Rudi 92
Ku, Lajos 120
Kubala, Ladsilav 18, 30, 40, 41, 44, 46, 47, 49, 57, 61, 69
Kurrat, 'Hoppy' 62

L
Lahden Reipas 77
Lambert, Raoul 119
Larque, Jean-Michel 111, *111*
Larsson, Bo 125
Larsson, Henrik *262-3*, 279
Latin Cup 10, 20
Lattek, Udo 106, 120, 143
Laudrup, Michael 160, 211
Law, Denis 65, 72, 74, 76
Lawler, Chris 61
Lawrence, Tommy 61
Lawrenson, Mark 155
Lazio 106, 238, 240, 244, 251
Leafe, Reg 44, 45
Leblond, Michel 21
Leduc, Marcel 178-9
Lee, Sammy 139
Leeds United 61, 84, 86, 87, 88, 106, 107, 108-9, 122, 191, 244
Legia Warsaw 40, 87, 211
Lehmann, Jens *277, 278*, 279
Lennox, Bobby 69, 71, 88
Lentini, Gianluigi 194
Lerby, Soren 136
Lesmes, Rafael 32
Levski Sofia 132, 197
Liedholm, Nils 26, 28
Limassol 76
Lineker, Gary 160, 186
Linfield 69, 197
Lippens, Martin 53
Lippi, Marcello 223, 224, 261
Litmanen, Jari 213, *250*
Ljungberg, Anders 125
Liverpool 52, 60, 61, 69, 84, 103, 106, 114, 115, 116-17, 118, 120-1, 122-3, 129, 136, 137, 138-9, 145, 148, 149, 150-1, 152, 154-5, 170, 251, 269, *269*, 270, 272, 274, *274*, 275, 276
Lobanovsky, Valeriy 110
Lobo, Francisco 100
Lodetti, Giovanni *77*
Lorenzo, Juan Carlos 103
Lorimer, Peter 87, 106, 108
Losada, Sebastian 182
Lovenkrands, Peter 275
Lung, Silviu *170*

Luxemburgo, Wanderley 275
Lyn Oslo 86
Lyon 263, 275

M
McBride, Joe 69, 71
McCoist, Ally 191
McDermott, Terry 116, *122-3*
Macedo, Evaristo de 40
McFarland, Roy 99
McGovern, John 99, *135*
Mackay, Dave 49
McLeish, Alex 275
McManaman, Steve 243, 255
McNeill, Billy 68-9, *68*, 70-1, 88, 89
Madjer, Rabah 182
Magdeburg 107
Magnusson, Roger 73
Magnini, Ardico 25
Maier, Josef 84
Maier, Sepp 102, 108
Makaay, Roy 264
Maldini, Cesare 54, 55, *55*, 57, *261*
Maldini, Paolo 26, 171, *174*, 175-7, *175*, *176*, *177*, 256, 261, *261*, 272
Malmo 76, 99, 123, 124-5
Manchester City 76
Manchester United 22-3, 24-5, 26-7, 31, *34-5*, 38, 53, 64-5, 72-3, 74-5, 76, 77, 196-7, 202-3, 217, 222, 223, 228-9, 230-1, 240, 241, 247, 251-2, 258, 264, 265, 275, *275*, 276
Manniche, Michael 149
Maradona, Diego 145, 157, 160, 164, 180, 182, 183
Marchi, Tony 48
Marquez, Rafael 278
Marsal, Ramon 20, 28
Marseille 99, 178-9, 182-3, 184-5, 191-3, 194-5, 236
Martins, Joao Baptista 19
Maschio, Humberto 57
Masek, Vaclav 73
Masopust, Josef 26, *60*
Mateos, Enrique 23, 25, 32
Matthaeus, Lothar 162, 204
Matthews, Stanley 25
Mazzola, Sandrino 58-9, 61, 63, 65, 71, 95, 96
Mazzola, Valentino *8*, 10
Meano, Francis 20
Meazza, Giuseppe 59
Mechelen 179
Mee, Bertie 95
Meisl, Hugo 9, 18, 90
Meisl, Willy 90
Mendibil, Jose Ortiz de 61
Mendieta, Gaizka 241
Mercer, Joe 76

Messi, Leo 276
Michels, Rinus 69, 79, 91, 96, 101
Milani, Aurelio 59
Milewski, Jurgen 135
Miljanic, Miljan 112
Millichip, Bert 156
Milne, Gordon 61
Millonarios 18
Milutinovic, Milos 19
Mitropa Cup 8-10
Moller, Andreas 219, *219*
Monaco 57, 198-9, 223, 264, 265, 266-7, 276
Monte, Girgio Dal 20
Montuori, Miguel 25
Mora, Bruno 53
Moratti, Angelo 56
Morgans, Ken 26
Morientes, Fernando 223, *224*, 225, *242*, 243, 264
Mortimore, John 165
Moscow Spartak 10, 183, 198, 210
Moscow Torpedo 118
Moulijn, Coen 52, 88, 120
Mourhino, Felix 38
Mourhino, Jose 38, 261, 265, 266, 267, 270, 271, *271*, 275, 276
MTK Budapest 69
Muhren, Gerrit 92, 96, 99
Mullen, Jimmy 40
Muller, Bennie 77
Muller, Gerd 102, 104, *104*, 107, 108, 109, 112, 113
Muller, Lucien 57
Munoz, Miguel 19, 20, 42, 65, 69
Murdoch, Bobby 71, 87, 88
Murray, Jimmy 40
Musampa, Kiki 211

N
Nadal, Miguel Angel 189, 200
Nancy 15
Nantes 65, 209, 210
Napoli 160, 164, 180, 183
Neal, Phil 116-17, 130, 138, 151
Nedved, Pavel 259, 260
Neeskens, Johan 96
Nendori Tirana 91, 145
Netzer, Gunter 94, 95, 112, 132
Neudecker, Wilhelm 83, 84, 108
Newcastle United 257
Nice 15, 23
Nicholson, Bill 48
Nielsen, Harald 61
Nordahl, Gunnar 26
Nottingham Forest 106, 122-3, 124-5, 133, 134-5, 136, 170
Nunez, Josep 157, 241
Nunweiler, Radu 103
Nurnberg 49, 76

O
OB Odense 148, 182
Offenbach 83
O'Leary, David 247
Oliveira, Antonio 165
Olympiakos Nicosia 86
Olympiakos Piraeus 227, 275
Onishenko, Vladimir 111
Orizaola, Enrique 46
Ostterreicher, Emil 30-1
Oulu Palloseura 137
Overmars, Marc 210

P
Pacheco, Jaime *181*
Pagliuca, Gianluca 189
Paintoni, Roger 32
Paisley, Bob 60, 114, 129, 139
Palloseura Helsinki 31
Panathinaikos 91, 92-3, 119, 187, 209, 211
Panchev, Darko 184, *185*
Panucci, Christian 200, 201
Papin, Jean-Pierre 179, *179*, 183, 191, 203
Paris St-Germain 203, 204, 278
Parma 238
Partizan Belgrade 15, 18-19, 57, 65, 66
Partizani 40, 165, 167
Pegg, David 22, 27
Peiro, Joaquin 63
Pele 30, 38, 50, 84
Penarol 49
Penverne, Armand 21, 31, 32
Pereira, Alberto Costa *50*, 51, *54*, 55, 63
Perez, Florentino 15, 42, 244
Persie, Robin Van 278
Petrovic, Ljubko 184
Pfaff, Jean-Marie 42
Phillips, Ted *52*
Piantoni, Roger 31
Piazza, Oswaldo 110, 111
Picchi, Armando *58*, 59, *63*
Piero, Alessandro Del 58, 209, *209*, 219, *256-7*, 261
Pieters-Graafland, Eddie 26, 27, 52, 88
Pinto, Joao 163, 199
Pirmajer, Josip 66
Pirri 65
Pivatelli, Gino 55
Platini, Michel 110, 131, 145, 147, 155, *160*
Portadown 182
Praag, Jaap Van 96
Prati, Pierino 76, 77, 78, 79, 86
Prini, Maurilio 23
PSV Eindhoven 56, 88, 113, 114, 161, 165, 166-7, 271
Puskas, Ferenc *9*, 10, 15, 22, 30-1, 32, 43, 44, 48, 49, *50*, 51, 57,

59, 61, 65, 79, *90*, 92
Puyol, Carlos 278, *279*

R
Ramallets, Antonio 46
Ramsey, Alf 52, 106, 157
Rangers 26, 31, *41*, 49, 56, 57, 61, 102, 182, 191, 193, 197, 275
Ranieri, Claudio 265
Rapid Bucharest 73
Rapid Vienna 9, 19, 23, 26, 45, 61, 76, 238
Rattin, Antonio 103
Raul 243, 247, 254, 259, 265
Ravanelli, Fabrizio 212
Real Madrid 15, 18, 19, 20-1, *20*, 23, 25, 26, 27, 28-9, 30, 31, 32, 38, 40, 41, 42-3, 44-5, 48-9, 50-1, 52, 53, 54, 56, 57, 59, 61, 64, 65, 66, 69, 73, 86, 87, 98, 99, 112-13, 118, 129, 132, 133, 137, 139-9, 161, 162, 165, 166, 179, 182, 183, 210, 220, 223, 224-5, 227, 228, 236-7, 239-40, 241, 242-3, 244, 247, 251, 253, 254, 258, 265, 274, 275, 277
Real Sociedad 50, 145, 264
Red Star Belgrade 23, 27, 40, 44, 61, 76, 91, 103, 169, 183, 184-5, 187, 191-2
Riedle, Karlheinz *218*, 219
Reims 15, 18, 19, 20-1, 30, 31, 32, 42, 44, 45, 53, 110, 274
Reina, Miguel 105
Remons, Mariano 99
Rensenbrink, Rob 114
Rep, Johnny 93, 100
Revie, Don 106
Rexach, Charly 106, 187
Reyes, Jose Antonio 278
Rial, Jose Hector 15, 19, 20, 21, 23, 26, 28, 42
Riediger, Hans-Jurgen 133
Riera, Fernando 53, 54, 62
Riise, John Arne 272
Rijkaard, Frank 169, 180, 181, 206, *206*, *207*, 278, 279
Rijnders, Nico 93
Rimmer, Jimmy 142
Riquelme, Juan Roman 277, *277*
Riva, Luigi 78
Rivaldo 241, *241*
River Plate 46
Rivera, Gianni 54, 55, 57, 58-9, 76, 77, 78, 79, 86-7
Rizzoli, Andrea 26
Robertson, John 122, *134*, , 135
Robson, Bobby 48, 157
Rocco, Nereo 48, 54, 55, 57, 77
Rocher, Roger 110
Rocheteau, Dominique 110, 113
Rodzik, Bruno 32

Roma 76, 150-1, 250, 251
Romanov, Vladimir 275
Romario 200, 203, 204
Ronaldinho 84, 278, 279
Ronaldo 84, 258, *258*
Ronaldo, Cristiano *275*
Rosenborg Trondheim 99, 215, 217, 221, 275
Rossi, Paolo 144, 145
Roth, Franz 84, 108, 113
Rous, Stanley 18
Ruiz, Antonio 32
Ruiz, Felix 57
Rummenigge, Karl-Heinz 84, 112
Rush, Ian *128*, 129-31, *129*, *131*, 150
Ryswick, Jacques Van 18

S
Sacchi, Arrigo 169, *169*, 171, 259
Sadler, David 73, 74
Saint-Etienne 73, 76, 84, 110, 112-13, 115
St John, Ian 61
Salgado, Michel 243
Sammer, Matthias 218, 250
Sampdoria 187, 188-9
Sani, Dino 54
Santamaria, Jose 42, 48, 49, 58, 65
Santana, Joaquin 38, 50
Santos 38, 50
Sar, Edwin van der 206, 212
Sarramagna, Christian 113
Sarti, Giuliano *24-5*, 25, 59, 63, 71
Saunders, Ron 141, *141*
Sauzee, Franck *194*
Savicevic, Dejan 169, 200-1, 205
Scaloni, Lionel 252
Schalke 31, 219
Schiaffino, Juan Alberto 26, 27, 28
Schmeichel, Peter 203, 228, 231
Schoenmaker, Lex 106
Scholes, Paul 275
Scholl, Mehmet 231
Schulenberg, Gerhard 100
Schuster, Bernd 157, *157*
Schwan, Robert 83, 84
Schwartz, Elek 62
Schwarzenbeck, 'Katsche' 83, 84
Seedorf, Clarence 260
Seeler, Dieter 45
Seeler, Uwe 31, *31*, 45
Segarra, Juan 46
Sekularac, Dragoslav 27
Senderos, Philippe 278
Serena, Fernando 66
Servette 19
Setubal, Vitoria 37
Sevilla 26, 32
Shankly, Bill 60, 69, 114, 116

Shankly, Bob 52, 53
Shamrock Rovers 26
Shaw, Gary 141
Sheffield Wednesday 27
Sheringham, Teddy *221*, 231
Shevchenko, Andriy 228,*239*, 259, 261, 273, *273*
Shilton, Peter 122
Showell, George 40
Sieloff, Klaus-Dieter 95
Simeon, Jan 120
Simoes, Antonio 50, 74
Simone, Marco 204, 206
Simonsen, Allan 116, 119
Simonsson, Agne 48, 50
Simpson, Ronnie 71
Sindelar, Matthias 9
Sinibaldi, Pierre 53
Sivori, Omar 31, 49, 52, 57
Skerlan, Karl 31
Smicer, Vladimir 272
Smith, Gordon 53
Smith, Tommy 116
Soldan, Narciso 28
Solich, Fleitas 42
Solskjaer, Ole-Gunnar *4-5*, *217*, 231
Solti, Dezso 100-1
Sorensen, Jan 121
Sormani, Benedetto 76, 77, 78, 79, *79*
Soskic, Milutin 65, 66, *67*
Souness, Graeme 118, 121, 130, 150-1, 153, *165*
Sousa, Paulo 218-19
Sparta Prague 9, 18, 65, 73, 187
Sparta Rotterdam 49
Spartak Trnava 76, 77, 99
Sparwasser, Jurgen 104, 106
Spink, Nigel 142-3
Sporting Clube de Portugal 18-19, 37
Sporting Clube of Lisbon 53, 66, 180
Standard Liege 31, 48, 49, 56, 87, 95, 184
Steaua Bucharest 40, 76, 158-9, 169, 170-1, 198, 200, 216, 279
Stefano, Alfredo Di 12-17, *12-13*, *14*, *15*, *17*, 18, 19, 20, 21, *21*, 23, *23*, *24-5*, 25, 27, 28, 30, 31, 32, 42, 43, 44, 45, 48, 49, 51, 54, 57, 59, 61, 71, 268, 274
Stein, Jock 68-9, 76, 87, 88, 99
Stepney, Alex 74, 75
Steven, Trevor 193
Stielike, Uli 132
Stiles, Nobby 65, 74, 77, *77*
Stoichkov, Hristo 199, 200, *202*, 203
Stuttgart 191
Suarez, Luis 40, *40*, 44, 46, 47, 57, 58, 59, 63, 65, 71
Suker, Davor *220*

Suurbier, Wim 91, 96
Swaart, Jackie 93
Swart, Sjaack 91
Szymaniak, Horst 57, 59

T
Tacchinardi, Alessio *216*
Tagnin, Carlo 59
Tapie, Bernard 178-9, *178*, 182-3, 191-2, 195
Tasic, Lazar 27
Taylor, Ernie 27
Taylor, Tommy 22, 27, *27*, 65
Tejada, Justo 49, 50, 51
Templin, Jean 21
Tendillo, Miguel 165
Terry, John 276
Tesanic, Branko 62
Thommen, Ernst 18
Thompson, Phil *138*
Tigana, Jean 166, 223
Tilkowski, Hans 57
TNS 275
Toppmoller, Klaus 252, 257
Torino 10
Torres, Jose 64, 74, 75
Torres, Miguel 25, 48, 54
Torstensson, Conny 84, 104-5, 109
Toshack, John 114
Tottenham Hotspur 48, 49, 72, 106, 136, 263
Totti, Francesco 58
TPs Turku 103
Trabzonspor 115
Trapattoni, Giovanni 55, 77
Tschenscher, Kurt 71

U
Ujpest Dozsa 45, 99, 103, 106, 107, 112
Union Luxembourg 53
Ure, Ian 53
UT Arad 91

V
Vadas, Gyorgy 56
Valdes, Victor 278
Valencia 43, 242-3, 246-7, 248-9, 256-7
Valenciennes 194
Valletta 182
Valur 76
Vasas Budapest 27, 48-9, 73
Vasco da Gama 21
Vasovic, Velibor 66, 77, 79, 93, *93*
Vava 31
Vejle 103
Venables, Terry *156*, 157
Verbiest, Laurent 53
Vialli, Gianluca 58, 189, *208*, 211, *213*
Viani, Gipo 27, 28

Vicente, Jose 59
Vieira, Patrick 247, 277
Vieri, Christian 217, 219
Vignola, Beniamino 161, *161*
Villa, Ricardo 136
Villalonga, Pepe 15, 20
Villarreal 277, *277*
Villaverde, Ramon 41
Vincent, Jean 32
Viollet, Dennis 22, 27, *27*
Virgili, 'Pecos Bill' 25
Vogts, Berti 94, 116
Vojvodina 69
Voros Lobogo 19
Vorwarts 40, 87
Vycpalek, Cestmir 100

W
Waddle, Chris 179, 184
Wallace, Willie 69, 88
Waterford 76
Weah, George *203*, 204
Webster, Colin 26
Weiner Sportclub 31
Weisweiler, Hennes 94
Wenger, Arsene 198, *198*, 257, 278, 279
Whelan, Billy 22, 23, 27
Widzew Lodz 145, 215
Wiederkehr, Gustav *57*, *73*
Williams, Evan *87*, 88, 99
Wilson, Bob 95
Wimmer, Herbert 94
Winterbottom, Walter 48
Wismut Chemnitz 26
Wolverhampton Wanderers 10, *10*, 18, 31, 40, 41
Wood, Ray *23*
Wright, Billy 40
Wulf, Peter 45
Wunder, Klaus 109

Y
Yonchev, Tzvetan 136
Yorath, Terry *106*
Yorke, Dwight 228
Young Boys Berne 31, 161
Younger, Tommy *19*

Z
Zabrze, Gornik 73
Zaccheroni, Alberto 251
Zaragoza 25, 28, 180
Zarraga, José Maria 20, 32, *33*
Zebec, Branko 132, 134
Zeman, Zdenek 212
Zidane, Zinedine 179, 214, 216, 219, 225, *225*, 226, *234*, 235-7, *235*, *236*, 237, 244, *247*, 250, 254, 259, 265, 275
Zoco, Ignacio 59, 66, 73
Zoff, Dino 100, *101*, 119, 147
Zubizarreta, Andoni 200

Acknowledgements

Special appreciation for 'leg work' at home and abroad to Paddy Agnew, Alberto da Silva, Sid Lowe, Karlheinz Wild and Colin Wood. Also to Martin Corteel at Carlton Books for essential supervision, Nigel Matheson for keeping the entire project up to speed, Tom Wright for picture research beyond the call of duty and Steve Dobell for his copy-editing. Thanks are also due to John Cookman for use of his excellent programme collection.

The Publishers would like to thank the following sources for their kind permission to reproduce the pictures in this book. Any location indicator (t-top, b-bottom, r-right, l-left).

Empics: /ANP: 76; /Abaca Press: 235; /Matthew Ashton: 4-5, 211, 239, 251, 264, 272; Barratts/Alpha: 33; /Luca Bruno/AP: 277t; /Jon Buckle: 279; /Istvan Bajdat/DPA: 107; Gareth Copley/PA: 246-247; /Adam Davy: 177, 258; /EPA: 91; /Mike Egerton: 2-3 274; /Laurence Griffiths: 215l; /Tim Hall: 6, 14, 36, 128, 174; /Alvaro Hernandez: 236; /Jasper Juinen/AP: 275; /Thomas Kienzle/AP: 273t; /Ross Kinnaird: 183b, 191, 196-197; /Le Monde Du Sport: 234; /Christian Liewig: 176; /Paul Marriott: 197; /Tony Marshall: 83, 172-173, 202, 205, 212, 216, 228, 240-241, 243, 269; /Andrew Medichini: 276; /Andrew Milligan: 262-263; /Steve Mitchell: 82, 238, 241; /Steve Morton: 245; /Rebecca Naden/PA: 271b, 278; /Phil O'Brien: 182, 190, 199, 200-201; /Tony O'Brien: 266; /PA: 7, 22, 34-35, 37, 54, 55t, 72, 74, 77, 87, 92-93, 106-107, 112-113, 113, 118, 136, 153; /Photonews: 215br; /Nick Potts/PA: 263; /Presse Sports: 32, 78; /Martin Ricketts: 265; /Peter Robinson: 109, 116-117, 117, 119, 120, 123, 124-125, 125, 129, 133, 134, 135, 137, 138, 142, 144-145, 150-151, 156, 158-159, 166-167, 170-171, 171; /S&G: 68; /S&G/Alpha: 10, 18, 31, 39, 48, 51br, 52, 93, 98, 105, 141; /SMG: 42-43, 89, 103, 165, 183t; /Neal Simpson: 188, 192-193, 216-217; /Michael Steele: 220, 226-227; /Studio Buzzi: 175; /Topham: 15, 17, 19, 30, 43, 44, 45, 49, 50, 53, 57, 58-59, 60, 61, 64, 65, 67, 69, 71, 73, 79, 139, 274-275; /Leo Vogelzang: 167; /John Walton: 273b, 252-253, 256-257; /Witters: 85, 154.

Getty Images: 230-231; /AFP: 102; /Central Press: 75; /Carl De Souza/AFP: 277b; /Hulton Archive: 46, 94; /Michael Webb/Keystone: 95; /Pascal Pavani/AFP 1; /Topical Press Agency: 11; /Wesley/Keystone: 90.

Offside Sports Photography: 20; /Farabolafoto: 8; /L'Equipe: 9, 12-13, 21, 23, 24-25, 26, 27, 28-29, 29, 40, 41, 47, 51t, 55b, 56, 59, 62-63, 63, 66-67, 70, 80-81, 86, 88-89, 96, 97, 99, 100-101, 101, 104, 108-109, 110, 111, 112-113, 114-115, 120-121, 126-127, 132, 140, 143, 146-147, 148, 149, 150, 152-153, 157, 159, 160, 161, 162, 162-163, 164, 168, 169, 178, 179, 180, 181, 184, 185t, 185b, 192, 194, 195, 198-199, 203, 206, 207t, 208, 209, 210, 214, 218, 244, 259, 267t, 267b, 268, 271t; /Mark Leech: 131, 145, 154-155, 186-187, 187, 189, 221, 222-223, 224, 225, 227, 228-229, 230, 222-223, 228-229, 232-233, 242, 250-251, 253, 254, 255, 260-261, 261; /Witters: 146, 207b, 219, 248-249, 249, 257.

Every effort has been made to acknowledge correctly and contact the source and/copyright holder of each picture, and Carlton Books Limited apologises for any unintentional errors or omissions, which will be corrected in further editions of this book.

Special thanks are due to Edd Griffin at Offside Sports Photography, Arnaud Jacob and Jean-Pierre Penel at Presse Sports, who greatly reduced the burdens of picture research.